PUBLIC REASON IN POLITICAL PHILOSOPHY

When people of good faith and sound mind disagree deeply about moral, religious, and other philosophical matters, how can we justify political institutions to all of them? The idea of public reason—of a shared public standard, despite disagreement—arose in the seventeenth and eighteenth centuries in the work of Hobbes, Locke, Rousseau, and Kant. At a time when John Rawls' influential theory of public reason has come under fire but its core idea remains attractive to many, it is important not to lose sight of earlier philosophers' answers to the problem of private conflict through public reason.

The distinctive selections from the great social contract theorists in this volume emphasize the pervasive theme of intractable disagreement and the need for public justification. New essays by leading scholars then put the historical work in context and provide a focus of debate and discussion. They also explore how the search for public reason has informed a wider body of modern political theory—in the work of Hume, Hegel, Bentham, and Mill—sometimes in surprising ways. The idea of public reason is revealed as an overarching theme in modern political philosophy—one very much needed today.

Piers Norris Turner is Associate Professor of Philosophy and (by courtesy) Political Science at Ohio State University. A co-editor of *Karl Popper, After The Open Society: Selected Social and Political Writings* (2008), his articles on John Stuart Mill's moral and political philosophy have appeared in a number of leading journals, including *Ethics* and the *Journal of the History of Philosophy*.

Gerald Gaus is the James E. Rogers Professor of Philosophy at the University of Arizona. Among his books are *The Order of Public Reason* (2011), *On Philosophy, Politics and Economics* (2008), *Justificatory Liberalism* (1996), and *Value and Justification* (1990). His most recent book is *The Tyranny of the Ideal* (2016). He was a founding editor of the journal *Politics, Philosophy, and Economics* and, with Fred D'Agostino, edited *The Routledge Companion to Social and Political Philosophy* (2013).

PUBLIC REASON IN POLITICAL PHILOSOPHY

Classic Sources and Contemporary Commentaries

Edited by Piers Norris Turner and Gerald Gaus

NEW YORK AND LONDON

First published 2018
by Routledge
711 Third Avenue, New York, NY 10017

and by Routledge
2 Park Square, Milton Park, Abingdon, Oxon, OX14 4RN

Routledge is an imprint of the Taylor & Francis Group, an informa business

© 2018 Taylor & Francis

The right of Piers Norris Turner and Gerald Gaus to be identified as the authors of the editorial material, and of the authors for their individual chapters, has been asserted in accordance with sections 77 and 78 of the Copyright, Designs and Patents Act 1988.

All rights reserved. No part of this book may be reprinted or reproduced or utilised in any form or by any electronic, mechanical, or other means, now known or hereafter invented, including photocopying and recording, or in any information storage or retrieval system, without permission in writing from the publishers.

Trademark notice: Product or corporate names may be trademarks or registered trademarks, and are used only for identification and explanation without intent to infringe.

Library of Congress Cataloging-in-Publication Data
A catalog record for this book has been requested

ISBN: 978-0-415-85559-4 (hbk)
ISBN: 978-1-315-11086-8 (ebk)

Typeset in Times New Roman
by codeMantra

Printed and bound in Great Britain by
TJ International Ltd, Padstow, Cornwall

CONTENTS

Acknowledgments		vii
Note on the Text		viii
Introduction Piers Norris Turner and Gerald Gaus		1

PART 1
Public Reason in Social Contract Theory   7

Hobbes	from *Leviathan* (1651),	9
	Critical Essay: S. A. Lloyd,	
	Public Reason in Hobbes	84
Locke	from *Second Treatise of Government* (1690),	108
	A Letter Concerning Toleration (1689),	149
	Critical Essay: Gerald Gaus,	
	Locke's Liberal Theory of Public Reason	163
Rousseau	from *A Discourse on Political Economy* (1755),	184
	The Social Contract (1762),	201
	Critical Essay: Christopher Bertram,	
	Rousseau on Public Reason	248
Kant	from *The Science of Right* (1796),	264
	The Principles of Political Right Considered in Connection with the Relation of Theory to Practice in the Right of the State (1793),	271
	Perpetual Peace (1795),	276
	What is Enlightenment? (1784),	278
	Critical Essay: Oliver Sensen,	
	Kant on Public Reason	282

PART 2
Public Reason in Broader Historical Context — 301

Hume   Critical Essay: Geoffrey Sayre-McCord,
Hume's Theory of Public Reason — 303

Hegel   Critical Essay: Kenneth R. Westphal,
*The Centrality of Public Reason in
Hegel's Moral Philosophy* — 330

Bentham   Critical Essay: Gerald J. Postema,
Jeremy Bentham: Theorist of Publicity — 354

Mill   Critical Essay: Piers Norris Turner,
Social Morality in Mill — 375

Index — 401

ACKNOWLEDGMENTS

Our deep thanks to our contributors in shaping this volume, not only through their excellent chapters but also by providing extensive advice on the historical selections. Early on in planning the project, we greatly benefited from a long discussion with Fred D'Agostino one summer's afternoon in Dubrovnik. We also wish to thank Andrew Beck and Vera Lochtefeld at Routledge for their uncommon patience and support as they awaited the completion of the manuscript.

NOTE ON THE TEXT

Classical selections from Rousseau and Kant were drawn from translations in the public domain (see those sections for references to the original translations). For the Hobbes selections we undertook to make them more accessible to the reader by simplifying the original spelling and capitalization while otherwise staying true to the original punctuation.

INTRODUCTION

Piers Norris Turner and Gerald Gaus

Most political philosophers and political theorists associate the idea of public reason primarily with John Rawls's political liberalism.[1] Indeed, many not only think that he provided the definitive statement of the idea, but that he invented it. While it is true that Rawls reshaped the project of liberal theory as he found it to reflect the commitments of public reason, the essays in this book show that the idea of public reason arose in the seventeenth and eighteenth centuries in response to two fundamental developments in modern political thought: the recognition of intractable disagreement, and the idea of a sovereign that expresses the will of all. Like Rawls, earlier public reason theorists tried to show that social, political, or legal institutions could be justified to everyone living under them—or at least to all those interested in sharing a common life together—despite their often deep moral, religious, and other differences. They grappled with the idea that public principles or rules could be justified not as implications of the *correct* moral principles, but by accommodating and respecting disagreement among people of good faith and sound mind. At a time when Rawls's own views have come under significant criticism but the idea of public reason remains attractive to many, it is important not to lose sight of the intellectual resources offered by earlier philosophers in their various approaches to the problem of intractable disagreement and public justification. Indeed, underlying the present volume is a stronger claim—that the idea of public reason has been a critical organizing motif in modern political theory, and so the study of modern political philosophy can be fruitfully organized around the evolution of this idea.

With that in mind, in the present volume we have tried to accomplish two main tasks. First, we have provided selections from Hobbes, Locke, Rousseau, and Kant that emphasize their contributions to the history of public reason in political philosophy and show its centrality to their political thought. Although these texts include familiar passages typically found in compendiums of the social contract tradition, they add a distinctive twist, emphasizing the pervasive theme of intractable disagreement and appropriate responses to it. We believe this helps the social contract tradition come alive to current students. It is not simply about states of nature, rights and agreements, but how those with enduring religious, moral, and philosophical disagreements can fruitfully live together— perhaps the most important question of our time. Second, we have invited chapters from leading scholars to put the historical work in context, not only making it accessible to contemporary theorists and students of public reason, but to provide a focus of debate and discussion. In Part I these essays are matched with selections from classical texts. In Part II a group of leading political philosophers explore how the search for public reason has informed a wider body of modern political theory—in the work of Hume, Hegel, Bentham, and Mill, each of whom (in their own way) addressed aspects of the public reason framework, sometimes in surprising ways. The result, we hope, is a valuable contribution to the study of public reason not just in the history of political philosophy, but for current debates as well.

Public Reason in Social Contract Theory

Private Reason and Disagreement in Hobbes and Locke

As S. A. Lloyd shows in her commentary, Hobbes is perhaps the pivotal figure in the history of public reason, for he was the first to analyze the crux of the modern political problem in terms of the sustained disagreement that results when individuals apply their reasoning and judgment to the problems of social life. Generations of students have been taught that the problem of conflict in Hobbesian theory was derived almost exclusively from conflicts of self-interest. Left free, selfish individuals inevitably compete and threaten each other, and so the sovereign is needed to awe them with its power and impose obedience to law. Of course this is a theme in Hobbes, but this common picture overlooks his repeated warning of the dangers of disagreement over a wide variety of matters, including theories and doctrines. He writes:

> And therefore, as when there is a controversy in an account, the parties must by their own accord, set up for right reason, the reason of some arbitrator, or judge, to whose sentence they will both stand, or their controversy must either come to blows, or be undecided, for want of a right reason constituted by nature; so is it also in all debates of what kind soever: and when men that think themselves wiser than all others, clamour and demand right reason for judge; yet seek no more, but that things should be determined, by no other men's reason but their own, it is as intolerable in the society of men, as it is in play after trump is

turned, to use for trump on every occasion that suit whereof they have most in their hand. For they do nothing else, that will have every of their passions, as it comes to bear sway in them, to be taken for right reason, and that in their own controversies: bewraying their want of right reason, by the claim they lay to it.[2]

Hobbes's world is one in which civil war arises over ideas and doctrines among those who each insist that their reason is "right reason" and that all should therefore conform to its conclusions. For Hobbes, only by constructing a public reason—a common reason and judgment, defined by an absolute sovereign authorized by all—can doctrinal disputes end and social peace and prosperity be secured.

In the canon, Locke is usually presented as Hobbes's antagonist. Whereas Hobbes provides a modern defense of absolutist claims, Locke is the voice of the emerging Whig view that citizens possess rights against the sovereign, and that Parliament expresses the will of the people. And for Jean Hampton, whereas Hobbes would make the sovereign our master, Locke depicts government as our agent—an agent that can be dismissed when it no longer performs its task.[3] This tendency to perceive Hobbes and Locke simply as antagonists obscures important, deep, agreements. Most fundamentally, Locke agrees that diversity of private judgment about religion is a basic social fact that must be reconciled with the demands of social order. Moreover, he accepts the crux of Hobbes's analysis of the causes of disputes about the laws of nature. Peace and justice, Locke holds, can only be secured when "all private judgment of every particular member being excluded, the community comes to be umpire by settled standing rules, indifferent, and the same to all parties."[4] As with Hobbes, the core problem of political philosophy is justifying the authority of the government over the private judgment of citizens. The clash of our private judgments leads us to see the need for a public determination of the law: justifying such authority is the central aim of the social contract. In his chapter, Gerald Gaus reconfigures the antagonism of Hobbes and Locke in light of this shared basic problem. Locke, he argues, is led to a very different, *liberal* resolution of the relation between private judgment and public reason.

The Public Will in Rousseau and Kant

The problem of disagreement permeates the writing of Hobbes, Locke, Rousseau, and Kant. For the latter two—whose theories of public reason are explored by Christopher Bertram and Oliver Sensen—a second feature of modernity becomes rather more prominent. Political associations encompass a variety of individuals, with their different wills and aims, and through law somehow forge a public will. The state is neither simply one individual imposing his will on others nor, as in Hobbes, the rest of us authorizing the judgment and will of the sovereign. The state forms a public will, with a public reason, that articulates the reason and will of all, qua members of a political community. Law, says Rousseau,

> is this celestial voice which dictates to each citizen the precepts of public reason, and teaches him to act according to the rules of his own judgment, and not to behave inconsistently with himself. It is with this voice alone that political rulers should speak when they command; for no sooner does one man, setting aside the law, claim to subject another to his private will, than he departs from the state of civil society, and confronts him face to face in the pure state of nature, in which obedience is prescribed solely by necessity.[5]

Public reason helps us not only to overcome conflicts, but also to live according to common law in a way that secures the freedom of each. As Sensen shows in his contribution, Kant too is centrally concerned with understanding the relation of each citizen's private judgment to the public laws, and under what conditions citizens can be said to will and endorse these laws.

Public Reason in Broader Historical Context

Hobbes, Locke, Rousseau, and Kant all developed the concept of public reason and systematically analyzed political philosophy in terms of the relation of private judgment and public reason. Part I of this book is therefore devoted to their contributions, matching the interpretive essays of Lloyd, Gaus, Bertram and Sensen with key text from these four groundbreaking theorists of public reason.

Often, however, while the idea of public reason is not at the forefront of a political philosophy, it is an organizing or fundamental theme. Having examined the great classical theorists of public reason, we can achieve a new perspective on modern political philosophy more generally. The essays on Hume, Hegel, Bentham, and Mill show how they address critical themes of the public reason tradition.

As Geoffrey Sayre-McCord shows, Hume—despite being the preeminent historical critic of the social contract tradition—was deeply engaged with the problem of public reason: "every particular man has a peculiar position with regard to others; and 'tis impossible we cou'd ever converse together on any reasonable terms, were each of us to consider characters and persons, only as they appear from his peculiar point of view."[6] He introduced the idea of the General Point of View precisely to establish conventions that could order our common lives together and allow for coordination. For Hegel, all reasoning is in some sense public. There is no avoiding the social. Kenneth Westphal argues that, on Hegel's view, it is an obligation of reason itself that we engage each other as equals and through mutual criticism attempt to solve our common problems. In doing so, he shows that Hegel's work can address many current questions about the value of public discourse and the significance of certain justice claims.

Gerald Postema's essay demonstrates the role that publicity plays in Bentham's utilitarian system. Bentham is revealed as anything but the simplistic act utilitarian calculator so commonly depicted. He was, in fact, keenly aware of the need for public standards for the purposes of accountability and deliberation, arguing not only that utility could provide such a standard but that it should be understood through subsidiary ends that could come to define the "universal interest." Piers Norris Turner then examines Mill, the other great utilitarian political philosopher. Turner also shows the central place of a shared, social, morality in Mill, one that is critical in solving an important puzzle about Mill's theory of morally right action. Mill not only articulates the need for social morality as a response to private conflict, he articulates a practice of public reason to revise social morality over time.

Each of these chapters provides a rich introduction to a particular thinker's approach to public reason. But part of the interest of these essays results from seeing that the core ideas of public reason end up playing central roles in very different theoretical frameworks, allowing us to see modern political philosophy in a new light. The problem of intractable disagreement is revealed as a persistent overarching problem in modern political philosophy. Once this is perceived, the classics of modern political philosophy become closer to us, analyzing pervasive disagreement and proposing solutions to guide a common life. This is our problem too, and can be ignored only at our peril. It is our hope that the classic selections and commentaries by contemporary philosophers will help to show the significance of public reason for political thought to both political philosophers and—even more—to students who come to the classics for the first time.

Notes

1. John Rawls, *Political Liberalism*, expanded edition (New York: Columbia University Press, 2005).
2. Hobbes, *Leviathan*, Chapter 5, ¶3 [9–10 – bracketed page numbers refer to selections in this volume].
3. Hampton, *Hobbes and the Social Contract Tradition* (Cambridge: Cambridge University Press, 1986), 224ff.
4. Locke, *Second Treatise*, §87 [125].
5. Jean-Jacques Rousseau, *A Discourse on Political Economy* in *The Social Contract and Discourses*, translated by G.D.H. Cole (London: J.M. Dent and Sons, 1923), 256–7 [188]. Emphasis added.
6. David Hume, *A Treatise of Human Nature*. Edited by D.F. Norton & M.J. Norton (Oxford: Oxford University Press, 2000), Book 3, Part 3, Section 1, ¶15.

Part I

PUBLIC REASON IN SOCIAL CONTRACT THEORY

1

THOMAS HOBBES (1588–1679)
Leviathan (1651)[1]

PART I: OF MAN

CHAPTER V

Of REASON and SCIENCE

When a man *reasoneth*, he does nothing else but conceive a sum total, from *addition* of parcels; or conceive a remainder, from *subtraction* of one sum from another: which (if it be done by words,) is conceiving of the consequence of the names of all the parts, to the name of the whole; or from the names of the whole and one part, to the name of the other part. ...Writers of politics, add together *pactions*, to find men's *duties*; and lawyers, *laws*, and *facts*, to find what is *right* and *wrong* in the actions of private men. In sum, in what matter soever there is place for *addition* and *subtraction*, there also is place for *reason*; and where these have no place, there *reason* has nothing at all to do.

Out of all which we may define, (that is to say determine,) what that is, which is meant by this word *reason*, when we reckon it amongst the faculties of the mind. For REASON, in this sense, is nothing but *reckoning* (that is, adding and subtracting) of the consequences of general names agreed upon, for the *marking* and *signifying* of our thoughts; I say *marking* them, when we reckon by ourselves; and *signifying*, when we demonstrate, or approve our reckonings to other men.

And as in arithmetic, unpractised men must, and professors themselves may often err, and cast up false; so also in any other subject of reasoning, the ablest, most attentive, and most practised men, may deceive themselves, and infer false conclusions; not but that reason itself is always right reason, as well as arithmetic is a certain and infallible art: but no one man's reason, nor the reason of any one number of men, makes the certainty; no more than an account is therefore well cast up, because a great many men have unanimously approved it. And therefore, as when there is a controversy in an account, the parties must by their own accord, set up for right reason, the reason of some arbitrator, or judge, to whose sentence they will both stand, or their controversy must either come to blows, or be undecided, for want of a right reason constituted by nature; so is it also in all debates of what kind soever: and when men that think themselves wiser than all others, clamour and demand right reason for judge; yet seek no more, but that things should be determined, by no other men's reason but their own, it is as intolerable in the society of men, as it is in play after trump is turned, to use for trump on every occasion that suit whereof they have most in their hand. For they do nothing else, that will have every of their passions, as it comes to bear sway in them, to be taken for right reason, and that in their own controversies: bewraying their want of right reason, by the claim they lay to it.

....

When a man reckons without the use of words, which may be done in particular things, (as when upon the sight of any one thing, we conjecture what was likely to have preceded, or is likely to follow upon it;) if that which he thought likely to follow, follows not; or that which he thought likely to have preceded it, hath not preceded it, this is called ERROR; to which even the most prudent men are subject. But when we reason in words of general signification, and fall upon a general inference which is false; though it be commonly called *error*, it is indeed an ABSURDITY, or senseless speech. For error is but a deception, in presuming that somewhat is past, or to come; of which, though it were not past, or not to come; yet there was no impossibility discoverable. But when we make a general assertion, unless it be a true one, the possibility of it is inconceivable. And words whereby we conceive nothing but the sound, are those we call *absurd, insignificant*, and *nonsense*. And therefore if a man should talk to me of a *round quadrangle*; or *accidents of bread in cheese*; or *immaterial substances*; or of *a free subject*; *a free will*; or any *free*, but free from being hindered by opposition, I should not say he were in an error, but that his words were without meaning; that is to say, absurd.

CHAPTER XII

Of Religion

Seeing there are no signs, nor fruit of *religion,* but in man only; there is no cause to doubt, but that the seed of *religion*, is also only in man; and consisteth in some peculiar quality, or at least in some eminent degree thereof, not to be found in other living creatures.

And first, it is peculiar to the nature of man, to be inquisitive into the causes of the events they see, some more, some less; but all men so much, as to be curious in the search of the causes of their own good and evil fortune.

Secondly, upon the sight of anything that hath a beginning, to think also it had a cause, which determined the same to begin, then when it did, rather than sooner or later.

Thirdly, whereas there is no other felicity of beasts, but the enjoying of their quotidian food, ease, and lusts; as having little, or no foresight of the time to come, for want of observation, and memory of the order, consequence, and dependence of the things they see; man observeth how one event hath been produced by another; and remembereth in them antecedence and consequence; and when he cannot assure himself of the true causes of things, (for the causes of good and evil fortune for the most part are invisible,) he supposes causes of them, either such as his own fancy suggesteth; or trusteth to the authority of other men, such as he thinks to be his friends, and wiser than himself.

The two first, make anxiety. For being assured that there be causes of all things that have arrived hitherto, or shall arrive hereafter; it is impossible for a man, who continually endeavoureth to secure himself against the evil he fears, and procure the good he desireth, not to be in a perpetual solicitude of the time to come; so that every man, especially those that are over-provident, are in an estate like to that of *Prometheus*. For as *Prometheus*, (which interpreted, is, *the prudent man,*) was bound to the hill *Caucasus*, a place of large prospect, where, an eagle feeding on his liver, devoured in the day, as much as was repaired in the night: so that man, which looks too far before him, in the care of future time, hath his heart all the day long gnawed on by fear of death, poverty, or other calamity; and has no repose, nor pause of his anxiety, but in sleep.

This perpetual fear, always accompanying mankind in the ignorance of causes, as it were in the dark, must needs have for object something. And therefore when there is nothing to be seen, there is nothing to accuse, either of their good, or evil fortune, but some *power*, or agent *invisible*: in which sense perhaps it was, that some of the old poets said, that the gods were at first created by human fear: which spoken of the gods, (that is to say, of the many gods of the Gentiles) is very true. But the acknowledging of one God eternal, infinite, and omnipotent, may more easily be derived, from the desire men have to know the causes of natural bodies, and their several virtues, and operations; than from the fear of what was to befall them in time to come. For he that from any effect he seeth come to pass, should reason to the next and immediate cause thereof, and from thence to the cause of that cause, and plunge himself profoundly into the pursuit of causes; shall at last come to this, that there must be (as even the heathen philosophers confessed) one First Mover; that is, a first, and an eternal cause of all things; which is that which men mean by the name of God: and all this without thought of their fortune; the solicitude whereof, both inclines to fear, and hinders them from the search of the causes of other things; and thereby gives occasion of feigning of as many gods, as there be men that feign them.

And for the matter, or substance of the invisible agents, so fancied; they could not by natural cogitation, fall upon any other concept, but that it was the same with that of the soul of man; and that the soul of man, was of the same substance, with that which appeareth in a dream, to one that sleepeth; or in a looking-glass, to one that is awake; which, men not knowing that such apparitions are nothing else but creatures of the fancy, think to be real, and external substances; and therefore call them ghosts; as the Latins called them *imagines*, and *umbrae*; and thought them spirits, that is, thin aerial bodies; and those invisible agents, which they feared, to be like them; save that they appear, and vanish when they please. But the opinion that such spirits were incorporeal, or immaterial, could never enter into the mind of any man by nature; because, though men may put together words of contradictory signification, as *spirit*, and *incorporeal*; yet they can never have the imagination of anything answering to them: and therefore, men that by their own meditation, arrive to the acknowledgement of one infinite, omnipotent, and eternal God, choose rather to confess he is incomprehensible, and above their understanding; than to define his nature by *spirit incorporeal*, and then confess their definition to be unintelligible: or if they give him such a title, it is not *dogmatically*, with intention to make the divine nature understood; but *piously*, to honour him with attributes, of significations, as remote as they can from the grossness of bodies visible.

. . . .

And in these four things, opinion of ghosts, ignorance of second causes, devotion towards what men fear, and taking of things casual for prognostics, consisteth the natural seed of *religion*; which, by reason of the different fancies, judgements, and passions of several men, hath grown up into ceremonies so different, that those which are used by one man, are for the most part ridiculous to another.

For these seeds have received culture from two sorts of men. One sort have been they, that have nourished, and ordered them, according to their own invention. The other, have done it, by God's commandment, and direction: but both sorts have done it, with a purpose to make those men that relied on them, the more apt to obedience, laws, peace, charity, and civil society. So that the religion of the former sort, is a part of human politics; and teacheth part of the duty which earthly kings require of their subjects. And the religion of the latter sort is divine politics; and containeth precepts to those that have yielded themselves subjects in the kingdom of God. Of the former sort, were all the founders of commonwealths, and the lawgivers of the Gentiles: of the latter sort, were *Abraham, Moses,* and our *blessed Saviour*; by whom have been derived unto us the laws of the kingdom of God.

....

And therefore the first founders, and legislators of commonwealths amongst the Gentiles, whose ends were only to keep the people in obedience, and peace, have in all places taken care; first, to imprint their minds a belief, that those precepts which they gave concerning religion, might not be thought to proceed from their own device, but from the dictates of some god, or other spirit; or else that they themselves were of a higher nature than mere mortals, that their laws might the more easily be received: so *Numa Pompilius* pretended to receive the ceremonies he instituted amongst the Romans, from the nymph *Egeria*: and the first king and founder of the kingdom of *Peru*, pretended himself and his wife to be the children of the sun: and Mahomet, to set up his new religion, pretended to have conferences with the Holy Ghost, in form of a dove. Secondly, they have had a care, to make it believed, that the same things were displeasing to the gods, which were forbidden by the laws. Thirdly, to prescribe ceremonies, supplications, sacrifices, and festivals, by which they were to believe, the anger of the gods might be appeased; and that ill success in war, great contagions of sickness, earthquakes, and each man's private misery, came from the anger of the gods; and their anger from the neglect of their worship, or the forgetting, or mistaking some point of the ceremonies required. And though amongst the ancient Romans, men were not forbidden to deny, that which in the poets is written of the pains, and pleasures after this life; which divers of great authority, and gravity in that state, have in their *harangues* openly derided; yet that belief was always more cherished, than the contrary.

And by these, and such other institutions, they obtained in order to their end, (which was the peace of the commonwealth,) that the common people in their misfortunes, laying the fault on neglect, or error in their ceremonies, or on their own disobedience to the laws, were the less apt to mutiny against their governors. And being entertained with the pomp, and pastime of festivals, and public games made in honour of the gods, needed nothing else but bread, to keep them from discontent, murmuring, and commotion against the state.

....

But where God himself, by supernatural revelation, planted religion; there he also made to himself a peculiar kingdom; and gave laws, not only of behaviour towards himself; but also towards one another; and thereby in the kingdom of God, the policy, and laws civil, are a part of religion; and therefore the distinction of temporal, and spiritual domination, hath there no place. It is true, that God is king of all the earth: yet may he be king of a peculiar, and chosen nation. For there is no more incongruity therein, than that he that hath the general command of the whole army, should have withal a peculiar regiment, or company of his own. God is king of all the earth by his power: but of his chosen people, he is king by covenant. But to speak more largely of the kingdom of God, both by nature, and covenant, I have in the following discourse assigned another place.

From the propagation of religion, it is not hard to understand the causes of the resolution of the same into its first seeds, or principles; which are only an opinion of a deity, and powers invisible, and supernatural; that can never be so abolished out of human nature, but that new religions may again be made to spring out of them, by the culture of such men as for such purpose are in reputation.

....

CHAPTER XIII

Of the NATURAL CONDITION of mankind, as concerning their felicity, and misery

Nature hath made men so equal, in the faculties of body, and mind; as that though there be found one man sometimes manifestly stronger in body, or of quicker mind than another; yet when all is reckoned together, the difference between man, and man, is not so considerable, as that one man can thereupon claim to himself any benefit, to which another may not pretend, as well as he. For as to the strength of body, the weakest has strength enough to kill the strongest, either by secret machination, or by confederacy with others, that are in the same danger with himself.

And as to the faculties of the mind, (setting aside the arts grounded upon words, and especially that skill of proceeding upon general, and infallible rules, called science; which very few have, and but in few things; as being not a native faculty, born with us; nor attained, (as prudence,) while we look after somewhat else,) I find yet a greater equality amongst men, than that of strength. For prudence, is but experience; which equal time, equally bestows on all men, in those things they equally apply themselves unto.

....

From this equality of ability, ariseth equality of hope in the attaining of our ends. And therefore if any two men desire the same thing, which nevertheless they cannot both enjoy, they become enemies; and in the way to their end, (which is principally their own conservation, and sometimes their delectation only,) endeavour to destroy, or subdue one another. And from hence it comes to pass, that where an invader hath no more to fear, than another man's single power; if one plant, sow, build, or possess a convenient seat, others may probably be expected to come prepared with forces united, to dispossess, and deprive him, not only of the fruit of his labour, but also of his life, or liberty. And the invader again is in the like danger of another.

And from this diffidence of one another, there is no way for any man to secure himself, so reasonable, as anticipation; that is, by force, or wiles, to master the persons of all men he can, so long, till he see no other power great enough to endanger him: and this is no more than his own conservation requireth, and is generally allowed. Also because there be some, that taking pleasure in contemplating their own power in the acts of conquest, which they pursue farther than their security requires; if others, that otherwise would be glad to be at ease within modest bounds, should not by invasion increase their power, they would not be able, long time, by standing only on their defence, to subsist. And by consequence, such augmentation of dominion over men, being necessary to a man's conservation, it ought to be allowed him.

Again, men have no pleasure, (but on the contrary a great deal of grief) in keeping company, where there is no power able to overawe them all. For every man looketh that his companion should value him, at the same rate he sets upon himself: and upon all signs of contempt, or undervaluing, naturally endeavours, as far as he dares (which amongst them that have no common power to keep them in quiet, is far enough to make them destroy each other,) to extort a greater value from his contemners, by damage; and from others, by the example.

So that in the nature of man, we find three principal causes of quarrel. First, competition; secondly, diffidence; thirdly, glory.

The first, maketh men invade for gain; the second, for safety; and the third, for reputation. The first use violence, to make themselves masters of other men's persons, wives, children, and cattle; the second, to defend them; the third, for trifles, as a word, a smile, a different opinion, and any other sign of undervalue, either direct in their persons or by reflection in their kindred, their friends, their nation, their profession, or their name.

Hereby it is manifest, that during the time men live without a common power to keep them all in awe, they are in that condition which is called war; and such a war, as is of every man, against every man. For WAR, consisteth not in battle only, or the act of fighting; but in a tract of time, wherein the will to contend by battle is sufficiently known: and therefore the notion of *time*, is to be considered in the nature of war; as it is in the nature of weather. For as the nature of foul weather, lieth not in a shower or two of rain; but in an inclination thereto of many days together: so the nature of war, consisteth not in actual fighting; but in the known disposition thereto, during all the time there is no assurance to the contrary. All other time is PEACE.

Whatsoever therefore is consequent to a time of war, where every man is enemy to every man; the same consequent to the time, wherein men live without other security, than what their own strength, and their own invention shall furnish them withal. In such condition, there is no place for industry; because the fruit thereof is uncertain: and consequently no culture of the earth; no navigation, nor use of the commodities that may be imported by sea; no commodious building; no instruments of moving, and removing such things as require much force; no knowledge of the face of the earth; no account of time; no arts; no letters; no society; and which is worst of all, continual fear, and danger of violent death; and the life of man, solitary, poor, nasty, brutish, and short.

It may seem strange to some man, that has not well weighed these things; that nature should thus dissociate, and render men apt to invade, and destroy one another: and he may therefore, not trusting to this inference, made from the passions, desire perhaps to have the same confirmed by experience. Let him therefore consider with himself, when taking a journey, he arms himself, and seeks to go well accompanied; when going to sleep, he locks his doors; when even in his house he locks his chests; and this when he knows there be laws, and public officers, armed, to revenge all injuries shall be done him; what opinion he has of his fellow subjects, when he rides armed; of his fellow citizens, when he locks his doors; and of his children, and servants, when he locks his chests. Does he not there as much accuse mankind by his actions, as I do by my words? But neither of us accuse man's nature in it. The desires, and other passions of man, are in themselves no sin. No more are the actions, that proceed from those passions, till they know a law that forbids them: which till laws be made they cannot know: nor can any law be made, till they have agreed upon the person that shall make it.

It may peradventure be thought, there was never such a time, nor condition of war as this; and I believe it was never generally so, over all the world: but there are many places, where they live so now. For the savage people in many places of *America*, except the government of small families, the concord whereof dependeth on natural lust, have no government at all; and live at this day in that brutish manner, as I said before. Howsoever, it may be perceived what manner of life there would be, where there were no common power to fear; by the manner of life, which men that have formerly lived under a peaceful government, use to degenerate into, in a civil war.

But though there had never been any time, wherein particular men were in a condition of war one against another; yet in all times, kings, and persons of sovereign authority, because of their independency, are in continual jealousies, and in the state and posture of gladiators; having their weapons pointing, and their eyes fixed on one another; that is, their forts, garrisons, and guns upon the frontiers of their kingdoms; and continual spies upon their neighbours, which is a posture of war. But because they uphold thereby, the industry of their subjects; there does not follow from it, that misery, which accompanies the liberty of particular men.

To this war of every man against every man, this also is consequent; that nothing can be unjust. The notions of right and wrong, justice and injustice have there no place. Where there is no common power, there is no law: where no law, no injustice. Force, and fraud, are in war the two cardinal virtues. Justice, and injustice are none of the faculties neither of the body, nor mind. If they were, they might be in a man that were alone in the world, as well as his senses, and passions. They are qualities, that relate to men in society, not in solitude. It is consequent also to the same condition, that there be no propriety, no dominion, no *mine* and *thine* distinct; but only that to be every man's, that he can get; and for so long, as he can keep it. And thus much for the ill condition, which man by mere nature is actually placed in; though with a possibility to come out of it, consisting partly in the passions, partly in his reason.

The passions that incline men to peace, are fear of death; desire of such things as are necessary to commodious living; and a hope by their industry to obtain them. And reason suggesteth convenient articles of peace, upon which men may be drawn to agreement. These articles, are they, which otherwise are called the laws of nature: whereof I shall speak more particularly, in the two following chapters.

CHAPTER XIV

Of the first and second NATURAL LAWS, and of CONTRACTS

The RIGHT OF NATURE, which writers commonly call *jus naturale*, is the liberty each man hath, to use his own power, as he will himself, for the preservation of his own nature; that is to say, of his own life; and consequently, of doing anything, which in his own judgement, and reason, he shall conceive to be the aptest means thereunto.

By LIBERTY, is understood, according to the proper signification of the word, the absence of external impediments: which impediments, may oft take away part of a man's power to do what he would; but cannot hinder him from using the power left him, according as his judgement, and reason shall dictate to him.

A LAW OF NATURE, (*lex naturalis*,) is a precept, or general rule, found out by reason, by which a man is forbidden to do, that, which is destructive of his life, or taketh away the means of preserving the same; and to omit, that, by which he thinketh it may be best preserved. For though they that speak of this subject, use to confound *jus* and *lex*, *right* and *law*; yet they ought to be distinguished; because RIGHT, consisteth in liberty to do, or to forbear; whereas LAW, determineth, and bindeth to one of them: so that law, and right, differ as much, as obligation, and liberty; which in one and the same matter are inconsistent.

And because the condition of man, (as hath been declared in the precedent chapter) is a condition of war of everyone against everyone; in which case everyone is governed by his own reason; and there is nothing he can make use of, that may not be a help unto him, in preserving his life against his enemies; it followeth, that in such a condition, every man has a right to everything; even to one another's body. And therefore, as long as this natural right of every man to everything endureth, there can be no security to any man, (how strong or wise soever he be,) of living out the time, which nature ordinarily alloweth men to live. And consequently it is a precept, or general rule of reason, *that every man, ought to endeavour peace, as far as he has hope of obtaining it; and when he cannot obtain it, that he may seek, and use, all helps, and advantages of war.* The first branch of which rule, containeth the first, and fundamental law of nature; which is, *to seek peace, and follow it.* The second, the sum of the right of nature; which is, *by all means we can, to defend ourselves.*

From this fundamental law of nature, by which men are commanded to endeavour peace, is derived this second law; *that a man be willing, when others are so too, as far-forth, as for peace, and defence of himself he shall think it necessary, to lay down this right to all things; and be contented with so much liberty against other men, as he would allow other men against himself.* For as long as every man holdeth this right, of doing anything he liketh; so long are all men in the condition of war. But if other men will not lay down their right, as well as he; then there is no reason for anyone, to divest himself of his: for that were to expose himself to prey, (which no man is bound to) rather than to dispose himself to peace. This is that law of the gospel; *Whatsoever you require that others should do to you, that do ye to them.* And that law of all men, *quod tibi fieri non vis, alteri ne feceris.*

To *lay down* a man's *right* to anything, is to *divest* himself of the *liberty*, of hindering another of the benefit of his own right to the same. For he that renounceth, or passeth away his right, giveth not to any other man a right which he had not before; because there is nothing to which every man had not right by nature: but only standeth out of his way, that he may enjoy his own original right, without hindrance from him; not without hindrance from another. So that the effect which redoundeth to one man, by another man's defect of right, is but so much diminution of impediments to the use of his own right original.

Right is laid aside, either by simply renouncing it; or by transferring it to another. By *simply* RENOUNCING; when he cares not to whom the benefit thereof redoundeth. By TRANSFERRING; when he intendeth the benefit thereof to some certain person, or persons. And when a man hath in either manner abandoned, or granted away his right; then is he said to be OBLIGED, or BOUND, not to hinder those, to whom such right is granted, or abandoned, from the benefit of it: and that he *ought*, and it is DUTY, not to make void that voluntary act of his own: and that such hindrance is INJUSTICE, and INJURY, as being *sine jure*; the right being before renounced, or transferred. So that *injury*, or *injustice*, in the controversies of the world, is somewhat like to that, which in the disputations of scholars is called *absurdity*. For as it is there called an absurdity, to contradict what one maintained in the beginning: so in the world it is called injustice, and injury, voluntarily to undo that, which from the beginning he had voluntarily done. The way by which a man either simply renounceth, or transferreth his right, is a declaration, or signification, by some voluntary and sufficient sign, or signs, that he doth so renounce, or transfer; or hath so renounced, or transferred the same, to him that accepteth it. And these signs are either words only, or actions only; or (as it happeneth most often) both words, and actions. And the same are the BONDS, by which men are bound, and obliged: bonds, that have their strength, not from their own nature, (for nothing is more easily broken than a man's word,) but from fear of some evil consequence upon the rupture.

Whensoever a man transferreth his right, or renounceth it; it is either in consideration of some right reciprocally transferred to himself; or for some other good he hopeth for thereby. For it is a voluntary act: and of the voluntary acts of every man, the object is some *good to himself.* And therefore there be some rights, which no man can be understood by any words, or other signs, to have abandoned, or transferred. As first a man cannot lay down the right of resisting them, that assault him by force, to take away his life; because he cannot be understood to aim thereby, at any good to himself. The same may be said of wounds, and chains, and imprisonment; both because there is no benefit consequent to such patience; as there is to the patience of suffering another to be wounded, or imprisoned: as also because a man cannot tell, when he seeth men proceed against him by violence, whether they intend his death or not. And lastly the motive, and end for which this renouncing and transferring of right is introduced, is nothing else but the security of a man's person, in his life, and in the means of so preserving life, as not to be weary of it. And therefore if a man by words, or other signs, seem to despoil himself of the end, for which those signs were intended; he is not to be understood as if he meant it, or that it was his will; but that he was ignorant of how such words and actions were to be interpreted.

The mutual transferring of right, is that which men call CONTRACT.

....

Signs of contract, are either *express*, or *by inference*. Express, are words spoken with understanding of what they signify: and such words are either of the time *present*, or *past*; as, *I give, I grant, I have given, I have granted, I will that this be yours*: or of the future; as, *I will give, I will grant*: which words of the future are called PROMISE.

Signs by inference, are sometimes the consequence of words; sometimes the consequence of silence; sometimes the consequence of actions; sometimes the consequence of forbearing an action: and generally a sign by inference, of any contract, is whatsoever sufficiently argues the will of the contractor.

....

If a covenant be made, wherein neither of the parties perform presently, but trust one another; in the condition of mere nature, (which is a condition of war of every man against every man,) upon any reasonable suspicion, it is void: but if there be a common power set over them both, with right and force sufficient to compel performance; it is not void. For he that performeth first, has no assurance the other will perform after; because the bonds of words are too weak to bridle men's ambition, avarice, anger, and other passions, without the fear of some coercive power; which in the condition of mere nature, where all men are equal, and judges of the justness of their own fears, cannot possibly be supposed. And therefore he which performeth first, does but betray himself to his enemy; contrary to the right (he can never abandon) of defending his life, and means of living.

But in a civil estate, where there a power set up to constrain those that would otherwise violate their faith, that fear is no more reasonable; and for that cause, he which by the covenant is to perform first, is obliged so to do.

The cause of fear, which maketh such a covenant invalid, must be always something arising after the covenant made; as some new fact, or other sign of the will not to perform: else it cannot make the covenant void. For that which could not hinder a man from promising, ought not to be admitted as a hindrance of performing.

....

To make covenant with God, is impossible, but by mediation of such as God speaketh to, either by revelation supernatural, or by his lieutenants that govern under him and in his name: for otherwise we know not whether our covenants be accepted, or not. And therefore they that vow anything contrary to any law of nature, vow in vain; as being a thing unjust to pay such vow. And if it be a thing commanded by the law of nature, it is not the vow, but the law that binds them.

....

Men are freed of their covenants two ways; by performing; or by being forgiven. For performance, is the natural end of obligation; and forgiveness, the restitution of liberty; as being a retransferring of that right, in which the obligation consisted.

Covenants entered into by fear, in the condition of mere nature, are obligatory. For example, if I covenant to pay a ransom, or service for my life, to an enemy; I am bound by it. For it is a contract, wherein one receiveth the benefit of life; the other is to receive money, or service for it; and consequently, where no other law (as in the condition, of mere nature) forbiddeth the performance, the covenant is valid. Therefore prisoners of war, if trusted with the payment of their ransom, are obliged to pay it: and if a weaker prince, make a disadvantageous peace with a stronger, for fear; he is bound to keep it; unless (as hath been said before) there ariseth some new, and just cause of fear, to renew the war. And even in commonwealths, if I be forced to redeem myself from a thief by promising him money, I am bound to pay it, till the civil law discharge me. For whatsoever I may lawfully do without obligation, the same I may lawfully covenant to do through fear: and what I lawfully covenant, I cannot lawfully break.

A former covenant makes void a later. For a man that hath passed away his right to one man today, hath it not to pass tomorrow to another: and therefore the later promise passeth no right, but is null.

A covenant not to defend myself from force, by force, is always void. For (as I have showed before) no man can transfer, or lay down his right to save himself from death, wounds, and imprisonment, (the avoiding whereof is the only end of laying down any right,) and therefore the promise of not resisting force, in no covenant transferreth any right; nor is obliging. For though a man may covenant thus, *unless I do so, or so, kill me*; he cannot covenant thus, *unless I do so, or so, I will not resist you when you come to kill me*. For man by nature chooseth the lesser evil, which is danger of death in resisting; rather than the greater, which is certain and present death in not resisting. And this is granted to be true by all men, in that they lead criminals to execution, and prison, with armed men, notwithstanding that such criminals have consented to the law, by which they are condemned.

A covenant to accuse oneself, without assurance of pardon, is likewise invalid. For in the condition of nature, where every man is judge, there is no place for accusation: and in the civil state, the accusation is followed with punishment; which being force, a man is not obliged not to resist. The same is also true, of the accusation of those, by whose condemnation a man falls into misery; as of a father, wife, or benefactor. For the testimony of such an accuser, if it be not willingly given, is presumed to be corrupted by nature; and therefore not to be received: and where a man's testimony is not to be credited, he is not bound to give it. Also accusations upon torture, are not to be reputed as testimonies. For torture is to be used but as means of conjecture, and light, in the further examination, and search of truth: and what is in that case confessed, tendeth to the ease of him that is tortured; not to the informing of the torturers: and therefore ought not to have the credit of a sufficient testimony: for whether he deliver himself by true, or false accusation, he does it by the right of preserving his own life.

The force of words, being (as I have formerly noted) too weak to hold men to the performance of their covenants; there are in man's nature, but two imaginable helps to strengthen it. And those are either a fear of the consequence of breaking their word; or a glory, or pride in appearing not to need to break it. This latter is a generosity too rarely found to be presumed on, especially in the pursuers of wealth, command, or sensual pleasure; which are the greatest part of mankind. The passion to be reckoned upon, is fear; whereof there be two very general objects: one, the power of spirits invisible; the other, the power of those men they shall therein offend. Of these two, though the former be the greater power, yet the fear of the latter is commonly the greater fear. The fear of the former is in every man, his own religion: which hath place in the nature of man before civil society. The latter hath not so; at least not place enough, to keep men to their promises; because in the condition of mere nature, the inequality of power is not discerned, but by the event of battle. So that before the time of civil society, or in the interruption thereof by war, there is nothing can strengthen a covenant of peace agreed on, against the temptations of avarice, ambition, lust, or other strong desire, but the fear of that invisible power, which they every one worship as God; and fear as a revenger of their perfidy. All therefore that can be done between two men not subject to civil power, is to put one another to swear by the God he feareth: which *swearing*, or OATH, is a *form of speech, added to a promise; by which he that promiseth, signifieth, that unless he perform, he renounceth the mercy of his God, or calleth to him for vengeance on himself.* Such was the heathen form, *Let* Jupiter *kill me else, as I kill this beast.* So is our form, *I shall do thus, and thus, so help me God.* And this, with the rites and ceremonies, which everyone useth in his own religion, that the fear of breaking faith might be the greater.

....

It appears also, that the oath adds nothing to the obligation. For a covenant, if lawful, binds in the sight of God, without the oath, as much as with it: if unlawful, bindeth not at all; though it be confirmed with an oath.

CHAPTER XV

Of other laws of nature

From that law of nature, by which we are obliged to transfer to another, such rights, as being retained, hinder the peace of mankind, there followeth a third; which is this, *that men perform their covenants made*: without which, covenants are in vain, and but empty words; and the right of all men to all things remaining, we are still in the condition of war.

And in this law of nature, consisteth the fountain and original of JUSTICE. For where no covenant hath preceded, there hath no right been transferred, and every man has right to everything; and consequently, no action can be unjust. But when a covenant is made, then to break it is *unjust*: and the definition of INJUSTICE, is no other than *the not performance of covenant*. And whatsoever is not unjust, is *just*.

But because covenants of mutual trust, where there is a fear of not performance on either part, (as hath been said in the former chapter,) are invalid; though the original of justice be the making of covenants; yet injustice actually there can be none, till the cause of such fear be taken away; which, while men are in the natural condition of war, cannot be done. Therefore before the names of just, and unjust can have place, there must be some coercive power, to compel men equally to the performance of their covenants, by the terror of some punishment, greater than the benefit they expect by the breach of their covenant; and to make good that propriety, which by mutual contract men acquire, in recompense of the universal right they abandon: and such power there is none before the erection of a commonwealth. And this is also to be gathered out of the ordinary definition of justice in the schools: for they say, that justice is the constant will of giving to every man his own. And therefore where there is no *own*, that is, no propriety, there is no injustice; and where there is no coercive power erected, that is, where there is no commonwealth, there is no propriety; all men having right to all things: therefore where there is no commonwealth, there nothing is unjust. So that the nature of justice, consisteth in keeping of valid covenants: but the validity of covenants begins not but with the constitution of a civil power, sufficient to compel men to keep them: and then it is also that propriety begins.

The fool hath said in his heart, there is no such thing as justice; and sometimes also with his tongue; seriously alleging, that every man's conservation, and contentment, being committed to his own care, there could be no reason, why every man might not do what he thought conduced thereunto: and therefore also to make, or not make; keep, or not keep covenants, was not against reason, when it conduced to one's benefit. He does not therein deny, that there be covenants; and that they are sometimes broken, sometimes kept; and that such breach of them may be called injustice, and the observance of them justice: but he questioneth, whether injustice, taking away the fear of God, (for the same fool hath said in his heart there is no God,) may not sometimes stand with that reason, which dictateth to every man his own good; and particularly then, when it conduceth to such a benefit, as shall put a man in a condition, to neglect not only the dispraise, and revilings, but also the power of other men. The kingdom of God is gotten by violence: but what if it could be gotten by unjust violence? Were it against reason so to get it, when it is impossible to receive hurt by it? And if it be not against reason, it is not against justice: or else justice is not to be approved for good. From such reasoning as this, successful wickedness hath obtained the name of virtue: and some that in all other things have disallowed the violation of faith; yet have allowed it, when it is for the getting of a kingdom. And the heathen that believed, that Saturn was deposed by his son *Jupiter*, believed nevertheless the same *Jupiter* to be the avenger of injustice: somewhat like to a piece of law in *Coke's* Commentaries on *Littleton*; where he says, if the right heir of the crown be attainted of treason; yet the crown shall descend to him, and *eo instante* the attainder be void: from which instances a man will be very prone to infer; that when the heir apparent of a kingdom, shall kill him that is in possession, though his father; you may call it injustice, or by what other name you will; yet it can never be against reason, seeing all the voluntary actions of men tend to the benefit of themselves; and those actions are most reasonable, that conduce most to their ends. This specious reasoning is nevertheless false.

For the question is not of promises mutual, where there is no security of performance on either side; as when there is no civil power erected over the parties promising; for such promises are no covenants: but either where one of the parties has performed already; or where there is a power to make him perform; there is the question whether it be against reason, that is, against the benefit of the other to perform, or not. And I say it is not against reason. For the manifestation whereof, we are to consider; first, that when a man doth a thing, which notwithstanding anything can be foreseen, and reckoned on, tendeth to his own destruction, howsoever some accident which he could not expect, arriving, may turn it to his benefit; yet such events do not make it reasonably or wisely done. Secondly, that in a condition of war, wherein every man to every man, for want of a common power to keep them all in awe, is an enemy, there is no man can hope by his own strength, or wit, to defend himself from destruction, without the help of confederates; where everyone expects the same defence by the confederation, that any one else does: and therefore he which declares he thinks it reason to deceive those that help him, can in reason expect no other means of safety, than what can be had from his own single power. He therefore that breaketh his covenant, and consequently declareth that he thinks he may with reason do so, cannot be received into any society, that unite themselves for peace and defence, but by the error of them that receive him; nor when he is received, be retained in it, without seeing the danger of their error; which errors a man cannot reasonably reckon upon as the means of his security: and therefore if he be left, or cast out of society, he perisheth; and if he live in society it is by the errors of other men, which he could not foresee, nor reckon upon; and consequently against the reason of his preservation; and so, as all men that contribute not to his destruction, forbear him only out of ignorance of what is good for themselves.

As for the instance of gaining the secure and perpetual felicity of heaven, by any way; it is frivolous: there being but one way imaginable; and that is not breaking, but keeping of covenant.

And for the other instance of attaining sovereignty by rebellion; it is manifest, that though the event follow, yet because it cannot reasonably be expected, but rather the contrary; and because by gaining it so, others are taught to gain the same in like manner, the attempt thereof is against reason. Justice therefore, that is to say, keeping of covenant, is a rule of reason, by which we are forbidden to do anything destructive to our life; and consequently a law of nature.

There be some that proceed further; and will not have the law of nature, to be those rules which conduce to the preservation of man's life on earth; but to the attaining of an eternal felicity after death; to which they think the breach of covenant may conduce; and consequently be just and reasonable; (such are they that think it a work of merit to kill, or depose, or rebel against, the sovereign power constituted over them by their own consent.) But because there is no natural knowledge of man's estate after death; much less of the reward that is then to be given to breach of faith; but only a belief grounded upon other men's saying, that they know it supernaturally, or that they know those that knew them, that knew others, that knew it supernaturally; breach of faith cannot be called a precept of reason, or nature.

Others, that allow for a law of nature, the keeping of faith, do nevertheless make exception of certain persons; as heretics, and such as use not to perform their covenant to others: and this also is against reason. For if any fault of a man, be sufficient to discharge our covenant made; the same ought in reason to have been sufficient to have hindered the making of it.

The names of just, and unjust, when they are attributed to men, signify one thing; and when they are attributed to actions, another. When they are attributed to men, they signify conformity, or inconformity of manners, to reason. But when they are attributed to actions, they signify the conformity, or inconformity to reason, not of manners, or manner of life, but of particular actions. A just man therefore, is he that taketh all the care he can, that his actions may be all just: and an unjust man, is he that neglecteth it. And such men are more often in our language styled by the names of righteous, and unrighteous; than just, and unjust; though the meaning be the same. Therefore a righteous man, does not lose that title, by one, or a few unjust actions, that proceed from sudden passion, or mistake of things, or persons: nor does an unrighteous man, lose his character, for such actions, as he does, or forbears to do, for fear: because his will is not framed by the justice, but by the apparent benefit of what he is to do. That which gives to human actions the relish of justice, is a certain nobleness or gallantness of courage, (rarely found,) by which a man scorns to be beholding for the contentment of his life, to fraud, or breach of promise. This justice of the manners, is that which is meant, where justice is called a virtue; and injustice, a vice.

But the justice of actions denominates men, not just, but guiltless: and the injustice of the same, (which is also called injury,) gives them but the name of guilty.

....

Whatsoever is done to a man, conformable to his own will signified to the doer, is no injury to him. For if he that doeth it, hath not passed away his original right to do what he please, by some antecedent covenant, there is no breach of covenant; and therefore no injury done him. And if he have; then his will to have it done being signified, is a release of that covenant: and so again there is no injury done him.

....

As justice dependeth on antecedent covenant; so does GRATITUDE depend on antecedent grace; that is to say, antecedent free gift: and is the fourth law of nature; which may be conceived in this form, *that a man which receiveth benefit from another of mere grace, endeavour that he which giveth it, have no reasonable cause to repent him of his good will.* For no man giveth, but with intention of good to himself; because gift is voluntary; and of all voluntary acts, the object is to every man his own good; of which if men see they shall be frustrated, there will be no beginning of benevolence, or trust; nor consequently of mutual help; nor of reconciliation of one man to another; and therefore they are to remain still in the condition of *war*, which is contrary to the first and fundamental law of nature, which commandeth men to *seek peace.* The breach of this law, is called *ingratitude*; and hath the same relation to grace, that injustice hath to obligation by covenant.

THOMAS HOBBES (1588-1679)

A fifth law of nature, is COMPLAISANCE; that is to say, *that every man strive to accommodate himself to the rest.* For the understanding whereof, we may consider, that there is in men's aptness to society, a diversity of nature, rising from their diversity of affections; not unlike to that we see in stones brought together for building of an edifice. For as that stone which by the asperity, and irregularity of figure, takes more room from others, than itself fills; and for the hardness, cannot be easily made plain, and thereby hindereth the building, is by the builders cast away as unprofitable, and troublesome: so also, a man that by asperity of nature, will strive to retain those things which to himself are superfluous, and to others necessary; and for the stubbornness of his passions, cannot be corrected, is to be left, or cast out of society, as cumbersome thereunto. For seeing every man, not only by right, but also by necessity of nature, is supposed to endeavour all he can, to obtain that which is necessary for his conservation; he that shall oppose himself against it, for things superfluous, is guilty of the war that thereupon is to follow; and therefore doth that, which is contrary to the fundamental law of nature, which commandeth *to seek peace*. The observers of this law, may be called SOCIABLE, (the Latins call them *commodi*;) the contrary, *stubborn, insociable, froward, intractable.*

A sixth law of nature, is this, *that upon caution of the future time, a man ought to pardon the offences past of them that repenting, desire it.* For PARDON, is nothing but granting of peace; which though granted to them that persevere in their hostility, be not peace, but fear; yet not granted to them that give caution of the future time, is sign of an aversion to peace; and therefore contrary to the law of nature.

A seventh is, *that in revenges,* (that is, retribution of evil for evil,) *men look not at the greatness of the evil past, but the greatness of the good to follow.* Whereby we are forbidden to inflict punishment with any other design, than for correction of the offender, or direction of others. For this law is consequent to the next before it, that commandeth pardon, upon security of the future time. Besides, revenge without respect to the example, and profit to come, is a triumph, or glorying in the hurt of another, tending to no end; (for the end is always somewhat to come;) and glorying to no end, is vain-glory, and contrary to reason; and to hurt without reason, tendeth to the introduction of war; which is against the law of nature; and is commonly styled by the name of *cruelty*.

And because all signs of hatred, or contempt, provoke to fight; insomuch as most men choose rather to hazard their life, than not to be revenged; we may in the eighth place, for a law of nature, set down this precept, *that no man by deed, word, countenance, or gesture, declare hatred, or contempt of another.* The breach of which law, is commonly called *contumely*.

The question who is the better man, has no place in the condition of mere nature; where, (as has been shown before,) all men are equal.

The inequality that now is, has been introduced by the laws civil. I know that *Aristotle* in the first book of his Politics, for a foundation of his doctrine, maketh men by nature, some more worthy to command, meaning the wiser sort (such as he thought himself to be for his philosophy;) others to serve, (meaning those that had strong bodies, but were not philosophers as he;) as if master and servant were not introduced by consent of men, but by difference of wit: which is not only against reason; but also against experience. For there are very few so foolish, that had not rather govern themselves, than be governed by others: nor when the wise in their own conceit, contend by force, with them who distrust their own wisdom, do they always, or often, or almost at any time, get the victory. If nature therefore have made men equal; that equality is to be acknowledged: or if nature have made men unequal; yet because men that think themselves equal, will not enter into conditions of peace, but upon equal terms, such equality must be admitted. And therefore for the ninth law of nature, I put this, *that every man acknowledge other for his equal by nature.* The breach of this precept is *pride.*

On this law, dependeth another, *that at the entrance into conditions of peace, no man require to reserve to himself any right, which he is not content should be reserved to every one of the rest.* As it is necessary for all men that seek peace, to lay down certain rights of nature; that is to say, not to have liberty to do all they list: so is it necessary for man's life, to retain some; as right to govern their own bodies; enjoy air, water, motion, ways to go from place to place; and all things else, without which a man cannot live, or not live well. If in this case, at the making of peace, men require for themselves, that which they would not have to be granted to others, they do contrary to the precedent law, that commandeth the acknowledgement of natural equality, and therefore also against the law of nature. The observers of this law, are those we call *modest*, and the breakers *arrogant* men. The Greeks call the violation of this law *pleonexia*; that is, a desire of more than their share.

Also, if *a man he trusted to judge between man and man*, it is a precept of the law of nature, *that he deal equally between them.* For without that, the controversies of men cannot be determined but by war. He therefore that is partial in judgement, doth what in him lies, to deter men from the use of judges, and arbitrators; and consequently, (against the fundamental law of nature) is the cause of war.

The observance of this law, from the equal distribution to each man of that which in reason belongeth to him, is called EQUITY, and (as I have said before) distributive justice: the violation, *acception of persons, prosopolepsia.*

And from this followeth another law, *that such things as cannot be divided, be enjoyed in common, if it can be; and if the quantity of the thing permit, without stint; otherwise proportionably to the number of them that have right.* For otherwise the distribution is unequal, and contrary to equity.

But some things there be, that can neither be divided, nor enjoyed in common. Then, the law of nature, which prescribeth equity, requireth, *that the entire right; or else, (making the use alternate,) the first possession, be determined by lot.* For equal distribution, is of the law of nature; and other means of equal distribution cannot be imagined.

Of *lots* there be two sorts, *arbitrary* and *natural*. Arbitrary, is that which is agreed on by the competitors: natural is either *primogeniture*, (which the Greek calls *kleronomia*, which signifies, *given by lot*;) or *first seizure*.

And therefore those things which cannot be enjoyed in common, nor divided, ought to be adjudged to the first possessor; and in some cases to the first born, as acquired by lot.

It is also a law of nature, *that all men that mediate peace, be allowed safe conduct.* For the law that commandeth peace, as the *end*, commandeth intercession, as the *means*; and to intercession the means is safe conduct.

And because, though men be never so willing to observe these laws, there may nevertheless arise questions concerning a man's action; first, whether it were done, or not done; secondly (if done) whether against the law, or not against the law; the former whereof, is called a question *of fact*; the latter a question *of right*; therefore unless the parties to the question, covenant mutually to stand to the sentence of another, they are as far from peace as ever. This other, to whose sentence they submit, is called an ARBITRATOR. And therefore it is of the law of nature, *that they that are at controversy, submit their right to the judgement of an arbitrator.*

And seeing every man is presumed to do all things in order to his own benefit, no man is a fit arbitrator in his own cause: and if he were never so fit; yet equity allowing to each party equal benefit, if one be admitted to be judge, the other is to be admitted also; and so the controversy, that is, the cause of war, remains, against the law of nature.

For the same reason no man in any cause ought to be received for arbitrator, to whom greater profit, or honour, or pleasure apparently ariseth out of the victory of one party, than of the other: for he hath taken (though an unavoidable bribe, yet) a bribe; and no man can be obliged to trust him. And thus also the controversy, and the condition of war remaineth, contrary to the law of nature.

And in a controversy of *fact*, the judge being to give no more credit to one, than to the other, (if there be no other arguments) must give credit to a third; or to a third and fourth; or more: for else the question is undecided, and left to force, contrary to the law of nature.

These are the laws of nature, dictating peace, for a means of the conservation of men in multitudes; and which only concern the doctrine of civil society. There be other things tending to the destruction of particular men; as drunkenness, and all other parts of intemperance; which may therefore also be reckoned amongst those things which the law of nature hath forbidden; but are not necessary to be mentioned, nor are pertinent enough to this place.

And though this may seem too subtle a deduction of the laws of nature, to be taken notice of by all men; whereof the most part are too busy in getting food, and the rest too negligent to understand; yet to leave all men inexcusable, they have been contracted into one easy sum, intelligible, even to the meanest capacity; and that is, *Do not that to another, which thou wouldest not have done to thyself;* which showeth him, that he has no more to do in learning the laws of nature, but, when weighing the actions of other men with his own, they seem too heavy, to put them into the other part of the balance, and his own into their place, that his own passions, and self-love, may add nothing to the weight; and then there is none of these laws of nature that will not appear unto him very reasonable.

The laws of nature oblige *in foro interno*; that is to say, they bind to a desire they should take place: but *in foro externo*; that is, to the putting them in act, not always. For he that should be modest, and tractable, and perform all he promises, in such time, and place, where no man else should do so, should but make himself a prey to others, and procure his own certain ruin, contrary to the ground of all laws of nature, which tend to nature's preservation. And again, he that having sufficient security, that others shall observe the same laws towards him, observes them not himself, seeketh not peace, but war; and consequently the destruction of his nature by violence.

And whatsoever laws bind *in foro interno*, may be broken, not only by a fact contrary to the law, but also by a fact according to it, in case a man think it contrary. For though his action in this case, be according to the law; yet his purpose was against the law; which where the obligation is *in foro interno*, is a breach.

The laws of nature are immutable and eternal; for injustice, ingratitude, arrogance, pride, iniquity, acception of persons, and the rest, can never be made lawful. For it can never be that war shall preserve life, and peace destroy it.

The same laws, because they oblige only to a desire, and endeavour, I mean an unfeigned and constant endeavour, are easy to be observed. For in that they require nothing but endeavour; he that endeavoureth their performance, fulfilleth them; and he that fulfilleth the law, is just.

And the science of them, is the true and only moral philosophy. For moral philosophy is nothing else but the science of what is *good,* and *evil,* in the conversation, and society of mankind. *Good,* and *evil,* are names that signify our appetites, and aversions; which in different tempers, customs, and doctrines of men, are different: and diverse men, differ not only in their judgement, on the senses of what is pleasant, and unpleasant to the taste, smell, hearing, touch, and sight; but also of what is conformable, or disagreeable to reason, in the actions of common life. Nay, the same man, in diverse times, differs from himself; and one time praiseth, that is, calleth good, what another time he dispraiseth, and calleth evil: from whence arise disputes, controversies, and at last war. And therefore so long a man is in the condition of mere nature, (which is a condition of war,) as private appetite is the measure of good, and evil: and consequently all men agree on this, that peace is good, and therefore also the way, or means of peace, which (as I have showed before) are *justice, gratitude, modesty, equity, mercy*, and the rest of the laws of nature, are good; that is to say, *moral virtues*; and their contrary *vices*, evil.

Now the science of virtue and vice, is moral philosophy; and therefore the true doctrine of the laws of nature, is the true moral philosophy. But the writers of moral philosophy, though they acknowledge the same virtues and vices; yet not seeing wherein consisted their goodness; nor that they come to be praised, as the means of peaceable, sociable, and comfortable living; place them in a mediocrity of passions: as if not the cause, but the degree of daring, made fortitude; or not the cause, but the quantity of a gift, made liberality.

These dictates of reason, men used to call by the name of laws, but improperly: for they are but conclusions, or theorems concerning what conduceth to the conservation and defence of themselves; whereas law, properly is the word of him, that by right hath command over others. But yet if we consider the same theorems, as delivered in the word of God, that by right commandeth all things; then are they properly called laws.

PART II: OF COMMONWEALTH

CHAPTER XVII

Of the causes, generation, and definition of a COMMONWEALTH

The final cause, end, or design of men, (who naturally love liberty, and dominion over others,) in the introduction of that restraint upon themselves, (in which we see them live in commonwealths,) is the foresight of their own preservation, and of a more contented life thereby; that is to say, of getting themselves out from that miserable condition of war, which is necessarily consequent (as hath been shown) to the natural passions of men, when there is no visible power to keep them in awe, and tie them by fear of punishment to the performance of their covenants, and observation of those laws of nature set down in the fourteenth and fifteenth chapters.

For the laws of nature (as *justice, equity, modesty, mercy*, and (in sum) *doing to others, as we would be done to*,) of themselves, without the terror of some power, to cause them to be observed, are contrary to our natural passions, that carry us to partiality, pride, revenge, and the like. And covenants, without the sword, are but words, and of no strength to secure a man at all. Therefore, notwithstanding the laws of nature, (which everyone hath then kept, when he has the will to keep them, when he can do it safely,) if there be no power erected, or not great enough for our security; every man will, and may lawfully rely on his own strength and art, for caution against all other men.

....

Nor is it the joining together of a small number of men, that gives them this security; because in small numbers, small additions on the one side or the other, make the advantage of strength so great, as is sufficient to carry the victory; and therefore gives encouragement to an invasion. The multitude sufficient to confide in for our security, is not determined by any certain number, but by comparison with the enemy we fear; and is then sufficient, when the odds of the enemy is not of so visible and conspicuous moment, to determine the event of war, as to move him to attempt.

And be there never so great a multitude; yet if their actions be directed according to their particular judgements, and particular appetites, they can expect thereby no defence, nor protection, neither against a common enemy, nor against the injuries of one another. For being distracted in opinions concerning the best use and application of their strength, they do not help, but hinder one another; and reduce their strength by mutual opposition to nothing: whereby they are easily, not only subdued by a very few that agree together; but also when there is no common enemy, they make war upon each other, for their particular interests. For if we could suppose a great multitude of men to consent in the observation of justice, and other laws of nature, without a common power to keep them all in awe; we might as well suppose all mankind to do the same; and then there neither would be, nor need to be any civil government, or commonwealth at all; because there would be peace without subjection.

Nor is it enough for the security, which men desire should last all the time of their life, that they be governed, and directed by one judgement, for a limited time; as in one battle, or one war. For though they obtain a victory by their unanimous endeavour against a foreign enemy; yet afterwards, when either they have no common enemy, or he that by one part is held for an enemy, is by another part held for a friend, they must needs by the difference of their interests dissolve, and fall again into a war amongst themselves.

It is true, that certain living creatures, as bees, and ants, live sociably one with another, (which are therefore by *Aristotle* numbered amongst political creatures;) and yet have no other direction, than their particular judgements and appetites; nor speech, whereby one of them can signify to another, what he thinks expedient for the common benefit: and therefore some man may perhaps desire to know, why mankind cannot do the same. To which I answer,

First, that men are continually in competition for honour and dignity, which these creatures are not; and consequently amongst men there ariseth on that ground, envy and hatred, and finally war; but amongst these not so.

Secondly, that amongst these creatures, the common good differeth not from the private; and being by nature inclined to their private, they procure thereby the common benefit. But man, whose joy consisteth in comparing himself with other men, can relish nothing but what is eminent.

Thirdly, that these creatures, having not (as man) the use of reason, do not see, nor think they see any fault, in the administration of their common business: whereas amongst men, there are very many, that think themselves wiser, and abler to govern the public, better than the rest; and these strive to reform and innovate, one this way, another that way; and thereby bring it into distraction and civil war.

Fourthly, that these creatures, though they have some use of voice, in making known to one another their desires, and other affections; yet they want that art of words, by which some men can represent to others, that which is good, in the likeness of evil; and evil, in the likeness of good; and augment, or diminish the apparent greatness of good and evil; discontenting men, and troubling their peace at their pleasure.

Fifthly, irrational creatures cannot distinguish between *injury*, and *damage*; and therefore as long as they be at ease, they are not offended with their fellows: whereas man is then most troublesome, when he is most at ease: for then it is that he loves to show his wisdom, and control the actions of them that govern the commonwealth.

Lastly, the agreement of these creatures is natural; that of men, is by covenant only, which is artificial: and therefore it is no wonder if there be somewhat else required (besides covenant) to make their agreement constant and lasting; which is a common power, to keep them in awe, and to direct their actions to the common benefit.

The only way to erect such a common power, as may be able to defend them from the invasion of foreigners, and the injuries of one another, and thereby to secure them in such sort, as that by their own industry, and by the fruits of the earth, they may nourish themselves and live contentedly; is, to confer all their power and strength upon one man, or upon one assembly of men, that may reduce all their wills, by plurality of voices, unto one will: which is as much as to say, to appoint one man, or assembly of men, to bear their person; and every one to own, and acknowledge himself to be author of whatsoever he that so beareth their person, shall act, or cause to be acted, in those things which concern the common peace and safety; and therein to submit their wills, everyone to his will, and their judgements to his judgement. This is more than consent, or concord; it is a real unity of them all, in one and the same person, made by covenant of every man with every man, in such manner, as if every man should say to every man, *I authorise and give up my right of governing myself, to this man, or to this assembly of men, on this condition, that thou give up thy right to him, and authorise all his actions in like manner.* This done, the multitude so united in one person, is called a COMMONWEALTH, in Latin CIVITAS. This is the generation of that great LEVIATHAN, or rather (to speak more reverently) of that *mortal god*, to which we owe under the *immortal God*, our peace and defence. For by this authority, given him by every particular man in the commonwealth, he hath the use of so much power and strength conferred on him, that by terror thereof, he is enabled to conform the wills of them all, to peace at home, and mutual aid against their enemies abroad. And in him consisteth the essence of the commonwealth; which (to define it,) is *one person, of whose acts a great multitude, by mutual covenants one with another, have made themselves every one the author, to the end he may use the strength and means of them all, as he shall think expedient, for their peace and common defence.*

And he that carryeth this person, is called SOVEREIGN, and said to have *sovereign power*; and every one besides, his SUBJECT.

The attaining to this sovereign power, is by two ways. One, by natural force; as when a man maketh his children, to submit themselves, and their children to his government, as being able to destroy them if they refuse; or by war subdueth his enemies to his will, giving them their lives on that condition. The other, is when men agree amongst themselves, to submit to some man, or assembly of men, voluntarily, on confidence to be protected by him against all others. This latter may be called a political commonwealth, or commonwealth by *institution*; and the former, a commonwealth by *acquisition*. And first, I shall speak of a commonwealth by institution.

CHAPTER XVIII

Of the RIGHTS of sovereigns by institution

A *commonwealth* is said to be *instituted*, when a *multitude* of men do agree, and *covenant, every one, with every one*, that to whatsoever *man*, or *assembly of men*, shall be given by the major part, the *right* to *present* the person of them all, (that is to say, to be their *representative*;) every one, as well he that *voted for it*, as he that *voted against it*, shall *authorize* all the actions and judgements, of that man, or assembly of men, in the same manner, as if they were his own, to the end, to live peaceably amongst themselves, and be protected against other men.

From this institution of a commonwealth are derived all the *rights* and *faculties* of him, or them, on whom the sovereign power is conferred by the consent of the people assembled.

First, because they covenant, it is to be understood, they are not obliged by former covenant to anything repugnant hereunto. And consequently they that have already instituted a commonwealth, being thereby bound by covenant, to own the actions, and judgements of one, cannot lawfully make a new covenant, amongst themselves, to be obedient to any other, in anything whatsoever, without his permission. And therefore, they that are subjects to a monarch, cannot without his leave cast off monarchy, and return to the confusion of a disunited multitude; nor transfer their person from him that beareth it, to another man, or other assembly of men: for they are bound, every man to every man, to own, and be reputed author of all, that he that already is their sovereign, shall do, and judge fit to be done: so that any one man dissenting, all the rest should break their covenant made to that man, which is injustice: and they have also every man given the sovereignty to him that beareth their person; and therefore if they depose him, they take from him that which is his own, and so again it is injustice. Besides, if he that attempteth to depose his sovereign, be killed, or punished by him for such attempt, he is author of his own punishment, as being by the institution, author of all his sovereign shall do: and because it is injustice for a man to do anything, for which he may be punished by his own authority, he is also upon that title, unjust. And whereas some men have pretended for their disobedience to their sovereign, a new covenant, made, not with men, but with God; this also is unjust: for there is no covenant with God, but by mediation of somebody that representeth God's person; which none doth but God's lieutenant who hath the sovereignty under God. But this pretence of covenant with God, is so evident a lie, even in the pretenders' own consciences, that it is not only an act of an unjust, but also of a vile, and unmanly disposition.

Secondly, because the right of bearing the person of them all, is given to him they make sovereign, by covenant only of one to another, and not of him to any of them; there can happen no breach of covenant on the part of the sovereign; and consequently none of his subjects, by any pretence of forfeiture, can be freed from his subjection. That he which is made sovereign maketh no covenant with his subjects beforehand, is manifest; because either he must make it with the whole multitude, as one party to the covenant; or he must make a several covenant with every man. With the whole, as one party, it is impossible; because as yet they are not one person: and if he make so many several covenants as there be men, those covenants after he hath the sovereignty are void, because what act soever can be pretended by any one of them for breach thereof, is the act both of himself, and of all the rest, because done in the person, and by the right of every one of them in particular. Besides, if any one, or more of them, pretend a breach of the covenant made by the sovereign at his institution; and others, or one other of his subjects, or himself alone, pretend there was no such breach, there is in this case, no judge to decide the controversy: it returns therefore to the sword again; and every man recovereth the right of protecting himself by his own strength, contrary to the design they had in the institution. It is therefore in vain to grant sovereignty by way of precedent covenant. The opinion that any monarch receiveth his power by covenant, that is to say on condition, proceedeth from want of understanding this easy truth, that covenants being but words, and breath, have no force to oblige, contain, constrain, or protect any man, but what it has from the public sword; that is, from the untied hands of that man, or assembly of men that hath the sovereignty, and whose actions are avouched by them all, and performed by the strength of them all, in him united. But when an assembly of men is made sovereign; then no man imagineth any such covenant to have passed in the institution; for no man is so dull as to say, for example, the people of *Rome*, made a covenant with the Romans, to hold the sovereignty on such or such conditions; which not performed, the Romans might lawfully depose the Roman people. That men see not the reason to be alike in a monarchy, and in a popular government, proceedeth from the ambition of some, that are kinder to the government of an assembly, whereof they may hope to participate, than of monarchy, which they despair to enjoy.

Thirdly, because the major part hath by consenting voices declared a sovereign; he that dissented must now consent with the rest; that is, be contented to avow all the actions he shall do, or else justly be destroyed by the rest. For if he voluntarily entered into the congregation of them that were assembled, he sufficiently declared thereby his will (and therefore tacitly covenanted) to stand to what the major part should ordain: and therefore if he refuse to stand thereto, or make protestation against any of their decrees, he does contrary to his covenant, and therefore unjustly. And whether he be of the congregation, or not; and whether his consent be asked, or not, he must either submit to their decrees, or be left in the condition of war he was in before; wherein he might without injustice be destroyed by any man whatsoever.

Fourthly, because every subject is by this institution author of all the actions, and judgements of the sovereign instituted; it follows, that whatsoever he doth, it can be no injury to any of his subjects; nor ought he to be by any of them accused of injustice. For he that doth anything by authority from another, doth therein no injury to him by whose authority he acteth: but by this institution of a commonwealth, every particular man is author of all the sovereign doth; and consequently he that complaineth of injury from his sovereign, complaineth of that whereof he himself is author; and therefore ought not to accuse any man but himself; no nor himself of injury; because to do injury to oneself, is impossible. It is true that they that have sovereign power, may commit iniquity; but not injustice, or injury in the proper signification.

Fifthly, and consequently to that which was said last, no man that hath sovereign power can justly be put to death, or otherwise in any manner by his subjects punished. For seeing every subject is author of the actions of his sovereign; he punisheth another, for the actions committed by himself.

And because the end of this institution, is the peace and defence of them all; and whosoever has right to the end, has right to the means; it belongeth of right, to whatsoever man, or assembly that hath the sovereignty, to be judge both of the means of peace and defence; and also of the hindrances, and disturbances of the same; and to do whatsoever he shall think necessary to be done, both beforehand, for the preserving of peace and security, by prevention of discord at home, and hostility from abroad; and, when peace and security are lost, for the recovery of the same. And therefore,

Sixthly, it is annexed to the sovereignty, to be judge of what opinions and doctrines are averse, and what conducing to peace; and consequently, on what occasions, how far, and what, men are to be trusted withal, in speaking to multitudes of people; and who shall examine the doctrines of all books before they be published. For the actions of men proceed from their opinions; and in the well-governing of opinions, consisteth the well-governing of men's actions, in order to their peace, and concord. And though in matter of doctrine, nothing ought to be regarded but the truth; yet this is not repugnant to regulating of the same by peace. For doctrine repugnant to peace, can no more be true, than peace and concord can be against the law of nature. It is true, that in a commonwealth, where by the negligence, or unskillfulness of governors and teachers, false doctrines are by time generally received; the contrary truths may be generally offensive: yet the most sudden, and rough bustling in of a new truth, that can be, does never break the peace, but only sometimes awake the war. For those men that are so remissly governed, that they dare take up arms, to defend, or introduce an opinion, are still in war; and their condition not peace, but only a cessation of arms for fear of one another; and they live, as it were, in the procincts of battle continually. It belongeth therefore to him that hath the sovereign power, to be judge, or constitute all judges of opinions and doctrines, as a thing necessary to peace; thereby to prevent discord and civil war.

Seventhly, is annexed to the sovereignty, the whole power of prescribing the rules, whereby every man may know, what goods he may enjoy, and what actions he may do, without being molested by any of his fellow subjects: and this is it men call *propriety*. For before constitution of sovereign power (as hath already been shown) all men had right to all things; which necessarily causeth war: and therefore this propriety, being necessary to peace, and depending on sovereign power, is the act of that power, in order to the public peace. These rules of propriety (or *meum* and *tuum*) and of *good, evil, lawful,* and *unlawful* in the actions of subjects, are the civil laws; that is to say, the laws of each commonwealth in particular; though the name of civil law be now restrained to the ancient civil laws of the city of *Rome;* which being the head of a great part of the world, her laws at that time were in these parts the civil law.

Eighthly, is annexed to the sovereignty, the right of judicature; that is to say, of hearing and deciding all controversies, which may arise concerning law, either civil, or natural, or concerning fact. For without the decision of controversies, there is no protection of one subject, against the injuries of another; the laws concerning *meum* and *tuum* are in vain; and to every man remaineth, from the natural and necessary appetite of his own conservation, the right of protecting himself by his private strength, which is the condition of war; and contrary to the end for which every commonwealth is instituted.

Ninthly, is annexed to the sovereignty, the right of making war, and peace with other nations, and commonwealths; that is to say, of judging when it is for the public good, and how great forces are to be assembled, armed, and paid for that end; and to levy money upon the subjects, to defray the expenses thereof. For the power by which the people are to be defended, consisteth in their armies; and the strength of an army, in the union of their strength under one command; which command the sovereign instituted, therefore hath; because the command of the *militia*, without other institution, maketh him that hath it sovereign. And therefore whosoever is made general of an army, he that hath the sovereign power is always generalissimo.

Tenthly, is annexed to the sovereignty, the choosing of all counsellors, ministers, magistrates, and officers, both in peace, and war. For seeing the sovereign is charged with the end, which is the common peace and defence; he is understood to have power to use such means, as he shall think most fit for his discharge.

Eleventhly, to the sovereign is committed the power of rewarding with riches, or honour; and of punishing with corporal, or pecuniary punishment, or with ignominy every subject according to the law he hath formerly made; or if there be no law made, according as he shall judge most to conduce to the encouraging of men to serve the commonwealth, or deterring of them from doing disservice to the same.

Lastly, considering what values men are naturally apt to set upon themselves; what respect they look for from others; and how little they value other men; from whence continually arise amongst them, emulation, quarrels, factions, and at last war, to the destroying of one another, and diminution of their strength against a common enemy; it is necessary that there be laws of honour, and a public rate of the worth of such men as have deserved, or are able to deserve well of the commonwealth; and that there be force in the hands of some or other, to put those laws in execution. But it hath already been shown, that not only the whole *militia*, or forces of the commonwealth; but also the judicature of all controversies, is annexed to the sovereignty. To the sovereign therefore it belongeth also to give titles of honour; and to appoint what order of place, and dignity, each man shall hold; and what signs of respect, in public or private meetings, they shall give to one another.

These are the rights, which make the essence of sovereignty; and which are the marks, whereby a man may discern in what man, or assembly of men, the sovereign power is placed, and resideth. For these are incommunicable, and inseparable. The power to coin money; to dispose of the estate and persons of infant heirs; to have pre-emption in markets; and all other statute prerogatives, may be transferred by the sovereign; and yet the power to protect his subjects be retained. But if he transfer the *militia*, he retains the judicature in vain, for want of execution of the laws: or if he grant away the power of raising money; the *militia* is in vain: or if he give away the government of doctrines, men will be frighted into rebellion with the fear of spirits. And so if we consider any one of the said rights, we shall presently see, that the holding of all the rest, will produce no effect, in the conservation of peace and justice, the end for which all commonwealths are instituted. And this division is it, whereof it is said, *a kingdom divided in itself cannot stand*: for unless this division precede, division into opposite armies can never happen. If there had not first been an opinion received of the greatest part of *England* that these powers were divided between the King and the Lords and the House of Commons, the people had never been divided, and fallen into this civil war; first between those that disagreed in politics; and after between the dissenters about the liberty of religion; which have so instructed men in this point of sovereign right, that there be few now (in England,) that do not see, that these rights are inseparable, and will be so generally acknowledged, at the next return of peace; and so continue, till their miseries are forgotten; and no longer, except the vulgar be better taught than they have hitherto been.

....

But a man may here object, that the condition of subjects is very miserable; as being obnoxious to the lusts, and other irregular passions of him, or them that have so unlimited a power in their hands. And commonly they that live under a monarch, think it the fault of monarchy; and they that live under the government of democracy, or other sovereign assembly, attribute all the inconvenience to that form of commonwealth; whereas the power in all forms, if they be perfect enough to protect them, is the same; not considering that the estate of man can never be without some incommodity or other; and that the greatest, that in any form of government can possibly happen to the people in general, is scarce sensible, in respect of the miseries, and horrible calamities, that accompany a civil war; or that dissolute condition of masterless men, without subjection to laws, and a coercive power to tie their hands from rapine, and revenge: nor considering that the greatest pressure of sovereign governors, proceedeth not from any delight, or profit they can expect in the damage, or weakening of their subjects, in whose vigour, consisteth their own strength and glory; but in the restiveness of themselves, that unwillingly contributing to their own defence, make it necessary for their governors to draw from them what they can in time of peace, that they may have means on any emergent occasion, or sudden need, to resist, or take advantage on their enemies. For all men are by nature provided of notable multiplying glasses, (that is their passions and self-love,) through which, every little payment appeareth a great grievance; but are destitute of those prospective glasses, (namely moral and civil science,) to see afar off the miseries that hang over them, and cannot without such payments be avoided.

CHAPTER XXI

Of the LIBERTY of subjects

LIBERTY, or FREEDOM, signifieth (properly) the absence of opposition; (by opposition, I mean external impediments of motion;) and may be applied no less to irrational, and inanimate creatures, than to rational. ... But when the impediment of motion, is in the constitution of the thing itself, we use not to say, it wants the liberty; but the power, to move; as when a stone lieth still, or a man is fastened to his bed by sickness.

And according to this proper, and generally received meaning of the word, *a* FREE-MAN, *is he, that in those things, which by his strength and wit he is able to do, is not hindered to do what he has a will to*. But when the words *free,* and *liberty,* are applied to anything but *bodies,* they are abused; for that which is not subject to motion, is not subject to impediment: ...Lastly, from the use of the word *free-will,* no liberty can be inferred of the will, desire, or inclination, but the liberty of the man; which consisteth in this, that he finds no stop, in doing what he has the will, desire, or inclination to do.

Fear, and liberty are consistent; as when a man throweth his goods into the sea for *fear* the ship should sink, he doth it nevertheless very willingly, and may refuse to do it if he will: it is therefore the action, of one that was *free*: so a man sometimes pays his debt, only for *fear* of imprisonment, which because nobody hindered him from detaining, was the action of a man at *liberty*. And generally all actions which men do in commonwealths, for *fear* of the law, are actions, which the doers had *liberty* to omit.

Liberty and *necessity* are consistent; as in the water, that hath not only *liberty*, but a *necessity* of descending by the channel; so likewise in the actions which men voluntarily do: which, because they proceed from their will, proceed from *liberty*; and yet, because every act of man's will, and every desire, and inclination proceedeth from some cause, and that from another cause, in a continual chain, (whose first link is in the hand of God the first of all causes,) they proceed from *necessity*. So that to him that could see the connection of those causes, the *necessity* of all men's voluntary actions, would appear manifest. And therefore God, that seeth, and disposeth all things, seeth also that the *liberty* of man in doing what he will, is accompanied with the *necessity* of doing that which God will, and no more, nor less.

....

But as men, for the attaining of peace, and conservation of themselves thereby, have made an artificial man, which we call a commonwealth; so also have they made artificial chains, called *civil laws*, which they themselves, by mutual covenants, have fastened at one end, to the lips of that man, or assembly, to whom they have given the sovereign power; and at the other to their own ears. These bonds, in their own nature but weak, may nevertheless be made to hold, by the danger, though not by the difficulty of breaking them.

In relation to these bonds only it is, that I am to speak now, of the *liberty of subjects*. For seeing there is no commonwealth in the world, wherein there be rules enough set down, for the regulating of all the actions, and words of men, (as being a thing impossible:) it followeth necessarily, that in all kinds of actions, by the laws pretermitted, men have the liberty, of doing what their own reasons shall suggest, for the most profitable to themselves. For if we take liberty in the proper sense, for corporal liberty; that is to say, freedom from chains, and prison, it were very absurd for men to clamour as they do, for the liberty they so manifestly enjoy. Again, if we take liberty, for an exemption from laws, it is no less absurd, for men to demand as they do, that liberty, by which all other men may be masters of their lives. And yet as absurd as it is, this is it they demand; not knowing that the laws are of no power to protect them, without a sword in the hands of a man, or men, to cause those laws to be put in execution. The liberty of a subject, lieth therefore only in those things, which in regulating their actions, the sovereign hath pretermitted: such as is the liberty to buy, and sell, and otherwise contract with one another; to choose their own abode, their own diet, their own trade of life, and institute their children as they themselves think fit; and the like.

Nevertheless we are not to understand, that by such liberty the sovereign power of life, and death, is either abolished, or limited. For it has been already shown, that nothing the sovereign representative can do to a subject, on what pretence soever, can properly be called injustice, or injury; because every subject is author of every act the sovereign doth; so that he never wanteth right to anything, otherwise, than as he himself is the subject of God, and bound thereby to observe the laws of nature. ... And the same holdeth also in a sovereign prince, that putteth to death an innocent subject. For though the action be against the law of nature, as being contrary to equity, (as was the killing of *Uriah*, by *David*;) yet it was not an injury to *Uriah*; but to *God*. Not to *Uriah*, because the right to do what he pleased, was given him by *Uriah* himself: and yet to *God*, because *David* was *God's* subject; and prohibited all iniquity by the law of nature.

....

The liberty, whereof there is so frequent, and honourable mention, in the histories, and philosophy of the ancient Greeks, and Romans, and in the writings, and discourse of those that from them have received all their learning in the politics, is not the liberty of particular men; but the liberty of the commonwealth: which is the same with that, which every man then should have, if there were no civil laws, nor commonwealth at all. And the effects of it also be the same. For as amongst masterless men, there is perpetual war, of every man against his neighbour; no inheritance, to transmit to the son, nor to expect from the father; no propriety of goods, or lands; no security; but a full and absolute liberty in every particular man: so in states, and commonwealths not dependent on one another, every commonwealth, (not every man) has an absolute liberty, to do what it shall judge (that is to say, what that man, or assembly that representeth it, shall judge) most conducing to their benefit. But withal, they live in the condition of a perpetual war, and upon the confines of battle, with their frontiers armed, and cannons planted against their neighbours round about. The *Athenians*, and *Romans* were free; that is, free commonwealths: not that any particular men had the liberty to resist their own representative; but that their representative had the liberty to resist, or invade other people. There is written on the turrets of the city of *Lucca* in great characters at this day, the word *LIBERTAS*; yet no man can thence infer, that a particular man has more liberty, or immunity from the service of the commonwealth there, than in *Constantinople*. Whether a commonwealth be monarchical, or popular, the freedom is still the same.

THOMAS HOBBES (1588-1679)

But it is an easy thing, for men to be deceived, by the specious name of liberty; and for want of judgement to distinguish, mistake that for their private inheritance, and birthright, which is the right of the public only. And when the same error is confirmed by the authority of men in reputation for their writings in this subject, it is no wonder if it produce sedition, and change of government. In these western parts of the world, we are made to receive our opinions concerning the institution, and rights of commonwealths, from *Aristotle*, *Cicero*, and other men, Greeks and Romans, that living under popular states, derived those rights, not from the principles of nature, but transcribed them into their books, out of the practice of their own commonwealths, which were popular; ...And by reading of these Greek, and Latin authors, men from their childhood have gotten a habit (under a false show of liberty,) of favouring tumults, and of licentious controlling the actions of their sovereigns; and again of controlling those controllers, with the effusion of so much blood; as I think I may truly say, there was never anything so dearly bought, as these western parts have bought the learning of the Greek and Latin tongues.

To come now to the particulars of the true liberty of a subject; that is to say, what are the things, which though commanded by the sovereign, he may nevertheless, without injustice, refuse to do; we are to consider, what rights we pass away, when we make a commonwealth; or (which is all one,) what liberty we deny ourselves, by owning all the actions (without exception) of the man or assembly we make our sovereign. For in the act of our *submission* consisteth both our *obligation*, and our *liberty*; which must therefore be inferred by arguments taken from thence; there being no obligation on any man, which ariseth not from some act of his own; for all men equally, are by nature free. And because such arguments, must either be drawn from the express words, *I authorise all his actions*, or from the intention of him that submitteth himself to his power, (which intention is to be understood by the end for which he so submitteth;) the obligation, and liberty of the subject, is to be derived, either from those words, (or others equivalent;) or else from the end of the institution of sovereignty; namely, the peace of the subjects within themselves, and their defence against a common enemy.

First therefore, seeing sovereignty by institution, is by covenant of every one to every one; and sovereignty by acquisition, by covenants of the vanquished to the victor, or child to the parent; it is manifest, that every subject has liberty in all those things, the right whereof cannot by covenant be transferred. I have shown before in the 14th chapter, that covenants, not to defend a man's own body, are void. Therefore,

If the sovereign command a man (though justly condemned,) to kill, wound, or maim himself; or not to resist those that assault him; or to abstain from the use of food, air, medicine, or any other thing, without which he cannot live; yet hath that man the liberty to disobey.

If a man be interrogated by the sovereign, or his authority, concerning a crime done by himself, he is not bound (without assurance of pardon) to confess it; because no man (as I have shown in the same chapter) can be obliged by covenant to accuse himself.

....

No man is bound by the words themselves, either to kill himself, or any other man; and consequently, that the obligation a man may sometimes have, upon the command of the sovereign to execute any dangerous, or dishonourable office, dependeth not on the words of our submission; but on the intention; which is to be understood by the end thereof. When therefore our refusal to obey, frustrates the end for which the sovereignty was ordained; then there is no liberty to refuse: otherwise, there is.

Upon this ground, a man that is commanded as a soldier to fight against the enemy, though his sovereign have right enough to punish his refusal with death, may nevertheless in many cases refuse, without injustice; as when he substituteth a sufficient soldier in his place: for in this case he deserteth not the service of the commonwealth. ...But he that enrolleth himself a soldier, or taketh impressed money, taketh away the excuse of a timorous nature; and is obliged, not only to go to the battle, but also not to run from it, without his captain's leave. And when the defence of the commonwealth, requireth at once the help of all that are able to bear arms, every one is obliged; because otherwise the institution of the commonwealth, which they have not the purpose, or courage to preserve, was in vain.

To resist the sword of the commonwealth, in defence of another man, guilty, or innocent, no man hath liberty; because such liberty, takes away from the sovereign, the means of protecting us; and is therefore destructive of the very essence of government. But in case a great many men together, have already resisted the sovereign power unjustly, or committed some capital crime, for which every one of them expecteth death, whether have they not the liberty then to join together, and assist, and defend one another? Certainly they have: for they but defend their lives, which the guilty man may as well do, as the innocent. There was indeed injustice in the first breach of their duty; their bearing of arms subsequent to it, though it be to maintain what they have done, is no new unjust act. And if it be only to defend their persons, it is not unjust at all. But the offer of pardon taketh from them, to whom it is offered, the plea of self-defence, and maketh their perseverance in assisting, or defending the rest, unlawful.

As for other liberties, they depend on the silence of the law. In cases where the sovereign has prescribed no rule, there the subject hath the liberty to do, or forbear, according to his own discretion. And therefore such liberty is in some places more, and in some less; and in some times more, in other times less, according as they that have the sovereignty shall think most convenient.

....

If a subject have a controversy with his sovereign, of debt, or of right of possession of lands or goods, or concerning any service required at his hands, or concerning any penalty, corporal or pecuniary, grounded on a precedent law; he hath the same liberty to sue for his right, as if it were against a subject; and before such judges, as are appointed by the sovereign. ...But if he demand, or take anything by pretence of his power; there lieth, in that case, no action of law: for all that is done by him in virtue of his power, is done by the authority of every subject, and consequently, he that brings an action against the sovereign, brings it against himself.

If a monarch, or sovereign assembly, grant a liberty to all, or any of his subjects, which grant standing, he is disabled to provide for their safety, the grant is void; unless he directly renounce, or transfer the sovereignty to another.

....

The obligation of subjects to the sovereign, is understood to last as long, and no longer, than the power lasteth, by which he is able to protect them. For the right men have by nature to protect themselves, when none else can protect them, can by no covenant be relinquished. The sovereignty is the soul of the commonwealth; which, once departed from the body, the members do no more receive their motion from it. The end of obedience is protection; which, wheresoever a man seeth it, either in his own, or in another's sword, nature applieth his obedience to it, and his endeavour to maintain it. And though sovereignty, in the intention of them that make it, be immortal; yet is it in its own nature, not only subject to violent death, by foreign war; but also through the ignorance, and passions of men, it hath in it, from the very institution, many seeds of a natural mortality, by intestine discord.

....

CHAPTER XXVI

Of Civil Laws

By CIVIL LAWS, I understand the laws, that men are therefore bound to observe, because they are members, not of this, or that commonwealth in particular, but of a commonwealth. For the knowledge of particular laws belongeth to them, that profess the study of the laws of their several countries; but the knowledge of civil law in general, to any man.

....

And first it is manifest, that law in general, is not counsel, but command; nor a command of any man to any man; but only of him, whose command is addressed to one formerly obliged to obey him. And as for civil law, it addeth only the name of the person commanding, which is *persona civitatis*, the person of the commonwealth.

Which considered, I define civil law in this manner. CIVIL LAW, *is to every subject, those rules, which the commonwealth hath commanded him, by word, writing, or other sufficient sign of the will, to make use of, for the distinction of right, and wrong; that is to say, of what is contrary, and what is not contrary to the rule.*

In which definition, there is nothing that is not at first sight evident. For every man seeth, that some laws are addressed to all the subjects in general; some to particular provinces; some to particular vocations; and some to particular men; and are therefore laws, to every of those to whom the command is directed; and to none else. As also, that laws are the rules of just, and unjust; nothing being reputed unjust, that is not contrary to some law. Likewise, that none can make laws but the commonwealth; because our subjection is to the commonwealth only: and that commands, are to be signified by sufficient signs; because a man knows not otherwise how to obey them. And therefore, whatsoever can from this definition by necessary consequence be deduced, ought to be acknowledged for truth. Now I deduce from it this that followeth.

1 The legislator in all commonwealths, is only the sovereign, be he one man, as in a monarchy, or one assembly of men, as in a democracy, or aristocracy. For the legislator, is he that maketh the law. And the commonwealth only, prescribes, and commandeth the observation of those rules, which we call law: therefore the commonwealth is the legislator. But the commonwealth is no person, nor has capacity to do anything, but by the representative, (that is, the sovereign;) and therefore the sovereign is the sole legislator. For the same reason, none can abrogate a law made, but the sovereign; because a law is not abrogated, but by another law, that forbiddeth it to be put in execution.

2 The sovereign of a commonwealth, be it an assembly, or one man, is not subject to the civil laws. For having power to make, and repeal laws, he may when he pleaseth, free himself from that subjection, by

repealing those laws that trouble him, and making of new; and consequently he was free before. For he is free, that can be free when he will: nor is it possible for any person to be bound to himself; because he that can bind, can release; and therefore he that is bound to himself only, is not bound.

3 When long use obtaineth the authority of a law, it is not the length of time that maketh the authority, but the will of the sovereign signified by his silence, (for silence is sometimes an argument of consent;) and it is no longer law, than the sovereign shall be silent therein.

....

4 The law of nature, and the civil law, contain each other, and are of equal extent. For the laws of nature, which consist in equity, justice, gratitude, and other moral virtues on these depending, in the condition of mere nature (as I have said before in the end of the 15th chapter,) are not properly laws, but qualities that dispose men to peace, and to obedience. When a commonwealth is once settled, then are they actually laws, and not before; as being then the commands of the commonwealth; and therefore also civil laws: for it is the sovereign power that obliges men to obey them. For in the differences of private men, to declare, what is equity, what is justice, and is moral virtue, and to make them binding, there is need of the ordinances of sovereign power, and punishments to be ordained for such as shall break them; which ordinances are therefore part of the civil law. The law of nature therefore is a part of the civil law in all commonwealths of the world. Reciprocally also, the civil law is a part of the dictates of nature. For justice, that is to say, performance of covenant, and giving to every man his own, is a dictate of the law of nature. But every subject in a commonwealth, hath covenanted to obey the civil law, (either one with another, as when they assemble to make a common representative, or with the representative itself one by one, when subdued by the sword they promise obedience, that they may receive life;) and therefore obedience to the civil law is part also of the law of nature. Civil, and natural law are not different kinds, but different parts of law; whereof one part being written, is called civil, the other unwritten, natural. But the right of nature, that is, the natural liberty of man, may by the civil law be abridged, and restrained: nay, the end of making laws, is no other, but such restraint; without the which there cannot possibly be any peace. And law was brought into the world for nothing else, but to limit the natural liberty of particular men, in such manner, as they might not hurt, but assist one another, and join together against a common enemy.

5 If the sovereign of one commonwealth, subdue a people that have lived under other written laws, and afterwards govern them by the same laws, by which they were governed before; yet those laws are the civil laws of the victor, and not of the vanquished commonwealth. For the legislator is he, not by whose authority the laws were first made, but by whose authority they now continue to be laws. ...But if an unwritten law, in all the provinces of a dominion, shall be generally observed, and no iniquity appear in the use thereof; that law can be no other but a law of nature, equally obliging all mankind.

....

7 That law can never be against reason, our lawyers are agreed; and that not the letter, (that is, every construction of it,) but that which is according to the intention of the legislator, is the law. And it is true: but the doubt is, of whose reason it is, that shall be received for law. It is not meant of any private reason; for then there would be as much contradiction in the laws, as there is in the schools; nor yet, (as Sir *Edward Coke* makes it,) an *artificial perfection of reason, gotten by long study, observation, and experience*, (as his was.) ...[T]herefore it is not that *juris prudentia*, or wisdom of subordinate judges; but the reason of this our artificial man the commonwealth, and his command, that maketh law: and the commonwealth being in their representative but one person, there cannot easily arise any contradiction in the laws; and when there doth, the same reason is able, by interpretation, or alteration, to take it away. In all courts of justice, the sovereign (which is the person of the commonwealth,) is he that judgeth: the subordinate judge, ought to have regard to the reason, which moved his sovereign to make such law, that his sentence may be according thereunto; which then is his sovereign's sentence; otherwise it is his own, and an unjust one.
8 From this, that the law is a command, and a command consisteth in declaration, or manifestation of the will of him that commandeth, by voice, writing, or some other sufficient argument of the same, we may understand, that the command of the commonwealth, is law only to those, that have means to take notice of it. Over natural fools, children, or madmen there is no law, no more than over brute beasts; nor are they capable of the title of just, or unjust; because they had never power to make any covenant, or to understand the consequences thereof; and consequently never took upon them to authorize the actions of any sovereign, as they must do that make to themselves a commonwealth. And as those from whom nature, or accident hath taken away the notice of all laws in general; so also every man, from

whom any accident, not proceeding from his own default, hath taken away the means to take notice of any particular law, is excused, if he observe it not; and to speak properly, that law is no law to him. It is therefore necessary, to consider in this place, what arguments, and signs be sufficient for the knowledge of what is the law; that is to say, what is the will of the sovereign, as well in monarchies, as in other forms of government.

And first, if it be a law that obliges all the subjects without exception, and is not written, nor otherwise published in such places as they may take notice thereof, it is a law of nature. For whatsoever men are to take knowledge of for law, not upon other men's words, but every one from his own reason, must be such as is agreeable to the reason of all men; which no law can be, but the law of nature. The laws of nature therefore need not any publishing, nor proclamation; as being contained in this one sentence, approved by all the world, *Do not that to another, which thou thinkest unreasonable to be done by another to thyself.*

....

The law of nature excepted, it belongeth to the essence of all other laws, to be made known, to every man that shall be obliged to obey them, either by word, or writing, or some other act, known to proceed from the sovereign authority. For the will of another, cannot be understood but by his own word, or act, or by conjecture taken from his scope and purpose; which in the person of the commonwealth, is to be supposed always consonant to equity and reason.

....

Nor is it enough the law be written, and published; but also that there be manifest signs, that it proceedeth from the will of the sovereign. For private men, when they have, or think they have force enough to secure their unjust designs, and convoy them safely to their ambitious ends, may publish for laws what they please, without, or against the legislative authority. There is therefore requisite, not only a declaration of the law, but also sufficient signs of the author, and authority. The author, or legislator is supposed in every commonwealth to be evident, because he is the sovereign, who having been constituted by the consent of every one, is supposed by every one to be sufficiently known. And though the ignorance, and security of men be such, for the most part, as that when the memory of the first constitution of their commonwealth is worn out, they do not consider, by whose power they use to be defended against their enemies, and to have their industry protected, and to be righted when injury is done them; yet because no man that considers, can make question of it, no excuse can be derived from the ignorance of where the sovereignty is placed. And it is a dictate of natural reason, and consequently an evident law of nature, that no man ought to weaken that power, the protection whereof he hath himself demanded, or wittingly received against others. Therefore of who is sovereign, no man, but by his own fault, (whatsoever evil men suggest,) can make any doubt.

....

The legislator known; and the laws, either by writing, or by the light of nature, sufficiently published; there wanteth yet another very material circumstance to make them obligatory. For it is not the letter, but the intendment, or meaning; that is to say, the authentic interpretation of the law (which is the sense of the legislator,) in which the nature of the law consisteth; and therefore the interpretation of all laws dependeth on the authority sovereign; and the interpreters can be none but those, which the sovereign, (to whom only the subject oweth obedience) shall appoint. For else, by the craft of an interpreter, the law may be made to bear a sense, contrary to that of the sovereign; by which means the interpreter becomes the legislator.

All laws, written, and unwritten, have need of interpretation. The unwritten law of nature, though it be easy to such, as without partiality, and passion, make use of their natural reason, and therefore leaves the violators thereof without excuse; yet considering there be very few, perhaps none, that in some cases are not blinded by self-love, or some other passion, it is now become of all laws the most obscure; and has consequently the greatest need of able interpreters. The written laws, if they be short, are easily misinterpreted, from the diverse significations of a word, or two: if long, they be more obscure by the diverse significations of many words: in so much as no written law, delivered in few, or many words, can be well understood, without a perfect understanding of the final causes, for which the law was made; the knowledge of which final causes is in the legislator. To him therefore there cannot be any knot in the law, insoluble; either by finding out the ends, to undo it by; or else by making what ends he will, (as *Alexander* did with his sword in the Gordian knot,) by the legislative power; which no other interpreter can do.

The interpretation of the laws of nature, in a commonwealth, dependeth not on the books of moral philosophy. The authority of writers, without the authority of the commonwealth, maketh not their opinions law, be they never so true. That which I have written in this treatise, concerning the moral virtues, and of their necessity, for the procuring, and maintaining peace, though it be evident truth, is not therefore presently law; but because in all commonwealths in the world, it is part of the civil law: for though it be naturally reasonable; yet it is by the sovereign power that it is law: otherwise, it were a great error, to call the laws of nature unwritten law; whereof we see so many volumes published by diverse authors, and in them so many contradictions of one another, and of themselves.

The interpretation of the law of nature, is the sentence of the judge constituted by the sovereign authority, to hear and determine such controversies, as depend thereon; and consisteth in the application of the law to the present case. For in the act of judicature, the judge doth no more but consider, whether the demand of the party, be consonant to natural reason, and equity; and the sentence he giveth, is therefore the interpretation of the law of nature; which interpretation is authentic; not because it is his private sentence; but because he giveth it by authority of the sovereign, whereby it becomes the sovereign's sentence; which is law for that time, to the parties pleading.

But because there is no judge subordinate, nor sovereign, but may err in a judgement of equity; if afterward in another like case he find it more consonant to equity to give a contrary sentence, he is obliged to do it. No man's error becomes his own law; nor obliges him to persist in it. Neither (for the same reason) becomes it a law to other judges, though sworn to follow it. For though a wrong sentence given by authority of the sovereign, if he know and allow it, in such laws as are mutable, be a constitution of a new law, in cases, in which every little circumstance is the same; yet in laws immutable, such as are the laws of nature, they are no laws to the same, or other judges, in the like cases for ever after. Princes succeed one another; and one judge passeth, another cometh; nay, heaven and earth shall pass; but not one tittle of the law of nature shall pass; for it is the eternal law of God. Therefore all the sentences of precedent judges that have ever been, cannot all together make a law contrary to natural equity: nor any examples of former judges, can warrant an unreasonable sentence, or discharge the present judge of the trouble of studying what is equity (in the case he is to judge,) from the principles of his own natural reason.

....

[A] judge may err in the interpretation even of written laws; but no error of a subordinate judge, can change the law, which is the general sentence of the sovereign.

In written laws, men use to make a difference between the letter, and the sentence of the law: and when by the letter, is meant whatsoever can be gathered from the bare words, it is well distinguished. For the significations of almost all words, are either in themselves, or in the metaphorical use of them, ambiguous; and may be drawn in argument, to make many senses; but there is only one sense of the law. But if by the letter, be meant the literal sense, then the letter, and the sentence or intention of the law, is all one. For the literal sense is that, which the legislator intended, should by the letter of the law be signified. Now the intention of the legislator is always supposed to be equity: for it were a great contumely for a judge to think otherwise of the sovereign. He ought therefore, if the words of the law do not fully authorize a reasonable sentence, to supply it with the law of nature; or if the case be difficult, to respite judgement till he have received more ample authority. ...So that the incommodity that follows the bare words of a written law, may lead him to the intention of the law, whereby to interpret the same the better; though no incommodity can warrant a sentence against the law. For every judge of right, and wrong, is not judge of what is commodious, or incommodious to the commonwealth.

....

The things that make a good judge, or good interpreter of the laws, are, first, *a right understanding* of that principal law of nature called *equity*; which depending not on the reading of other men's writings, but on the goodness of a man's own natural reason, and meditation, is presumed to be in those most, that had most leisure, and had the most inclination to meditate thereon. Secondly, *contempt of unnecessary riches*, and preferments. Thirdly, *to be able in judgement to divest himself of all fear, anger, hatred, love,* and *compassion*. Fourthly, and lastly, *patience to hear; diligent attention in hearing; and memory to retain, digest and apply what he hath heard.*

....

Another division of laws, is into *natural* and *positive*. *Natural* are those which have been laws from all eternity; and are called not only *natural*, but also *moral* laws; consisting in the moral virtues, as justice, equity, and all habits of the mind that conduce to peace, and charity; of which I have already spoken in the fourteenth and fifteenth chapters.

Positive, are those which have not been from eternity; but have been made laws by the will of those that have had the sovereign power over others; and are either written, or made known to men, by some other argument of the will of their legislator.

Again, of positive laws some are *human*, some *divine*: and of human positive laws, some are *distributive*, some *penal*...

Divine positive laws (for natural laws being eternal, and universal, are all divine,) are those, which being the commandments of God, (not from all eternity, nor universally addressed to all men, but only to a certain people, or to certain persons,) are declared for such, by those whom God hath authorized to declare them. But this authority of man to declare what be these positive of God, how can it be known? God may command a man by a supernatural way, to deliver laws to other men. But because it is of the essence of law, that he who is to be obliged, be assured of the authority of him that declareth it, which we cannot naturally take notice to be from God, *how can a man without supernatural revelation be assured of the revelation received by the declarer?* and *how can he be bound to obey them?* For the first question, how a man can be assured of the revelation of another, without a revelation particularly to himself, it is evidently impossible: for though a man may be induced to believe such revelation, from the miracles they see him do, or from seeing the extraordinary sanctity of his life, or from seeing the extraordinary wisdom, or extraordinary felicity of his actions, all which are marks of God's extraordinary favour; yet they are not assured evidences of special revelation. Miracles are marvellous works: but that which is marvellous to one, may not be so to another. Sanctity may be feigned; and the visible felicities of this world, are most often the work of God by natural and ordinary causes. And therefore no man can infallibly know by natural reason, that another has had a supernatural revelation of God's will; but only a belief; every one (as the signs thereof shall appear greater, or lesser) a firmer, or a weaker belief.

But for the second, how he can be bound to obey them; it is not so hard. For if the law declared, be not against the law of nature (which is undoubtedly God's law) and he undertake to obey it, he is bound by his own act; bound I say to obey it, but not bound to believe it: for men's belief, and interior cogitations, are not subject to the commands, but only to the operation of God, ordinary, or extraordinary. Faith of supernatural law, is not a fulfilling, but only an assenting to the same; and not a duty that we exhibit to God, but a gift which God freely giveth to whom he pleaseth; as also unbelief is not a breach of any of his laws; but a rejection of them all, except the laws natural. ...[T]here is no place in the world where men are permitted to pretend other commandments of God, than are declared for such by the commonwealth. Christian states punish those that revolt from Christian religion, and all other states, those that set up any religion by them forbidden. For in whatsoever is not regulated by the commonwealth, it is equity (which is the law of nature, and therefore an eternal law of God) that every man equally enjoy his liberty.

....

I find the words *lex civilis,* and *jus civile,* that is to say, *law* and *right civil,* promiscuously used for the same thing, even in the most learned authors; which nevertheless ought not to be so. For *right* is *liberty,* namely that liberty which the civil law leaves us: but *civil law* is an *obligation*; and takes from us the liberty which the law of nature gave us. Nature gave a right to every man to secure himself by his own strength, and to invade a suspected neighbor, by way of prevention: but the civil law takes away that liberty, in all cases where the protection of the law may be safely stayed for. Insomuch as *lex* and *jus*, are as different as *obligation* and *liberty*.

CHAPTER XXVII

Of CRIMES, EXCUSES, and EXTENUATIONS

A *sin*, is not only a transgression of a law, but also any contempt of the legislator. For such contempt, is a breach of all his laws at once. And therefore may consist, not only in the *commission* of a fact, or the speaking of words by the laws forbidden, or the *omission* of what the law commandeth, but also in the *intention*, or purpose to transgress.

....

A CRIME, is a sin, consisting in the committing (by deed, or word) of that which the law forbiddeth, or the omission of what it hath commanded. So that every crime is a sin; but not every sin a crime.

....

From this relation of sin to the law, and of crime to the civil law, may be inferred, first, that where the law ceaseth, sin ceaseth. But because the law of nature is eternal, violation of covenants, ingratitude, arrogance, and all facts contrary to any moral virtue, can never cease to be sin.

....

[N]ot every fear justifies the action it produceth, but the fear only of corporeal hurt, which we call *bodily fear*, and from which a man cannot see how to be delivered, but by the action. A man is assaulted, fears present death, from which he sees not how to escape, but by wounding him that assaulteth him; if he wound him to death, this is no crime; because no man is supposed at the making of a commonwealth, to have abandoned the defence of his life, or limbs, where the law cannot arrive time enough to his assistance. But to kill a man, because from his actions, or his threatenings, I may argue he will kill me when he can, (seeing I have time, and means to demand protection, from the sovereign power,) is a crime. Again, a man receives words of disgrace or some little injuries (for which they that made the laws, had assigned no punishment, nor thought it worthy of a man that hath the use of reason, to take notice of,) and is afraid, unless he revenge it, he shall fall into contempt, and consequently be obnoxious to the like injuries from others; and to avoid this breaks the law, and protects himself for the future, by the terror of his private revenge. This is a crime: for the hurt is not corporeal, but fantastical, and (though, in this corner of the world, made sensible by a custom not many years since begun, amongst young and vain men,) so light, as a gallant man, and one that is assured of his own courage, cannot take notice of. Also a man may stand in fear of spirits, either through his own superstition, or through too much credit given to other men, that tell him of strange dreams and visions; and thereby be made believe they will hurt him, for doing, or omitting diverse things, which nevertheless, to do, or omit, is contrary to the laws; and that which is so done, or omitted, is not to be excused by this fear; but is a crime. For (as I have shown before in the second chapter) dreams be naturally but the fancies remaining in sleep, after the impressions our senses had formerly received waking; and when men are by any accident unassured they have slept, seem to be real visions; and therefore he that presumes to break the law upon his own, or another's dream, or pretended vision, or upon other fancy of the power of invisible spirits, than is permitted by the commonwealth, leaveth the law of nature, which is a certain offence, and followeth the imagery of his own, or another private man's brain, which he can never know whether it signifieth anything, or nothing, nor whether he that tells his dream, say true, or lie; which if every private man should have leave to do, (as they must by the law of nature, if any one have it) there could no law be made to hold, and so all commonwealth would be dissolved.

CHAPTER XXIX

*Of those things that weaken, or tend to the
DISSOLUTION of a commonwealth*

Though nothing can be immortal, which mortals make; yet, if men had the use of reason they pretend to, their commonwealths might be secured, at least, from perishing by internal diseases. For by the nature of their institution, they are designed to live, as long as mankind, or as the laws of nature, or as justice itself, which gives them life. Therefore when they come to be dissolved, not by external violence, but intestine disorder, the fault is not in men, as they are the *matter*; but as they are the *makers*, and orderers of them. For men, as they become at last weary of irregular jostling, and hewing one another, and desire with all their hearts, to conform themselves into one firm and lasting edifice; so for want, both of the art of making fit laws, to square their actions by, and also of humility, and patience, to suffer the rude and cumbersome points of their present greatness to be taken off, they cannot without the help of a very able architect, be compiled, into any other than a crazy building, such as hardly lasting out their own time, must assuredly fall upon the heads of their posterity.

Amongst the *infirmities* therefore of a commonwealth, I will reckon in the first place, those that arise from an imperfect institution, and resemble the diseases of a natural body, which proceed from a defectuous procreation.

Of which, this is one, *that a man to obtain a kingdom, is sometimes content with less power, than to the peace, and defence of the commonwealth is necessarily required.* From whence it cometh to pass, that when the exercise of the power laid by, is for the public safety to be resumed, it hath the resemblance of an unjust act; which disposeth great numbers of men (when occasion is presented) to rebel...

. . . .

In the second place, I observe the *diseases* of a commonwealth, that proceed from the poison of seditious doctrines; whereof one is, *that every private man is judge of good and evil actions.* This is true in the condition of mere nature, where there are no civil laws; and also under civil government, in such cases as are not determined by the law. But otherwise, it is manifest, that the measure of good and evil actions, is the civil law; and the judge the legislator, who is always the representative of the commonwealth. From this false doctrine, men are disposed to debate with themselves, and dispute the commands of the commonwealth; and afterwards to obey, or disobey them, as in their private judgments they shall think fit. Whereby the commonwealth is distracted and *weakened.*

Another doctrine repugnant to civil society, is, that *whatsoever a man does against his conscience, is sin*; and it dependeth on the presumption of making himself judge of good and evil. For a man's conscience, and his judgement is the same thing; and as the judgement, so also the conscience may be erroneous. Therefore, though he that is subject to no civil law, sinneth in all he does against his conscience, because he has no other rule to follow but his own reason; yet it is not so with him that lives in a commonwealth; because the law is the public conscience, by which he hath already undertaken to be guided. Otherwise in such diversity, as there is of private consciences, which are but private opinions, the commonwealth must needs be distracted, and no man dare to obey the sovereign power, farther than it shall seem good in his own eyes.

It hath been also commonly taught, *that faith and sanctity, are not to be attained by study and reason, but by supernatural inspiration, or infusion.* Which granted, I see not why any man should render a reason of his faith; or why every Christian should not be also a prophet; or why any man should take the law of his country, rather than his own inspiration, for the rule of his action. And thus we fall again into the fault of taking upon us to judge of good and evil; or to make judges of it, such private men as pretend to be supernaturally inspired, to the dissolution of all civil government. Faith comes by hearing, and hearing by those accidents, which guide us into the presence of them that speak to us; which accidents are all contrived by God Almighty; and yet are not supernatural, but only, for the great number of them that concur to every effect, unobservable. Faith, and sanctity, are indeed not very frequent; but yet they are not miracles, but brought to pass by education, discipline, correction, and other natural ways, by which God worketh them in his elect, at such time as he thinketh fit. And these three opinions, pernicious to peace and government, have in this part of the world, proceeded chiefly from tongues, and pens of unlearned divines; who joining the words of Holy Scripture together, otherwise than is agreeable to reason, do what they can, to make men think, that sanctity and natural reason, cannot stand together.

A fourth opinion, repugnant to the nature of a commonwealth, is this, *that he that hath the sovereign power, is subject to the civil laws*. It is true, that sovereigns are all subject to the laws of nature; because such laws be divine, and cannot by any man, or commonwealth be abrogated. But to those laws which the sovereign himself, that is, which the commonwealth maketh, he is not subject. ...Which error, because it setteth the laws above the sovereign, setteth also a judge above him, and a power to punish him; which is to make a new sovereign; and again for the same reason a third, to punish the second; and so continually without end, to the confusion, and dissolution of the commonwealth.

A fifth doctrine, that tendeth to the dissolution of a commonwealth, is, *that every private man has an absolute propriety in his goods; such, as excludeth the right of the sovereign*. Every man has indeed a propriety that excludes the right of every other subject: and he has it only from the sovereign power; without the protection whereof, every other man should have equal right to the same. But if the right of the sovereign also be excluded, he cannot perform the office they have put him into; which is, to defend them both from foreign enemies, and from the injuries of one another; and consequently there is no longer a commonwealth.

And if the propriety of subjects, exclude not the right of the sovereign representative to their goods; much less to their offices of judicature, or execution, in which they represent the sovereign himself.

There is a sixth doctrine, plainly, and directly against the essence of a commonwealth; and it is this, *that the sovereign power may be divided*. For what is it to divide the power of a commonwealth, but to dissolve it; for powers divided mutually destroy each other.

....

And as false doctrine, so also oftentimes the example of different government in a neighbouring nation, disposeth men to alteration of the form already settled. ...And I doubt not, but many men, have been contented to see the late troubles in *England,* out of an imitation of the Low Countries; supposing there needed no more to grow rich, than to change, as they had done, the form of their government. For the constitution of man's nature, is of itself subject to desire novelty: when therefore they are provoked to the same, by the neighbourhood also of those that have been enriched by it, it is almost impossible for them, not to be content with those that solicit them to change.

....

And as to rebellion in particular against monarchy; one of the most frequent causes of it, is the reading of the books of policy, and histories of the ancient Greeks, and Romans; ...From the reading, I say, of such books, men have undertaken to kill their kings, because the Greek and Latin writers, in their books, and discourses of policy, make it lawful, and laudable, for any man so to do; provided before he do it, he call him tyrant. For they say not *regicide,* that is, killing of a king, but *tyrannicide,* that is, killing of a tyrant is lawful. From the same books, they that live under a monarch conceive an opinion, that the subjects in a popular commonwealth enjoy liberty; but that in a monarchy they are all slaves. I say, they that live under a monarchy conceive such an opinion; not they that live under a popular government: for they find no such matter. In sum, I cannot imagine, how anything can be more prejudicial to a monarchy, than the allowing of such books to be publicly read, without present applying such correctives of discreet masters, as are fit to take away their venom.

....

As there have been doctors, that hold there be three souls in a man; so there be also that think there may be more souls, (that is, more sovereigns,) than one, in a commonwealth; and set up a *supremacy* against the *sovereignty*; *canons* against *laws*; and a *ghostly authority* against the *civil*; working on men's minds, with words and distinctions, that of themselves signify nothing, but bewray (by their obscurity) that there walketh (as some think invisibly) another kingdom, as it were a kingdom of fairies, in the dark. Now seeing it is manifest, that the civil power, and the power of the commonwealth is the same thing; and that supremacy, and the power of making canons, and granting faculties, implieth a commonwealth; it followeth, that where one is sovereign, another supreme; where one can make laws, and another make canons; there must needs be two commonwealths, of one and the same subjects; which is a kingdom divided in itself, and cannot stand. For notwithstanding the insignificant distinction of *temporal*, and *ghostly*, they are still two kingdoms, and every subject is subject to two masters. For seeing the *ghostly* power challengeth the right to declare what is sin, it challengeth by consequence to declare what is law, (sin being nothing but the transgression of the law;) and again, the civil power challenging to declare what is law, every subject must obey two masters, who both will have their commands be observed as law; which is impossible. Or, if it be but one kingdom, either the *civil*, which is the power of the commonwealth, must be subordinate to the *ghostly*, and then there is no sovereignty but the *ghostly*; or the *ghostly* must be subordinate to the *temporal*, and then there is no *supremacy* but the *temporal*. When therefore these two powers oppose one another, the commonwealth cannot but be in great danger of civil war, and dissolution. For the *civil* authority being more visible, and standing in the clearer light of natural reason, cannot choose but draw to it in all times a very considerable part of the people: and the *spiritual*, though it stand in the darkness of School distinctions, and hard words; yet, because the fear of darkness, and ghosts, is greater than other fears, cannot want a party sufficient to trouble, and sometimes to destroy a commonwealth. ...[I]n the body politic, when the spiritual power, moveth the members of a commonwealth, by the terror of punishments, and hope of rewards (which are the nerves of it,) otherwise than by the civil power (which is the soul of the commonwealth) they ought to be moved; and by strange, and hard words suffocates their understanding, it must needs thereby distract the people, and either overwhelm the commonwealth with oppression, or cast it into the fire of a civil war.

Sometimes also in the merely civil government, there be more than one soul: as when the power of levying money, (which is the nutritive faculty,) has depended on a general assembly; the power of conduct and command, (which is the motive faculty,) on one man; and the power of making laws, (which is the rational faculty,) on the accidental consent, not only of those two, but also of a third; this endangereth the commonwealth, sometimes for want of consent to good laws; but most often for want of such nourishment, as is necessary to life, and motion. For although few perceive, that such government, is not government, but division of the commonwealth into three factions, and call it mixed monarchy; yet the truth is, that it is not one independent commonwealth, but three independent factions; nor one representative person, but three. In the kingdom of God, there may be three persons independent, without breach of unity in God that reigneth; but where men reign, that be subject to diversity of opinions, it cannot be so.

....

Lastly, when in a war (foreign, or intestine,) the enemies get a final victory; so as (the forces of the commonwealth keeping the field no longer) there is no farther protection of subjects in their loyalty; then is the commonwealth DISSOLVED, and every man at liberty to protect himself by such courses as his own discretion shall suggest unto him. For the sovereign, is the public soul, giving life and motion to the commonwealth; which expiring, the members are governed by it no more, than the carcass of a man, by his departed (though immortal) soul. For though the right of a sovereign monarch cannot be extinguished by the act of another; yet the obligation of the members may. For he that wants protection, may seek it anywhere; and, when he hath it, is obliged (without fraudulent pretence of having submitted himself out of fear,) to protect his protection as long as he is able. But when the power of an assembly is once suppressed, the right of the same perisheth utterly; because the assembly itself is extinct; and consequently, there is no possibility for the sovereignty to re-enter.

CHAPTER XXX

Of the OFFICE of the sovereign representative

The OFFICE of the sovereign, (be it a monarch, or an assembly,) consisteth in the end, for which he was trusted with the sovereign power, namely the procuration of *the safety of the people*; to which he is obliged by the law of nature, and to render an account thereof to God, the author of that law, and to none but him. But by safety here, is not meant a bare preservation, but also all other contentments of life, which every man by lawful industry, without danger, or hurt to the commonwealth, shall acquire to himself.

And this is intended should be done... by a general providence, contained in public instruction, both of doctrine, and example; and in the making, and executing of good laws, to which individual persons may apply their own cases.

And because, if the essential rights of sovereignty (specified before in the eighteenth chapter) be taken away, the commonwealth is thereby dissolved, and every man returneth into the condition, and calamity of a war with every other man, (which is the greatest evil that can happen in this life;) it is the office of the sovereign, to maintain those rights entire... Secondly, it is against his duty, to let the people be ignorant, or misinformed of the grounds, and reasons of those his essential rights.

....

And the grounds of these rights, have the rather need to be diligently, and truly taught; because they cannot be maintained by any civil law, or terror of legal punishment. For a civil law, that shall forbid rebellion, (and such is all resistance to the essential rights of sovereignty,) is not (as a civil law) any obligation, but by virtue only of the law of nature, that forbiddeth violation of faith; which natural obligation if men know not, they cannot know the right of any law the sovereign maketh.

....

But they say again, that though the principles be right, yet common people are not of capacity enough to be made to understand them. I should be glad, that the rich, and potent subjects of a kingdom, or those that are accounted the most learned, were no less incapable than they. But all men know, that the obstructions to this kind of doctrine, proceed not so much from the difficulty of the matter, as from the interest of them that are to learn. Potent men, digest hardly anything that setteth up a power to bridle their affections; and learned men, anything that discovereth their errors, and thereby lesseneth their authority: whereas the common people's minds, unless they be tainted with dependence on the potent, or scribbled over with the opinions of their doctors, are like clean paper, fit to receive whatsoever by public authority shall be imprinted in them. ...I conclude therefore, that in the instruction of the people in the essential rights (which are the natural, and fundamental laws) of sovereignty, there is no difficulty, (whilst a sovereign has his power entire,) but what proceeds from his own fault, or the fault of those whom he trusteth in the administration of the commonwealth; and consequently, it is his duty, to cause them so to be instructed; and not only his duty, but his benefit also, and security, against the danger that may arrive to himself in his natural person, from rebellion.

And (to descend to particulars) the people are to be taught, first, that they ought not to be in love with any form of government they see in their neighbour nations, more than with their own, nor (whatsoever present prosperity they behold in nations that are otherwise governed than they,) to desire change. For the prosperity of a people ruled by an aristocratical, or democratical assembly, cometh not from aristocracy, nor from democracy, but from the obedience, and concord of the subjects: nor do the people flourish in a monarchy, because one man has the right to rule them, but because they obey him. Take away in any kind of state, the obedience, (and consequently the concord of the people,) and they shall not only not flourish, but in short time be dissolved. And they that go about by disobedience, to do no more than reform the commonwealth, shall find they do thereby destroy it; like the foolish daughters of *Peleus* (in the fable;) which desiring to renew the youth of their decrepit father, did by the counsel of *Medea*, cut him in pieces, and boil him, together with strange herbs, but made not of him a new man.

....

Secondly, they are to be taught, that they ought not to be led with admiration of the virtue of any of their fellow subjects, how high soever he stand, nor how conspicuously soever he shine in the commonwealth; nor of any assembly, (except the sovereign assembly,) so as to defer to them any obedience, or honour, appropriate to the sovereign only, whom (in their particular stations) they represent; nor to receive any influence from them, but such as is conveyed by them from the sovereign authority.

....

Thirdly, in consequence to this, they ought to be informed, how great a fault it is, to speak evil of the sovereign representative, (whether one man, or an assembly of men;) or to argue and dispute his power, or any way to use his name irreverently, whereby he may be brought into contempt with his people, and their obedience (in which the safety of the commonwealth consisteth) slackened.

....

Fourthly, seeing people cannot be taught this, nor when it is taught, remember it, nor after one generation past, so much as know in whom the sovereign power is placed, without setting apart from their ordinary labour, some certain times, in which they may attend those that are appointed to instruct them; it is necessary that some such times be determined, wherein they may assemble together, and (after prayers and praises given to God, the sovereign of sovereigns) hear those their duties told them, and the positive laws, such as generally concern them all, read and expounded, and be put in mind of the authority that maketh them laws. To this end had the *Jews* every seventh day, a *sabbath*, in which the law was read and expounded; and in the solemnity whereof they were put in mind, that their king was God.

....

Again, every sovereign ought to cause justice to be taught, which (consisting in taking from no man what is his) is as much as to say, to cause men to be taught not to deprive their neighbours, by violence, or fraud, of anything which by the sovereign authority is theirs. Of things held in propriety, those that are dearest to a man are his own life, and limbs; and in the next degree, (in most men,) those that concern conjugal affection; and after them riches and means of living. Therefore the people are to be taught, to abstain from violence to one another's person, by private revenges; from violation of conjugal honour; and from forcible rapine, and fraudulent surreption of one another's goods. For which purpose also it is necessary they be showed the evil consequences of false judgment, by corruption either of judges or witnesses, whereby the distinction of propriety is taken away, and justice becomes of no effect: all which things are intimated in the sixth, seventh, eighth, and ninth commandments.

Lastly, they are to be taught, that not only the unjust facts, but the designs and intentions to do them, (though by accident hindered,) are injustice; which consisteth in the pravity of the will, as well as in the irregularity of the act. And this is the intention of the tenth commandment, and the sum of the second table; which is reduced all to this one commandment of mutual charity, *Thou shalt love thy neighbour as thy self*: as the sum of the first table is reduced to *the love of God*; whom they had then newly received as their king.

. . . .

CHAPTER XXXI

Of the KINGDOM OF GOD BY NATURE

That the condition of mere nature, that is to say, of absolute liberty, such as is theirs, that neither are sovereigns, nor subjects, is anarchy, and the condition of war: that the precepts, by which men are guided to avoid that condition, are the laws of nature: that a commonwealth, without sovereign power, is but a word, without substance, and cannot stand: that subjects owe to sovereigns, simple obedience, in all things, wherein their obedience is not repugnant to the laws of God, I have sufficiently proved, in that which I have already written. There wants only, for the entire knowledge of civil duty, to know what are those laws of God. For without that, a man knows not, when he is commanded anything by the civil power, whether it be contrary to the law of God, or not: and so, either by too much civil obedience, offends the Divine Majesty, or through fear of offending God, transgresses the commandments of the commonwealth. To avoid both these rocks, it is necessary to know what are the laws divine. And seeing the knowledge of all law, dependeth on the knowledge of the sovereign power; I shall say something in that which followeth, of the KINGDOM OF GOD.

God is king, let the earth rejoice, saith the psalmist. And again, *God is king though the nations be angry: and he that sitteth on the cherubims, though the earth be moved.* Whether men will or not, they must be subject always to the divine power. By denying the existence, or providence of God, men may shake off their ease, but not their yoke. But to call this power of God, which extendeth itself not only to man, but also to beasts, and plants, and bodies inanimate, by the name of kingdom, is but a metaphorical use of the word. For he only is properly said to reign, that governs his subjects, by his word, and by promise of rewards to those that obey it, and by threatening them with punishment that obey it not. Subjects therefore in the kingdom of God, are not bodies inanimate, nor creatures irrational; because they understand no precepts as his: nor atheists; nor they that believe not that God has any care of the actions of mankind; because they acknowledge no word for his, nor have hope of his rewards, or fear of his threatenings. They therefore that believe there is a God that governeth the world, and hath given precepts, and propounded rewards, and punishments to mankind, are God's subjects; all the rest, are to be understood as enemies.

To rule by words, requires that such words be manifestly made known; for else they are no laws: for to the nature of laws, belongeth a sufficient, and clear promulgation, such as may take away the excuse of ignorance; which in the laws of men is but of one only kind, and that is, proclamation, or promulgation by the voice of man. But God declareth his laws three ways; by the dictates of *natural reason*, by *revelation*, and by the *voice* of some *man*, to whom by the operation of miracles, he procureth credit with the rest. From hence there ariseth a triple word of God, *rational, sensible,* and *prophetic*: to which correspondeth a triple hearing; *right reason, sense supernatural,* and *faith*. As for sense supernatural, which consisteth in revelation, or inspiration, there have not been any universal laws so given, because God speaketh not in that manner, but to particular persons, and to diverse men diverse things.

From the difference between the other two kinds of God's word, *rational,* and *prophetic*, there may be attributed to God, a twofold kingdom, *natural*, and *prophetic*: natural, wherein he governeth as many of mankind as acknowledge his providence, by the natural dictates of right reason; and prophetic, wherein having chosen out one peculiar nation (the Jews) for his subjects, he governed them, and none but them, not only by natural reason, but by positive laws, which he gave them by the mouths of his holy prophets. Of the natural kingdom of God I intend to speak in this chapter.

The right of nature, whereby God reigneth over men, and punisheth those that break his laws, is to be derived, not from his creating them as if he required obedience, as of gratitude for his benefits; but from his *irresistible power*. I have formerly shown, how the sovereign right ariseth from pact: to show how the same right may arise from nature, requires no more, but to show in what case it is never taken away. Seeing all men by nature had right to all things, they had right every one to reign over all the rest. But because this right could not be obtained by force, it concerned the safety of every one, laying by that right, to set up men (with sovereign authority) by common consent, to rule and defend them: whereas if there had been any man of power irresistible; there had been no reason, why he should not by that power have ruled, and defended both himself, and them, according to his own discretion. To those therefore whose power is irresistible, the dominion of all men adhereth naturally by their excellence of power; and consequently it is from that power, that the kingdom over men, and the right of afflicting men at his pleasure, belongeth naturally to God Almighty; not as Creator and gracious; but as omnipotent. And though punishment be due for sin only, because by that word is understood affliction for sin; yet the right of afflicting, is not always derived from men's sin, but from God's power.

This question, *why evil men often prosper, and good men suffer adversity*, has been much disputed by the ancient, and is the same with this of ours, *by what right God dispenseth the prosperities and adversities of this life*; and is of that difficulty, as it hath shaken the faith, not only of the vulgar, but of philosophers, and which is more, of the saints, concerning the Divine Providence. *How good* (saith *David*) *is the God of Israel to those that are upright in heart; and yet my feet were almost gone, my treadings had well-nigh slipped; for I was grieved at the wicked, when I saw the ungodly in such prosperity.* And *Job*, how earnestly does he expostulate with God, for the many afflictions he suffered, notwithstanding his righteousness? This question in the case of *Job*, is decided by God himself, not by arguments derived from *Job's* sin, but his own power. For whereas the friends of *Job* drew their arguments from his affliction to his sin, and he defended himself by the conscience of his innocence, God himself taketh up the matter, and having justified the affliction by arguments drawn from his power, such as this, *Where wast thou when I laid the foundations of the earth*, and the like both approved *Job's* innocence, and reproved the erroneous doctrine of his friends. Conformable to this doctrine is the sentence of our Saviour, concerning the man that was born blind, in these words, *Neither hath this man sinned, nor his fathers; but that the works of God might be made manifest in him.* And though it be said, *that death entered into the world by sin*, (by which is meant that if *Adam* had never sinned, he had never died, that is, never suffered any separation of his soul from his body,) it follows not thence, that God could not justly have afflicted him, though he had not sinned, as well as he afflicteth other living creatures, that cannot sin.

Having spoken of the right of God's sovereignty, as grounded only on nature; we are to consider next, what are the divine laws, or dictates of natural reason; which laws concern either the natural duties of one man to another, or the honour naturally due to our Divine Sovereign.

The first are the same laws of nature, of which I have spoken already in the 14th and 15th chapters of this treatise; namely, equity, justice, mercy, humility, and the rest of the moral virtues. It remaineth therefore that we consider, what precepts are dictated to men, by their natural reason only, without other word of God, touching the honour and worship of the Divine Majesty.

Honour consisteth in the inward thought, and opinion of the power, and goodness of another: and therefore to honour God, is to think as highly of his power and goodness, as is possible. And of that opinion, the external signs appearing in the words, and actions of men, are called *worship*.

....

From internal honour, consisting in the opinion of power and goodness, arise three passions; *love*, which hath reference to goodness; and *hope*, and *fear*, that relate to power: and three parts of external worship; *praise*, *magnifying*, and *blessing*: the subject of praise, being goodness; the subject of magnifying, and blessing, being power, and the effect thereof felicity. Praise, and magnifying are signified both by words, and actions: by words, when we say a man is good, or great: by actions, when we thank him for his bounty, and obey his power. The opinion of the happiness of another, can only be expressed by words.

There be some signs of honour, (both in attributes and actions,) that be naturally so; as amongst attributes, *good, just, liberal*, and the like; and amongst actions, *prayers, thanks*, and *obedience*. Others are so by institution, or custom of men; and in some times and places are honourable; in others, dishonourable; in others indifferent: such as are the gestures in salutation, prayer, and thanksgiving, in different times and places, differently used. The former is *natural*; the latter *arbitrary* worship.

....

Again, there is a *public*, and a *private* worship. Public, is the worship that a commonwealth performeth, as one person. Private, is that which a private person exhibiteth. Public, in respect of the whole commonwealth, is free; but in respect of particular men it is not so. Private, is in secret free; but in the sight of the multitude, it is never without some restraint, either from the laws, or from the opinion of men; which is contrary to the nature of liberty.

The end of worship amongst men, is power. For where a man seeth another worshipped, he supposeth him powerful, and is the readier to obey him; which makes his power greater. But God has no ends: the worship we do him, proceeds from our duty, and is directed according to our capacity, by those rules of honour, that reason dictateth to be done by the weak to the more potent men, in hope of benefit, for fear of damage, or in thankfulness for good already received from them.

That we may know what worship of God is taught us by the light of nature, I will begin with his attributes. Where, first, it is manifest, we ought to attribute to him *existence*: for no man can have the will to honour that, which he thinks not to have any being.

Secondly, that those philosophers, who said the world, or the soul of the world was God, spake unworthily of him; and denied his existence: for by God, is understood the cause of the world; and to say the world is God, is to say there is no cause of it, that is, no God.

Thirdly, to say the world was not created, but eternal, (seeing that which is eternal has no cause,) is to deny there is a God.

Fourthly, that they who attributing (as they think) ease to God, take from him the care of mankind; take from him his honour: for it takes away men's love, and fear of him; which is the root of honour.

Fifthly, in those things that signify greatness, and power; to say he is *finite*, is not to honour him: for it is not a sign of the will to honour God, to attribute to him less than we can; and finite, is less than we can; because to finite it is easy to add more.

....

He that will attribute to God, nothing but what is warranted by natural reason, must either use such negative attributes, as *infinite, eternal, incomprehensible*; or superlatives, as *most high, most great*, and the like; or indefinite, as *good, just, holy, creator*; and in such sense, as if he meant not to declare what he is, (for that were to circumscribe him within the limits of our fancy,) but how much we admire him, and how ready we would be to obey him; which is a sign of humility, and of a will to honour him as much as we can: for there is but one name to signify our conception of his nature, and that is, I AM: and but one name of his relation to us, and that is *God*; in which is contained Father, King, and Lord.

Concerning the actions of divine worship, it is a most general precept of reason, that they be signs of the intention to honour God; such as are, first, *prayers*: for not the carvers, when they made images, were thought to make them gods; but the people that *prayed* to them.

Secondly, *thanksgiving*; which differeth from prayer in divine worship, no otherwise, than that prayers precede, and thanks succeed the benefit; the end both of the one, and the other, being to acknowledge God, for author of all benefits, as well past, as future.

Thirdly, *gifts*; that is to say, *sacrifices*, and *oblations*, (if they be of the best,) are signs of honour: for they are thanksgivings.

Fourthly, *not to swear by any but God*, is naturally a sign of honour: for it is a confession that God only knoweth the heart; and that no man's wit, or strength can protect a man against God's vengeance on the perjured.

Fifthly, it is a part of rational worship, to speak considerately of God; for it argues a fear of him, and fear, is a confession of his power. Hence followeth, that the name of God is not to be used rashly, and to no purpose; for that is as much, as in vain: and it is to no purpose, unless it be by way of oath, and by order of the commonwealth, to make judgements certain; or between commonwealths, to avoid war. And that disputing of God's nature is contrary to his honour: for it is supposed, that in this natural kingdom of God, there is no other way to know anything, but by natural reason; that is, from the principles of natural science; which are so far from teaching us anything of God's nature, as they cannot teach us our own nature, nor the nature of the smallest creature living. And therefore, when men out of the principles of natural reason, dispute of the attributes of God, they but dishonour him: for in the attributes which we give to God, we are not to consider the signification of philosophical truth; but the signification of pious intention, to do him the greatest honour we are able. From the want of which consideration, have proceeded the volumes of disputation about the nature of God, that tend not to his honour, but to the honour of our own wits, and learning; and are nothing else but inconsiderate, and vain abuses of his sacred name.

....

Seventhly, reason directeth not only to worship God in secret; but also, and especially, in public, and in the sight of men: for without that, (that which in honour is most acceptable) the procuring others to honour him is lost.

Lastly, obedience to his laws (that is, in this case to the laws of nature,) is the greatest worship of all. For as obedience is more acceptable to God than sacrifice; so also to set light by his commandments, is the greatest of all contumelies. And these are the laws of that divine worship, which natural reason dictateth to private men.

But seeing a commonwealth is but one person, it ought also to exhibit to God but one worship; which then it doth, when it commandeth it to be exhibited by private men, publicly. And this is public worship; the property whereof, is to be *uniform*: for those actions that are done differently, by different men, cannot be said to be a public worship. And therefore, where many sorts of worship be allowed, proceeding from the different religions of private men, it cannot be said there is any public worship, nor that the commonwealth is of any religion at all.

And because words (and consequently the attributes of God) have their signification by agreement, and constitution of men; those attributes are to be held significative of honour, that men intend shall so be; and whatsoever may be done by the wills of particular men, where there is no law but reason, may be done by the will of the commonwealth, by laws civil. And because a commonwealth hath no will, nor makes no laws, but those that are made by the will of him, or them that have the sovereign power; it followeth, that those attributes which the sovereign ordaineth, in the worship of God, for signs of honour, ought to be taken and used for such, by private men in their public worship.

But because not all actions are signs by constitution; but some are naturally signs of honour, others of contumely, these latter (which are those that men are ashamed to do in the sight of them they reverence) cannot be made by human power a part of divine worship; nor the former (such as are decent, modest, humble behavior) ever be separated from it. But whereas there be an infinite number of actions, and gestures, of an indifferent nature; such of them as the commonwealth shall ordain to be publicly and universally in use, as signs of honour, and part of God's worship, are to be taken and used for such by the subjects. And that which is said in the Scripture, *It is better to obey God than men*, hath place in the kingdom of God by pact, and not by nature.

Having thus briefly spoken of the natural kingdom of God, and his natural laws, I will add only to this chapter a short declaration of his natural punishments. There is no action of man in this life, that is not the beginning of so long a chain of consequences, as no human providence, is high enough, to give a man a prospect to the end. And in this chain, there are linked together both pleasing and unpleasing events; in such manner, as he that will do anything for his pleasure, must engage himself to suffer all the pains annexed to it; and these pains, are the natural punishments of those actions, which are the beginning of more harm than good. And hereby it comes to pass, that intemperance, is naturally punished with diseases; rashness, with mischances; injustice, with the violence of enemies; pride, with ruin; cowardice, with oppression; negligent government of princes, with rebellion; and rebellion, with slaughter. For seeing punishments are consequent to the breach of laws; natural punishments must be naturally consequent to the breach of the laws of nature; and therefore follow them as their natural, not arbitrary effects.

And thus far concerning the constitution, nature, and right of sovereigns; and concerning the duty of subjects, derived from the principles of natural reason. And now, considering how different this doctrine is, from the practice of the greatest part of the world, especially of these western parts, that have received their moral learning from *Rome* and *Athens*; and how much depth of moral philosophy is required, in them that have the administration of the sovereign power; I am at the point of believing this my labour, as useless, as the commonwealth of *Plato*; for he also is of opinion that it is impossible for the disorders of state, and change of governments by civil war, ever to be taken away, till sovereigns be philosophers. But when I consider again, that the science of natural justice, is the only science necessary for sovereigns, and their principal ministers; and that they need not be charged with the sciences mathematical, (as by *Plato* they are,) further, than by good laws to encourage men to the study of them; and that neither *Plato*, nor any other philosopher hitherto, hath put into order, and sufficiently, or probably proved all the theorems of moral doctrine, that men may learn thereby, both how to govern and how to obey; I recover some hope, that one time or other, this writing of mine, may fall into the hands of a sovereign, who will consider it himself, (for it is short, and I think clear,) without the help of any interested, or envious interpreter; and by the exercise of entire sovereignty, in protecting the public teaching of it, convert this truth of speculation, into the utility of practice.

PART III: OF A CHRISTIAN COMMONWEALTH

CHAPTER XXXII

Of the principles of CHRISTIAN POLITICS

I have derived the rights of sovereign power, and the duty of subjects hitherto, from the principles of nature only; such as experience has found true, or consent (concerning the use of words) has made so; that is to say, from the nature of men, known to us by experience, and from definitions (of such words as are essential to all political reasoning) universally agreed on. But in that I am next to handle, which is the nature and rights of a CHRISTIAN COMMONWEALTH, whereof there dependeth much upon supernatural revelations of the will of God; the ground of my discourse must be, not only the natural word of God, but also the prophetical.

Nevertheless, we are not to renounce our senses, and experience; nor (that which is the undoubted word of God) our natural reason. For they are the talents which he hath put into our hands to negotiate, till the coming again of our blessed Saviour; and therefore not to be folded up in the napkin of an implicit faith, but employed in the purchase of justice, peace, and true religion. For though there be many things in God's word above reason; that is to say, which cannot by natural reason be either demonstrated, or confuted; yet there is nothing contrary to it; but when it seemeth so, the fault is either in our unskilful interpretation, or erroneous ratiocination.

THOMAS HOBBES (1588-1679)

Therefore, when anything therein written is too hard for our examination, we are bidden to captivate our understanding to the words; and not to labour in sifting out a philosophical truth by logic, of such mysteries as are not comprehensible, nor fall under any rule of natural science. For it is with the mysteries of our religion, as with wholesome pills for the sick, which swallowed whole, have the virtue to cure; but chewed, are for the most part cast up again without effect.

But by the captivity of our understanding, is not meant a submission of the intellectual faculty, to the opinion of any other man; but of the will to obedience, where obedience is due. For sense, memory, understanding, reason, and opinion are not in our power to change; but always, and necessarily such, as the things we see, hear, and consider suggest unto us; and therefore are not effects of our will, but our will of them. We then captivate our understanding and reason, when we forbear contradiction; when we so speak, as (by lawful authority) we are commanded; and when we live accordingly; which in sum, is trust, and faith reposed in him that speaketh, though the mind be incapable of any notion at all from the words spoken.

When God speaketh to man, it must be either immediately; or by mediation of another man, to whom he had formerly spoken by himself immediately. How God speaketh to a man immediately, may be understood by those well enough, to whom he hath so spoken; but how the same should be understood by another, is hard, if not impossible, to know. For if a man pretend to me, that God hath spoken to him supernaturally, and immediately, and I make doubt of it, I cannot easily perceive what argument he can produce, to oblige me to believe it. It is true, that if he be my sovereign, he may oblige me to obedience, so, as not by act or word to declare I believe him not; but not to think any otherwise than my reason persuades me. But if one that hath not such authority over me, shall pretend the same, there is nothing that exacteth either belief, or obedience.

For to say that God hath spoken to him in the Holy Scripture, is not to say God hath spoken to him immediately, but by mediation of the prophets, or of the Apostles, or of the church, in such manner as he speaks to all other Christian men. To say he hath spoken to him in a dream, is no more than to say he dreamed that God spake to him; which is not of force to win belief from any man, that knows dreams are for the most part natural, and may proceed from former thoughts; and such dreams as that, from self-conceit, and foolish arrogance, and false opinion of a man's own goodliness, or other virtue, by which he thinks he hath merited the favour of extraordinary revelation. To say he hath seen a vision, or heard a voice, is to say, that he dreamed between sleeping and waking: for in such manner a man doth many times naturally take his dream for a vision, as not having well observed his own slumbering. To say he speaks by supernatural inspiration, is to say he finds an ardent desire to speak, or some strong opinion of himself, for which he can allege no natural and sufficient reason. So that though God Almighty can speak to a man, by dreams, visions, voice, and inspiration; yet he obliges no man to believe he hath so done to him that pretends it; who (being a man) may err, and (which is more) may lie.

How then can he, to whom God hath never revealed his will immediately (saving by the way of natural reason) know when he is to obey, or not to obey his word, delivered by him, that says he is a prophet? Of 400 prophets, of whom the king of *Israel* asked counsel, concerning the war he made against *Ramoth Gilead*, only *Micaiah* was a true one. The prophet that was sent to prophesy against the altar set up by *Jeroboam*, though a true prophet, and that by two miracles done in his presence appears to be a prophet sent from God, was yet deceived by another old prophet, that persuaded him as from the mouth of God, to eat and drink with him. If one prophet deceive another, what certainty is there of knowing the will of God, by other way than that of reason? To which I answer out of the Holy Scripture, that there be two marks, by which together, not asunder, a true prophet is to be known. One is the doing of miracles; the other is the not teaching any other religion than that which is already established. Asunder (I say) neither of these is sufficient.

....

So that it is manifest, that the teaching of the religion which God hath established, and the showing of a *present* miracle, joined together, were the only marks whereby the Scripture would have a true prophet, that is to say, immediate revelation to be acknowledged; neither of them being singly sufficient to oblige any other man to regard what he saith.

Seeing therefore miracles now cease, we have no sign left, whereby to acknowledge the pretended revelations, or inspirations of any private man; nor obligation to give ear to any doctrine, farther than it is conformable to the Holy Scriptures, which since the time of our Saviour, supply the place, and sufficiently recompense the want of all other prophecy; and from which, by wise and learned interpretation, and careful ratiocination, all rules and precepts necessary to the knowledge of our duty both to God and man, without enthusiasm, or supernatural inspiration, may easily be deduced. And this Scripture is it, out of which I am to take the principles of my discourse, concerning the rights of those that are the supreme governors on earth, of Christian commonwealths; and of the duty of Christian subjects towards their sovereigns.

....

THOMAS HOBBES (1588-1679)

CHAPTER XLIII

Of what is NECESSARY *for a man's reception into the kingdom of heaven*

The most frequent pretext of sedition, and civil war, in Christian commonwealths hath a long time proceeded from a difficulty, not yet sufficiently resolved, of obeying at once, both God, and man, then when their commandments are one contrary to the other. It is manifest enough, that when a man receiveth two contrary commands, and knows that one of them is God's, he ought to obey that, and not the other, though it be the command even of his lawful sovereign (whether a monarch, or a sovereign assembly,) or the command of his father. The difficulty therefore consisteth in this, that men when they are commanded in the name of God, know not in diverse cases, whether the command be from God, or whether he that commandeth, do but abuse God's name for some private ends of his own. For as there were in the church of the Jews, many false prophets, that sought reputation with the people, by feigned dreams, and visions; so there have been in all times in the church of Christ, false teachers, that seek reputation with the people, by fantastical and false doctrines; and by such reputation (as is the nature of ambition,) to govern them for their private benefit.

But this difficulty of obeying both God, and the civil sovereign on earth, to those that can distinguish between what is *necessary*, and what is not *necessary* for their *reception* into the *kingdom of God*, is of no moment. For if the command of the civil sovereign be such, as that it may be obeyed, without the forfeiture of life eternal; not to obey it is unjust; and the precept of the apostle takes place; *Servants obey your masters in all things*; and, *Children, obey your parents in all things*; and the precept of our Saviour, *The Scribes and Pharisees sit in Moses' chair, all therefore they shall say, that observe, and do*. But if the command be such, as cannot be obeyed, without being damned to eternal death, then it were madness to obey it, and the counsel of our Saviour takes place, (*Matt.* 10.28.) *Fear not those that kill the body, but cannot kill the soul*. All men therefore that would avoid, both the punishments that are to be in this world inflicted, for disobedience to their earthly sovereign, and those that shall be inflicted in the world to come for disobedience to God, have need be taught to distinguish well between what is, and what is not necessary to eternal salvation.

All that is NECESSARY *to salvation*, is contained in two virtues, *faith in Christ*, and *obedience to laws*. The latter of these, if it were perfect, were enough to us. But because we are all guilty of disobedience to God's law, not only originally in Adam, but also actually by our own transgressions, there is required at our hands now, not only *obedience* for the rest of our time, but also a *remission* of sins for the time past; which remission is the reward of our faith in Christ. That nothing else is necessarily required to salvation, is manifest from this, that the kingdom of heaven is shut to none but to sinners; that is to say, to the disobedient, or transgressors of the law; nor to them, in case they repent, and believe all the articles of Christian faith, necessary to salvation.

The obedience required at our hands by God, that accepteth in all our actions the will for the deed, is a serious endeavour to obey him; and is called also by all such names as signify that endeavour. And therefore obedience, is sometimes called by the names of *charity*, and *love*, because they imply a will to obey; and our Saviour himself maketh our love to God, and to one another, a fulfilling of the whole law: and sometimes by the name of *righteousness*; for righteousness is but the will to give to every one his own, that is to say, the will to obey the laws: and sometimes by the name of *repentance*; because to repent, implieth a turning away from sin, which is the same, with the return of the will to obedience. Whosoever therefore unfeignedly desireth to fulfil the commandments of God, or repenteth him truly of his transgressions, or that loveth God with all his heart, and his neighbour as himself, hath all the obedience necessary to his reception into the kingdom of God: for if God should require perfect innocence, there could no flesh be saved.

But what commandments are those that God hath given us? Are all those laws which were given to the Jews by the hand of Moses, the commandments of God? If they be, why are not Christians taught to obey them? If they be not, what others are so, besides the law of nature? For our Saviour Christ hath not given us new laws, but counsel to observe those we are subject to; that is to say, the laws of nature, and the laws of our several sovereigns: nor did he make any new law to the Jews in his Sermon on the Mount, but only expounded the laws of Moses, to which they were subject before. The laws of God therefore are none but the laws of nature, whereof the principal is, that we should not violate our faith, that is, a commandment to obey our civil sovereigns, which we constituted over us, by mutual pact one with another. And this law of God, that commandeth obedience to the law civil, commandeth by consequence obedience to all the precepts of the Bible; which (as I have proved in the precedent chapter) is there only law, where the civil sovereign hath made it so; and in other places but counsel; which a man at his own peril, may without injustice refuse to obey.

....

The (*unum necessarium*) only article of faith, which the Scripture maketh simply necessary to salvation, is this, that JESUS IS THE CHRIST. By the name of *Christ*, is understood the king, which God had before promised by the prophets of the Old Testament, to send into the world, to reign (over the Jews, and over such of other nations as should believe in him) under himself eternally; and to give them that eternal life, which was lost by the sin of Adam. Which when I have proved out of Scripture, I will further show when, and in what sense some other articles may be also called *necessary*.

....

Having thus shown what is necessary to salvation; it is not hard to reconcile our obedience to God, with our obedience to the civil sovereign; who is either Christian, or infidel. If he be a Christian, he alloweth the belief of this article, that *Jesus is the Christ*; and of all the articles that are contained in, or are by evident consequence deduced from it: which is all the faith necessary to salvation. And because he is a sovereign, he requireth obedience to all his own, that is, to all the civil laws; in which also are contained all the laws of nature, that is, all the laws of God: for besides the laws of nature, and the laws of the church, which are part of the civil law, (for the church that can make laws is the commonwealth,) there be no other laws divine. Whosoever therefore obeyeth his Christian sovereign, is not thereby hindered, neither from believing, nor from obeying God. But suppose that a Christian king should from this foundation *Jesus is the Christ*, draw some false consequences, that is to say, make some superstructions of hay, or stubble, and command the teaching of the same; yet seeing St. Paul says, he shall be saved; much more shall he be saved, that teacheth them by his command; and much more yet, he that teaches not, but only believes his lawful teacher. And in case a subject be forbidden by the civil sovereign to profess some of those his opinions, upon what just ground can he disobey? Christian kings may err in deducing a consequence, but who shall judge? Shall a private man judge, when the question is of his own obedience? Or shall any man judge but he that is appointed thereto by the church, that is, by the civil sovereign that representeth it? Or if the pope, or an apostle judge, may he not err in deducing of a consequence? Did not one of the two, St. Peter, or St. Paul err in a superstructure, when St. Paul withstood St. Peter to his face? There can therefore be no contradiction between the laws of God, and the laws of a Christian commonwealth.

And when the civil sovereign is an infidel, every one of his own subjects that resisteth him, sinneth against the laws of God (for such are the laws of nature,) and rejecteth the counsel of the apostles, that admonisheth all Christians to obey their princes, and all children and servants to obey their parents, and masters in all things. And for their *faith*, it is internal, and invisible; they have the license that Naaman had, and need not put themselves into danger for it. But if they do, they ought to expect their reward in heaven, and not complain of their lawful sovereign; much less make war upon him. For he that is not glad of any just occasion of martyrdom, has not the faith he professeth, but pretends it only, to set some colour upon his own contumacy. But what infidel king is so unreasonable, as knowing he has a subject, that waiteth for the second coming of Christ, after the present world shall be burnt, and intendeth then to obey him (which is the intent of believing that Jesus is the Christ,) and in the meantime thinketh himself bound to obey the laws of that infidel king, (which all Christians are obliged in conscience to do,) to put to death, or to persecute such a subject?

And thus much shall suffice, concerning the kingdom of God, and policy ecclesiastical. Wherein I pretend not to advance any position of my own, but only to show what are the consequences that seem to me deducible from the principles of Christian politics, (which are the Holy Scriptures,) in confirmation of the power of civil sovereigns, and the duty of their subjects.

....

CHAPTER XLVII

Of the BENEFIT that proceedeth from such darkness, and to whom it accrueth

Cicero maketh honourable mention of one of the *Cassii*, a severe judge amongst the Romans, for a custom he had, in criminal causes, (when the testimony of the witnesses was not sufficient,) to ask the accusers, *cui bono*; that is to say, what profit, honour, or other contentment, the accused obtained, or expected by the fact. For amongst presumptions, there is none that so evidently declareth the author, as doth the BENEFIT of the action. By the same rule I intend in this place to examine, who they may be, that have possessed the people so long in this part of Christendom, with these doctrines, contrary to the peaceable societies of mankind.

And first, to this error, *that the present church now militant on earth, is the kingdom of God,* (that is, the kingdom of glory, or the land of promise; not the kingdom of grace, which is but a promise of the land,) are annexed these worldly benefits; first, that the pastors, and teachers of the church, are entitled thereby, as God's public ministers, to a right of governing the church; and consequently (because the church and commonwealth are the same persons) to be rectors, and governors of the commonwealth. By this title it is, that the pope prevailed with the subjects of all Christian princes, to believe, that to disobey him, was to disobey Christ himself; and in all differences between him and other princes, (charmed with the word *power spiritual*,) to abandon their lawful sovereigns; which is in effect an universal monarchy over all Christendom. For though they were first invested in the right of being supreme teachers of Christian doctrine, by, and under Christian emperors, within the limits of the Roman empire (as is acknowledged by themselves) by the title of *Pontifex Maximus*, who was an officer subject to the civil state; yet after the empire was divided, and dissolved, it was not hard to obtrude upon the people already subject to them, another title, namely, the right of St. Peter; not only to save entire their pretended power; but also to extend the same over the same Christian provinces, though no more united in the empire of Rome. This benefit of an universal monarchy, (considering the desire of men to bear rule) is a sufficient presumption, that the popes that pretended to it, and for a long time enjoyed it, were the authors of the doctrine, by which it was obtained; namely, that the church now on earth, is the kingdom of Christ. For that granted, it must be understood, that Christ hath some lieutenant amongst us, by whom we are to be told what are his commandments.

....

The authors therefore of this darkness in religion, are the Roman, and the presbyterian clergy.

To this head, I refer also all those doctrines, that serve them to keep the possession of this spiritual sovereignty after it is gotten. As first, that the *pope in his public capacity cannot err.* For who is there, that believing this to be true, will not readily obey him in whatsoever he commands?

....

Fifthly, the teaching that matrimony is a sacrament, giveth to the clergy the judging of the lawfulness of marriages; and thereby, of what children are legitimate; and consequently, of the right of succession to hereditary kingdoms.

Sixthly, the denial of marriage to priests, serveth to assure this power of the pope over kings. For if a king be a priest, he cannot marry, and transmit his kingdom to his posterity; if he be not a priest then the pope pretendeth this authority ecclesiastical over him, and over his people.

Seventhly, from auricular confession, they obtain, for the assurance of their power, better intelligence of the designs of princes, and great persons in the civil state, than these can have of the designs of the state ecclesiastical.

Eighthly, by the canonization of saints, and declaring who are martyrs, they assure their power, in that they induce simple men into an obstinacy against the laws and commands of their civil sovereigns even to death, if by the pope's excommunication, they be declared heretics or enemies to the church; that is, (as they interpret it,) to the pope.

Ninthly, they assure the same, by the power they ascribe to every priest, of making Christ; and by the power of ordaining penance; and of remitting, and retaining of sins.

Tenthly, by the doctrine of purgatory, of justification by external works, and of indulgences, the clergy is enriched.

Eleventhly, by their demonology, and the use of exorcism, and other things appertaining thereto, they keep (or think they keep) the people more in awe of their power.

Lastly, the metaphysics, ethics, and politics of Aristotle, the frivolous distinctions, barbarous terms, and obscure language of the Schoolmen, taught in the universities, (which have been all erected and regulated by the pope's authority,) serve them to keep these errors from being detected, and to make men mistake the *ignis fatuus* of vain philosophy, for the light of the Gospel.

To these, if they sufficed not, might be added other of their dark doctrines, the profit whereof redoundeth manifestly, to the setting up of an unlawful power over the lawful sovereigns of Christian people; or for the sustaining of the same, when it is set up; or to the worldly riches, honour, and authority of those that sustain it. And therefore by the aforesaid rule, of *cui bono*, we may justly pronounce for the authors of all this spiritual darkness, the pope, and Roman clergy, and all those besides that endeavour to settle in the minds of men this erroneous doctrine, that the church now on earth, is that kingdom of God mentioned in the Old and New Testament.

But the emperors, and other Christian sovereigns, under whose government these errors, and the like encroachments of ecclesiastics upon their office, at first crept in, to the disturbance of their possessions, and of the tranquillity of their subjects, though they suffered the same for want of foresight of the sequel, and of insight into the designs of their teachers, may nevertheless be esteemed accessories to their own, and the public damage: for without their authority there could at first no seditious doctrine have been publicly preached. I say they might have hindered the same in the beginning: but when the people were once possessed by those spiritual men, there was no human remedy to be applied, that any man could invent.

....

But as the inventions of men are woven, so also are they ravelled out; the way is the same, but the order is inverted: the web begins at the first elements of power, which are wisdom, humility, sincerity, and other virtues of the apostles, whom the people converted, obeyed, out of reverence, not by obligation: their consciences were free, and their words and actions subject to none but the civil power. Afterwards the presbyters (as the flocks of Christ increased) assembling to consider what they should teach, and thereby obliging themselves to teach nothing against the decrees of their assemblies, made it to be thought the people were thereby obliged to follow their doctrine, and when they refused, refused to keep them company, (that was then called excommunication,) not as being infidels, but as being disobedient: and this was the first knot upon their liberty. And the number of presbyters increasing, the presbyters of the chief city or province got themselves an authority over the parochial presbyters, and appropriated to themselves the names of bishops: and this was a second knot on Christian liberty. Lastly, the bishop of Rome, in regard of the imperial city, took upon him an authority (partly by the wills of the emperors themselves, and by the title of *Pontifex Maximus*, and at last when the emperors were grown weak, by the priviliges of St. Peter) over all other bishops of the empire: which was the third and last knot, and the whole *synthesis* and *construction* of the pontifical power.

And therefore the *analysis*, or *resolution* is by the same way; but beginneth with the knot that was last tied; as we may see in the dissolution of the preterpolitical church government in England. First, the power of the popes was dissolved totally by Queen Elizabeth; and the bishops, who before exercised their functions in right of the pope, did afterwards exercise the same in right of the queen and her successors; though by retaining the phrase of *jure divino*, they were thought to demand it by immediate right from God: and so was untied the first knot. After this, the presbyterians lately in England obtained the putting down of episcopacy: and so was the second knot dissolved: and almost at the same time, the power was taken also from the presbyterians: and so we are reduced to the independency of the primitive Christians to follow Paul, or Cephas, or Apollos, every man as he liketh best: which, if it be without contention, and without measuring the doctrine of Christ, by our affection to the person of his minister, (the fault which the apostle reprehended in the Corinthians,) is perhaps the best: first, because there ought to be no power over the consciences of men, but of the word itself, working faith in every one, not always according to the purpose of them that plant and water, but of God himself, that giveth the increase: and secondly, because it is unreasonable in them, who teach there is such danger in every little error, to require of a man endued with reason of his own, to follow the reason of any other man, or of the most voices of many other men; which is little better, than to venture his salvation at cross and pile.

....

But who knows that this spirit of Rome, now gone out, and walking by missions through the dry places of China, Japan, and the Indies, that yield him little fruit, may not return, or rather an assembly of spirits worse than he, enter, and inhabit this clean-swept house, and make the end thereof worse than the beginning? For it is not the Roman clergy only, that pretends the kingdom of God to be of this world, and thereby to have a power therein, distinct from that of the civil state. And this is all I had a design to say, concerning the doctrine of the POLITICS. Which when I have reviewed, I shall willingly expose it to the censure of my country.

A REVIEW, *and* CONCLUSION

From the contrariety of some of the natural faculties of the mind, one to another, as also of one passion to another, and from their reference to conversation, there has been an argument taken, to infer an impossibility that any one man should be sufficiently disposed to all sorts of civil duty. The severity of judgement, they say, makes men censorious, and unapt to pardon the errors and infirmities of other men: and on the other side, celerity of fancy, makes the thoughts less steady than is necessary, to discern exactly between right and wrong. Again, in all deliberations, and in all pleadings, the faculty of solid reasoning is necessary: for without it, the resolutions of men are rash, and their sentences unjust: and yet if there be not powerful eloquence, which procureth attention and consent, the effect of reason will be little. But these are contrary faculties; the former being grounded upon principles of truth; the other upon opinions already received, true, or false; and upon the passions and interests of men, which are different and mutable.

....

To which I answer, that these are indeed great difficulties, but not impossibilities: for by education, and discipline, they may be, and are sometimes reconciled. Judgement, and fancy may have place in the same man; but by turns; as the end which he aimeth at requireth. As the Israelites in Egypt, were sometimes fastened to their labour of making bricks, and other times were ranging abroad to gather straw: so also may the judgement sometimes be fixed upon one certain consideration, and the fancy at another time wandering about the world. So also reason, and eloquence, (though not perhaps in the natural sciences, yet in the moral) may stand very well together. For wheresoever there is place for adorning and preferring of error, there is much more place for adorning and preferring of truth, if they have it to adorn. Nor is there any repugnancy between fearing the laws, and not fearing a public enemy; nor between abstaining from injury, and pardoning it in others. There is therefore no such inconsistence of human nature, with civil duties, as some think.

....

THOMAS HOBBES (1588-1679)

To the laws of nature, declared in the 15th chapter, I would have this added, *that every man is bound by nature, as much as in him lieth, to protect in war, the authority, by which he is himself protected in time of peace.* For he that pretendeth a right of nature to preserve his own body, cannot pretend a right of nature to destroy him, by whose strength he is preserved: it is a manifest contradiction of himself. And though this law may be drawn by consequence, from some of those that are there already mentioned; yet the times require to have it inculcated, and remembered.

....

In the 29th chapter I have set down for one of the causes of the dissolutions of commonwealths, their imperfect generation, consisting in the want of an absolute and arbitrary legislative power; for want whereof, the civil sovereign is fain to handle the sword of justice unconstantly, and as if it were too hot for him to hold: one reason whereof (which I have not there mentioned) is this, that they will all of them justify the war, by which their power was at first gotten, and whereon (as they think) their right dependeth, and not on the possession. As if, for example, the right of the kings of England did depend on the goodness of the cause of *William* the Conqueror, and upon their lineal, and directest descent from him; by which means, there would perhaps be no tie of the subjects' obedience to their sovereign at this day in all the world: wherein whilst they needlessly think to justify themselves, they justify all the successful rebellions that ambition shall at any time after raise against them, and their successors. Therefore I put down for one of the most effectual seeds of the death of any state, that the conquerors require not only a submission of men's actions to them for the future, but also an approbation of all their actions past; when there is scarce a commonwealth in the world, whose beginnings can in conscience be justified.

....

And as to the whole doctrine, I see not yet, but the principles of it are true and proper; and the ratiocination solid. For I ground the civil right of sovereigns, and both the duty and liberty of subjects, upon the known natural inclinations of mankind, and upon the articles of the law of nature; of which no man, that pretends but reason enough to govern his private family, ought to be ignorant. And for the power ecclesiastical of the same sovereigns, I ground it on such texts, as are both evident in themselves, and consonant to the scope of the whole Scripture. And therefore am persuaded, that he that shall read it with a purpose only to be informed, shall be informed by it. But for those that by writing, or public discourse, or by their eminent actions, have already engaged themselves to the maintaining of contrary opinions, they will not be so easily satisfied. For in such cases, it is natural for men, at one and the same time, both to proceed in reading, and to lose their attention, in the search of objections to that they had read before: of which, in a time wherein the interests of men are changed (seeing much of that doctrine, which serveth to the establishing of a new government, must needs be contrary to that which conduced to the dissolution of the old,) there cannot choose but be very many.

In that part which treateth of a Christian commonwealth, there are some new doctrines, which, it may be, in a state where the contrary were already fully determined, were a fault for a subject without leave to divulge, as being an usurpation of the place of a teacher. But in this time, that men call not only for peace, but also for truth, to offer such doctrine as I think true, and that manifestly tend to peace and loyalty, to the consideration of those that are yet in deliberation, is no more, but to offer new wine, to be put into new casks, that both may be preserved together. And I suppose, that then, when novelty can breed no trouble, nor disorder in a state, men are not generally so much inclined to the reverence of antiquity, as to prefer ancient errors, before new and well-proved truth.

. . . .

To conclude, there is nothing in this whole discourse, nor in that I wrote before of the same subject in Latin, as far as I can perceive, contrary either to the word of God, or to good manners; or tending to the disturbance of the public tranquillity. Therefore I think it may be profitably printed, and more profitably taught in the universities, in case they also think so, to whom the judgement of the same belongeth. For seeing the universities are the fountains of civil, and moral doctrine, from whence the preachers, and the gentry, drawing such water as they find, use to sprinkle the same (both from the pulpit, and in their conversation) upon the people, there ought certainly to be great care taken, to have it pure, both from the venom of heathen politicians, and from the incantation of deceiving spirits. And by that means the most men, knowing their duties, will be the less subject to serve the ambition of a few discontented persons, in their purposes against the state; and be the less grieved with the contributions necessary for their peace, and defence; and the governors themselves have the less cause, to maintain at the common charge any greater army, than is necessary to make good the public liberty, against the invasions and encroachments of foreign enemies.

And thus I have brought to an end my discourse of civil and ecclesiastical government, occasioned by the disorders of the present time, without partiality, without application, and without other design, than to set before men's eyes the mutual relation between protection and obedience;

of which the condition of human nature, and the laws divine, (both natural and positive) require an inviolable observation. And though in the revolution of states, there can be no very good constellation for truths of this nature to be born under, (as having an angry aspect from the dissolvers of an old government, and seeing but the backs of them that erect a new;) yet I cannot think it will be condemned at this time, either by the public judge of doctrine, or by any that desires the continuance of public peace. And in this hope I return to my interrupted speculation of bodies natural; wherein, (if God give me health to finish it,) I hope the novelty will as much please, as in the doctrine of this artificial body it useth to offend. For such truth, as opposeth no man's profit, nor pleasure, is to all men welcome.

Note

1 Many thanks to Sharon Lloyd for her guidance on these Hobbes selections. Lavender McKittrick-Sweitzer and Daniel Olson aided in their preparation. In preparing this original edition, we gratefully referred to Richard Tuck's (Cambridge, 1991) and Edwin Curley's (Hackett, 1994) editions for help in correcting errors and checking punctuation.

PUBLIC REASON IN HOBBES

S. A. Lloyd[1]

1 Introduction

When we ask whether a political philosophy contains a conception of public reason, we may have in mind either of two quite distinct questions: Does it require an appeal to public reasons in order to justify its overarching political framework, or proposed form of regime? Alternatively, does it require political actors within its justified political system to appeal to public reasons in political deliberation? We may be tempted to think that these are not distinct questions if we're inclined toward the view that no political framework permitting the state's coercive power to enforce decisions (made at any level) that are not supported by public reasons could be justified. But Hobbes's political philosophy shows us that these questions are indeed separate.

Hobbes's theory also proves fruitful in thinking about our current debate over whether a public reason requirement is better conceived as requiring reasons that appeal to interests, values, or beliefs all parties share (consensus), or rather as requiring that each party has a reason that supports the same policy as the different reasons of others (convergence). Hobbes deploys both conceptions in a coherent and well-designed system.

Hobbes's political philosophy addresses the problem of ensuring a society's domestic stability. He was vividly impressed by the "miseries, and horrible calamities, that accompany a civil war,"[2] having lived through the terrifying and destructive English Civil War and the chaotic period of political upheaval that followed it. Hobbes analyzed that war as the result of people's embracing mistaken views, many religiously rooted, about the character and limits of governmental authority. Many of Hobbes's fellow subjects took themselves to have a religious duty or justification for taking up arms against the existing political authority and they were willing to risk or even to sacrifice their lives in pursuit of their *transcendent* interests in fulfilling what they understood to be their religious duties and securing their eternal prospects. Hobbes comments on his writing of *Leviathan* that "the cause of my writing that book was the consideration of what the ministers before and in the beginning of the civil war, by their preaching and writing did contribute thereunto"[3] and that

> it was written in a time when the pretence of Christ's kingdom was made use of for the most horrid actions that can be imagined; and it was in just indignation of that, that I desired to see the bottom of that doctrine of the kingdom of Christ, which divers ministers then preached for a pretence to their rebellion.[4]

For Hobbes, the English Civil War largely issued from a perceived division between civil authority and religious authority, which he graphically symbolized in his frontispiece to *Leviathan*. But other ways of dividing political authority, or limiting it, may also invite civil war. Hobbes undertook the project of discovering how to design an everlasting commonwealth so internally stable that it will not be "destroyed, but by foreign war."[5]

Hobbes's general plan for addressing the problem of domestic disorder is to begin from the interests his readers actually affirm as their own and then to provide each with reasons linked to those interests for adhering to a principle of practically unconditional obedience to the effective political authority under which they live. An effective political authority is one that protects its citizens.[6] Hobbes offers a confluence of reasons for obeying such an authority, including narrowly prudential reasons, moral reasons from both natural duty and obligation, and religious reasons from Christian duty and Christians' special-prudential interest in receiving eternal life. Hobbes conjectures that, taken together, these reasons will prove sufficient to motivate most of the people most of the time to obey enough of the political authority's commands that domestic peace can be maintained indefinitely. Over time, political institutions will narrow the range of disagreement among citizens, forging a broader consensus in citizens' beliefs and conceptions of their interests through education and other mandated social practices.

Although Hobbes was writing to a specifically Christian audience, splintered into many opposed factions, some of which hoped to use state power to achieve a Biblically directed commonwealth, both his problem and his intended solution have continuing relevance for us today. Sectarian religious conflict, frequently violent, as well as pervasive disagreement over the proper scope and exercise of governmental authority even within liberal democracies, persists on almost every continent, disrupting domestic peace. Still today, multiple authorities make competing claims on the same populations, often resulting in civil war. People acting on transcendent interests in fulfilling their duties to God, or in securing self-determination, or social justice, or the good of future generations, continue to take up arms to bring down political regimes they judge to have overstepped the limits of their authority or to have failed to fulfill their obligations. Hobbes provides us with conceptual resources for engaging these problems our age shares with his.

2 The Need for Government

Hobbes begins from the plausible supposition that when human beings living together in a group exercise their own private judgments about how to conduct their common business, they are apt to disagree. Not only will their private judgments diverge over questions of fact and of value, urgency, and strategy but they may also diverge over which matters should be regarded as common business and which to leave to individual choice. Unlike ants and bees and other naturally "sociable creatures" whose consensus on a coordinated pattern of behavior in their community is hardwired,[7] we humans come to differing judgments about matters of right and wrong, good and bad, yours and mine, fine and base, pious and irreligious, acceptable and unacceptable; and these differing private judgments can put us at odds over how to conduct our community.

We need not assume that human beings are vicious or even selfish in order to account for divergence in private judgments. Hobbes identifies a variety of morally neutral causes of our disagreement in private judgments. Differences in our bodily constitutions can affect our temperaments, degrees of optimism, patience, aggressiveness, and capacities for complex reasoning. Differences in our tastes and interests affect our judgments of desirability, usefulness, and urgency. Differences in our upbringing, and in our life experiences, have a pervasive effect on our judgments across a wide range of issues.[8] And our education, or socialization, both formal and informal, profoundly affects the content of our private judgments on everything from religious truths to gender roles to attitudes about the proper scope of community claims on the individual. The specific things different individuals desire or fear or hope for "the constitution individual, and particular education do so vary" that only God can really know what they are.[9] Although the differences mentioned suffice to account for wide disagreement in private judgments, when we add to them the undeniable fact that people often do make judgments under the influence of self-partiality, their judgments are likely to diverge even further.

Although our own experience confirms Hobbes's account of the sources of divergence in private judgments, we may think that he exaggerates the degree of our disagreement. But that, Hobbes would say, is because we have all grown up and live in societies where public authorities strongly influence or even condition the content of our private judgments. Precisely because we live in politically ordered communities, our upbringing and education and experiences largely conform to the judgments imposed by government, churches, schools, and other social institutions. One function of public institutions is to adjudicate conflicts among competing private judgments; but another equally important function is to create consensus in private judgment. We can hardly dismiss Hobbes's argument that we require government in order to address the problem of disagreement in private judgment on the ground that such disagreements are few and unimportant, if the explanation for the fact that they are few and unimportant is that we have been brought up under a government that has conditioned our consensus in private judgment on most, and the most important, matters.

To assess Hobbes's contention, we would have to consider what life would be like were we to try to live together while each governing ourselves according to our own private judgment. This is in fact the thought experiment Hobbes proposes when he considers "the condition of mere nature," a condition of universal, unbridled private judgment over every question. Such a condition requires more than just the absence of a government; it requires that we assume that no one has any obligation to obey or to defer to the private judgment of anyone else in anything. No government, church, teacher, or parent has any authority to impose its judgment on another. Because no one has a duty to defer to the private judgment of anyone else, each individual permissibly exercises her own private judgment over all matters, including how to act. Thus in the condition of mere nature, each enjoys a liberty right (though not a claim right) to act as she thinks best.

No such condition has ever actually existed, nor even could, Hobbes grants, because everyone is born under an obligation of obedience to (at the very least) the parent or other person who has sustained his or her life. He notes that "a son cannot be understood to be at any time in the state of nature, as being under... the command of them to whom he owes protection as soon as ever he is born."[10] Because Hobbes thinks that we are all born under an obligation of obedience to those who have sustained our lives, he says that in the state of nature we must "consider men as if but even now sprung up out of the earth, and suddenly, like mushrooms, come to full maturity without all kinds of engagement to each other."[11] By "engagements" Hobbes has in mind undertakings of obligations to obey, as we see in his description of the imagined condition as "considering men therefore again in the state of nature, without covenants or subjection one to another, as if they were but even now all at once created [adult] male and female."[12] Subsequent thinkers, notably Locke, denied that we are born under any obligations of obedience at all, even to parents; such a position will make Hobbes's characterization of the state of nature as entirely devoid of obligations to obey even more appropriate for modeling our pre-political moral position.

Hobbes defines the state of nature as a condition of universal private judgment, writing that "so long a man is in the condition of mere nature... as private appetite is the measure of good, and evil."[13] But it is important to notice that something close to this condition can obtain even in the presence of various entities that claim political or religious authority to command others, if their commands cannot be jointly satisfied, because in such cases every individual must use his or her private judgment to decide which if any of those authorities to obey. This phenomenon is clear enough in the case of a civil war: Different entities claim authority over the same population, and each member of that population is thrown back on her own private judgment to determine which party she (and in her judgment others) should obey as legitimate. And because private judgments diverge, for all the reasons just surveyed, it's no surprise that when multiple contenders to authority emerge—whether they be secular versus religious, federal versus state, executive versus legislative, or hereditary versus popular—civil wars should result.

Is a condition of universal private judgment satisfactory? Hobbes argues that while it works fine for some insect communities, it won't do for us. Because our private judgments diverge, governance by individual private judgment leads to *conflict*. We're sufficiently equal in the sorts of capacities needed to dominate others or to resist others—bodily strength, intelligence, ingenuity, wiles—that none of us can reasonably expect to impose our own private judgment on everyone else. Even if we are marginally superior to others in all the qualities mentioned, others can combine their talents to outdo us. So not only can we expect conflict when we all try to make the world conform to our private judgment, but we can expect that *conflict to be perpetual and irresoluble* because there just are no superhumans who can bend the wills of everyone else to conform to their private judgment. People who are operationally equal in these ways will have similar hope to achieve their ends and will see no reason why they should defer to others rather than the other way around.

In a condition of universal private judgment, we can expect that people will disagree over what is of value, what ends are worth pursing, how best to achieve ends, and all the rest. This sort of disagreement is bound to result in mutual interference in one another's plans, in dispute over control of resources, and in attempted constraints on our liberty of action. Hobbes goes so far as to say that there is nothing those others may not claim a right to in order to advance their plans—even other people's bodies.[14] We may be shocked by that claim until we recall innumerable historical incidents, continuing today, of people claiming rights to control or to use other people's bodies: men over women's to use as wives, concubines, and mothers for their children, masters over slaves, impressed workers, conscripted soldiers, captives of war, prisoner laborers, debtor laborers, not to mention human sacrifices to deities, destruction of witches, heretics and apostates, and garden variety cannibalism. Some may judge that all such uses of other people are wrong, but why should others who disagree defer to those people's private judgments rather than rely on their own?[15] Hobbes argues that if it is permissible for you to judge the correctness of my judgments about how to act, it must be equally permissible for me to judge the correctness of your judgment about the correctness of my judgment.[16] As equals, our judgments stand on the same footing; and to imagine that all humans each governing themselves by their private judgment and equal enough to press their claims against others' competing claims would somehow each decide to leave everyone else in their reach untouched is pure fantasy. Hobbes appears to be correct that a permanent state of universal unbridled private judgment would result in perpetual irresoluble conflict.

Hobbes contrasts the form of life we could expect to have in a world of universal private judgment (outside commonwealth) with life within political societies: "out of it, there is a dominion of passions, war, fear, poverty, slovenliness, solitude, barbarism, ignorance, cruelty; in it, the dominion of reason, peace, security, riches, decency, society, elegancy, sciences, and benevolence."[17] In one of the most famous passages of *Leviathan*, Hobbes concludes of the state of nature that

> In such condition, there is no place for industry; because the fruit thereof is uncertain: and consequently no culture of the earth; no navigation, nor use of the commodities that may be imported by sea; no commodious building; no instruments of moving, and removing such things as require much force; no knowledge of the face of the earth; no account of time; no arts; no letters; no society; and which is worst of all, continual fear, and danger of violent death; and the life of man, solitary, poor, nasty, brutish, and short.[18]

This sounds very bad indeed. But why wouldn't we have all those valuable human achievements? Hobbes's simple answer is that universal private judgment *undermines individuals' agency*. We humans, who think of ourselves as agents who do things rather than as mere objects being acted on, value achieving our ends or purposes. That our agency be effective matters to us. More strongly, humans, qua rational agents, *necessarily* desire to make their agency effective. We may have lots of personally idiosyncratic desires, and other widely shared but not universal desires to pursue such ends as comfort, luxury, honor, fame, bodily self-preservation, or eternal life. The objects of human desire and their relative strength differ greatly among individuals, but the one thing we all must want, no matter what else we want, is that our actions in pursuit of our desires not be futile. But the interference of other people with our plans, our use of resources, our control even of our own bodies, undermines our capacity to effect our goals. Our agency may be expected to be systematically thwarted in the sort of free-for-all social world where private judgments rule. It follows that we must desire to avoid such a world.

3 The Duty to Submit to Government

The obvious solution to the impasse created by universal private judgment is to defer some matters to a *public* judgment. If we set up a mutually agreeable public judge of our private disputes, and agree mutually to stand by its decisions, we can begin to create a social environment in which we get out of each other's way enough that we can each hope to achieve our purposes, at least the most important ones, much of the time. The public judge would be an arbitrator of disputes, or an umpire, or judge. Hobbes terms the socially constructed body authorized to arbitrate disputes "the sovereign." A sovereign is an artificially constructed "person," that is, an entity or body that can exercise the personal qualities of deliberating, judging, willing, and acting. It is constructed when many individuals regard themselves as under an obligation to defer their private judgment to its public judgment, that is, to treat its will as if it were their own will. The existence of a sovereign does not rely on any actual historical process in which people make an agreement to abide by the decisions of a particular entity; rather, sovereignty exists when people act *as if* they had undertaken an obligation to defer their private judgments to the public entity. The idea is to erect an entity

> that may reduce all their wills... unto one will: which is as much as to say, to appoint one man, or assembly of men, to bear their person; and every one to own, and acknowledge himself to be author of whatsoever he that so beareth their person, shall act, or cause to be acted, in those things which concern the common peace and safety; and therein to submit their wills, everyone to his will, and their judgements to his judgement... in such manner, *as if* every man should say to every man, *I authorise and give up my right of governing myself, to this man, or to this assembly of men, on this condition, that thou give up thy right to him, and authorise all his actions in like manner.*[19]

The first thing to notice is that in Hobbes's system, a sovereign *constitutes* public reason for all internal purposes of political decision-making. Whatever reason the sovereign offers *is* a public reason, regardless of its content. When citizens cite to one another the public reasons for, e.g., paying a tax, enlisting in the military, or attending services of the state church, those reasons are simply that the sovereign judges such actions to be required (or perhaps merely desirable, as the case may be). Thus in Hobbes's system, internal public reason, the deliberative reason of citizens, is purely procedural. It picks out a unique locus of decision-making, or of judgment, which is to be treated as authoritative. There are no enforceable substantive constraints on the content of public reasons, although, as we'll see, the law of nature constrains the consciences of sovereigns and limits what sorts of considerations can count as reasons at all, whether public or private. The reasons to which the sovereign appeals will usually be couched in the language of the common good, the commonwealth's peace and defense, or the good of the population, but to enforce any limit on the sorts of reasons that the sovereign could lay down to support its judgments of what laws or policies serve the public good would be to decide that the ultimate arbitrator of all disputes was subject to review of its decisions, hence no ultimate arbitrator at all.

We'll return later to some of the questions posed by this Hobbesian conception of internal public reason as entirely formal or procedural. We note it now only to help distinguish the character of Hobbes's argument for the necessity of erecting a public reason to advance our shared and necessary interest in securing conditions for the effective exercise of our agency. That argument addresses the higher level question whether public reasons are required in order to justify a political framework or form of regime. Indeed they are, in Hobbes's view, and at that level public reasons cannot be merely procedural and substance-free.[20] They must engage a variety of non-procedural reason-giving interests, some shared, others converging, and all respecting a reciprocity constraint on what can count as a reason.

Hobbes's state of nature argument permits us to see that we have a *shared* reason to agree to defer our private judgments to a common arbitrator of our disputes (a sovereign), namely, that we can expect to be better able to achieve our ends in an ordered social environment that specifies rules of the road so that we take turns in standing out of each other's way than we could in the free-for-all of a government-less state of nature. That shared reason appeals to our shared interest in effecting our ends.

But shared desires or interests are not enough to settle our political obligations. To have even a universal reason or motive to subordinate one's private judgment to a public political authority (that is, to obey a public authority) is not yet to have any moral duty to do so. We can believe that it is in our personal interest for us to do something without believing it is wrong for us neglect to do that thing. On some accounts of justification, we have no genuine *justification* of political authority until we identify a moral requirement on everyone to undertake that obligation of obedience. Such accounts may reason that because political authority deploys coercive force to compel compliance with its decisions, and the use of force on unwilling others requires justification, whatever interests we may share in deferring to an arbitrator will not amount to political obligation unless it would be wrong—morally fault-worthy—of people to resist the imposition of that force on themselves.

The challenge, then, is to identify a ground of moral obligation to submit to the arbitrating authority that we can so clearly see it is in our common interest to do. Hobbes provides this in his idea of the laws of nature. These laws are rules of conduct discoverable by anyone who exercises her natural reason in thinking about human nature and the human condition, the observance of which helps to secure harmonious human communities.

4 The Reciprocity Requirement of the Law of Nature

Hobbes insists that we each have a moral duty to submit to the institutions we require others to submit to. If our desire to make our own agency effective compels us to insist that others must defer their disputes to a public judgment, then we must do so ourselves. His argument for this conclusion again begins from our shared human self-conception as rational agents, but this time unfolds the meaning of rationality. Rationality involves much more than instrumental fitting of means to desired ends. When Hobbes investigates what "accords with reason," he is asking what sorts of considerations reasonable people could advance to justify to others the things they do that will impact those others. For Hobbes, to be rational is to act for a reason, where a reason is understood to be a justifying consideration that one is prepared not only to offer to others but to accept from them as well. Hobbes observes a *consistency* requirement on rationality. A rational person is prepared to offer justifying reasons for her own judgments and is willing to accept from others those very same reasons to justify their judgments.[21] This is because the basic reciprocity requirement of natural law is that we not do what we are prepared to fault, or blame, others for doing. So if we would fault them for attempting to justify their action by resort to a particular consideration (reason), then neither may we deploy that consideration. On this distinctively Hobbesian conception, for a consideration to count as a reason at all it must be to some degree public because it commits us to consistency in our treatment of reasons across all people. But reasons won't necessarily be fully public, because they depend on judgments of blameworthiness, and such judgments are perspectival. If, for example, a theist offers her religious belief as a reason for her action, she is committed to accepting others' religious beliefs as an equally good reason for their like actions; whereas an atheist, lacking any religious beliefs may consistently refuse to count anyone's religious beliefs as providing reasons. Given the variability in people's private judgments of blameworthiness, we shouldn't expect there to be a single set of universal public reasons. This means that although reasons can be less than fully public, they must be more than purely private if they are to count as reasons at all.[22]

We might then imagine that, considering our diversity in private judgment, imposing a reciprocity requirement on everyone would only entrench alienation. In fact, it pulls us together. When we accept that morality dictates that the claims we impose on others we must also accept ourselves, we feel a moral pressure to do what our narrow self-interest has already dictated, namely, to acquiesce with everyone else in deferring our private judgment to a sovereign public judgment. This moral imperative not only operates to induce us to enter the arrangement we can see it is in our prudential interest to sustain, but it also gives us greater assurance that others will do the same.

5 The Scope of Political Obligation

One of the most controversial features of Hobbes's system is his insistence that sovereign authority should be neither divided nor limited. Authority to conduct the various functions needed to settle all private disputes and to enforce those settlements—Hobbes terms these the "essential rights of sovereignty," which include legislation, adjudication, punishment, taxation, power to declare war, education, and interpretation of religion—should not be divided among different bodies.[23] The reason Hobbes calls these rights essential is that all are needed and none can be effective in securing peace without possession of the others. A right to adjudicate disputes, for example, will not secure peace if those decisions are not enforced; and a right to declare war to defend the nation will not succeed in doing so without funding of the war effort. Furthermore, Hobbes insists that the sovereign's authority to exercise these functions must not be limited by a body of rules (for instance a constitution) or external decision-makers such as churches. In making this argument, Hobbes follows his reasoning against the desirability of universal private judgment through to its logical conclusion.

In characterizing the sort of public authority needed to overcome the problems that attend the state of nature, Hobbes defines a commonwealth as

> *one person, of whose acts a great multitude, by mutual covenants one with another, have made themselves every one the author, to the end he may use the strength and means of them all, as he shall think expedient, for their peace and common defence.*[24]

We noted earlier that Hobbes is speaking of an artificial entity we treat as issuing judgments to which we should defer. This entity is afforded the authority to tax us (use our means) and call on us to perform functions like military or jury service, administration or law enforcement (use our strength), in pursuit of a particular and limited end—our "peace and common defence." Because the proper end of government is limited, we might suppose that governmental authority is limited. That would be a mistake, Hobbes argues. He writes of subjects that

> if any one, or more of them, pretend a breach of the covenant made by the sovereign at his institution; and others, or one other of his subjects, or himself alone, pretend there was no such breach, there is in this case, no judge to decide the controversy: it therefore returns to the sword again.[25]

Our purpose in submitting to government is to resolve disputes among private judgments. If we limit governmental authority, the question immediately arises as to when those limits have been overstepped. Who decides? If the decision whether the limits have been overstepped belongs to each and every individual, we find ourselves again, or are still, in a condition of universal private judgment. People are apt to disagree on this question as they do on all others; and because there is no public authority to settle their dispute, civil war looms. And as we saw, in civil wars, all are thrown back on their own private judgments. To allow each individual to evaluate the government's performance at all points is to treat its judgment as just another private judgment, and so to remain in the very state of nature we all have reason to escape.

To avoid this, we might try to set up some further authority external to the sovereign to make the judgment whether the sovereign has overstepped the limits of its commission. Historically, entities like the Pope (conceived as a "universal sovereign of Christendom") or a church court or even a document like Magna Carta have been offered as such authorities. What happens when the sovereign and its overseeing authority disagree on whether it has properly exercised its authority? If the judgment of the overseeing authority is decisive in all cases, then it is actually the sovereign, and the other was merely a functionary exercising delegated powers. If, for instance, the Pope can delegitimize or excommunicate a national sovereign for ruling incorrectly, thereby releasing its subjects from any obligation to obey it, then the Pope is the actual sovereign, and kings are exercising delegated powers at the pleasure of the real sovereign.[26] But notice, Hobbes says, that if this is what's going on, sovereignty remains unlimited. The sovereign is unlimited, we've just misidentified the sovereign.

Alternatively, suppose that the limiting body is not authoritative, but is itself limited so that the question arises as to whether it has correctly exercised its oversight powers, leaving unsettled the issue as to which to obey.

If we are not to allow each individual to decide this question (returning us to condition of universal private judgment), we need yet another body to adjudicate the dispute between the sovereign and the limiting body. Call this a meta-sovereign. The same question arises again: Is this meta-sovereign the final authority? If so, it is actually sovereign, and its authority is unlimited. If not, we need yet a further meta-meta-sovereign, inviting a perpetual regress. Hobbes's point is that if we are to escape the miseries of private judgment, we must collectively defer to a public judgment, conceived as a *final* judgment, at which the buck finally stops. And for that to be the case, the final authority must also have final authority to decide whether it has properly exercised its own authority.

We can see this requirement in Hobbes's definition of a commonwealth as an artificial person that uses the means and strength of citizens *as it deems fit* for their peace and common defense. The sovereign alone decides what policies comport with its mandate. This is what turns a limited commission—of securing peace and common defense—into an absolute, unlimited authority. And this is why whatever reason, regardless of its content, the sovereign offers in support of its mandate counts as a public justifying reason, for the question whether some reason is or is not a proper basis for justifying laws or policies is to be decided by the sovereign itself.

Although no person or group is entitled to enforce limits on the sovereign's rule, the law of nature does provide standards for correct rule, binding on the conscience of the sovereign and for which God will hold the sovereign accountable. The sovereign's job is "the procuration of *the safety of the people*; to which he is obliged by the law of nature, and to render an account thereof to God, the author of that law, and to none but him"[27] under pain of damnation. Hobbes construes "safety" or the "good of the people" broadly, to include not just domestic peace and national defense, but also subjects' prosperity and enrichment, their enjoyment of an expansive sphere of "harmless liberty," and even efforts to facilitate their eternal good in the next life.[28] It is thus incorrect to suppose that because the scope of sovereign authority is unlimited, there are no moral limits on its proper exercise. We may fear that the sovereign will "take all, spoil all, kill all," but "though by right... he may do it, yet he cannot do it justly, that is, without breach of the natural laws and injury against God."[29] This consideration, that misrule is morally wrong and invites divine punishment, along with the fact that (whether justified or not) people will rebel against tyrannical misrule, puts some pressure on sovereigns to rule within the bounds of the law of nature.

Hobbes thus recognizes that affording a sovereign such unlimited authority is unnerving, but concludes that doing so is better than the alternative: "And though of so unlimited a Power, men may fancy many evil consequences, yet the consequences of the want of it, which is perpetual war of every man against his neighbor, are much worse."[30] This is because of all inconveniences or "incommodities"

> the greatest, that in any form of government can possibly happen *to the people in general*, is scarce sensible, in respect of the miseries, and horrible calamities, that accompany a civil war; or that dissolute condition of masterless men, without subjection to laws.[31]

Of interest for our purpose is not whether Hobbes was right about this, but rather whether concern for things other than a commodious earthly life might deprive Hobbes's argument for absolute authority of its justifying power.

6 The Christian Problem

So far Hobbes has argued for the absolute authority of a sovereign to determine all questions, basing that argument on our necessary interest in securing a stable peaceful environment in which to act effectively, and on the moral requirement that we do our part in creating that environment. But these are not the only interests people have, and Hobbes's Christian readership in particular affirms a distinct and, for some, overriding interest in fulfilling the requirements of their faith. Should those requirements be incompatible with obeying the sovereign's commands, Hobbes's argument would prove insufficient to motivate their compliance, and more importantly, would fail to justify to them the requirement of political obedience.

Hobbes acknowledges this problem when he writes

> The most frequent pretext of sedition, and civil war, in Christian commonwealths hath a long time proceeded from a difficulty, not yet sufficiently resolved, of obeying at once both God, and man, then when their commandments are one contrary to the other. It is manifest enough, that when a man receiveth two contrary commands, and knows that one of them is God's, he ought to obey that, and not the other, though it be the command even of his lawful sovereign.[32]

This problem of a perceived conflict between religious and civil duty was, Hobbes is claiming, the usual cause of civil strife in Christian states, and it was a problem that had not yet been satisfactorily addressed. His own work must offer a solution.

Were we to translate Hobbes's argument for submitting to sovereign authority into a principle of political obligation stating the conditions under which citizens are to obey their existing political authority, we would think the best candidate principle was "Obey the political authority in all of its commands." As it happens, however, Hobbes's own principle of political obligation is nowhere near that absolute. His principle is this: "subjects owe to sovereigns, simple obedience, in all things, wherein their obedience is not repugnant to the laws of God."[33] When those commands are repugnant to God's laws, Hobbes has said that we ought instead to obey God's laws, and further that "if the [sovereign's] command be such, as cannot be obeyed, without being damned to eternal death, then it were madness to obey it."[34]

This exemption from the requirement of obedience to an effective sovereign has the potential to completely undermine political stability. If many people refuse to obey the sovereign's commands, exempting themselves from political obedience, it may be unable to sustain order and the rule of law, the conditions needed for people to hope to act effectively. If the population divides over whether the sovereign's commands are to be obeyed, civil war may ensue, again thwarting effective agency. Recall that Hobbes's strategy for addressing civil instability was to identify a principle of political obligation that would, if followed, ensure perpetual domestic stability, and then to provide each person with something they could see in their own terms to be a sufficient reason to adhere to that principle. Any principle that did not contain a duty to God exemption would be rejected by those whose religious interests are of paramount importance. But a principle, like Hobbes's, that does contain such an exemption may prove incapable of securing social stability, even when all faithfully follow it, if it licenses widespread refusal to obey the sovereign.

Confronting this challenge, the obvious first question to ask is what our duties to God are. And so Hobbes writes at the end of the first half of *Leviathan*

> that subjects owe to sovereigns, simple obedience, in all things, wherein their obedience is not repugnant to the laws of God, I have sufficiently proved, in that which I have already written. There wants only, for the entire knowledge of civil duty, to know what are those laws of God. For without that, a man knows not, when he is commanded anything by the civil power, whether it be contrary to the law of God, or not... [and so] it is necessary to know what are the laws divine.[35]

How can we definitively ascertain the laws of God? To do so in a way convincing to Christians requires arguing from the sources of religious knowledge they accept as authoritative. Hobbes identifies three such sources: natural reason, personal revelation, and Scripture (understood as the accumulated revelations of the true prophets). Hobbes will argue that none of these sources gives Christians any reason to refuse to obey their sovereign's commands, even those commands that concern the specification or interpretation of divine law, or the profession or practice of Christian religion. On the contrary, both natural reason and Scripture positively direct us to defer to our sovereign's judgment in such matters. If successful, Hobbes's argument renders the duty to God exemption from political obedience harmless; the set of commands the sovereign could issue that would require us to violate our duty to God is empty, and so adherence to Hobbes's principle of political obligation should produce as much stability as would the unacceptable principle lacking any religious exemption.

To the difficulty of knowing what are God's laws, Hobbes answers that the laws we can be certain are God's are the laws of nature (which require reciprocity and can be summed up by the Golden Rule), because these laws are accessible through an exercise of unaided natural reason. These precepts of behavior to sustain human communities make claims on us because we have the nature God gave us. All theists can accept these precepts as divine laws.[36]

Other rules alleged to be God's laws by those who claim to have received direct personal revelation, that is, self-identified prophets, have a different status. The private person who honestly believes that God has spoken to her immediately in a dream or vision or auditory event and given that person a command does permissibly (and perhaps prudently) treat that belief as revealing a command *she* should obey. But the revelations she alleges are not God's laws to anyone else, because *they* cannot know that God has caused her experiences; and being a mere private person, she has no authority to require others to defer to her belief that God has spoken immediately to her. Hobbes cites Scripture on how far we are to credit the claims of those who allege personal revelation. The two marks of a true prophet are teaching the established religion and performance of miracles, each necessary but only jointly sufficient to require others to acknowledge the prophet's claims as God's word. Hobbes gleans from Scripture the definition of a miracle as "a work of God, (besides his operation by the way of nature, ordained in the Creation,) done for the making manifest to his elect, the mission of an extraordinary minister for their salvation."[37] Miracles are extraordinary events for which we can find no naturalistic explanation. But of course, what a person will count as a miracle will depend on both her experience and her degree of scientific sophistication; producing a Polaroid photograph might operate as a miracle for members of some isolated tribe, but "the same thing, may be a miracle to one, and not to another."[38] And while it would seem a miracle that a lame man suddenly walks when the alleged prophet declares him healed, there is nothing at all miraculous about a man who is pretending to be lame walking when his confederate "heals" him. Hobbes's point is that people disagree about whether a miracle has been performed, so "in this also we must have recourse to God's lieutenant; to whom in all doubtful cases, we have submitted our private judgments."[39] Because decision about whether the marks of a true prophet have been satisfied must be made "according to the public reason, i.e., according to the reason of him who has sovereign power in the commonwealth,"[40] the alleged personal revelations of private individuals do not provide sources of religious knowledge that could require resisting the sovereign's dictates in matters of religion.

In contrast, when someone whom others are already obligated to obey commands them to take the alleged revelations of prophets as God's law, then the precepts revealed become genuine positive divine laws for them.[41] On Hobbes's account, when Moses, who was sovereign by consent of the Hebrews following him out of Egypt, commanded them to take the prescriptions on the tablets he brought down from the mountain to be God's laws, those prescriptions became God's laws for those people. Similarly, when Roman emperors converted to Christianity, their command made the precepts contained in the canonical books of the Bible God's positive law to their subjects. Before then, the Scriptures contained teaching and advice intended to attract belief and to persuade; but they were not law. Laws, says Hobbes, are commands from one we are antecedently obligated to obey; and compliance with them may permissibly be compelled by coercion. By Hobbes's interpretation of Biblical texts, the commission of Jesus himself was only to teach and preach but not to rule, command, or coerce. Jesus himself did not make law but rather exhorted his followers to obey earthly authorities until such time as his own kingdom should come. If Jesus was not the sovereign of a presently existing kingdom, neither having nor claiming authority to impose law, then neither were his apostles nor the church that followed them. So again, directives based on personal revelation become laws only when they are commanded to be observed as such by those who have political authority. Hobbes concludes that God's laws are the laws of nature and those precepts from divine revelation that have been made law to subjects by those having political authority over them.

This Hobbesian answer to the obvious first question concerning what God's law is, reveals that the *crucial* question is, as always, who has the *right to decide*. In the case of God's laws of nature, which do not apply themselves but rather require interpretation, who has the right to decide what they require? The answer Hobbes gives is that *the laws themselves tell us to defer* this question, as all other contested questions, to a public authority, that is, to a sovereign. The laws of nature are *self-effacing*, meaning that they refer interpretation of their own content to the very civil authority they demand we establish. For instance, the laws of nature require that we keep our valid covenants, but who has authority to decide whether a covenant is valid or whether some specific performance counts as keeping it? That authority belongs to the very arbitrator of all disputes the natural law has directed us to establish. And if we have a dispute over whether the civil law properly specifies the requirements of natural law, natural law tells us to look for resolution to the public political authority.

Who then has the right to decide whether the sovereign's command conflicts with subjects' duties to God as these are laid down in divine *positive* law, as contained in Scripture? If that right belongs to each individual person, we may find ourselves with as many different answers as there are individuals. This leaves us again too close for comfort to the state of nature and certainly invites civil war. Hobbes writes, "If it be lawful then for subjects to resist the king when he commands anything that is against the Scripture, that is, contrary to the command of God, and to be judge of the meaning of Scripture, it is impossible that the life of any king, or the peace of any Christian kingdom, can long be secure."[42] For all to exercise private judgment about the requirements of divine positive law invites war. The law of nature requires all to submit to a public judgment, and so

> for a private man, without the authority of the commonwealth... to interpret the law by his own spirit, is another error in the politics [of the universities]... And are not the Scriptures, in all places where they are law, made law by the authority of the commonwealth, and consequently, a part of the civil law?[43]

So again, the right to decide lies with the public authority.

Hobbes concludes that none of the sources of religious knowledge his Christian audience takes to be authoritative gives any reason for resisting any command the sovereign might issue as being contrary to their duty to God. Further than this, Hobbes offers Scriptural texts in support of a positive duty to obey the civil sovereign in all matters, even if the sovereign is not merely mistaken in matters of doctrine, but is even an infidel. Far from providing a reason to resist the sovereign's authority, Christian doctrine, properly understood, demands obedience to it.

Still, sovereigns are by no means infallible, as Hobbes concedes.[44] If people believe that God will fault them, and punish them, for following their sovereign's mistaken directives concerning religion, they will have the strongest of motives for insisting on relying on their own private judgment in such matters. It is thus imperative to Hobbes's argument that he persuades his Christian audience that God imposes a *hierarchy of responsibility* according to which subjects are responsible to God for obeying their sovereign's commands, while sovereigns alone are responsible to God for the correctness of the content of their commands. When a sovereign issues a wrongful command, God will hold it alone responsible for every action subjects do in obedience to that command. What subjects do in obedience to laws, and not from their own private judgment, is considered to be the sovereign's act and not their own.[45] By this account, not only do Christians have no duty to resist their sovereign's erroneous religious commands—let alone to martyr themselves standing on private conscience—God will actually fault them for doing so. This completes Hobbes's defense of his absolutist principle of political obligation in response to the Christian problem.

7 Overview of Hobbes's Argumentative Approach

The fundamental problem for peaceful human communal living is that we disagree in our private judgments. Hobbes insightfully observes that *what* one believes is very often a function of *whom* one believes. Our beliefs, apart from those based on direct sense perceptions, are virtually all taken on authority. What we believe about history, religion, science, and current events we believe on the authority of others such as, to name just a few, parents, teachers, pastors, reporters and the authors of records, documents, and books, including the so-called holy books like those that comprise Judeo-Christian Scripture. In matters of religious belief, it is incorrect to say we believe God himself, for God does not speak to us personally without intermediaries. It would also be incorrect for Christians to say they believe Jesus, when they at best believe accounts of the reports of those who claim to have heard Jesus speak. In matters of religious belief, virtually everyone believes some merely human interpreter or inventor of stories, doctrines, or dogmas.[46] And when different people believe different authorities, their judgments are bound to diverge.

Were we all to take the very same source to be authoritative, our disagreements in judgment would be much narrowed. Seeing this, Hobbes seeks to transform substantive disagreements about which beliefs are true into the question of whose judgment we should take as authoritative. If we can finally agree on a single authority, the range of our disagreement will narrow dramatically, as that authority comes not only to reflect, but also to condition consensus in our judgments. Instead of characterizing our duty to God as a duty to believe x, profess y, and practice z (where each variable stands for a specific, contestable, item), Hobbes suggests our duty to God is more properly characterized as a duty to believe, profess, and practice as the appropriate authority in matters of religion dictates. He then argues that whoever that authority is will also have secular civil authority. This is an elaborate process carried out in Part III of *Leviathan,* which requires showing that there do not exist two concurrent realms that could have distinct authorities to govern them; there can be no distinct sovereign of the kingdom of God because that kingdom does not presently exist; there is no distinct spiritual sovereign because people do not have immortal souls existing separately from their bodies that could require a distinct governor;[47] and there can be no temporal religious sovereign distinct from the temporal secular one because the essential right of sovereignty to make laws and coerce compliance was not claimed or granted to ecclesiastics by Jesus as part of their persuasive mission.

Once Hobbes establishes that there is only one authority in matters both civil and religious over any given Christian subject, all that remains is to determine who that authority is. An easy test for sovereignty is the reciprocity test imposed by the law of nature: "to whose dominion we require our fellow subjects to yield obedience for our good, his dominion we acknowledge to be legitimate by that very request."[48] This test picks out one's national civil sovereign. But Hobbes also offers a formal argument to the same conclusion, beginning from his definition of a church as a lawful congregation of Christians united in the person of one sovereign. Because Christians live in different commonwealths with different sovereigns, a church must be the same thing as a civil commonwealth consisting of Christians. Thus, there is no universal church that all Christians are bound to obey because there is no earthly power to which all other commonwealths are subject. Hobbes concludes that the appropriate authority in all matters is the national civil sovereign. It is "that one chief pastor" "according to the law of Nature," and also the entity "to whom the Scripture hath assigned that Office."[49]

We can see, then, Hobbes's approach to dealing with the substantive disagreements among people in their conceptions of their duty to God arising from their belief in different authorities. It is to redescribe those interests less substantively and more formally (as involving not what, but rather whom, we believe), so that religious duty becomes, finally, practicing and professing as the sovereign dictates. That the sovereign's command could conflict with our religious duty becomes all but impossible.

8 Public Reason in Hobbes's System

We are now in a position to identify ideas of public reason in Hobbes's political system. At the level of internal political deliberation over law and policy, there are no substantive constraints on justifying reasons, for any reason the sovereign offers is to be treated as justifying. The sovereign constitutes public reason at this level. When citizens offer one another reasons for accepting particular laws, those reasons are all the same and purely procedural: the law has been judged by the public authority to conduce to the common good. But at the more basic level of justification of the political framework, or form of regime, Hobbes seeks to ensure that each individual has by her own standards a sufficient reason to accept an obligation to defer her private judgment to a public political authority.

In his effort to ensure that each finds sufficient reason, Hobbes offers multiple reasons. We share a prudential reason to want to live in an environment ordered by a public political authority: such an environment promises best to satisfy our necessary desire to achieve our ends. This gives us all a prudential reason to insist that others should accept the political obligation needed to create that environment, and not to attempt to undermine that environment ourselves.[50] That's one reason.

But the law of nature, requiring reciprocity, tells us that if we will insist that others accept political obligation, we have a moral duty to do so ourselves. Natural laws requiring equity or fairness and against pride impose on us a natural duty to hold ourselves to the same standards we require of others. What motivates us to fulfill this natural duty of reciprocity is our desire to justify ourselves to others. This desire—to be seen as right by others—is powerful in almost everyone. We share the desire to justify our actions to others that motivates our acceptance of the natural duty of reciprocity. That duty provides a second reason to accept political obligation.

Natural duties do not exhaust moral claims on us. We can undertake additional moral obligations through voluntary acts of our own. The person who promises to fulfill the terms of a business contract or marriage contract assumes a moral obligation not incumbent on others, an obligation underwritten by the natural duty to honor contractual agreements. Similarly, the person who undertakes an obligation of political obedience, either by expressly swearing an oath as in the case of naturalized citizens, or tacitly, by living openly under the state's protection and accepting its benefits, has an additional moral reason—a reason from obligation to obey their political authority. How many people we think have such obligations will depend in part on our views of the bindingness of tacit consent, or of even express consent when it is coerced by circumstance.[51] But if voluntary undertakings can create moral obligations, those who have undertaken political obligations will have a third reason to defer to the public authority.

The fourth reason Hobbes advances is that fulfillment of our duty to God demands political obedience. His effort to establish that the laws of nature are divine laws and entail a duty to defer to government has potential resonance with not just Christians and Jews but also Muslims, indeed any theist. His arguments, relying on specific Scriptural passages,[52] are intended to drive home to Christians their duty under divine positive law to obey earthly authorities.

Hobbes argues finally that salvation depends on fulfilling our duties to God. The only necessary conditions for salvation are *"faith in Christ,* and *obedience to laws*," those laws being "none but the laws of nature, whereof the principal is... a commandment to obey our civil sovereigns."[53] Here, he offers a distinct fifth reason for Christians to accept political authority. The interest in achieving salvation or avoiding damnation is a distinctive form of self-interest; it is a special-prudential interest in our survival and commodious living in the afterlife. This interest was transcendent for many of Hobbes's readers, and so offers what was perhaps the most powerful for them of the reasons Hobbes offers for adhering to his principle of political obligation.

We can see that some of the five distinct reasons Hobbes has offered can be expected to be shared, while others cannot. Atheists may accept the first three while rejecting the last two. If disruptive transcendent interests tend to be religious, and atheists lack them, reasons from prudence, duty, and obligation may suffice for atheists.[54] Christians require further reasons, while Muslims would presumably require the same sorts of further reasons, but with different authoritative texts adduced in support of those reasons. Whether the Qur'an could plausibly be interpreted to provide reinforcing divine positive law duties is a question Hobbes himself did not address. Non-salvationist religions such as Judaism will not be moved by Hobbes's fifth proffered reason, but may find the fourth very important. This allows us to see that founding political obligation on our shared prudential and moral interests is probably necessary, but not necessarily sufficient. A convergence of reasons drawn from our various unshared comprehensive doctrines will be needed if each of us is to have something we will recognize as a *sufficient* reason to defer to a public authority. But all of our reasons, whether offered on the basis of shared interests or sectarian ones, will be constrained by the reciprocity requirement of the law of nature that we be willing to accept from others the same kinds of reasons we offer them. In Hobbes, a commitment to offering others only reasons we think it would be reasonable to accept turns out to be built into the very idea of what it is to have a reason, and so even sectarian reasons will have a public aspect, no matter what their content.

Notes

1. Professor of Philosophy and Law, University of Southern California.
2. XVIII.20 [40]. References to Hobbes's *Leviathan* are by chapter and paragraph number. [Page numbers in brackets refer to the Hobbes selections in this volume—eds.]
3. *Six Lessons to the Savilain Professors of the Mathematics,* The English Works of Thomas Hobbes, edited by William Molesworth (hereafter EW) Volume VII, 335.
4. *Seven Philosophical Problems,* EW Volume VII, 5.
5. XX.19.

6 If a government becomes unable to protect the citizen, her obligation to obey it is extinguished. Although it is up to the individual to judge whether the government can protect her, the government may permissibly attempt to punish those whom it deems to have judged incorrectly (for instance, the soldier who runs from battle, or the person who unreasonably claims self-defense in killing another).
7 See XVII.6–12 [32–33].
8 A contemporary illustration of this might be race-related differences in judgments of police trustworthiness.
9 Introduction to *Leviathan*.
10 *De Cive*, I.10n.
11 *De Cive*, VIII.1.
12 *Elements of Law*, II.3.2.
13 XV.40 [31].
14 LXIV.4.
15 John Stuart Mill famously dismissed the answer we may be tempted to give, namely that others should defer to our judgments because we are right, while we should not defer to theirs because they are wrong, as "the logic of persecutors" (see *On Liberty*, chapter 4).
16 Hobbes writes,

> say that another man is judge. Why now, because he judgeth of what concerns me, by the same reason, because we are equal by nature, will I judge also of things which do belong to him. Therefore it agrees with right reason, that is, it is the right of nature that I judge of his opinion.
> (*De Cive*, I.9)

17 *De Cive*, X.1.
18 XIII.9 [16].
19 XVII.13 [34], first emphasis added.
20 As they would be if, for example, the justification of political authority were simply that God requires us to submit to it.
21 This means that under an objective, non-indexical description of the action and the reason, we are also willing to accept from others the very reason we offer them. For example, if I propose to exempt myself from obedience for the reason that religion requires it, I must be willing to allow you to exempt yourself when you judge that what you believe to be true religion requires it, even though we disagree about what the true religion is or about what it requires.
22 For a fuller discussion of Hobbes's account, see S.A. Lloyd, *Morality in the Philosophy of Thomas Hobbes: Cases in the Law of Nature* (Cambridge: Cambridge University Press, 2009), hereafter CLN, 222–30.
23 XXX.3 [60; see also XVIII.16 [39] for those "rights, which make the essence of sovereignty"—eds.].
24 XVII.13 [34].
25 XVIII.4 [36].
26 Thomas Aquinas defends a similar understanding of the relationship between Pontiffs and Christian kings in *Summa Theologica,* Question 12, Article 2, and in Question 104, Article 6, Reply to Objection 3.
27 XXX.1 [60].
28 See CLN, 33–9 for textual documentation.
29 *De Cive*, VI.13.
30 XX.18.

31 XVIII.20 [40], emphasis added. By "the people in general" Hobbes means all or most of the population.
32 XLIII.1 [73].
33 XXXI.1 [63].
34 XLIII.2 [73].
35 XXXI.1 [63].
36 Hobbes thinks it is natural for us to posit the existence of a single omnipotent god because our persistent inquiry into the causes of the effects we see will lead us back eventually to the idea of a first uncaused cause of the entire causal chain of all that exists, including the laws of nature, and this first cause we term "god" (XI.25).
37 XXXVII.7.
38 XXXVII.5.
39 XXXVII.13.
40 XXXVII.13, Latin variant.
41 Hobbes sharply distinguishes between deference to authority and belief. Belief cannot be compelled, and inquisition into it is contrary to the law of nature. Belief is not a matter of the will. All that can reasonably be required is that we outwardly act in conformity with law.
42 *Behemoth*, 50. Hobbes expresses disdain at the suggestion that individuals should determine the meaning of Scripture when he comments that one effect of the translation of the Bible into vulgar languages was that

> after the Bible was translated into English, every man, nay every boy and wench, that could read English, thought they spoke with God Almighty, and understood what he said, when by a certain number of chapters a day they had read the Scriptures one or twice over... every man became a judge of religion, and an interpreter of the Scriptures to himself.
>
> (*Behemoth*, 28)

43 XLVI.38.
44 XXVI.24 [75].
45 XLII.106; XVI.7.
46 Hobbes writes that

> all formed religion, is founded at first, upon the faith which a multitude has in some one person, whom they believe not only to be a wise man, and to labor to procure their happiness, but also to be a holy man, to whom God himself vouchsafeth to declare his will supernaturally.
>
> (XII.24)

Hobbes argues that the "seeds" of religion (which include curiosity about causes and fear for the future) have been cultivated by individuals "with a purpose to make those men that relied on them, the more apt to obedience," or in the variant phrase of the Latin Leviathan, to make "their initiates more obedient to themselves" (XII.12 [12]). Cf. XII.20, where Hobbes explains how founders of commonwealth have encouraged their subjects to believe that their laws came from some god so that the laws would be more easily accepted.

47 "It is true," Hobbes writes,

> that the bodies of the faithful, after the resurrection shall be not only spiritual, but eternal; but in this life they are gross, and corruptible. There is therefore no other government in this life, neither of state, nor religion, but temporal;
>
> (XXXIX.5)

Hobbes continues,

> And that governor must be one, or else there must needs follow faction, and civil war in the commonwealth, between the Church and the State; between spiritualists, and temporalists; ... and... in every Christian man's own breast, between the Christian, and the man.

48 *De Cive*, XIV.12.
49 XXXIX.5.
50 This is the import of Hobbes's famous discussion in Chapter XV of *Leviathan* of the "fool" who thinks (assuming there is no God to punish his iniquity) that maybe it is in his rational self-interest to defect from the political obedience he requires of others.
51 That proves a much greater challenge to a theorist like Locke, who rests political obligation (to a legitimate regime) entirely on consent, than it does to Hobbes, for whom this is just another reason among many, indeed the least important reason of all.
52 For instance, Titus 3.1, Matthew 23.2.3, Colossians 3.22 and 3.20.
53 XLIII.5 [74]; Hobbes offers elaborate Scriptural support for these claims in that chapter.
54 Atheists may have other sorts of transcendent interests in such things as liberty or justice, which might militate against political obligation. Hobbes recognizes the potential transcendence of interests in securing liberty or justice, and offers arguments that these ends are best secured through a stable political society. See S.A. Lloyd, *Ideals as Interests in Hobbes's Leviathan* (Cambridge, 1992), Chapter 8 for his arguments.

JOHN LOCKE (1632–1704)
Second Treatise of Government (1690)[1]

CHAPTER I

....

§ 3. Political power, then, I take to be a right of making laws with penalties of death, and consequently all less penalties for the regulating and preserving of property, and of employing the force of the community, in the execution of such laws, and in the defence of the commonwealth from foreign injury; and all this only for the public good.

CHAPTER II

Of the state of nature

§ 4. To understand political power right, and derive it from its original, we must consider what state all men are naturally in, and that is, a state of perfect freedom to order their actions and dispose of their possessions and persons, as they think fit, within the bounds of the law of nature; without asking leave, or depending upon the will of any other man.

A state also of equality, wherein all the power and jurisdiction is reciprocal, no one having more than another; there being nothing more evident, than that creatures of the same species and rank, promiscuously born to all the same advantages of nature, and the use of the same faculties, should also be equal one amongst another without subordination or subjection: unless the lord and master of them all should, by any manifest declaration of his will, set one above another, and confer on him, by an evident and clear appointment, an undoubted right to dominion and sovereignty.

....

JOHN LOCKE (1632-1704)

§ 6. But though this be a state of liberty, yet it is not a state of licence: though man in that state have an uncontrolable liberty to dispose of his person or possessions, yet he has not liberty to destroy himself, or so much as any creature in his possession, but where some nobler use than its bare preservation calls for it. The state of nature has a law of nature to govern it, which obliges every one: and reason, which is that law, teaches all mankind, who will but consult it, that being all equal and independent, no one ought to harm another in his life, health, liberty, or possessions: for men being all the workmanship of one omnipotent and infinitely wise Maker; all the servants of one sovereign master, sent into the world by his order, and about his business; they are his property, whose workmanship they are, made to last during his, not another's pleasure: and being furnished with like faculties, sharing all in one community of nature, there cannot be supposed any such subordination among us, that may authorize us to destroy another, as if we were made for one another's uses, as the inferior ranks of creatures are for ours. Every one, as he is bound to preserve himself, and not to quit his station wilfully, so by the like reason, when his own preservation comes not in competition, ought he, as much as he can, to preserve the rest of mankind, and may not, unless it be to do justice to an offender, take away or impair the life, or what tends to the preservation of life, the liberty, health, limb, or goods of another.

§ 7. And that all men may be restrained from invading others rights, and from doing hurt to one another, and the law of nature be observed, which willeth the peace and preservation of all mankind, the execution of the law of nature is, in that state, put into every man's hands, whereby every one has a right to punish the transgressors of that law to such a degree as may hinder its violation: for the law of nature would, as all other laws that concern men in this world, be in vain, if there were nobody that in the state of nature had a power to execute that law, and thereby preserve the innocent and restrain offenders. And if any one in the state of nature may punish another for any evil he has done, every one may do so: for in that state of perfect equality, where naturally there is no superiority or jurisdiction of one over another, what any may do in prosecution of that law, every one must needs have a right to do.

§ 8. And thus, in the state of nature, "one man comes by a power over another;" but yet no absolute or arbitrary power, to use a criminal, when he has got him in his hands, according to the passionate heats, or boundless extravagancy of his own will; but only to retribute to him, so far as calm reason and conscience dictate, what is proportionate to his transgression; which is so much as may serve for reparation and restraint: for these two are the only reasons, why one man may lawfully do harm to another, which is that we call punishment. In transgressing the law of nature, the offender declares himself to live by another rule than that of reason and common equity, which is that measure God has set to the actions of men, for their mutual security; and so he becomes dangerous to mankind, the tye, which is to secure them from injury and violence, being slighted and broken by him. Which being a trespass against the whole species, and the peace and safety of it, provided for by the law of nature; every man upon this score, by the right he hath to preserve mankind in general, may restrain, or, where it is necessary, destroy things noxious to them, and so may bring such evil on any one, who hath transgressed that law, as may make him repent the doing of it, and thereby deter him, and by his example others, from doing the like mischief. And in this case, and upon this ground, "every man hath a right to punish the offender, and be executioner of the law of nature."

§ 9. I doubt not but this will seem a very strange doctrine to some men: but before they condemn it, I desire them to resolve me, by what right any prince or state can put to death, or punish any alien, for any crime he commits in their country. It is certain their laws, by virtue of any sanction they receive from the promulgated will of the legislative, reach not a stranger: they speak not to him, nor, if they did, is he bound to hearken to them. The legislative authority, by which they are in force over the subjects of that commonwealth, hath no power over him. Those who have the supreme power of making laws in England, France, or Holland, are to an Indian but like the rest of the world, men without authority: and therefore, if by the law of nature every man hath not a power to punish offences against it, as he soberly judges the case to require, I see not how the magistrates of any community can punish an alien of another country; since, in reference to him, they can have no more power than what every man naturally may have over another.

§ 10. Besides the crime which consists in violating the law, and varying from the right rule of reason, whereby a man so far becomes degenerate, and declares himself to quit the principles of human nature, and to be a noxious creature, there is commonly injury done to some person or other, and some other man receives damage by his transgression: in which case he who hath received any damage, has, besides the right of punishment common to him with other men, a particular right to seek reparation from him that has done it: and any other person, who finds it just, may also join with him that is injured, and assist him in recovering from the offender so much as may make satisfaction for the harm he has suffered.

§ 11. From these two distinct rights, the one of punishing the crime for restraint, and preventing the like offence, which right of punishing is in every body; the other of taking reparation, which belongs only to the injured party; comes it to pass that the magistrate, who by being magistrate hath the common right of punishing put into his hands, can often, where the public good demands not the execution of the law, remit the punishment of criminal offences by his own authority, but yet cannot remit the satisfaction due to any private man for the damage he has received. That, he who has suffered the damage has a right to demand in his own name, and he alone can remit: the damnified person has this power of appropriating to himself the goods or service of the offender, by right of self-preservation, as every man has a power to punish the crime, to prevent its being committed again, "by the right he has of preserving all mankind;" and doing all reasonable things he can in order to that end: and thus it is, that every man, in the state of nature, has a power to kill a murderer, both to deter others from doing the like injury, which no reparation can compensate, by the example of the punishment that attends it from every body; and also to secure men from the attempts of a criminal, who having renounced reason, the common rule and measure God hath given to mankind, hath, by the unjust violence and slaughter he hath committed upon one, declared war against all mankind; and therefore may be destroyed as a lion or a tiger, one of those wild savage beasts, with whom men can have no society nor security: and upon this is grounded that great law of nature, "Whoso sheddeth man's blood, by man shall his blood be shed." And Cain was so fully convinced, that every one had a right to destroy such a criminal, that after the murder of his brother, he cries out, "Every one that findeth me, shall slay me;" so plain was it writ in the hearts of mankind.

§ 12. By the same reason may a man in the state of nature punish the lesser breaches of that law. It will perhaps be demanded, with death? I answer, each transgression may be punished to that degree, and with so much severity, as will suffice to make it an ill bargain to the offender, give him cause to repent, and terrify others from doing the like. Every offence, that can be committed in the state of nature, may in the state of nature be also punished equally, and as far forth, as it may in a commonwealth: for though it would be beside my present purpose, to enter here into the particulars of the law of nature, or its measures of punishment, yet it is certain there is such a law, and that too as intelligible and plain to a rational creature, and a studier of that law, as the positive laws of commonwealths: nay, possibly plainer, as much as reason is easier to be understood, than the fancies and intricate contrivances of men, following contrary and hidden interests put into words; for so truly are a great part of the municipal laws of countries, which are only so far right, as they are founded on the law of nature, by which they are to be regulated and interpreted.

§ 13. To this strange doctrine, viz. That "in the state of nature every one has the executive power" of the law of nature, I doubt not but it will be objected, that it is unreasonable for men to be judges in their own cases, that self love will make men partial to themselves and their friends; and on the other side, that ill-nature, passion, and revenge will carry them too far in punishing others; and hence nothing but confusion and disorder will follow: and that therefore God hath certainly appointed government to restrain the partiality and violence of men. I easily grant, that civil government is the proper remedy for the inconveniencies of the state of nature, which must certainly be great, where men may be judges in their own case; since it is easy to be imagined, that he who was so unjust as to do his brother an injury, will scarce be so just as to condemn himself for it: but I shall desire those who make this objection, to remember, that absolute monarchs are but men; and if government is to be the remedy of those evils, which necessarily follow from men's being judges in their own cases, and the state of nature is therefore not to be endured; I desire to know what kind of government that is, and how much better it is than the state of nature, where one man commanding a multitude, has the liberty to be judge in his own case, and may do to all his subjects whatever he pleases, without the least liberty to any one to question or control those who execute his pleasure? and in whatsoever he doth, whether led by reason, mistake or passion, must be submitted to? much better it is in the state of nature, wherein men are not bound to submit to the unjust will of another: and if he that judges, judges amiss in his own, or any other case, he is answerable for it to the rest of mankind.

§ 14. It is often asked as a mighty objection, "where are, or ever were there any men in such a state of nature?" To which it may suffice as an answer at present, that since all princes and rulers of independent governments, all through the world, are in a state of nature, it is plain the world never was, nor ever will be, without numbers of men in that state. I have named all governors of independent communities, whether they are, or are not, in league with others: for it is not every compact that puts an end to the state of nature between men, but only this one of agreeing together mutually to enter into one community, and make one body politic; other promises and compacts men may make one with another, and yet still be in the state of nature. The promises and bargains for truck, &c. between the two men in the desert island, mentioned by Garcilasso de la Vega, in his history of Peru; or between a Swiss and an Indian, in the woods of America; are binding to them, though they are perfectly in a state of nature, in reference to one another: for truth and keeping of faith belongs to men as men, and not as members of society.

§ 15. To those that say, there were never any men in the state of nature, I will not only oppose the authority of the judicious Hooker, Eccl. Pol. lib. 1. sect. 10, where he says, "The laws which have been hitherto mentioned," i. e. the laws of nature, "do bind men absolutely, even as they are men, although they have never any settled fellowship, never any solemn agreement amongst themselves what to do, or not to do; but forasmuch as we are not by ourselves sufficient to furnish ourselves with competent store of things, needful for such a life as our nature doth desire, a life fit for the dignity of man; therefore to supply those defects and imperfections which are in us, as living singly and solely by ourselves, we are naturally induced to seek communion and fellowship with others. This was the cause of men's uniting themselves at first in politic societies." But I moreover affirm, that all men are naturally in that state, and remain so, till by their own consents they make themselves members of some politic society; and I doubt not in the sequel of this discourse to make it very clear.

CHAPTER III

Of the state of War

§ 16. The state of war is a state of enmity and destruction: and therefore declaring by word or action, not a passionate and hasty, but a sedate settled design upon another man's life, puts him in a state of war with him against whom he has declared such an intention, and so has exposed his life to the other's power to be taken away by him, or any one that joins with him in his defence, and espouses his quarrel; it being reasonable and just, I should have a right to destroy that which threatens me with destruction; for, by the fundamental law of nature, man being to be preserved as much as possible, when all cannot be preserved, the safety of the innocent is to be preferred: and one may destroy a man who makes war upon him, or has discovered an enmity to his being, for the same reason that he may kill a wolf or a lion; because such men are not under the ties of the common law of reason, have no other rule, but that of force and violence, and so may be treated as beasts of prey, those dangerous and noxious creatures, that will be sure to destroy him whenever he falls into their power.

§ 17. And hence it is, that he who attempts to get another man into his absolute power, does thereby put himself into a state of war with him; it being to be understood as a declaration of a design upon his life: for I have reason to conclude, that he who would get me into his power without my consent, would use me as he pleased when he got me there, and destroy me too when he had a fancy to it; for nobody can desire to have me in his absolute power, unless it be to compel me by force to that which is against the right of my freedom, i. e. make me a slave. To be free from such force is the only security of my preservation; and reason bids me look on him, as an enemy to my preservation, who would take away that freedom which is the fence to it; so that he who makes an attempt to enslave me, thereby puts himself into a state of war with me. He that, in the state of nature, would take away the freedom that belongs to any one in that state, must necessarily be supposed to have a design to take away every thing else, that freedom being the foundation of all the rest; as he that, in the state of society, would take away the freedom belonging to those of that society or commonwealth, must be supposed to design to take away from them every thing else, and so be looked on as in a state of war.

§ 18. This makes it lawful for a man to kill a thief, who has not in the least hurt him, nor declared any design upon his life, any farther than, by the use of force, so to get him in his power, as to take away his money, or what he pleases, from him; because using force, where he has no right, to get me into his power, let his pretence be what it will, I have no reason to suppose, that he, who would take away my liberty, would not, when he had me in his power, take away every thing else. And therefore it is lawful for me to treat him as one who has put himself into a state of war with me, i. e. kill him if I can; for to that hazard does he justly expose himself, whoever introduces a state of war, and is aggressor in it.

§ 19. And here we have the plain "difference between the state of nature and the state of war," which however some men have confounded, are as far distant, as a state of peace, good-will, mutual assistance and preservation, and a state of enmity, malice, violence and mutual destruction, are one from another. Men living together according to reason, without a common superiour on earth, with authority to judge between them, is properly the state of nature. But force, or a declared design of force, upon the person of another, where there is no common superiour on earth to appeal to for relief, is the state of war: and it is the want of such an appeal gives a man the right of war even against an aggressor, though he be in society and a fellow-subject. Thus a thief, whom I cannot harm, but by appeal to the law, for having stolen all that I am worth, I may kill, when he sets on me to rob me but of my horse or coat; because the law, which was made for my preservation, where it cannot interpose to secure my life from present force, which, if lost, is capable of no reparation, permits me my own defence, and the right of war, a liberty to kill the aggressor, because the aggressor allows not time to appeal to our common judge, nor the decision of the law, for remedy in a case where the mischief may be irreparable. Want of a common judge with authority, puts all men in a state of nature: force without right, upon a man's person, makes a state of war, both where there is, and is not, a common judge.

§ 20. But when the actual force is over, the state of war ceases between those that are in society, and are equally on both sides subjected to the fair determination of the law; because then there lies open the remedy of appeal for the past injury, and to prevent future harm: but where no such appeal is, as in the state of nature, for want of positive laws, and judges with authority to appeal to, the state of war once begun, continues with a right to the innocent party to destroy the other whenever he can, until the aggressor offers peace, and desires reconciliation on such terms as may repair any wrongs he has already done, and secure the innocent for the future: nay, where an appeal to the law, and constituted judges, lies open, but the remedy is denied by a manifest perverting of justice, and a barefaced wresting of the laws to protect or indemnify the violence or injuries of some men, or party of men; there it is hard to imagine any thing but a state of war: for wherever violence is used, and injury done, though by hands appointed to administer justice, it is still violence and injury, however coloured with the name, pretences, or forms of law, the end whereof being to protect and redress the innocent, by an unbiassed application of it, to all who are under it; wherever that is not bona fide done, war is made upon the sufferers, who having no appeal on earth to right them, they are left to the only remedy in such cases, an appeal to heaven.

§ 21. To avoid this state of war (wherein there is no appeal but to heaven, and wherein every the least difference is apt to end, where there is no authority to decide between the contenders) is one great reason of men's putting themselves into society, and quitting the state of nature: for where there is an authority, a power on earth, from which relief can be had by appeal, there the continuance of the state of war is excluded, and the controversy is decided by that power. Had there been any such court, any superior jurisdiction on earth, to determine the right between Jephthah and the Ammonites, they had never come to a state of war: but we see he was forced to appeal to heaven: "The Lord the Judge," says he, "be judge this day, between the children of Israel and the children of Ammon," Judg. xi. 27, and then prosecuting, and relying on his appeal, he leads out his army to battle: and therefore in such controversies, where the question is put, who shall be judge? it cannot be meant, who shall decide the controversy; every one knows what Jephthah here tells us, that "the Lord the Judge" shall judge. Where there is no judge on earth, the appeal lies to God in heaven. That question then cannot mean, who shall judge, whether another hath put himself in a state of war with me, and whether I may, as Jephthah did, appeal to heaven in it? of that I myself can only be judge in my own conscience, as I will answer it, at the great day, to the supreme judge of all men.

...

CHAPTER V

Of property

§ 25. Whether we consider natural reason, which tells us, that men, being once born, have a right to their preservation, and consequently to meat and drink, and such other things as nature affords for their subsistence; or revelation, which gives us an account of those grants God made of the world to Adam, and to Noah, and his sons; it is very clear, that God, as king David says, Psal. cxv. 16, "has given the earth to the children of men;" given it to mankind in common. But this being supposed, it seems to some a very great difficulty how any one should ever come to have a property in any thing: I will not content myself to answer, that if it be difficult to make out property, upon a supposition, that God gave the world to Adam, and his posterity in common, it is impossible that any man, but one universal monarch, should have any property upon a supposition, that God gave the world to Adam, and his heirs in succession, exclusive of all the rest of his posterity. But I shall endeavour to show, how men might come to have a property in several parts of that which God gave to mankind in common, and that without any express compact of all the commoners.

§ 26. God, who hath given the world to men in common, hath also given them reason to make use of it to the best advantage of life, and convenience. The earth, and all that is therein, is given to men for the support and comfort of their being. And though all the fruits it naturally produces, and beasts it feeds, belong to mankind in common, as they are produced by the spontaneous hand of nature; and nobody has originally a private dominion, exclusive of the rest of mankind, in any of them, as they are thus in their natural state; yet being given for the use of men, there must of necessity be a means to appropriate them some way or other, before they can be of any use, or at all beneficial to any particular man. The fruit, or venison, which nourishes the wild Indian, who knows no enclosure, and is still a tenant in common, must be his, and so his, i.e. a part of him, that another can no longer have any right to it, before it can do him any good for the support of his life.

§ 27. Though the earth, and all inferiour creatures, be common to all men, yet every man has a property in his own person: this nobody has any right to but himself. The labour of his body, and the work of his hands, we may say, are properly his. Whatsoever then he removes out of the state that nature hath provided, and left it in, he hath mixed his labour with, and joined to it something that is his own, and thereby makes it his property. It being by him removed from the common state nature hath placed it in, it hath by this labour something annexed to it, that excludes the common right of other men. For this labour being the unquestionable property of the labourer, no man but he can have a right to what that is once joined to, at least where there is enough, and as good, left in common for others.

§ 28. He that is nourished by the acorns he picked up under an oak, or the apples he gathered from the trees in the wood, has certainly appropriated them to himself. Nobody can deny but the nourishment is his. I ask then, when did they begin to be his? when he digested? or when he eat? or when he boiled? or when he brought them home? or when he picked them up? and it is plain, if the first gathering made them not his, nothing else could. That labour put a distinction between them and common: that added something to them more than nature, the common mother of all, had done; and so they became his private right. And will any one say he had no right to those acorns or apples he thus appropriated, because he had not the consent of all mankind to make them his? was it a robbery thus to assume to himself what belonged to all in common? If such a consent as that was necessary, man had starved, notwithstanding the plenty God had given him. We see in commons, which remain so by compact, that it is the taking any part of what is common, and removing it out of the state nature leaves it in, which begins the property; without which the common is of no use. And the taking of this or that part does not depend on the express consent of all the commoners. Thus the grass my horse has bit; the turfs my servant has cut; and the ore I have digged in any place, where I have a right to them in common with others; become my property, without the assignation or consent of any body. The labour that was mine, removing them out of that common state they were in, hath fixed my property in them.

§ 29. By making an explicit consent of every commoner necessary to any one's appropriating to himself any part of what is given in common, children or servants could not cut the meat, which their father or master had provided for them in common, without assigning to every one his peculiar part. Though the water running in the fountain be every one's, yet who can doubt, but that in the pitcher is his only who drew it out? His labour hath taken it out of the hands of nature, where it was common, and belonged equally to all her children, and hath thereby appropriated it to himself.

§ 30. Thus this law of reason makes the deer that Indian's who hath killed it; it is allowed to be his goods, who hath bestowed his labour upon it, though before it was the common right of every one. And amongst those who are counted the civilized part of mankind, who have made and multiplied positive laws to determine property, this original law of nature, for the beginning of property, in what was before common, still takes place; and by virtue thereof, what fish any one catches in the ocean, that great and still remaining common of mankind: or what ambergrise any one takes up here, is by the labour that removes it out of that common state nature left it in, made his property, who takes that pains about it. And even amongst us, the hare that any one is hunting, is thought his who pursues her during the chace: for being a beast that is still looked upon as common, and no man's private possession; whoever has employed so much labour about any of that kind, as to find and pursue her, has thereby removed her from the state of nature, wherein she was common, and hath begun a property.

§ 31. It will perhaps be objected to this, that "if gathering the acorns, or other fruits of the earth, &c. makes a right to them, then any one may engross as much as he will." To which I answer, Not so. The same law of nature, that does by this means give us property, does also bound that property too. "God has given us all things richly," I Tim. vi. 17, is the voice of reason confirmed by inspiration. But how far has he given it us? To enjoy. As much as any one can make use of to any advantage of life before it spoils, so much he may by his labour fix a property in: whatever is beyond this, is more than his share, and belongs to others. Nothing was made by God for man to spoil or destroy. And thus, considering the plenty of natural provisions there was a long time in the world, and the few spenders; and to how small a part of that provision the industry of one man could extend itself, and engross it to the prejudice of others; especially keeping within the bounds, set by reason, of what might serve for his use; there could be then little room for quarrels or contentions about property so established.

§ 32. But the chief matter of property being now not the fruits of the earth, and the beasts that subsist on it, but the earth itself; as that which takes in, and carries with it all the rest; I think it is plain, that property in that too is acquired as the former. As much land as a man tills, plants, improves, cultivates, and can use the product of, so much is his property. He by his labour does, as it were, enclose it from the common. Nor will it invalidate his right, to say every body else has an equal title to it, and therefore he cannot appropriate, he cannot enclose, without the consent of all his fellow commoners, all mankind. God, when he gave the world in common to all mankind, commanded man also to labour, and the penury of his condition required it of him. God and his reason commanded him to subdue the earth, i. e. improve it for the benefit of life, and therein lay out something upon it that was his own, his labour. He that, in obedience to this command of God, subdued, tilled, and sowed any part of it, thereby annexed to it something that was his property, which another had no title to, nor could without injury take from him.

§ 33. Nor was this appropriation of any parcel of land, by improving it, any prejudice to any other man, since there was still enough, and as good left; and more than the yet unprovided could use. So that, in effect, there was never the less left for others because of his enclosure for himself: for he that leaves as much as another can make use of, does as good as take nothing at all. Nobody could think himself injured by the drinking of another man, though he took a good draught, who had a whole river of the same water left him to quench his thirst; and the case of land and water, where there is enough for both, is perfectly the same.

§ 34. God gave the world to men in common; but since he gave it them for their benefit, and the greatest conveniences of life they were capable to draw from it, it cannot be supposed he meant it should always remain common and uncultivated. He gave it to the use of the industrious and rational, (and labour was to be his title to it) not to the fancy or covetousness of the quarrelsome and contentious. He that had as good left for his improvement, as was already taken up, needed not complain, ought not to meddle with what was already improved by another's labour: if he did, it is plain he desired the benefit of another's pains, which he had no right to, and not the ground which God had given him in common with others to labour on, and whereof there was as good left, as that already possessed, and more than he knew what to do with, or his industry could reach to.

§ 35. It is true, in land that is common in England, or any other country, where there is plenty of people under government, who have money and commerce, no one can enclose or appropriate any part, without the consent of all his fellow-commoners; because this is left common by compact, i. e. by the law of the land, which is not to be violated. And though it be common, in respect of some men, it is not so to all mankind, but is the joint property of this country, or this parish. Besides, the remainder, after such enclosure, would not be as good to the rest of the commoners, as the whole was when they could all make use of the whole; whereas in the beginning and first peopling of the great common of the world, it was quite otherwise. The law man was under, was rather for appropriating. God commanded, and his wants forced him to labour. That was his property which could not be taken from him wherever he had fixed it. And hence subduing or cultivating the earth, and having dominion, we see are joined together. The one gave title to the other. So that God, by commanding to subdue, gave authority so far to appropriate: and the condition of human life, which requires labour and materials to work on, necessarily introduces private possessions.

§ 36. The measure of property nature has well set by the extent of men's labour, and the conveniences of life: no man's labour could subdue or appropriate all; nor could his enjoyment consume more than a small part; so that it was impossible for any man, this way, to intrench upon the right of another, or acquire to himself a property, to the prejudice of his neighbour, who would still have room for as good, and as large a possession (after the other had taken out his) as before it was appropriated. This measure did confine every man's possession to a very moderate proportion, and such as he might appropriate to himself, without injury to any body, in the first ages of the world, when men were more in danger to be lost, by wandering from their company, in the then vast wilderness of the earth, than to be straitened for want of room to plant in. And the same measure may be allowed still without prejudice to any body, as full as the world seems: for supposing a man, or family, in the state they were at first peopling of the world by the children of Adam, or Noah; let him plant in some inland, vacant places of America, we shall find that the possessions he could make himself, upon the measures we have given, would not be very large, nor, even to this day, prejudice the rest of mankind, or give them reason to complain, or think themselves injured by this man's encroachment; though the race of men have now spread themselves to all the corners of the world, and do infinitely exceed the small number was at the beginning. Nay, the extent of ground is of so little value, without labour, that I have heard it affirmed, that in Spain itself a man may be permitted to plough, sow, and reap, without being disturbed, upon land he has no other title to, but only his making use of it. But, on the contrary, the inhabitants think themselves beholden to him, who by his industry on neglected, and consequently waste land, has increased the stock of corn, which they wanted. But be this as it will, which I lay no stress on; this I dare boldly affirm, that the same rule of propriety, (viz.) that every man should have as much as he could make use of, would hold still in the world, without straitening any body; since there is land enough in the world to suffice double the inhabitants, had not the invention of money, and the tacit agreement of men to put a value on it, introduced (by consent) larger possessions, and a right to them; which, how it has done, I shall by and by show more at large.

§ 37. This is certain, that in the beginning, before the desire of having more than man needed had altered the intrinsic value of things, which depends only on their usefulness to the life of man; or had agreed, that a little piece of yellow metal, which would keep without wasting or decay, should be worth a great piece of flesh, or a whole heap of corn; though men had a right to appropriate, by their labour, each one to himself as much of the things of nature as he could use: yet this could not be much, nor to the prejudice of others, where the same plenty was still left to those who would use the same industry. To which let me add, that he who appropriates land to himself by his labour, does not lessen, but increase the common stock of mankind: for the provisions serving to the support of human life, produced by one acre of enclosed and cultivated land, are (to speak much within compass) ten times more than those which are yielded by an acre of land of an equal richness lying waste in common. And therefore he that encloses land, and has a greater plenty of the conveniencies of life from ten acres, than he could have from an hundred left to nature, may truly be said to give ninety acres to mankind: for his labour now supplies him with provisions out of ten acres, which were by the product of an hundred lying in common. I have here rated the improved land very low, in making its product but as ten to one, when it is much nearer an hundred to one: for I ask, whether in the wild woods and uncultivated waste of America, left to nature, without any improvement, tillage, or husbandry, a thousand acres yield the needy and wretched inhabitants as many conveniencies of life, as ten acres equally fertile land do in Devonshire, where they are well cultivated.

Before the appropriation of land, he who gathered as much of the wild fruit, killed, caught, or tamed, as many of the beasts as he could; he that so employed his pains about any of the spontaneous products of nature, as any way to alter them from the state which nature put them in, by placing any of his labour on them, did thereby acquire a propriety in them: but if they perished, in his possession, without their due use; if the fruits rotted, or the venison putrified, before he could spend it; he offended against the common law of nature, and was liable to be punished: he invaded his neighbour's share, for he had no right, farther than his use called for any of them, and they might serve to afford him conveniencies of life.

§ 38. The same measures governed the possession of land too: whatsoever he tilled and reaped, laid up and made use of, before it spoiled, that was his peculiar right; whatsoever he enclosed, and could feed, and make use of, the cattle and product was also his. But if either the grass of his inclosure rotted on the ground, or the fruit of his planting perished without gathering and laying up; this part of the earth, notwithstanding his inclosure, was still to be looked on as waste, and might be the possession of any other. Thus at the beginning, Cain might take as much ground as he could till, and make it his own land, and yet leave enough to Abel's sheep to feed on; a few acres would serve for both their possessions. But as families increased, and industry enlarged their stocks, their possessions enlarged with the need of them; but yet it was commonly without any fixed property in the ground they made use of, till they incorporated, settled themselves together, and built cities; and then, by consent, they came in time to set out the bounds of their distinct territories, and agree on limits between them and their neighbours; and by laws within themselves settled the properties of those of the same society: for we see, that in that part of the world which was first inhabited, and therefore like to be best peopled, even as low down as Abraham's time, they wandered with their flocks, and their herds, which was their substance, freely up and down; and this Abraham did, in a country where he was a stranger. Whence it is plain, that at least a great part of the land lay in common: that the inhabitants valued it not, nor claimed property in any more than they made use of. But when there was not room enough in the same place, for their herds to feed together, they by consent, as Abraham and Lot did, Gen. xiii. 5, separated and enlarged their pasture, where it best liked them. And for the same reason Esau went from his father, and his brother, and planted in mount Seir, Gen. xxxvi. 6.

...

§ 40. Nor is it so strange, as perhaps before consideration it may appear, that the property of labour should be able to over-balance the community of land: for it is labour indeed that put the difference of value on every thing; and let any one consider what the difference is between an acre of land planted with tobacco or sugar, sown with wheat or barley, and an acre of the same land lying in common, without any husbandry upon it, and he will find, that the improvement of labour makes the far greater part of the value. I think it will be but a very modest computation to say, that of the products of the earth useful to the life of man, nine tenths are the effects of labour: nay, if we will rightly estimate things as they come to our use, and cast up the several expences about them, what in them is purely owing to nature, and what to labour, we shall find, that in most of them ninety-nine hundredths are wholly to be put on the account of labour.

§ 41. There cannot be a clearer demonstration of any thing, than several nations of the Americans are of this, who are rich in land, and poor in all the comforts of life; whom nature having furnished as liberally as any other people, with the materials of plenty, i. e. a fruitful soil, apt to produce in abundance what might serve for food, raiment, and delight; yet for want of improving it by labour, have not one hundredth part of the conveniencies we enjoy: and a king of a large and fruitful territory there feeds, lodges, and is clad worse than a day-labourer in England.

§ 42. To make this a little clear, let us but trace some of the ordinary provisions of life, through their several progresses, before they come to our use, and see how much of their value they receive from human industry. Bread, wine, and cloth, are things of daily use, and great plenty: yet notwithstanding, acorns, water, and leaves, or skins, must be our bread, drink, and cloathing, did not labour furnish us with these more useful commodities: for whatever bread is more worth than acorns, wine than water, and cloth or silk, than leaves, skins, or moss, that is wholly owing to labour and industry: the one of these being the food and raiment which unassisted nature furnishes us with: the other, provisions which our industry and pains prepare for us; which how much they exceed the other in value, when any one hath computed, he will then see how much labour makes the far greatest part of the value of things we enjoy in this world: and the ground which produces the materials, is scarce to be reckoned in, as any, or, at most, but a very small part of it: so little, that even amongst us, land that is left wholly to nature, that hath no improvement of pasturage, tillage, or planting, is called, as indeed it is, waste; and we shall find the benefit of it amount to little more than nothing.

...

§ 44. From all which it is evident, that though the things of nature are given in common, yet man, by being master of himself, and "proprietor of his own person, and the actions or labour of it, had still in himself the great foundation of property;" and that, which made up the greater part of what he applied to the support or comfort of his being, when invention and arts had improved the conveniencies of life, was perfectly his own, and did not belong in common to others.

...

§ 46. The greatest part of things really useful to the life of man, and such as the necessity of subsisting made the first commoners of the world look after, as it doth the Americans now, are generally things of short duration; such as, if they are not consumed by use, will decay and perish of themselves: gold, silver, and diamonds, are things that fancy or agreement hath put the value on, more than real use, and the necessary support of life. Now of those good things which nature hath provided in common, every one had a right, (as hath been said) to as much as he could use, and property in all that he could effect with his labour; all that his industry could extend to, to alter from the state nature had put it in, was his. He that gathered a hundred bushels of acorns or apples, had thereby a property in them, they were his goods as soon as gathered. He was only to look, that he used them before they spoiled, else he took more than his share, and robbed others. And indeed it was a foolish thing, as well as dishonest, to hoard up more than he could make use of. If he gave away a part to any body else, so that it perished not uselessly in his possession, these he also made use of. And if he also bartered away plums, that would have rotted in a week, for nuts that would last good for his eating a whole year, he did no injury; he wasted not the common stock; destroyed no part of the portion of the goods that belonged to others, so long as nothing perished uselessly in his hands. Again, if he would give his nuts for a piece of metal, pleased with its colour; or exchange his sheep for shells, or wool for a sparkling pebble or a diamond, and keep those by him all his life, he invaded not the right of others, he might heap as much of these durable things as he pleased; the exceeding of the bounds of his just property not lying in the largeness of his possession, but the perishing of any thing uselessly in it.

§ 47. And thus came in the use of money, some lasting thing that men might keep without spoiling, and that by mutual consent men would take in exchange for the truly useful, but perishable supports of life.

§ 48. And as different degrees of industry were apt to give men possessions in different proportions, so this invention of money gave them the opportunity to continue and enlarge them: for supposing an island, separate from all possible commerce with the rest of the world, wherein there were but an hundred families, but there were sheep, horses, and cows, with other useful animals, wholesome fruits, and land enough for corn for a hundred thousand times as many, but nothing in the island, either because of its commonness, or perishableness, fit to supply the place of money; what reason could any one have there to enlarge his possessions beyond the use of his family and a plentiful supply to its consumption, either in what their own industry produced, or they could barter for like perishable, useful commodities with others? Where there is not something, both lasting and scarce, and so valuable to be hoarded up, there men will not be apt to enlarge their possessions of land, were it ever so rich, ever so free for them to take: for I ask, what would a man value ten thousand, or an hundred thousand acres of excellent land, ready cultivated and well stocked too with cattle, in the middle of the inland parts of America, where he had no hopes of commerce with other parts of the world, to draw money to him by the sale of the product? It would not be worth the enclosing, and we should see him give up again to the wild common of nature, whatever was more than would supply the conveniencies of life to be had there for him and his family.

§ 49. Thus in the beginning all the world was America, and more so than that is now; for no such thing as money was any where known. Find out something that hath the use and value of money amongst his neighbours, you shall see the same man will begin presently to enlarge his possessions.

§ 50. But since gold and silver, being little useful to the life of man in proportion to food, raiment, and carriage, has its value only from the consent of men, whereof labour yet makes, in great part, the measure; it is plain, that men have agreed to a disproportionate and unequal possession of the earth, they having, by a tacit and voluntary consent, found out a way how a man may fairly possess more land than he himself can use the product of, by receiving in exchange for the overplus, gold and silver, which may be hoarded up without injury to any one; these metals not spoiling or decaying in the hands of the possessor. This partage of things in an inequality of private possessions, men have made practicable out of the bounds of society, and without compact; only by putting a value on gold and silver, and tacitly agreeing in the use of money: for in governments, the laws regulate the right of property, and the possession of land is determined by positive constitutions.

§ 51. And thus, I think, it is very easy to conceive, "how labour could at first begin a title of property" in the common things of nature, and how the spending it upon our uses bounded it. So that there could then be no reason of quarrelling about title, nor any doubt about the largeness of possession it gave. Right and conveniency went together; for as a man had a right to all he could employ his labour upon, so he had no temptation to labour for more than he could make use of. This left no room for controversy about the title, nor for encroachment on the right of others; what portion a man carved to himself, was easily seen: and it was useless, as well as dishonest, to carve himself too much, or take more than he needed.

...

JOHN LOCKE (1632–1704)

CHAPTER VII

Of political or civil society

...

§ 87. Man being born, as has been proved, with a title to perfect freedom, and uncontrolled enjoyment of all the rights and privileges of the law of nature, equally with any other man, or number of men in the world, hath by nature a power, not only to preserve his property, that is, his life, liberty, and estate, against the injuries and attempts of other men; but to judge of and punish the breaches of that law in others, as he is persuaded the offence deserves, even with death itself, in crimes where the heinousness of the fact, in his opinion, requires it. But because no political society can be, nor subsist, without having in itself the power to preserve the property, and, in order thereunto, punish the offences of all those of that society; there and there only is political society, where every one of the members hath quitted his natural power, resigned it up into the hands of the community in all cases that excludes him not from appealing for protection to the law established by it. And thus all private judgment of every particular member being excluded, the community comes to be umpire by settled standing rules, indifferent, and the same to all parties; and by men having authority from the community, for the execution of those rules, decides all the differences that may happen between any members of that society concerning any matter of right; and punishes those offences which any member hath committed against the society, with such penalties as the law has established, whereby it is easy to discern, who are, and who are not, in political society together. Those who are united into one body, and have a common established law and judicature to appeal to, with authority to decide controversies between them, and punish offenders, are in civil society one with another: but those who have no such common appeal, I mean on earth, are still in the state of nature, each being, where there is no other, judge for himself, and executioner: which is, as I have before showed, the perfect state of nature.

§ 88. And thus the commonwealth comes by a power to set down what punishment shall belong to the several transgressions which they think worthy of it, committed amongst the members of that society, (which is the power of making laws) as well as it has the power to punish any injury done unto any of its members, by any one that is not of it, (which is the power of war and peace,) and all this for the preservation of the property of all the members of that society, as far as is possible. But though every man who has entered into civil society, and is become a member of any commonwealth, has thereby quitted his power to punish offences against the law of nature, in prosecution of his own private judgment; yet with the judgment of offences, which he has given up to the legislative in all cases, where he can appeal to the magistrate, he has given a right to the commonwealth to employ his force, for the execution of the judgments of the commonwealth, whenever he shall be called to it; which indeed are his own judgments, they being made by himself, or his representative. And herein we have the original of the legislative and executive power of civil society, which is to judge by standing laws, how far offences are to be punished, when committed within the commonwealth; and also to determine, by occasional judgments founded on the present circumstances of the fact, how far injuries from without are to be vindicated; and in both these to employ all the force of all the members, when there shall be need.

§ 89. Whenever therefore any number of men are so united into one society, as to quit every one his executive power of the law of nature, and to resign it to the public, there and there only is a political, or civil society. And this is done, wherever any number of men, in the state of nature, enter into society to make one people, one body politic, under one supreme government; or else when any one joins himself to, and incorporates with any government already made: for hereby he authorizes the society, or, which is all one, the legislative thereof, to make laws for him, as the public good of the society shall require; to the execution whereof, his own assistance (as to his own degrees) is due. And this puts men out of a state of nature into that of a commonwealth, by setting up a judge on earth, with authority to determine all the controversies, and redress the injuries that may happen to any member of the commonwealth: which judge is the legislative, or magistrate appointed by it. And wherever there are any number of men, however associated, that have no such decisive power to appeal to, there they are still in the state of nature.

§ 90. Hence it is evident, that absolute monarchy, which by some men is counted the only government in the world, is indeed inconsistent with civil society, and so can be no form of civil government at all; for the end of civil society being to avoid and remedy these inconveniencies of the state of nature, which necessarily follow from every man being judge in his own case, by setting up a known authority, to which every one of that society may appeal upon any injury received, or controversy that may arise, and which every one of the society ought to obey;[2] wherever any persons are, who have not such an authority to appeal to for the decision of any difference between them, there those persons are still in the state of nature; and so is every absolute prince, in respect of those who are under his dominion.

§ 91. For he being supposed to have all, both legislative and executive power in himself alone, there is no judge to be found, no appeal lies open to any one, who may fairly, and indifferently, and with authority decide, and from whose decision relief and redress may be expected of any injury or inconveniency that may be suffered from the prince, or by his order: so that such a man, however intitled, czar, or grand seignior, or how you please, is as much in the state of nature, with all under his dominion, as he is with the rest of mankind: for wherever any two men are, who have no standing rule, and common judge to appeal to on earth, for the determination of controversies of right betwixt them, there they are still in the state of nature,[3] and under all the inconveniencies of it, with only this woful difference to the subject, or rather slave of an absolute prince; that whereas in the ordinary state of nature he has a liberty to judge of his right, and, according to the best of his power, to maintain it; now, whenever his property is invaded by the will and order of his monarch, he has not only no appeal, as those in society ought to have, but, as if he were degraded from the common state of rational creatures, is denied a liberty to judge of, or to defend his right; and so is exposed to all the misery and inconveniencies, that a man can fear from one, who being in the unrestrained state of nature, is yet corrupted with flattery, and armed with power.

...

CHAPTER VIII

Of the beginning of political societies

§ 95. Men being, as has been said, by nature, all free, equal, and independent, no one can be put out of this estate, and subjected to the political power of another, without his own consent. The only way, whereby any one divests himself of his natural liberty, and puts on the bonds of civil society, is by agreeing with other men to join and unite into a community, for their comfortable, safe, and peaceable living one amongst another, in a secure enjoyment of their properties, and a greater security against any, that are not of it. This any number of men may do, because it injures not the freedom of the rest; they are left as they were in the liberty of the state of nature. When any number of men have so consented to make one community or government, they are thereby presently incorporated, and make one body politic, wherein the majority have a right to act and conclude the rest.

§ 96. For when any number of men have, by the consent of every individual, made a community, they have thereby made that community one body, with a power to act as one body, which is only by the will and determination of the majority: for that which acts any community, being only the consent of the individuals of it, and it being necessary to that which is one body to move one way; it is necessary the body should move that way whither the greater force carries it, which is the consent of the majority: or else it is impossible it should act or continue one body, one community, which the consent of every individual that united into it, agreed that it should; and so every one is bound by that consent to be concluded by the majority. And therefore we see, that in assemblies, impowered to act by positive laws, where no number is set by that positive law which impowers them, the act of the majority passes for the act of the whole, and of course determines; as having, by the law of nature and reason, the power of the whole.

§ 97. And thus every man, by consenting with others to make one body politic under one government, puts himself under an obligation, to every one of that society, to submit to the determination of the majority, and to be concluded by it; or else this original compact, whereby he with others incorporate into one society, would signify nothing, and be no compact, if he be left free, and under no other ties than he was in before in the state of nature. For what appearance would there be of any compact? what new engagement if he were no farther tied by any decrees of the society, than he himself thought fit, and did actually consent to? This would be still as great a liberty, as he himself had before his compact, or any one else in the state of nature hath, who may submit himself, and consent to any acts of it if he thinks fit.

§ 98. For if the consent of the majority shall not, in reason, be received as the act of the whole, and conclude every individual; nothing but the consent of every individual can make any thing to be the act of the whole: but such a consent is next to impossible ever to be had, if we consider the infirmities of health, and avocations of business, which in a number, though much less than that of a commonwealth, will necessarily keep many away from the public assembly. To which if we add the variety of opinions, and contrariety of interest, which unavoidably happen in all collections of men, the coming into society upon such terms would be only like Cato's coming into the theatre, only to go out again. Such a constitution as this would make the mighty leviathan of a shorter duration, than the feeblest creatures, and not let it outlast the day it was born in: which cannot be supposed, till we can think, that rational creatures should desire and constitute societies only to be dissolved; for where the majority cannot conclude the rest, there they cannot act as one body, and consequently will be immediately dissolved again.

§ 99. Whosoever therefore out of a state of nature unite into a community, must be understood to give up all the power, necessary to the ends for which they unite into society, to the majority of the community, unless they expressly agreed in any number greater than the majority. And this is done by barely agreeing to unite into one political society, which is all the compact that is, or needs be, between the individuals, that enter into, or make up a commonwealth. And thus that, which begins and actually constitutes any political society, is nothing, but the consent of any number of freemen capable of a majority, to unite and incorporate into such a society. And this is that, and that only, which did, or could give beginning to any lawful government in the world.

...

§ 119. Every man being, as has been showed, naturally free, and nothing being able to put him into subjection to any earthly power, but only his own consent; it is to be considered, what shall be understood to be a sufficient declaration of a man's consent, to make him subject to the laws of any government. There is a common distinction of an express and a tacit consent, which will concern our present case. Nobody doubts but an express consent, of any man entering into any society, makes him a perfect member of that society, a subject of that government. The difficulty is, what ought to be looked upon as a tacit consent, and how far it binds, i. e. how far any one shall be looked upon to have consented, and thereby submitted to any government, where he has made no expressions of it at all. And to this I say, that every man, that hath any possessions, or enjoyment of any part of the dominions of any government, doth thereby give his tacit consent, and is as far forth obliged to obedience to the laws of that government, during such enjoyment, as any one under it; whether this his possession be of land, to him and his heirs for ever, or a lodging only for a week; or whether it be barely travelling freely on the highway: and, in effect, it reaches as far as the very being of any one within the territories of that government.

§ 120. To understand this the better, it is fit to consider, that every man, when he at first incorporates himself into any commonwealth, he, by his uniting himself thereunto, annexes also, and submits to the community, those possessions which he has, or shall acquire, that do not already belong to any other government: for it would be a direct contradiction, for any one to enter into society with others for the securing and regulating of property, and yet to suppose, his land, whose property is to be regulated by the laws of the society, should be exempt from the jurisdiction of that government, to which he himself, the proprietor of the land, is a subject. By the same act therefore, whereby any one unites his person, which was before free, to any commonwealth; by the same he unites his possessions, which were before free, to it also: and they become, both of them, person and possession, subject to the government and dominion of that commonwealth, as long as it hath a being. Whoever therefore, from thenceforth, by inheritance, purchase, permission, or otherways, enjoys any part of the land so annexed to, and under the government of that commonwealth, must take it with the condition it is under; that is, of submitting to the government of the commonwealth, under whose jurisdiction it is, as far forth as any subject of it.

§ 121. But since the government has a direct jurisdiction only over the land, and reaches the possessor of it, (before he has actually incorporated himself in the society) only as he dwells upon, and enjoys that; the obligation any one is under, by virtue of such enjoyment, to "submit to the government, begins and ends with the enjoyment:" so that whenever the owner, who has given nothing but such a tacit consent to the government, will, by donation, sale, or otherwise, quit the said possession, he is at liberty to go and incorporate himself into any other commonwealth; or to agree with others to begin a new one, in vacuis locis, in any part of the world they can find free and unpossessed: whereas he, that has once, by actual agreement, and any express declaration, given his consent to be of any commonwealth, is perpetually and indispensably obliged to be, and remain unalterably a subject to it, and can never be again in the liberty of the state of nature; unless, by any calamity, the government he was under comes to be dissolved, or else by some public act cuts him off from being any longer a member of it.

§ 122. But submitting to the laws of any country, living quietly, and enjoying privileges and protection under them, makes not a man a member of that society: this is only a local protection and homage due to and from all those, who, not being in a state of war, come within the territories belonging to any government, to all parts whereof the force of its laws extends. But this no more makes a man a member of that society, a perpetual subject of that commonwealth, than it would make a man a subject to another, in whose family he found it convenient to abide for some time, though, whilst he continued in it, he were obliged to comply with the laws, and submit to the government he found there. And thus we see, that foreigners, by living all their lives under another government, and enjoying the privileges and protection of it, though they are bound, even in conscience, to submit to its administration, as far forth as any denison; yet do not thereby come to be subjects or members of that commonwealth. Nothing can make any man so, but his actually entering into it by positive engagement, and express promise and compact. This is that, which I think, concerning the beginning of political societies, and that consent which makes any one a member of any commonwealth.

CHAPTER IX

Of the ends of political society and government

§ 123. If man in the state of nature be so free, as has been said; if he be absolute lord of his own person and possessions, equal to the greatest, and subject to nobody, why will he part with his freedom? why will he give up his empire, and subject himself to the dominion and control of any other power? To which it is obvious to answer, that though in the state of nature he hath such a right, yet the enjoyment of it is very uncertain, and constantly exposed to the invasion of others; for all being kings as

JOHN LOCKE (1632-1704)

much as he, every man his equal, and the greater part no strict observers of equity and justice, the enjoyment of the property he has in this state is very unsafe, very unsecure. This makes him willing to quit a condition, which, however free, is full of fears and continual dangers: and it is not without reason, that he seeks out, and is willing to join in society with others, who are already united, or have a mind to unite, for the mutual preservation of their lives, liberties, and estates, which I call by the general name, property.

§ 124. The great and chief end, therefore, of men's uniting into commonwealths, and putting themselves under government, is the preservation of their property. To which in the state of nature there are many things wanting.

First, There wants an established, settled, known law, received and allowed by common consent to be the standard of right and wrong, and the common measure to decide all controversies between them: for though the law of nature be plain and intelligible to all rational creatures; yet men being biassed by their interest, as well as ignorant for want of studying it, are not apt to allow of it as a law binding to them in the application of it to their particular cases.

§ 125. Secondly, In the state of nature there wants a known and indifferent judge, with authority to determine all differences according to the established law: for every one in that state being both judge and executioner of the law of nature, men being partial to themselves, passion and revenge is very apt to carry them too far, and with too much heat, in their own cases; as well as negligence, and unconcernedness, to make them too remiss in other men's.

§ 126. Thirdly, In the state of nature, there often wants power to back and support the sentence when right, and to give it due execution. They who by any injustice offend, will seldom fail, where they are able, by force to make good their injustice; such resistance many times makes the punishment dangerous, and frequently destructive, to those who attempt it.

§ 127. Thus mankind, notwithstanding all the privileges of the state of nature, being but in an ill condition, while they remain in it, are quickly driven into society. Hence it comes to pass that we seldom find any number of men live any time together in this state. The inconveniencies that they are therein exposed to, by the irregular and uncertain exercise of the power every man has of punishing the transgressions of others, make them take sanctuary under the established laws of government, and therein seek the preservation of their property. It is this makes them so willingly give up every one his single power of punishing, to be exercised by such alone, as shall be appointed to it amongst them; and by such rules as the community, or those authorized by them to that purpose, shall agree on. And in this we have the original right of both the legislative and executive power, as well as of the governments and societies themselves.

§ 128. For in the state of nature, to omit the liberty he has of innocent delights, a man has two powers.

The first is to do whatsoever he thinks fit for the preservation of himself and others within the permission of the law of nature: by which law, common to them all, he and all the rest of mankind are one community, make up one society, distinct from all other creatures. And, were it not for the corruption and viciousness of degenerate men, there would be no need of any other; no necessity that men should separate from this great and natural community, and by positive agreements combine into smaller and divided associations.

The other power a man has in the state of nature, is the power to punish the crimes committed against that law. Both these he gives up, when he joins in a private, if I may so call it, or particular politic society, and incorporates into any commonwealth, separate from the rest of mankind.

§ 129. The first power, viz. "of doing whatsoever he thought fit for the preservation of himself," and the rest of mankind, he gives up to be regulated by laws made by the society, so far forth as the preservation of himself and the rest of that society shall require; which laws of the society in many things confine the liberty he had by the law of nature.

§ 130. Secondly, The power of punishing he wholly gives up, and engages his natural force, (which he might before employ in the execution of the law of nature, by his own single authority, as he thought fit) to assist the executive power of the society, as the law thereof shall require: for being now in a new state, wherein he is to enjoy many conveniencies, from the labour, assistance, and society of others in the same community, as well as protection from its whole strength; he is to part also, with as much of his natural liberty, in providing for himself, as the good, prosperity, and safety of the society shall require; which is not only necessary, but just, since the other members of the society do the like.

§ 131. But though men, when they enter into society, give up the equality, liberty, and executive power they had in the state of nature, into the hands of the society, to be so far disposed of by the legislative, as the good of the society shall require; yet it being only with an intention in every one the better to preserve himself, his liberty and property; (for no rational creature can be supposed to change his condition with an intention to be worse) the power of the society, or legislative constituted by them, can never be supposed to extend farther, than the common good; but is obliged to secure every one's property, by providing against those three defects above mentioned, that made the state of nature so unsafe and uneasy. And so whoever has the legislative or supreme power of any commonwealth, is bound to govern by established standing laws, promulgated and known to the people, and not by extempary decrees; by indifferent and upright judges, who are to decide controversies by those laws; and to employ the force of the community at home, only in the execution of such laws; or abroad to prevent or redress foreign injuries, and secure the community from inroads and invasion. And all this to be directed to no other end, but the peace, safety, and public good of the people.

....

CHAPTER XV

Of paternal, political, and despotical power, considered together

§ 169. Though I have had occasion to speak of these separately before, yet the great mistakes of late about government having, as I suppose, arisen from confounding these distinct powers one with another, it may not, perhaps, be amiss to consider them here together.

§ 170. First, then, Paternal or parental power is nothing but that which parents have over their children, to govern them for the children's good, till they come to the use of reason, or a state of knowledge, wherein they may be supposed capable to understand that rule, whether it be the law of nature, or the municipal law of their country, they are to govern themselves by: capable, I say, to know it, as well as several others, who live as freemen under that law. The affection and tenderness which God hath planted in the breast of parents towards their children, makes it evident that this is not intended to be a severe arbitrary government, but only for the help, instruction, and preservation of their offspring. But happen it as it will, there is, as I have proved, no reason why it should be thought to extend to life and death, at any time, over their children, more than over any body else; neither can there be any pretence why this parental power should keep the child, when grown to a man, in subjection to the will of his parents, any farther than having received life and education from his parents, obliges him to respect, honour, gratitude, assistance and support, all his life, to both father and mother. And thus, it is true, the paternal is a natural government, but not at all extending itself to the ends and jurisdictions of that which is political. The power of the father doth not reach at all to the property of the child, which is only in his own disposing.

§ 171 Secondly, Political power is that power, which every man having in the state of nature, has given up into the hands of the society, and therein to the governors, whom the society hath set over itself, with this express or tacit trust, that it shall be employed for their good, and the preservation of their property: now this power, which every man has in the state of nature, and which he parts with to the society in all such cases where the society can secure him, is to use such means for the preserving of his own property, as he thinks good, and nature allows him; and to punish the breach of the law of nature in others, so as (according to the best of his reason) may most conduce to the preservation of himself, and the rest of mankind. So that the end and measure of this power, when in every man's hands in the state of nature, being the preservation of all of his society, that is, all mankind in general; it can have no other end or measure, when in the hands of the magistrate, but to preserve the members of that society in their lives, liberties, and possessions; and so cannot be an absolute arbitrary power, over their lives and fortunes, which are as much as possible to be preserved; but a power to make laws, and annex such penalties to them, as may tend to the preservation of the whole, by cutting off those parts, and those only, which are so corrupt, that they threaten the sound and healthy, without which no severity is lawful. And this power has its original only from compact and agreement, and the mutual consent of those who make up the community.

§ 172. Thirdly, Despotical power is an absolute, arbitrary power one man has over another, to take away his life, whenever he pleases. This is a power, which neither nature gives, for it has made no such distinction between one man and another; nor compact can convey: for man not having such an arbitrary power over his own life, cannot give another man such a power over it; but it is the effect only of forfeiture which the aggressor makes of his own life, when he puts himself into the state of war with another; for having quitted reason, which God hath given to be the rule betwixt man and man, and the common bond whereby human kind is united into one fellowship and society; and having renounced the way of peace which that teaches, and made use of the force of war, to compass his unjust ends upon another, where he has no right; and so revolting from his own kind to that of beasts, by making force, which is theirs, to be his rule of right; he renders himself liable to be destroyed by the injured person, and the rest of mankind, that will join with him in the execution of justice, as any other wild beast, or noxious brute, with whom mankind can have neither society nor security.[4] And thus captives, taken in a just and lawful war, and such only, are subject to a despotical power; which, as it arises not from compact, so neither is it capable of any, but is the state of war continued: for what compact can be made with a man that is not master of his own life? what condition can he perform? and if he be once allowed to be master of his own life, the despotical arbitrary power of his master ceases. He that is master of himself, and his own life, has a right too to the means of preserving it; so that, as soon as compact enters, slavery ceases, and he so far quits his absolute power, and puts an end to the state of war, who enters into conditions with his captive.

§ 173. Nature gives the first of these, viz. paternal power, to parents for the benefit of their children during their minority, to supply their want of ability and understanding how to manage their property. (By property I must be understood here, as in other places, to mean that property which men have in their persons as well as goods.) Voluntary agreement gives the second, viz. political power to governors for the benefit of their subjects, to secure them in the possession and use of their properties. And forfeiture gives the third despotical power to lords, for their own benefit, over those who are stripped of all property.

§ 174. He, that shall consider the distinct rise and extent, and the different ends of these several powers, will plainly see, that paternal power comes as far short of that of the magistrate, as despotical exceeds it; and that absolute dominion, however placed, is so far from being one kind of civil society, that it is as inconsistent with it, as slavery is with property. Paternal power is only where minority makes the child incapable to manage his property; political, where men have property in their own disposal; and despotical, over such as have no property at all.

....

CHAPTER XVII

Of usurpation

§ 197. As conquest may be called a foreign usurpation, so usurpation is a kind of domestic conquest; with this difference, that an usurper can never have right on his side, it being no usurpation but where one is got into the possession of what another has right to. This, so far as it is usurpation, is a change only of persons, but not of the forms and rules of the government; for if the usurper extend his power beyond what of right belonged to the lawful princes, or governors of the commonwealth, it is tyranny added to usurpation.

§ 198. In all lawful governments, the designation of the persons, who are to bear rule, is as natural and necessary a part, as the form of the government itself; and is that which had its establishment originally from the people; the anarchy being much alike to have no form of government at all, or to agree, that it shall be monarchical, but to appoint no way to design the person that shall have the power, and be the monarch.—Hence all commonwealths, with the form of government established, have rules also of appointing those who are to have any share in the public authority, and settled methods of conveying the right to them: for the anarchy is much alike to have no form of government at all, or to agree that it shall be monarchical, but to appoint no way to know or design the person that shall have the power and be the monarch. Whoever gets into the exercise of any part of the power, by other ways than what the laws of the community have prescribed, hath no right to be obeyed, though the form of the commonwealth be still preserved; since he is not the person the laws have appointed, and consequently not the person the people have consented to. Nor can such an usurper, or any deriving from him, ever have a title, till the people are both at liberty to consent, and have actually consented to allow, and confirm in him the power he hath till then usurped.

CHAPTER XVIII

Of tyranny

§ 199. As usurpation is the exercise of power, which another hath a right to, so tyranny is the exercise of power beyond right, which nobody can have a right to. And this is making use of the power any one has in his hands, not for the good of those who are under it, but for his own private separate advantage.—When the governor, however intitled, makes not the law, but his will, the rule; and his commands and actions are not directed to the preservation of the properties of his people, but the satisfaction of his own ambition, revenge, covetousness, or any other irregular passion.

....

§ 202. Wherever law ends, tyranny begins, if the law be transgressed to another's harm; and whosoever in authority exceeds the power given him by the law, and makes use of the force he has under his command, to compass that upon the subject, which the law allows not, ceases in that to be a magistrate; and, acting without authority, may be opposed as any other man, who by force invades the right of another. This is acknowledged in subordinate magistrates. He that hath authority to seize my person in the street, may be opposed as a thief and a robber if he endeavours to break into my house to execute a writ, notwithstanding that I know he has such a warrant, and such a legal authority, as will impower him to arrest me abroad. And why this should not hold in the highest, as well as in the most inferiour magistrate, I would gladly be informed. Is it reasonable that the eldest brother, because he has the greatest part of his father's estate, should thereby have a right to take away any of his younger brother's portions? or, that a rich man, who possessed a whole country, should from thence have a right to seize, when he pleased, the cottage and garden of his poor neighbour? The being rightfully possessed of great power and riches, exceedingly beyond the greatest part of the sons of Adam, is so far from being an excuse, much less a reason for rapine and oppression, which the endamaging another without authority is, that it is a great aggravation of it: for the exceeding the bounds of authority is no more a right in a great, than in a petty officer; no more justifiable in a king than a constable; but is so much the worse in him, in that he has more trust put in him, has already a much greater share than the rest of his brethren, and is supposed, from the advantages of his education, employment, and counsellors, to be more knowing in the measures of right and wrong.

JOHN LOCKE (1632-1704)

§ 203. "May the commands then of a prince be opposed? may he be resisted as often as any one shall find himself aggrieved, and but imagine he has not right done him? This will unhinge and overturn all polities, and, instead of government and order, leave nothing but anarchy and confusion."

§ 204. To this I answer, that force is to be opposed to nothing but to unjust and unlawful force; whoever makes any opposition in any other case, draws on himself a just condemnation both from God and man; and so no such danger or confusion will follow, as is often suggested: for,

§ 205. First, As, in some countries, the person of the prince by the law is sacred; and so, whatever he commands or does, his person is still free from all question or violence, not liable to force, or any judicial censure or condemnation. But yet opposition may be made to the illegal acts of any inferiour officer, or other commissioned by him; unless he will, by actually putting himself into a state of war with his people, dissolve the government, and leave them to that defence which belongs to every one in the state of nature: for of such things who can tell what the end will be? and a neighbour kingdom has showed the world an odd example. In all other cases the sacredness of the person exempts him from all inconveniencies, whereby he is secure, whilst the government stands, from all violence and harm whatsoever; than which there cannot be a wiser constitution; for the harm he can do in his own person not being likely to happen often, nor to extend itself far; nor being able by his single strength to subvert the laws, nor oppress the body of the people; should any prince have so much weakness and ill-nature as to be willing to do it, the inconveniency of some particular mischiefs that may happen sometimes, when a heady prince comes to the throne, are well recompensed by the peace of the public, and security of the government, in the person of the chief magistrate, thus set out of the reach of danger: it being safer for the body that some few private men should be sometimes in danger to suffer, than that the head of the republic should be easily, and upon slight occasions, exposed.

§ 206. Secondly, But this privilege belonging only to the king's person, hinders not, but they may be questioned, opposed, and resisted, who use unjust force, though they pretend a commission from him, which the law authorizes not; as is plain in the case of him that has the king's writ to arrest a man, which is a full commission from the king; and yet he that has it cannot break open a man's house to do it, nor execute this command of the king upon certain days, nor in certain places, though this commission have no such exception in it; but they are the limitations of the law, which if any one transgress, the king's commission excuses him not: for the king's authority being given him only by the law, he cannot impower any one to act against the law, or justify him, by his commission, in so doing; the commission or command of any magistrate, where he has no authority, being as void and insignificant, as that of any private man; the difference between the one and the other being that the magistrate has some authority so far, and to such ends, and the private man has none at all: for it is not the commission, but the authority, that gives the right of acting; and against the laws there can be no authority. But notwithstanding such resistance, the king's person and authority are still both secured, and so no danger to governor or government.

§ 207. Thirdly, supposing a government wherein the person of the chief magistrate is not thus sacred; yet this doctrine of the lawfulness of resisting all unlawful exercises of his power, will not upon every slight occasion endanger him, or embroil the government: for where the injured party may be relieved, and his damages repaired by appeal to the law, there can be no pretence for force, which is only to be used where a man is intercepted from appealing to the law: for nothing is to be accounted hostile force, but where it leaves not the remedy of such an appeal: and it is such force alone, that puts him that uses it into a state of war, and makes it lawful to resist him. A man with a sword in his hand, demands my purse in the highway, when perhaps I have not twelve-pence in my pocket: this man I may lawfully kill. To another I deliver £100 to hold only whilst I alight, which he refuses to restore me, when I am got up again, but draws his sword to defend the possession of it by force, if I endeavour to retake it. The mischief this man does me is an hundred, or possibly a thousand times more than the other perhaps intended me (whom I killed before he really did me any;) and yet I might lawfully kill the one, and cannot so much as hurt the other lawfully. The reason whereof is plain; because the one using force, which threatened my life, I could not have time to appeal to the law to secure it: and when it was gone, it was too late to appeal. The law could not restore life to my dead carcase, the loss was irreparable: which to prevent, the law of nature gave me a right to destroy him, who had put himself into a state of war with me, and threatened my destruction. But in the other case, my life not being in danger, I may have the benefit of appealing to the law, and have reparation for my £100 that way.

§ 208. Fourthly, But if the unlawful acts done by the magistrate be maintained (by the power he has got) and the remedy which is due by law, be by the same power obstructed: yet the right of resisting, even in such manifest acts of tyranny, will not suddenly, or on slight occasions, disturb the government: for if it reach no farther than some private men's cases, though they have a right to defend themselves, and to recover by force what by unlawful force is taken from them: yet the right to do so will not easily engage them in a contest, wherein they are sure to perish; it being as impossible for one, or a few oppressed men to disturb the government, where the body of the people do not think themselves concerned in it, as for a raving madman, or heady malecontent, to overturn a well-settled state, the people being as little apt to follow the one, as the other.

§ 209. But if either these illegal acts have extended to the majority of the people; or if the mischief and oppression has lighted only on some few, but in such cases, as the precedent and consequences seem to threaten all; and they are persuaded in their consciences, that their laws, and with them their estates, liberties, and lives are in danger, and perhaps their religion too: how they will be hindered from resisting illegal force, used against them, I cannot tell. This is an inconvenience, I confess, that attends all governments whatsoever, when the governors have brought it to this pass, to be generally suspected of their people; the most dangerous state which they can possibly put themselves in; wherein they are less to be pitied, because it is so easy to be avoided; it being as impossible for a governor, if he really means the good of his people, and the preservation of them, and their laws together, not to make them see and feel it, as it is for the father of a family, not to let his children see he loves and takes care of them.

§ 210. But if all the world shall observe pretences of one kind, and actions of another; arts used to elude the law, and the trust of prerogative, (which is an arbitrary power in some things left in the prince's hand to do good, not harm, to the people) employed contrary to the end for which it was given: if the people shall find the ministers and subordinate magistrates chosen suitable to such ends, and favoured, or laid by, proportionably as they promote or oppose them: if they see several experiments made of arbitrary power, and that religion underhand favoured (though publicly proclaimed against) which is readiest to introduce it; and the operators in it supported, as much as may be; and when that cannot be done, yet approved still, and liked the better: if a long train of actions show the councils all tending that way; how can a man any more hinder himself from being persuaded in his own mind, which way things are going; or from casting about how to save himself, than he could from believing the captain of the ship he was in, was carrying him, and the rest of the company, to Algiers, when he found him always steering that course, though cross winds, leaks in his ship, and want of men and provisions did often force him to turn his course another way for some time, which he steadily returned to again, as soon as the wind, weather, and other circumstances would let him?

CHAPTER XIX

Of the dissolution of government

§ 211. He that will with any clearness speak of the dissolution of government, ought in the first place to distinguish between the dissolution of the society and the dissolution of the government. That which makes the community, and brings men out of the loose state of nature into one politic society, is the agreement which every one has with the rest to incorporate, and act as one body, and so be one distinct commonwealth. The usual, and almost only way whereby this union is dissolved, is the inroad of foreign force making a conquest upon them; for in that case, (not being able to maintain and support themselves, as one entire and independent body) the union belonging to that body which consisted therein, must necessarily cease, and so every one return to the state he was in before, with a liberty to shift for himself, and provide for his own safety, as he thinks fit, in some other society. Whenever the society is dissolved, it is certain the government of that society cannot remain. Thus conquerors swords often cut up governments by the roots, and mangle societies to pieces, separating the subdued or scattered multitude from the protection of, and dependance on, that society which ought to have preserved them from violence. The world is too well instructed in, and too forward to allow of, this way of dissolving of governments, to need any more to be said of it; and there wants not much argument to prove, that where the society is dissolved, the government cannot remain; that being as impossible, as for the frame of a house to subsist when the materials of it are scattered and dissipated by a whirlwind, or jumbled into a confused heap by an earthquake.

§ 212. Besides this overturning from without, governments are dissolved from within.

First, When the legislative is altered. Civil society being a state of peace, amongst those who are of it, from whom the state of war is excluded by the umpirage, which they have provided in their legislative, for the ending all differences that may arise amongst any of them; it is in their legislative, that the members of a commonwealth are united, and combined together into one coherent living body. This is the soul that gives form, life, and unity to the commonwealth: from hence the several members have their mutual influence, sympathy, and connexion; and therefore, when the legislative is broken, or dissolved, dissolution and death follows: for, the essence and union of the society consisting in having one will, the legislative, when once established by the majority, has the declaring, and as it were keeping of that will. The constitution of the legislative is the first and fundamental act of society, whereby provision is made for the continuation of their union, under the direction of persons, and bonds of laws, made by persons authorized thereunto, by the consent and appointment of the people; without which no one man, or number of men, amongst them, can have authority of making laws that shall be binding to the rest. When any one, or more, shall take upon them to make laws, whom the people have not appointed so to do, they make laws without authority, which the people are not therefore bound to obey; by which means they come again to be out of subjection, and may constitute to themselves a new legislative, as they think best, being in full liberty to resist the force of those, who without authority would impose any thing upon them. Every one is at the disposure of his own will, when those who had, by the delegation of the society, the declaring of the public will, are excluded from it, and others usurp the place, who have no such authority or delegation.

....

§ 214. ... [W]hen such a single person, or prince, sets up his own arbitrary will in place of the laws, which are the will of the society, declared by the legislative, then the legislative is changed: for that being in effect the legislative, whose rules and laws are put in execution, and required to be obeyed; when other laws are set up, and other rules pretended, and enforced, than what the legislative, constituted by the society, have enacted, it is plain that the legislative is changed. Whoever introduces new laws, not being thereunto authorized, by the fundamental appointment of the society, or subverts the old; disowns and overturns the power by which they were made, and so sets up a new legislative.

....

§ 220. In these and the like cases, when the government is dissolved, the people are at liberty to provide for themselves, by erecting a new legislative, differing from the other, by the change of persons, or form, or both, as they shall find it most for their safety and good: for the society can never, by the fault of another, lose the native and original right it has to preserve itself; which can only be done by a settled legislative, and a fair and impartial execution of the laws made by it. But the state of mankind is not so miserable that they are not capable of using this remedy, till it be too late to look for any. To tell people they may provide for themselves, by erecting a new legislative, when by oppression, artifice, or being delivered over to a foreign power, their old one is gone, is only to tell them, they may expect relief when it is too late, and the evil is past cure. This is in effect no more than to bid them first be slaves, and then to take care of their liberty; and when their chains are on, tell them, they may act like freemen. This, if barely so, is rather mockery than relief; and men can never be secure from tyranny, if there be no means to escape it till they are perfectly under it: and therefore it is, that they have not only a right to get out of it, but to prevent it.

§ 221. There is, therefore, secondly, another way whereby governments are dissolved, and that is, when the legislative, or the prince, either of them, act contrary to their trust.

First, The legislative acts against the trust reposed in them, when they endeavour to invade the property of the subject, and to make themselves, or any part of the community, masters, or arbitrary disposers of the lives, liberties, or fortunes of the people.

§ 222. The reason why men enter into society, is the preservation of their property; and the end why they choose and authorize a legislative, is, that there may be laws made, and rules set, as guards and fences to the properties of all the members of the society: to limit the power, and moderate the dominion, of every part and member of the society: for since it can never be supposed to be the will of the society, that the legislative should have a power to destroy that which every one designs to secure by entering into society, and for which the people submitted themselves to legislators of their own making; whenever the legislators endeavour to take away and destroy the property of the people, or to reduce them to slavery under arbitrary power, they put themselves into a state of war with the people, who are thereupon absolved from any farther obedience, and are left to the common refuge, which God hath provided for all men, against force and violence. Whensoever therefore the legislative shall transgress this fundamental rule of society; and either by ambition, fear, folly or corruption, endeavour to grasp themselves, or put into the hands of any other, an absolute power over the lives, liberties, and estates of the people; by this breach of trust they forfeit the power the people had put into their hands for quite contrary ends, and it devolves to the people, who have a right to resume their original liberty, and, by the establishment of a new legislative, (such as they shall think fit) provide for their own safety and security, which is the end for which they are in society. What I have said here, concerning the legislative in general, holds true also concerning the supreme executor, who having a double trust put in him, both to have a part in the legislative, and the supreme execution of the law, acts against both, when he goes about to set up his own arbitrary will as the law of the society. He acts also contrary to his trust, when he either employs the force, treasure, and offices of the society to corrupt the representatives, and gain them to his purposes; or openly pre-engages the electors, and prescribes to their choice, such, whom he has, by solicitations, threats, promises, or otherwise, won to his designs: and employs them to bring in such, who have promised beforehand what to vote, and what to enact. Thus to regulate candidates and electors, and new-model the ways of election, what is it but to cut up the government by the roots, and poison the very fountain of public security? for the people having reserved to themselves the choice of their representatives, as the fence to their properties, could do it for no other end, but that they might always be freely chosen, and so chosen, freely act, and advise, as the necessity of the commonwealth, and the public good should, upon examination and mature debate, be judged to require. This, those who give their votes before they hear the debate, and have weighed the reasons on all sides, are not capable of doing. To prepare such an assembly as this, and endeavour to set up the declared abettors of his own will, for the true representatives of the people, and the law-makers of the society, is certainly as great a breach of trust, and as perfect a declaration of a design to subvert the government, as is possible to be met with. To which if one shall add rewards and punishments visibly employed to the same end, and all the arts of perverted law made use of, to take off and destroy all that stand in the way of such a design, and will not comply and consent to betray the liberties of their country, it will be past doubt what is doing. What power they ought to have in the society, who thus employ it contrary to the trust that went along with it in its first institution, is easy to determine; and one cannot but see, that he, who has once attempted any such thing as this, cannot any longer be trusted.

§ 223. To this perhaps it will be said, that the people being ignorant, and always discontented, to lay the foundation of government in the unsteady opinion and uncertain humour of the people, is to expose it to certain ruin; and no government will be able long to subsist, if the people may set up a new legislative, whenever they take offence at the old one. To this I answer, quite the contrary. People are not so easily got out of their old forms as some are apt to suggest. They are hardly to be prevailed with to amend the acknowledged faults in the frame they have been accustomed to. And if there be any original defects, or adventitious ones introduced by time, or corruption: it is not an easy thing to get them changed, even when all the world sees there is an opportunity for it. This slowness and aversion in the people to quit their old constitutions, has in the many revolutions which have been seen in this kingdom, in this and former ages, still kept us to, or, after some interval of fruitless attempts, still brought us back again to, our old legislative of king, lords, and commons: and whatever provocations have made the crown be taken from some of our princes heads, they never carried the people so far as to place it in another line.

§ 224. But it will be said, this hypothesis lays a ferment for frequent rebellion. To which I answer,

First, no more than any other hypothesis: for when the people are made miserable, and find themselves exposed to the ill-usage of arbitrary power, cry up their governors as much as you will, for sons of Jupiter; let them be sacred or divine, descended, or authorized from heaven; give them out for whom or what you please, the same will happen. The people generally ill-treated, and contrary to right, will be ready upon any occasion to ease themselves of a burden that sits heavy upon them. They will wish, and seek for the opportunity, which in the change, weakness, and accidents of human affairs, seldom delays long to offer itself. He must have lived but a little while in the world, who has not seen examples of this in his time; and he must have read very little, who cannot produce examples of it in all sorts of governments in the world.

§ 225. Secondly, I answer, such revolutions happen not upon every little mismanagement in public affairs. Great mistakes in the ruling part, many wrong and inconvenient laws, and all the slips of human frailty, will be borne by the people without mutiny or murmur. But if a long train of abuses, prevarications and artifices, all tending the same way, make the design visible to the people, and they cannot but feel what they lie under, and see whither they are going; it is not to be wondered, that they should then rouse themselves, and endeavour to put the rule into such hands which may secure to them the ends for which government was at first erected; and without which, ancient names, and specious forms, are so far from being better, that they are much worse, than the state of nature, or pure anarchy; the inconveniencies being all as great and as near, but the remedy farther off and more difficult.

§ 226. Thirdly, I answer, that this doctrine of a power in the people of providing for their safety anew, by a new legislative, when their legislators have acted contrary to their trust, by invading their property, is the best fence against rebellion, and the probablest means to hinder it: for rebellion being an opposition, not to persons, but authority, which is founded only in the constitutions and laws of the government; those, whoever they be, who by force break through, and by force justify their violation of them, are truly and properly rebels: for when men, by entering into society and civil government, have excluded force, and introduced laws for the preservation of property, peace, and unity amongst themselves; those who set up force again in opposition to the laws, do rebel are, that is, bring back again the state of war, and are properly rebels; which they who are in power, (by the pretence they have to authority, the temptation of force they have in their hands, and the flattery of those about them) being likeliest to do; the properest way to prevent the evil, is to show them the danger and injustice of it, who are under the greatest temptation to run into it.

§ 227. In both the forementioned cases, when either the legislative is changed, or the legislators act contrary to the end for which they were constituted, those who are guilty are guilty of rebellion; for if any one by force takes away the established legislative of any society, and the laws by them made pursuant to their trust, he thereby takes away the umpirage, which every one had consented to, for a peaceable decision of all their controversies, and a bar to the state of war amongst them. They who remove, or change the legislative, take away this decisive power, which nobody can have but by the appointment and consent of the people; and so destroying the authority which the people did, and nobody else can set up, and introducing a power which the people hath not authorized, they actually introduce a state of war, which is that of force without authority; and thus by removing the legislative established by the society, (in whose decisions the people acquiesced and united, as to that of their own will) they untie the knot, and expose the people anew to the state of war. And if those, who by force take away the legislative, are rebels, the legislators themselves, as has been shown, can be no less esteemed so; when they, who were set up for the protection and preservation of the people, their liberties and properties, shall by force invade and endeavour to take them away; and so they putting themselves into a state of war with those who made them the protectors and guardians of their peace, are properly, and with the greatest aggravation, *rebellantes*, rebels.

§ 228. But if they, who say, "it lays a foundation for rebellion," mean that it may occasion civil wars, or intestine broils, to tell the people they are absolved from obedience when illegal attempts are made upon their liberties or properties, and may oppose the unlawful violence of those who were their magistrates, when they invade their properties contrary to the trust put in them; and that therefore this doctrine is not to be allowed, being so destructive to the peace of the world: they may as well say, upon the same ground, that honest men may not oppose robbers or pirates, because this may occasion disorder or bloodshed. If any mischief come in such cases, it is not to be charged upon him who defends his own right, but on him that invades his neighbour's. If the innocent honest man must quietly quit all he has, for peace sake, to him who will lay violent hands upon it, I desire it may be considered, what a kind of peace there will be in the world, which consists only in violence and rapine; and which is to be maintained only for the benefit of robbers and oppressors. Who would not think it an admirable peace betwixt the mighty and the mean, when the lamb, without resistance, yielded his throat to be torn by the imperious wolf? Polyphemus's den gives us a perfect pattern of such a peace, and such a government, wherein Ulysses and his companions had nothing to do, but quietly to suffer themselves to be devoured. And no doubt Ulysses, who was a prudent man, preached up passive obedience, and exhorted them to a quiet submission, by representing to them of what concernment peace was to mankind; and by showing the inconveniencies might happen, if they should offer to resist Polyphemus, who had now the power over them.

§ 229. The end of government is the good of mankind: and which is best for mankind, that the people should be always exposed to the boundless will of tyranny; or that the rulers should be sometimes liable to be opposed, when they grow exorbitant in the use of their power, and employ it for the destruction, and not the preservation of the properties of their people?

§ 230. Nor let any one say, that mischief can arise from hence, as often as it shall please a busy head, or turbulent spirit, to desire the alteration of the government. It is true, such men may stir, whenever they please; but it will be only to their own just ruin and perdition: for till the mischief be grown general, and the ill designs of the rulers become visible, or their attempts sensible to the greater part, the people, who are more disposed to suffer than right themselves by resistance, are not apt to stir. The examples of particular injustice or oppression, of here and there an unfortunate man, moves them not. But if they universally have a persuasion, grounded upon manifest evidence, that designs are carrying on against their liberties, and the general course and tendency of things cannot but give them strong suspicions of the evil intention of their governors, who is to be blamed for it? Who can help it, if they, who might avoid it, bring themselves into this suspicion? Are the people to be blamed, if they have the sense of rational creatures, and can think of things no otherwise than as they find and feel them? And is it not rather their fault, who put things into such a posture, that they would not have them thought to be as they are? I grant, that the pride, ambition, and turbulency of private men, have sometimes caused great disorders in commonwealths, and factions have been fatal to states and kingdoms. But whether the mischief hath oftener begun in the people's wantonness, and a desire to cast off the lawful authority of their rulers, or in the rulers insolence, and endeavours to get and exercise an arbitrary power over their people; whether oppression, or disobedience, gave the first rise to the disorder; I leave it to impartial history to determine. This I am sure, whoever, either ruler or subject, by force goes about to invade the rights of either prince or people, and lays the foundation for overturning the constitution and frame of any just government; is highly guilty of the greatest crime, I think, a man is capable of; being to answer for all those mischiefs of blood, rapine, and desolation, which the breaking to pieces of governments bring on a country. And he who does it, is justly to be esteemed the common enemy and pest of mankind, and is to be treated accordingly.

§ 231. That subjects or foreigners, attempting by force on the properties of any people, may be resisted with force, is agreed on all hands. But that magistrates, doing the same thing, may be resisted, hath of late been denied: as if those who had the greatest privileges and advantages by the law, had thereby a power to break those laws, by which alone they were set in a better place than their brethren: whereas their offence is thereby the greater, both as being ungrateful for the greater share they have by the law, and breaking also that trust which is put into their hands by their brethren.

. . . .

§ 240. Here, it is like, the common question will be made, "Who shall be judge, whether the prince or legislative act contrary to their trust?" This, perhaps, ill-affected and factious men may spread amongst the people, when the prince only makes use of his due prerogative. To this I reply, "The people shall be judge;" for who shall be judge whether his trustee or deputy acts well, and according to the trust reposed in him, but he who deputes him, and must by having deputed him, have still a power to discard him, when he fails in his trust? If this be reasonable in particular cases of private men, why should it be otherwise in that of the greatest moment, where the welfare of millions is concerned, and also where the evil, if not prevented, is greater, and the redress very difficult, dear, and dangerous?

§ 241. But farther, this question, ("Who shall be judge?") cannot mean that there is no judge at all: for where there is no judicature on earth, to decide controversies amongst men, God in heaven is judge. He alone, it is true, is judge of the right. But every man is judge for himself, as in all other cases, so in this, whether another hath put himself into a state of war with him, and whether he should appeal to the supreme judge, as Jephthah did.

§ 242. If a controversy arise betwixt a prince and some of the people, in a matter where the law is silent, or doubtful, and the thing be of great consequence, I should think the proper umpire, in such a case, should be the body of the people: for in cases where the prince hath a trust reposed in him, and is dispensed from the common ordinary rules of the law; there, if any men find themselves aggrieved, and think the prince acts contrary to, or beyond that trust, who so proper to judge as the body of the people, (who, at first, lodged that trust in him) how far they meant it should extend? But if the prince, or whoever they be in the administration, decline that way of determination, the appeal then lies no where but to heaven; force between either persons, who have no known superior on earth, or which permits no appeal to a judge on earth, being properly a state of war, wherein the appeal lies only to heaven; and in that state the injured party must judge for himself, when he will think fit to make use of that appeal, and put himself upon it.

§ 243. To conclude, The power that every individual gave the society, when he entered into it, can never revert to the individuals again, as long as the society lasts, but will always remain in the community; because without this there can be no community, no commonwealth, which is contrary to the original agreement: so also when the society hath placed the legislative in any assembly of men, to continue in them and their successors, with direction and authority for providing such successors, the legislative can never revert to the people whilst that government lasts; because, having provided a legislative with power to continue for ever, they have given up their political power to the legislative, and cannot resume it. But if they have set limits to the duration of their legislative, and made this supreme power in any person, or assembly, only temporary; or else, when by the miscarriages of those in authority, it is forfeited; upon the forfeiture, or at the determination of the time set, it reverts to the society, and the people have a right to act as supreme, and continue the legislative in themselves; or erect a new form, or under the old form place it in new hands, as they think good.

Notes

1 From John Locke, *The Works of John Locke in Nine Volumes,* twelfth edition (London: Rivington, 1824), vol. IV.

2 The public power of all society is above every soul contained in the same society; and the principal use of that power is, to give laws unto all that are under it, which laws in such cases we must obey, unless there be reason showed which may necessarily inforce, that the law of reason, or of God, doth enjoin the contrary.

Hook. Eccl. Pol. l. i. sect. 16

3 "To take away all such mutual grievances, injuries and wrongs," i.e. such as attend men in the state of nature,

> there was no way but only by growing into composition and agreement amongst themselves, by ordaining some kind of government public, and by yielding themselves subject thereunto, that unto whom they granted authority to rule and govern, by them the peace, tranquillity, and happy state of the rest might be procured. Men always knew that where force and injury was offered, they might be defenders of themselves; they knew that however men may seek their own commodity, yet if this were done with injury unto others, it was not to be suffered, but by all men, and all good means to be withstood. Finally, they knew that no man might in reason take upon him to determine his own right, and according to his own determination proceed in maintenance thereof, in as much as every man is towards himself, and them whom he greatly affects, partial; and therefore that strifes and troubles would be endless, except they gave their common consent, all to be ordered by some, whom they should agree upon, without which consent there would be no reason that one man should take upon him to be lord or judge over another.

Hooker's Eccl. Pol. l. i. sect. 10

4 Another copy, corrected by Mr. Locke, has it thus, "Noxious brute that is destructive to their being."

A LETTER CONCERNING TOLERATION (1689)[1]

To the Reader

The ensuing Letter Concerning Toleration, first printed in Latin this very year, in Holland, has already been translated both into Dutch and French. So general and speedy an approbation may therefore bespeak its favourable reception in England. I think indeed there is no nation under heaven, in which so much has already been said upon that subject, as ours. But yet certainly there is no people that stand in more need of having something further both said and done amongst them, in this point, than we do.

Our government has not only been partial in matters of religion; but those also who have suffered under that partiality, and have therefore endeavoured by their writings to vindicate their own rights and liberties, have for the most part done it upon narrow principles, suited only to the interests of their own sects.

This narrowness of spirit on all sides has undoubtedly been the principal occasion of our miseries and confusions. But whatever have been the occasions, it is now high time to seek for a thorough cure. We have need of more generous remedies than what have yet been made use of in our distemper. It is neither declarations of indulgence, nor acts of comprehension, such as have yet been practised or projected amongst us, that can do the work. The first will but palliate, the second increase our evil.

Absolute liberty, just and true liberty, equal and impartial liberty, is the thing that we stand in need of. Now though this has indeed been much talked of, I doubt it has not been much understood; I am sure not at all practised, either by our governors towards the people in general, or by any dissenting parties of the people towards one another.

I cannot therefore but hope that this discourse, which treats of that subject, however briefly, yet more exactly than any we have yet seen, demonstrating both the equitableness and practicableness of the thing, will be esteemed highly seasonable, by all men who have souls large enough to prefer the true interest of the public, before that of a party.

It is for the use of such as are already so spirited, or to inspire that spirit into those that are not, that I have translated it into our language. But the thing itself is so short, that it will not bear a longer preface. I leave it therefore to the consideration of my countrymen, and heartily wish they may make the use of it that it appears to be designed for.

A Letter Concerning Toleration

Honoured Sir,

Since you are pleased to inquire what are my thoughts about the mutual toleration of christians in their different professions of religion, I must needs answer you freely, that I esteem that toleration to be the chief characteristical mark of the true church. For whatsoever some people boast of the antiquity of places and names, or of the pomp of their outward worship; others, of the reformation of their discipline; all of the orthodoxy of their faith, for every one is orthodox to himself: these things, and all others of this nature, are much rather marks of men's striving for power and empire over one another, than of the church of Christ. Let any one have ever so true a claim to all these things, yet if he be destitute of charity, meekness, and goodwill in general towards all mankind, even to those that are not christians, he is certainly yet short of being a true christian himself. "The kings of the gentiles exercise lordship over them," said our Saviour to his disciples, "but ye shall not be so," Luke xxii. 25, 26. The business of true religion is quite another thing. It is not instituted in order to the erecting an external pomp, nor to the obtaining of ecclesiastical dominion, nor to the exercising of compulsive force; but to the regulating of men's lives according to the rules of virtue and piety. Whosoever will list himself under the banner of Christ, must, in the first place and above all things, make war upon his own lusts and vices. It is in vain for any man to usurp the name of christian, without holiness of life, purity of manners, and benignity and meekness of spirit. "Let every one that nameth the name of Christ, depart from iniquity." 2 Tim. ii. 19. "Thou, when thou art converted, strengthen thy brethren," said our Lord to Peter, Luke xxii. 32. It would indeed be very hard for one that appears careless about his own salvation, to persuade me that he were extremely concerned for mine. For it is impossible that those should sincerely and heartily apply themselves to make other people christians, who have not really embraced the christian religion in their own hearts. If the gospel and the apostles may be credited, no man can be a christian without charity, and without that faith which works, not by force, but by love. Now I appeal to the consciences of those that persecute, torment, destroy, and kill other men upon pretence of religion, whether they do it out of friendship and kindness towards them, or no: and I shall then indeed, and not till then, believe they do so, when I shall see those fiery zealots correcting, in the same manner, their friends and familiar acquaintance, for the manifest sins they commit against the precepts of the gospel; when I shall see them prosecute with fire and sword the members of their own communion that are tainted with enormous vices, and without amendment are in danger of eternal perdition; and when I shall see them thus express their love and desire of the salvation of their souls, by the infliction of torments, and exercise of all manner of cruelties. For if it be out of a principle of charity, as they pretend, and love to men's souls, that they deprive them of their estates, maim them with corporal punishments, starve and torment them in noisome prisons, and in the end even take away their lives; I say, if all this be done merely to make men christians, and procure their salvation, why then do they suffer "whoredom, fraud, malice, and such like enormities," which, according to the apostle, Rom. i. manifestly relish of heathenish corruption, to predominate so much and abound amongst their flocks and people? These, and such like things, are certainly more contrary to the glory of God, to the purity of the church, and to the salvation of souls, than any conscientious dissent from ecclesiastical decision, or separation from public worship, whilst accompanied with innocency of life. Why then does this burning zeal for God, for the church, and for the salvation of souls; burning, I say literally, with fire and faggot; pass by those moral vices and wickednesses, without any chastisement, which are acknowledged by all men to be diametrically opposite to the profession of christianity; and bend all its nerves either to the introducing of ceremonies, or to the establishment of opinions, which for the most part are about nice and intricate matters, that exceed the capacity of ordinary understandings? Which of the parties contending about these things is in the right, which of them is guilty of schism or heresy, whether those that domineer or those that suffer, will then at last be manifest, when the cause of their separation comes to be judged of. He certainly that follows Christ, embraces his doctrine, and bears his yoke, though he forsake both father and mother, separate from the public assemblies and ceremonies of his country, or whomsoever, or whatsoever else he relinquishes, will not then be judged an heretic.

Now, though the divisions that are among sects should be allowed to be ever so obstructive of the salvation of souls; yet nevertheless "adultery, fornication, uncleanness, lasciviousness, idolatry, and such like things, cannot be denied to be works of the flesh;" concerning which the apostle has expressly declared, that "they who do them shall not inherit the kingdom of God." Gal. v. 21. Whosoever therefore is sincerely solicitous about the kingdom of God, and thinks it his duty to endeavour the enlargement of it amongst men, ought to apply himself with no less care and industry to the rooting out of these immoralities than to the extirpation of sects. But if any one do otherwise, and whilst he is cruel and implacable towards those that differ from him in opinion, he be indulgent to such iniquities and immoralities as are unbecoming the name of a christian, let such a one talk ever so much of the church, he plainly demonstrates by his actions, that it is another kingdom he aims at, and not the advancement of the kingdom of God.

That any man should think fit to cause another man, whose salvation he heartily desires, to expire in torments, and that even in an unconverted state, would, I confess, seem very strange to me, and, I think, to any other also. But nobody, surely, will ever believe that such a carriage can proceed from charity, love or goodwill. If any one maintain that men ought to be compelled by fire and sword to profess certain doctrines, and conform to this or that exterior worship, without any regard had unto their morals; if any one endeavour to convert those that are erroneous unto the faith, by forcing them to profess things that they do not believe, and allowing them to practise things that the gospel does not permit; it cannot be doubted indeed, that such a one is desirous to have a numerous assembly joined in the same profession with himself; but that he principally intends by those means to compose a truly christian church, is altogether incredible. It is not therefore to be wondered at, if those who do not really contend for the advancement of the true religion, and of the church of Christ, make use of arms that do not belong to the christian warfare. If, like the captain of our salvation, they sincerely desired the good of souls, they would tread in the steps and follow the perfect example of that prince of peace, who sent out his soldiers to the subduing of nations, and gathering them into his church, not armed with the sword, or other instruments of force, but prepared with the gospel of peace, and with the exemplary holiness of their conversation. This was his method. Though if infidels were to be converted by force, if those that are either blind or obstinate were to be drawn off from their errors by armed soldiers, we know very well that it was much more easy for him to do it with armies of heavenly legions, than for any son of the church, how potent soever, with all his dragoons.

The toleration of those that differ from others in matters of religion, is so agreeable to the gospel of Jesus Christ, and to the genuine reason of mankind, that it seems monstrous for men to be so blind, as not to perceive the necessity and advantage of it, in so clear a light. I will not here tax the pride and ambition of some, the passion and uncharitable zeal of others. These are faults from which human affairs can perhaps scarce ever be perfectly freed; but yet such as nobody will bear the plain imputation of, without covering them with some specious colour; and so pretend to commendation, whilst they are carried away by their own irregular passions. But however, that some may not colour their spirit of persecution and unchristian cruelty, with a pretence of care of the public weal, and observation of the laws; and that others, under pretence of religion, may not seek impunity for their libertinism and licentiousness; in a word, that none may impose either upon himself or others, by the pretences of loyalty and obedience to the prince, or of tenderness and sincerity in the worship of God; I esteem it above all things necessary to distinguish exactly the business of civil government from that of religion, and to settle the just bounds that lie between the one and the other. If this be not done, there can be no end put to the controversies that will be always arising between those that have, or at least pretend to have, on the one side, a concernment for the interest of men's souls, and, on the other side, a care of the commonwealth.

The commonwealth seems to me to be a society of men constituted only for the procuring, preserving, and advancing their own civil interests.

Civil interest I call life, liberty, health, and indolency of body; and the possession of outward things, such as money, lands, houses, furniture, and the like.

It is the duty of the civil magistrate, by the impartial execution of equal laws, to secure unto all the people in general, and to every one of his subjects in particular, the just possession of these things belonging to this life. If any one presume to violate the laws of public justice and equity, established for the preservation of these things, his presumption is to be checked by the fear of punishment, consisting in the deprivation or diminution of those civil interests, or goods, which otherwise he might and ought to enjoy. But seeing no man does willingly suffer himself to be punished by the deprivation of any part of his goods, and much less of his liberty or life, therefore is the magistrate armed with the force and strength of all his subjects, in order to the punishment of those that violate any other man's rights.

Now that the whole jurisdiction of the magistrate reaches only to these civil concernments; and that all civil power, right, and dominion, is bounded and confined to the only care of promoting these things; and that it neither can nor ought in any manner to be extended to the salvation of souls; these following considerations seem unto me abundantly to demonstrate.

First, Because the care of souls is not committed to the civil magistrate, any more than to other men. It is not committed unto him, I say, by God; because it appears not that God has ever given any such authority to one man over another, as to compel any one to his religion. Nor can any such power be vested in the magistrate by the consent of the people; because no man can so far abandon the care of his own salvation, as blindly to leave it to the choice of any other, whether prince or subject, to prescribe to him what faith or worship he shall embrace. For no man can, if he would, conform his faith to the dictates of another. All the life and power of true religion consists in the inward and full persuasion of the mind; and faith is not faith, without believing. Whatever profession we make, to whatever outward worship we conform, if we are not fully satisfied in our own mind that the one is true, and the other well-pleasing unto God, such profession and such practice, far from being any furtherance, are indeed great obstacles to our salvation. For in this manner, instead of expiating other sins by the exercise of religion, I say in offering thus unto God Almighty such a worship as we esteem to be displeasing unto him, we add unto the number of our other sins, those also of hypocrisy, and contempt of his Divine Majesty.

In the second place, The care of souls cannot belong to the civil magistrate, because his power consists only in outward force: but true and saving religion consists in the inward persuasion of the mind, without which nothing can be acceptable to God. And such is the nature of the understanding, that it cannot be compelled to the belief of any thing by outward force. Confiscation of estate, imprisonment, torments, nothing of that nature can have any such efficacy as to make men change the inward judgment that they have framed of things.

It may indeed be alleged, that the magistrate may make use of arguments, and thereby draw the heterodox into the way of truth, and procure their salvation. I grant it; but this is common to him with other men. In teaching, instructing, and redressing the erroneous by reason, he may certainly do what becomes any good man to do. Magistracy does not oblige him to put off either humanity or christianity. But it is one thing to persuade, another to command; one thing to press with arguments, another with penalties. This the civil power alone has a right to do; to the other, good-will is authority enough. Every man has commission to admonish, exhort, convince another of errour, and by reasoning to draw him into truth: but to give laws, receive obedience, and compel with the sword, belongs to none but the magistrate. And upon this ground I affirm, that the magistrate's power extends not to the establishing of any article of faith, or forms of worship, by the force of his laws. For laws are of no force at all without penalties, and penalties in this case are absolutely impertinent; because they are not proper to convince the mind. Neither the profession of any articles of faith, nor the conformity to any outward form of worship, as has been already said, can be available to the salvation of souls, unless the truth of the one, and the acceptableness of the other unto God, be thoroughly believed by those that so profess and practise. But penalties are no ways capable to produce such belief. It is only light and evidence that can work a change in men's opinions; and that light can in no manner proceed from corporal sufferings, or any other outward penalties.

In the third place, The care of the salvation of men's souls cannot belong to the magistrate; because, though the rigour of laws and the force of penalties were capable to convince and change men's minds, yet would not that help at all to the salvation of their souls. For, there being but one truth, one way to heaven; what hopes is there that more men would be led into it, if they had no other rule to follow but the religion of the court, and were put under a necessity to quit the light of their own reason, to oppose the dictates of their own consciences, and blindly to resign up themselves to the will of their governors, and to the religion which either ignorance, ambition, or superstition had chanced to establish in the countries where they were born? In the variety and contradiction of opinions in religion, wherein the princes of the world are as much divided as in their secular interests, the narrow way would be much straitened; one country alone would be in the right, and all the rest of the world put under an obligation of following their princes in the ways that lead to destruction: and that which heightens the absurdity, and very ill suits the notion of a deity, men would owe their eternal happiness or misery to the places of their nativity.

These considerations, to omit many others that might have been urged to the same purpose, seem unto me sufficient to conclude, that all the power of civil government relates only to men's civil interests, is confined to the care of the things of this world, and hath nothing to do with the world to come.

Let us now consider what a church is. A church then I take to be a voluntary society of men, joining themselves together of their own accord in order to the public worshipping of God, in such a manner as they judge acceptable to him, and effectual to the salvation of their souls.

I say, it is a free and voluntary society. Nobody is born a member of any church; otherwise the religion of parents would descend unto children, by the same right of inheritance as their temporal estates, and every one would hold his faith by the same tenure he does his lands; than which nothing can be imagined more absurd. Thus therefore that matter stands. No man by nature is bound unto any particular church or sect, but every one joins himself voluntarily to that society in which he believes he has found that profession and worship which is truly acceptable to God. The hopes of salvation, as it was the only cause of his entrance into that communion, so it can be the only reason of his stay there. For if afterwards he discover any thing either erroneous in the doctrine, or incongruous in the worship of that society to which he has joined himself, why should it not be as free for him to go out as it was to enter? No member of a religious society can be tried with any other bonds but what proceed from the certain expectation of eternal life. A church then is a society of members voluntarily uniting to this end.

It follows now that we consider what is the power of this church, and unto what laws it is subject.

Forasmuch as no society, how free soever, or upon whatsoever slight occasion instituted (whether of philosophers for learning, of merchants for commerce, or of men of leisure for mutual conversation and discourse,) no church or company, I say, can in the least subsist and hold together, but will presently dissolve and break to pieces, unless it be regulated by some laws, and the members all consent to observe some order. Place and time of meeting must be agreed on; rules for admitting and excluding members must be established: distinction of officers, and putting things into a regular course, and such like, cannot be omitted. But since the joining together of several members into this church-society, as has already been demonstrated, is absolutely free and spontaneous, it necessarily follows, that the right of making its laws can belong to none but the society itself, or at least, which is the same thing, to those whom the society by common consent has authorised thereunto...

The end of a religious society, as has already been said, is the public worship of God, and by means thereof the acquisition of eternal life. All discipline ought therefore to tend to that end, and all ecclesiastical laws to be thereunto confined. Nothing ought, nor can be transacted in this society, relating to the possession of civil and worldly goods. No force is here to be made use of, upon any occasion whatsoever: for force belongs wholly to the civil magistrate, and the possession of all outward goods is subject to his jurisdiction....

These things being thus determined, let us inquire in the next place, how far the duty of Toleration extends, and what is required from every one by it.

And first, I hold, that no church is bound by the duty of Toleration to retain any such person in her bosom, as after admonition continues obstinately to offend against the laws of the society. For these being the condition of communion, and the bond of society, if the breach of them were permitted without any animadversion, the society would immediately be thereby dissolved. But nevertheless in all such cases care is to be taken that the sentence of excommunication, and the execution thereof, carry with it no rough usage, of word or action, whereby the ejected person may any ways be damnified in body or estate. For all force, as has often been said, belongs only to the magistrate, nor ought any private persons, at any time, to use force; unless it be in self-defence against unjust violence. Excommunication neither does nor can deprive the excommunicated person of any of those civil goods that he formerly possessed. All those things belong to the civil government, and are under the magistrate's protection. The whole force of excommunication consists only in this, that the resolution of the society in that respect being declared, the union that was between the body and some member, comes thereby to be dissolved; and that relation ceasing, the participation of some certain things which the society communicated to its members, and unto which no man has any civil right, comes also to cease. For there is no civil injury done unto the excommunicated person by the church minister's refusing him that bread and wine, in the celebration of the Lord's supper, which was not bought with his, but other men's money.

Secondly: no private person has any right in any manner to prejudice another person in his civil enjoyments, because he is of another church or religion. All the rights and franchises that belong to him as a man, or as a denison, are inviolably to be preserved to him. These are not the business of religion. No violence nor injury is to be offered him, whether he be christian or pagan. Nay, we must not content ourselves with the narrow measures of bare justice: charity, bounty, and liberality must be added to it. This the Gospel enjoins, this reason directs, and this that natural fellowship we are born into requires of us. If any man err from the right way, it is his own misfortune, no injury to thee: nor therefore art thou to punish him in the things of this life, because thou supposest he will be miserable in that which is to come.

What I say concerning the mutual toleration of private persons differing from one another in religion, I understand also of particular churches; which stand as it were in the same relation to each other as private persons among themselves; nor has any one of them any manner of jurisdiction over any other, no not even when the civil magistrate, as it sometimes happens, comes to be of this or the other communion. For the civil government can give no new right to the church, nor the church to the civil government. So that whether the magistrate join himself to any church, or separate from it, the church remains always as it was before, a free and voluntary society. It neither acquires the power of the sword by the magistrate's coming to it, nor does it lose the right of instruction and excommunication by his going from it. This is the fundamental and immutable right of a spontaneous society, that it has to remove any of its members who transgress the rules of its institution: but it cannot, by the accession of any new members, acquire any right of jurisdiction over those that are not joined with it. And therefore peace, equity, and friendship, are always mutually to be observed by particular churches, in the same manner as by private persons, without any pretence of superiority or jurisdiction over one another....

In the third place: Let us see what the duty of toleration requires from those who are distinguished from the rest of mankind, from the laity, as they please to call us, by some ecclesiastical character and office; whether they be bishops, priests, presbyters, ministers, or however else dignified or distinguished. It is not my business to enquire here into the original of the power or dignity of the clergy. This only I say, that whencesoever their authority be sprung, since it is ecclesiastical, it ought to be confined within the bounds of the church, nor can it in any manner be extended to civil affairs; because the church itself is a thing absolutely separate and distinct from the commonwealth. The boundaries on both sides are fixed and immoveable. He jumbles heaven and earth together, the things most remote and opposite, who mixes these societies, which are, in their original, end, business, and in every thing, perfectly distinct, and infinitely different from each other. No man therefore, with whatsoever ecclesiastical office he be dignified, can deprive another man that is not of his church and faith, either of liberty, or of any part of his worldly goods, upon the account of that difference which is between them in religion. For whatsoever is not lawful to the whole church cannot by any ecclesiastical right, become lawful to any of its members....

In the last place. Let us now consider what is the magistrate's duty in the business of toleration: which is certainly very considerable.

We have already proved that the care of souls does not belong to the magistrate: not a magisterial care, I mean, if I may so call it, which consists in prescribing by laws, and compelling by punishments. But a charitable care, which consists in teaching, admonishing, and persuading, cannot be denied unto any man. The care therefore of every man's soul belongs unto himself, and is to be left unto himself....

But after all, the principal consideration, and which absolutely determines this controversy, is this: Although the magistrate's opinion in religion be sound, and the way that he appoints be truly evangelical, yet if I be not thoroughly persuaded thereof in my own mind, there will be no safety for me in following it. No way whatsoever that I shall walk in against the dictates of my conscience, will ever bring me to the mansions of the blessed. I may grow rich by an art that I take not delight in; I may be cured of some disease by remedies that I have not faith in; but I cannot be saved by a religion that I distrust, and by a worship that I abhor. It is in vain for an unbeliever to take up the outward show of another man's profession. Faith only, and inward sincerity, are the things that procure acceptance with God. The most likely and most approved remedy can have no effect upon the patient, if his stomach reject it as soon as taken; and you will in vain cram a medicine down a sick man's throat, which his particular constitution will be sure to turn into poison. In a word; Whatsoever may be doubtful in religion, yet this at least is certain, that no religion, which I believe not to be true, can be either true or profitable unto me. In vain therefore do princes compel their subjects to come into their church-communion, under pretence of saving their souls. If they believe, they will come of their own accord; if they believe not, their coming will nothing avail them. How great soever, in fine, may be the pretence of good-will and charity, and concern for the salvation of men's souls, men cannot be forced to be saved whether they will or no; and therefore when all is done, they must be left to their own consciences....

These religious societies I call churches: and these I say the magistrate ought to tolerate. For the business of these assemblies of the people is nothing but what is lawful for every man in particular to take care of;

A LETTER CONCERNING TOLERATION (1689)

I mean the salvation of their souls: nor in this case is there any difference between the national church, and other separated congregations.

But as in every church there are two things especially to be considered; the outward form and rites of worship, and the doctrines and articles of faith; these things must be handled each distinctly, that so the whole matter of toleration may the more clearly be understood.

Concerning outward worship, I say, in the first place, that the magistrate has no power to enforce by law either in his own church, or much less in another, the use of any rites or ceremonies whatsoever in the worship of God. And this, not only because these churches are free societies, but because whatsoever is practised in the worship of God, is only so far justifiable as it is believed by those that practise it to be acceptable unto him.—Whatsoever is not done with that assurance of faith, is neither well in itself, nor can it be acceptable to God. To impose such things therefore upon any people, contrary to their own judgment, is in effect to command them to offend God; which, considering that the end of all religion is to please him, and that liberty is essentially necessary to that end, appears to be absurd beyond expression....

But some may ask, "What if the magistrate should enjoin any thing by his authority, that appears unlawful to the conscience of a private person?" I answer, that if government be faithfully administered, and the counsels of the magistrate be indeed directed to the public good, this will seldom happen. But if perhaps it do so fall out, I say, that such a private person is to abstain from the actions that he judges unlawful; and he is to undergo the punishment, which is not unlawful for him to bear; for the private judgment of any person concerning a law enacted in political matters, for the public good, does not take away the obligation of that law, nor deserve a dispensation. But if the law indeed be concerning things that lie not within the verge of the magistrate's authority; as for example, that the people, or any party amongst them, should be compelled to embrace a strange religion, and join in the worship and ceremonies of another church; men are not in these cases obliged by that law, against their consciences; for the political society is instituted for no other end, but only to secure every man's possession of the things of this life. The care of each man's soul, and of the things of heaven, which neither does belong to the commonwealth, nor can be subjected to it, is left entirely to every man's self. Thus the safeguard of men's lives, and of the things that belong unto this life, is the business of the commonwealth; and the preserving of those things unto their owners is the duty of the magistrate; and therefore the magistrate cannot take away these worldly things from this man, or party, and give them to that; nor change property amongst fellow-subjects, no not even by a law, for a cause that has no relation to the end of civil government; I mean for their religion; which, whether it be true or false, does no prejudice to the worldly concerns of their fellow-subjects, which are the things that only belong unto the care of the commonwealth.

"But what if the magistrate believe such a law as this to be for the public good?" I answer: as the private judgment of any particular person, if erroneous, does not exempt him from the obligation of law, so the private judgment, as I may call it, of the magistrate, does not give him any new right of imposing laws upon his subjects, which neither was in the constitution of the government granted him, nor ever was in the power of the people to grant: and least of all, if he make it his business to enrich and advance his followers and fellow-sectaries with the spoils of others. But what if the magistrate believe that he has a right to make such laws, and that they are for the public good; and his subjects believe the contrary? Who shall be judge between them? I answer, God alone; for there is no judge upon earth between the supreme magistrate and the people. God, I say, is the only judge in this case, who will retribute unto every one at the last day according to his deserts; that is, according to his sincerity and uprightness in endeavouring to promote piety, and the public weal and peace of mankind. But what shall be done in the mean while? I answer: the principal and chief care of every one ought to be of his own soul first, and, in the next place, of the public peace: though yet there are few will think it is peace there, where they see all laid waste. There are two sorts of contests amongst men: the one managed by law, the other by force; and they are of that nature, that where the one ends the other always begins. But it is not my business to inquire into the power of the magistrate in the different constitutions of nations. I only know what usually happens where controversies arise, without a judge to determine them. You will say, then the magistrate being the stronger will have his will, and carry his point. Without doubt. But the question is not here concerning the doubtfulness of the event, but the rule of right.

But to come to particulars. I say, First, No opinions contrary to human society, or to those moral rules which are necessary to the preservation of civil society, are to be tolerated by the magistrate. But of those indeed examples in any church are rare. For no sect can easily arrive to such a degree of madness, as that it should think fit to teach, for doctrines of religion, such things as manifestly undermine the foundations of society, and are therefore condemned by the judgment of all mankind: because their own interest, peace, reputation, every thing would be thereby endangered.

Another more secret evil, but more dangerous to the commonwealth, is when men arrogate to themselves, and to those of their own sect, some peculiar prerogative covered over with a specious show of deceitful words, but in effect opposite to the civil rights of the community. For example: We cannot find any sect that teaches expressly and openly, that men are not obliged to keep their promise; that princes may be dethroned by those that differ from them in religion; or that the dominion of all things belongs only to themselves. For these things, proposed thus nakedly and plainly, would soon draw on them the eye and hand of the magistrate, and awaken all the care of the commonwealth to a watchfulness against the spreading of so dangerous an evil. But nevertheless, we find those that say the same things in other words. What else do they mean, who teach that, "faith is not to be kept with heretics?" Their meaning, forsooth, is, that the privilege of breaking faith belongs unto themselves: for they declare all that are not of their communion to be heretics, or at least may declare them so whensoever they think fit. What can be the meaning of their asserting that "kings excommunicated forfeit their crowns and kingdoms?" It is evident that they thereby arrogate unto themselves the power of deposing kings: because they challenge the power of excommunication as the peculiar right of their hierarchy. "That dominion is founded in grace," is also an assertion by which those that maintain it do plainly lay claim to the possession of all things. For they are not so wanting to themselves as not to believe, or at least as not to profess, themselves to be the truly pious and faithful. These therefore, and the like, who attribute unto the faithful, religious, and orthodox, that is, in plain terms, unto themselves, any peculiar privilege or power above other mortals, in civil concernments; or who, upon pretence of religion, do challenge any manner of authority over such as are not associated with them in their ecclesiastical communion; I say these have no right to be tolerated by the magistrate; as neither those that will not own and teach the duty of tolerating all men in matters of mere religion. For what do all these and the like doctrines signify, but that they may, and are ready upon any occasion to seize the government, and possess themselves of the estates and fortunes of their fellow-subjects; and that they only ask leave to be tolerated by the magistrates so long, until they find themselves strong enough to effect it?

Again: That church can have no right to be tolerated by the magistrate, which is constituted upon such a bottom, that all those who enter into it, do thereby ipso facto deliver themselves up to the protection and service of another prince. For by this means the magistrate would give way to the settling of a foreign jurisdiction in his own country, and suffer his own people to be listed, as it were, for soldiers against his own government. Nor does the frivolous and fallacious distinction between the court and the church afford any remedy to this inconvenience; especially when both the one and the other are equally subject to the absolute authority of the same person; who has not only power to persuade the members of his church to whatsoever he lists, either as purely religious, or as in order thereunto; but can also enjoin it them on pain of eternal fire. It is ridiculous for any one to profess himself to be a mahometan only in religion, but in every thing else a faithful subject to a christian magistrate, whilst at the same time he acknowledges himself bound to yield blind obedience to the mufti of Constantinople; who himself is entirely obedient to the Ottoman emperor, and frames the feigned oracles of that religion according to his pleasure. But this mahometan living amongst christians, would yet more apparently renounce their government, if he acknowledged the same person to be head of his church, who is the supreme magistrate in the state.

Lastly, Those are not at all to be tolerated who deny the being of God. Promises, covenants, and oaths, which are the bonds of human society, can have no hold upon an atheist. The taking away of God, though but even in thought, dissolves all. Besides also, those that by their atheism undermine and destroy all religion, can have no pretence of religion whereupon to challenge the privilege of a toleration. As for other practical opinions, though not absolutely free from all errour, yet if they do not tend to establish domination over others, or civil impunity to the church in which they are taught, there can be no reason why they should not be tolerated....

Note

1 From John Locke, *The Works of John Locke in Nine Volumes,* twelfth edition (London: Rivington, 1824), vol. V.

LOCKE'S LIBERAL THEORY OF PUBLIC REASON

Gerald Gaus[1]

1 Lockean Rights and Disagreement

It would seem that of all the classical social contract theories—Hobbes', Locke's, Rousseau's and Kant's—Locke's has least to do with the idea that social and political life requires constructing a sphere of public reason, and so to some extent, setting aside one's private judgment.[2] Indeed, many read Locke's overall account as inclining toward a sort of anarchism, in which each is guided exclusively by her own judgment, rather than in the direction of creating a public sphere defined by common reasoning. This interpretation appears, at least at first inspection, well grounded in familiar passages.[3] All individuals, says Locke,

> are naturally in... a state of perfect freedom to order their actions and dispose of their possessions and persons, as they think fit, within the bounds of the law of nature; without asking leave, or depending upon the will of any other man.
> (ST: §4 [108])[4]

This is also a condition of

> equality, wherein all the power and jurisdiction is reciprocal, no one having more than another; there being nothing more evident, than that creatures of the same species and rank, promiscuously born to all the same advantages of nature, and the use of the same faculties, should also be equal one amongst another without subordination or subjection.
> (ST: §4 [108])

However, Locke's state of nature, while one of natural freedom, is not one of "licence" in which one can do whatever one wishes.

> The state of nature has a law of nature to govern it, which obliges every one: and reason, which is that law, teaches all mankind,

> who will but consult it, that being all equal and independent, no one ought to harm another in his life, health, liberty, or possessions.
>
> (ST: §6 [109])

In addition to each possessing natural rights, each has the right to enforce the law of nature:

> that all men may be restrained from invading others' rights, and from doing hurt to one another, and the law of nature be observed, which willeth the peace and preservation of all mankind, the execution of the law of nature is, in that state, put into every man's hands, whereby every one has a right to punish the transgressors of that law to such a degree as may hinder its violation.
>
> (ST: §7 [109])

The question for interpreters of Locke is how conflictual such a condition is. Because the state of nature is a condition of perfect equality in which no one has superior authority to determine the dictates of natural law and decide on appropriate enforcement, each has an equal right to do so. But each being a judge in his own case—having the right to interpret and enforce the law of nature—leads to great "inconveniencies": "self love will make men partial to themselves and their friends; and on the other side, that ill-nature, passion, and revenge will carry them too far in punishing others; and hence nothing but confusion and disorder will follow" (ST: §13 [111]). Locke, though not all his contemporary followers, grants that "civil government is the proper remedy for the inconveniencies of the state of nature" (ST: §13 [112]): government employs political power, "making laws with penalties of death, and consequently all less penalties for the regulating and preserving of property, and of employing the force of the community, in the execution of such laws" (ST: §3 [108]). However, he also points to "Every man being, as has been showed, naturally free, and nothing being able to put him into subjection to any earthly power, but only his own consent" (ST: §119 [129]). Thus only if individuals actually consent to form a political society and institute a government are they bound to obey political authority. Many insist that because this demanding test is seldom if ever met, there are few if any legitimate governments.

What we might call the "anarchist strain" among Lockean interpreters stresses either (*i*) that these inconveniencies could be handled within the state of nature or, (*ii*) even if a central state organization is required to facilitate coordination, it is not really essential that people consent to obey it. The first option examines various ways that organizations, such as private enterprise enforcement and adjudication firms, could arise within the state of nature to solve the problems of disagreement.[5] The second strain argues that, while legitimate governments could arise, widespread consent to obey is neither to be expected, nor is it very important. Because most people have not, in fact, consented to government, most are not bound to obey; most continue to have their full rights to interpret and enforce the law of nature as their own judgment dictates.[6] Their original jurisdictional rights are retained. But this does not mean that they will disobey the law. Given all the relevant moral considerations, this type of Lockean anarchist may well decide that it is best to do as the current civil government directs (say, because these common directions allow individuals to coordinate their activity). The critical point is that our Lockean anarchist does not perform an act simply because the law says she must—because she is obligated to obey. She decides on the right thing to do, taking account of the fact that there is a legal directive, which many will follow, and this may produce moral benefits. The definitive feature of this type of Lockean anarchism is that, as a matter of fact, almost all individuals retain their *full right of private judgment* even if there is a state that gives legal directives. Such non-consenting individuals may do as others do and obey, but only if their own judgment instructs them to.

2 The Inconvenience of Retaining Private Judgment

Lockean anarchists typically see their proposals as friendly amendments to Locke, perhaps noting that he was rather too quick to jump to government as a solution to the "inconveniencies" of the state of nature, though his basic moral outlook remains pretty much intact.[7] For them, it is the theory of rights that is the core of Locke's theory, not his analysis of the inevitable disputes that arise from differing private judgment: the important thing is to act on your rights, and do what you think is demanded by morality. So long as people are rational, and see important benefits in cooperation, they should be able to act both morally and cooperate with each other. I believe that the problem of conflicting private judgment about morality is much more severe than anarchistically inclined Lockeans believe. Only a more radical solution—one that creates an umpire or judge that gives an authoritative public judgment, can solve Locke's problem.

That problem is: (1)

> Man being born... with a title to perfect freedom, and uncontrolled enjoyment of all the rights and privileges of the law of nature, equally with any other man... hath by nature a power, not only to preserve his property, that is, his life, liberty, and estate, against the injuries and attempts of other men; *but to judge of and punish the breaches of that law in others, as he is persuaded*

the offence deserves, even with death itself, in crimes where the heinousness of the fact, in his opinion, requires it.

(ST: §87 [125], emphasis added)

(2) But we judge differently. Thus not only are we led into conflict about whether or not punishment is appropriate, but we have conflicting judgments about what our rights are. It is important that our concern is not simply about coordination on what Locke calls "indifferent" matters (FLT: 30). I might disagree with you about which side of the road we should drive on, but we both can clearly see that we need to coordinate, and so I will be ready to do what most others do, rather than insist on what I think is best. The law certainly can serve as a simple coordination device here: the state announces through a law that "Drivers shall drive on the right side of the road" and even if I prefer the left side, I will go along. This is simply a matter of interests. In matters of justice or natural rights, one's moral sentiments are evoked; a good education, Locke stressed, teaches a person to detest the vice of injustice as an ingrained habit (TCE: 101). So, once a person has formed a judgment of justice, compromising with views she considers unjust is apt to be difficult and unstable. Judgments of justice involve moral emotions and ingrained habits.

The Lockean anarchist would have us think that she can secure coordination benefits despite this. Thus, as she would have it, our Lockean anarchist could see that if some law, which she thinks violates natural rights (but not in too grievous a way), is critical in helping to coordinate effectively with others, she may rationally act on it. While maintaining her judgment that the law is unjust, she could still see the coordination benefits of identifying the contours of our rights and stopping cycles of punishment and counter-punishment; thus she may do as the law directs even though, in her view, these are not the just boundaries of rights. But once we have taken seriously that one believes that the other is acting *unjustly* (not just counter to my interests), and so it is apt to invoke one's "detestation of this shameful vice" (TCE: 102), this looks less likely. Given the importance of acting as one judges morality requires, we might expect anarchistic Lockeans, who also recognize the importance of coordinating on what morality requires, to have the following ordering of outcomes: 1st—we coordinate on what I think is just; 2nd—I act alone on what I think is just; 3rd—I act on what you think is just while you act on what I think is just (at least one person does the just thing!); 4th—we coordinate on what you think is just (we achieve coordination but no justice). This is the ordering of people who care most about acting as morality requires and detest the vice of injustice, but also value coordination when it does not prevent justice. As Figure 2.1 shows, if rational, such people will fail to coordinate.

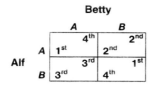

Figure 2.1 Where Commitment to Morality Prevents Coordination.

In this game the sole equilibrium is that Alf acts on his view (*A*), and Betty acts on her view (*B*), of justice. At either of the coordination solutions (when both play *A* or both play *B*), one of the parties would do better by changing her move, and acting on her favored interpretation of natural law. Thus they have no real interest in coordinating, even though they see considerable value in coordinating. As Locke says, in this case "confusion and disorder will follow" (ST: §13 [111])—a case in which each is devoted to her private judgment about morality. In order to coordinate, at least one of the parties must prefer coordination with the other to acting alone as she thinks is right: doing what the other believes to be right for the sake of coordination. Such an agent places great value on coordination, and less value on doing what her private judgment deems the right thing. It is hard to believe that people devoted to natural rights typically would have such valuings.

3 Excluding Private Judgment in Favor of Public Judgment

I am not, of course, maintaining that this was Locke's analysis, though he certainly did believe in a fundamental distinction between acting from morality and acting from interests, and thought that a good education instilled strong reactions to acting unjustly. The point, rather, is that many Lockean anarchists underestimate the difficulties in achieving coordination on what the law of nature requires when each has arrived at a discordant private judgment about it. Even two who appreciate the important benefits of coordination on the requirements of the law of nature may not be able to secure it. However, if individuals unite in a "political society" effective coordination and order can be achieved. In a political society

> every one of the members hath quitted his natural power, resigned it up into the hands of the community in all cases that excludes him not from appealing for protection to the law established by it. *And thus all private judgment of every particular member being excluded,* the community comes to be umpire by settled

> standing rules, indifferent, and the same to all parties; and by men having authority from the community, for the execution of those rules, decides all the differences that may happen between any members of that society concerning any matter of right....
>
> .... And this puts men out of a state of nature into that of a commonwealth, by setting up a judge on earth, with authority to determine all the controversies, and redress the injuries that may happen to any member of the commonwealth: which judge is the legislative, or magistrate appointed by it.
>
> ... for the end of civil society being to avoid and remedy these inconveniencies of the state of nature, which necessarily follow from every man being judge in his own case, *by setting up a known authority*, to which every one of that society may appeal upon any injury received, or controversy that may arise, and which every one of the society ought to obey.
>
> (ST: §§87, 89, 90 [125–6]; emphasis added)

What, then, does Locke mean by "all private judgment of every particular member being excluded?" It seems insufficient to interpret this as simply claiming that individuals in a political society do not *act* on their private judgment but, instead, obey the law. This implies that, while they may do as the law says, they still maintain their full rights to authoritatively judge what natural law requires. But then we would not be in a position very different than Figure 2.1: an individual's reasoning would easily incline him to disobey the law when, on his view, it is not just.

As Locke insists in the above passage, what is critical is that the government has the "authority to determine all the controversies"—that a citizen recognizes the magistrate's judgments as authoritative even if, we might say, her private opinion leads to a different result. The essence of the Lockean contract is that a citizen gives up, not her private opinion as to what natural law requires, but its *claim to authority*. In a political society one has no authority to insist that others conform to one's view of the law of nature, or to enforce one's judgment. Indeed, it is not even authoritative for oneself: if one sees the magistrate as authoritative on this matter, one accepts that his judgment, not one's own, determines what ought to be done. Thus, we find the

> end of civil society being to avoid and remedy these inconveniencies of the state of nature, which necessarily follow from every man being judge in his own case, *by setting up a known authority*, to which every one of that society may appeal upon any injury received, or controversy that may arise, and *which every one of the society ought to obey*.
>
> (ST: §90 [126]; emphasis added)[8]

It is important that the authority must be impartial:

> In the state of nature there wants a known and indifferent [impartial] judge, with authority to determine all differences according to the established law: for every one in that state being both judge and executioner of the law of nature, men being partial to themselves, passion and revenge is very apt to carry them too far, and with too much heat, in their own cases.
> (ST: §125 [131])

Anyone interested in correctly determining the law of nature and applying it to resolve disputes should recognize her own tendency to self-bias, and so consider her own opinion of the merits of her case to be a generally unreliable guide, for herself as well as others.

There is nothing odd about the stance Locke requires of us—that we have an opinion but renounce its authority. Consider a prosaic example, such as a game of baseball. The batter hits the ball, runs to first base, and the impartial umpire calls her out. In her opinion she was safe, and perhaps she even gives the umpire an exasperated look. But she knows that her opinion counts for naught—not only does it fail to be directive for others, it is not directive for her. The only judgment that really matters is the umpire's.

Our baseball example illuminates another feature of public authority: we must know who the umpire is. Locke repeatedly stresses the importance of setting up a *known* authority. It is not enough to recognize the necessity of an impartial judge with the authority to decide disputes: we must be able to agree on who has that authority. "For if this remains disputable, all the rest will be to very little purpose" (FT: §106).[9] Thus the end of civil society is a publicly known authority who can resolve our disputes about morality by providing public, determinate judgments as to the boundaries of our rights and who has abridged the rights of others.

4 Drawing Liberal Boundaries: Reasonable Disputes about Natural Law

What, then, are the bounds of the competency of public authority in Locke's theory? In contrast to Hobbes, who spends so much effort seeking to establish that limits and bounds cannot be set to the authority of the sovereign, Lockean theory is all about setting the bounds of public judgment and its authority. That is why Locke's is a liberal theory of public reason: within the bounds of certain sorts of disputes, the reasoning of the public authorities is definitive, but outside of these bounds the judgment of the magistrate is simply one more private judgment.

Because individuals in the state of nature disagree about the interpretation of the law of nature, we have seen that they require a public judgment with authority to umpire their disputes. However, Locke's theory of revolution supposes that, while the range of disagreement among rational persons is wide, it is not unlimited. At some point a citizen could well conclude the government has exceeded its justified authority by giving decisions that cannot plausibly be construed as a good-faith attempt to umpire disputes about the laws of nature. In cases of individual dissent, where the citizen believes that the civil government is forcing him to act against his conscience, Locke recommends civil disobedience.

> What if the magistrate should enjoin any thing by his authority, that appears unlawful to the conscience of a private person?... I say, that such a private person is to abstain from the actions that he judges unlawful; and he is to undergo the punishment, which is not unlawful for him to bear; for the private judgment of any person concerning a law enacted in political matters, for the public good, does not take away the obligation of that law, nor deserve a dispensation.
> (FLT: 43 [159])

However, Locke is convinced that lone dissent will not produce civil instability: "the body of the people do not think themselves concerned in it, as for a raving madman, or heady malecontent, to overturn a well-settled state, the people being as little apt to follow the one, as the other" (ST: §208 [138]). However, if the overwhelming majority becomes convinced "in their consciences, that their laws, and with them their estates, liberties, and lives are in danger, and perhaps their religion too,"

> if a long train of abuses, prevarications and artifices, all tending the same way, make the design visible to the people, and they cannot but feel what they lie under, and see whither they are going; it is not to be wondered, that they should then rouse themselves, and endeavour to put the rule into such hands which may secure to them the ends for which government was at first erected.
> (ST: §, 225 [144])

In these cases the people "*universally have a persuasion, grounded upon manifest evidence, that designs are carrying on against their liberties, and the general course and tendency of things cannot but give them strong suspicions of the evil intention of their governors*" (ST: §230 [146]; emphasis added).

For Locke, then, there is some range of reasonable interpretative dispute that is defined by the convergence of judgments of the great body of people about the plausible interpretations of natural law. Locke allows that there will always be outliers, but "the people" speak when the judgments of citizens overwhelming concur; in this case a collective judgment has been made that the government has exceeded its authority. We might say that the Lockean public sphere is defined by a certain consensus about the broad requirements of morality; within this broad consensus we have a wide variety of disputes, especially about the application to specific cases. So long as the government remains within this broad consensus it will be seen by the great majority of citizens as performing its proper role of umpiring disputes generated by disagreements in private judgments about the law of nature; within its proper scope, the public authority of the umpire excludes all private judgment about the requirement of morality. However, when in the view of the citizens the decisions of government are systematically outside of the range of reasonable judgments—it makes decisions that our private judgments converge upon in deeming manifestly immoral—the people will conclude that it violates their conscience and is tyrannical. In the end, of course, they must rely on their private judgments about this: so while in one way (within certain bounds) private judgment is excluded, in the end, if citizens decide that the government has exceeded its authority, they can only act as they see fit, appealing to God to be the final judge of their case. "[H]e that appeals to heaven must be sure he has right on his side; and a right too that is worth the trouble and cost of the appeal, as he will answer at a tribunal that cannot be deceived" (ST: §176).[10] We might sum up Locke's view in five critical theses.

1 Individuals employing their private judgment disagree about the requirements of the law of nature, especially in cases in which one's interests are involved.
2 Consequently, a peaceful cooperative social life, in which people have a common understanding of their rights, requires a known and impartial public umpire to provide a public, definitive, and authoritative resolution of the disputes between citizens. This is an authoritative public judgment that excludes the authority of conflicting private judgments. Recall our discussion in Section 3: one may continue to have a private opinion, but renounce its authority for both others and oneself.
3 The range of the authority of the umpire is not unlimited; the umpire only has the authority to make impartial judgments within the bounds of reasonable dispute about the law of nature.
4 The boundary of reasonable disputes is determined by the general consensus of the private judgments or reasoning of citizens.
5 When the umpire acts outside these bounds it has no public authority.

5 Drawing Liberal Boundaries: The Public and Private Spheres

One important liberal feature of Locke's view, then, is that public authority is limited by natural rights. But in contrast to the anarchist, who insists that each individual's private judgment about her rights is determinative for her (and so essentially denies the existence of public authority), on Locke's view an umpire is required to publicly, authoritatively, interpret natural rights. And this requires citizens to set aside (as non-authoritative) their private judgments on these matters. Nevertheless citizens do not renounce making private determinations: they remain active in ensuring that the umpire does not become a threat to the rights of citizens. In normal contexts private judgment must be self-effacing, disclaiming any authority to rule action, but it always remains, ready to assert itself should the proper bounds of public authority be crossed.

A second important boundary for any liberal theory of political life is that between the public and the private—concerns that are the proper scope of public authority and those matters that are private, and over which the state has no authority. Locke identifies a clear boundary to public authority:

> The commonwealth seems to me to be a society of men constituted only for the procuring, preserving, and advancing their own civil interests.
>
> Civil interest I call life, liberty, health, and indolency of body; and the possession of outward things, such as money, lands, houses, furniture, and the like.
>
> It is the duty of the civil magistrate, by the impartial execution of equal laws, to secure unto all the people in general, and to every one of his subjects in particular, the just possession of these things belonging to this life. If any one presume to violate the laws of public justice and equity, established for the preservation of these things, his presumption is to be checked by the fear of punishment, consisting in the deprivation or diminution of those civil interests, or goods, which otherwise he might and ought to enjoy....
>
> the whole jurisdiction of the magistrate reaches only to these civil concernments; and that all civil power, right, and dominion, is bounded and confined to the only care of promoting these things....
>
> (FLT: 10 [153])

These are the ends of government, and securing them is the reason free people enter it: no others should be admitted (SLT: 119). These define the public, political, sphere. Locke is especially concerned with demonstrating that religious matters lie outside the political realm. "I esteem it above all things necessary," Locke insisted,

> to distinguish exactly the business of civil government from that of religion, and to settle the just bounds that lie between the one and the other. If this be not done, there can be no end put to the controversies that will be always arising between those that have, or at least pretend to have, on the one side, a concernment for the interest of men's souls, and, on the other side, a care of the commonwealth.
> (FLT: 9–10 [153])

Outside of matters of civil interests and morality, the government has no authority—the judgment of the magistrate does not stand for public reason:

> as the private judgment of any particular person, if erroneous, does not exempt him from the obligation of law, so the private judgment, as I may call it, of the magistrate, does not give him any new right of imposing laws upon his subjects [in matters such as religion], which neither was in the constitution of the government granted him, nor ever was in the power of the people to grant.
> (FLT: 45 [160])

On the other hand, churches are voluntary organizations, and thus have no political authority over their members or right to use force (FLT: 17, 19 [155, 157]). Thus, Locke insists, "the church itself is a thing absolutely separate and distinct from the commonwealth. The boundaries on both sides are fixed and immoveable" (FLT: 21 [157]).

6 Locke and Rawlsian Public Reason

Locke, then, manifestly and repeatedly distinguishes the realm of the civil sphere, where the public authority of the umpire about rights and core civil interests excludes the authority of private judgment, from the religious sphere, in which each rightfully acts on her private judgment, and where the judgment of the umpire is just one more opinion—it has no claim to public authority. Let us inquire further into the nature of this "fixed and immoveable" boundary between the civil and the religious.

One possibility is that Locke's entire theory of public authority, which I have explicated thus far, depends on purely secular arguments about civil interests and abjures all appeal to religious doctrines. If religion is a purely private matter, we might reason, it cannot enter into the case for a public authority; the argument for public authority must be premised only on the "worldly welfare of the commonwealth" (FLT: 54). This would be what John Rawls would call a "freestanding," secular, political argument.[11] Rawls distinguishes two phases of a public reason justification.[12] The first phase articulates and defends a theory of political right on the basis of a "freestanding" argument—one that is based simply on the shared, secular, reasons of all citizens, which ground the public sphere. If, as Rawls and Locke both recognize, we have deep and enduring disagreements about matters such as religion, then it looks as if we must "bracket" or set aside these reasons when defining the common, political, realm. In the second stage of justification, which Rawls calls "full justification," citizens draw on their own religious convictions, and beliefs about the good, to see if they can find support in these doctrines for the conclusions of the freestanding political argument. If many different religious doctrines support the freestanding political theory, then we can say that there is an "overlapping consensus" on the political theory. When such an overlapping consensus obtains, citizens are not torn between the demands of the political and the religious, and so we can expect a more stable compliance with the public laws.

Now it is quite clear that Locke engages in extensive argumentation that we would today classify under "overlapping consensus."[13] Throughout his *Letters on Toleration* Locke argues that the limitation of the magistrate's authority to civil interests is endorsed from religious perspectives. Thus, in arguing that the civil government has no authority over belief, Locke appeals to the nature of true religious belief: "The care of souls cannot belong to the civil magistrate, because his power consists only in outward force: but true and saving religion consists in the inward persuasion of the mind, without which nothing can be acceptable to God" (FLT: 11 [158]). The aim, then, is to demonstrate to religious citizens that their religion does not conflict with the government observing a "fixed and immoveable" boundary between the civil and the religious; the religious should welcome this, since true religion and salvation cannot be achieved through the tools of law. One who accepts the law acknowledges that one's private opinion about morality is without authority, but the law does not determine one's private opinion. And salvation depends on genuine private belief. In any event, even if government could shape belief, a religious person should realize the folly of giving any government such power.

> For, there being but one truth, one way to heaven; what hopes is there that more men would be led into it, if they had no other rule to follow but the religion of the court [ruler], and were put under a necessity to quit the light of their own reason, to oppose the

dictates of their own consciences, and blindly to resign up themselves to the will of their governors, and to the religion which either ignorance, ambition, or superstition had chanced to establish in the countries where they were born? In the variety and contradiction of opinions in religion, wherein the princes of the world are as much divided as in their secular interests, the narrow way would be much straitened; one country alone would be in the right, and all the rest of the world put under an obligation of following their princes in the ways that lead to destruction: and that which heightens the absurdity, and very ill suits the notion of a deity, men would owe their eternal happiness or misery to the places of their nativity.

(FLT: 12–13 [155])

Again and again, Locke employs a type of "overlapping consensus" strategy to show that, from within the perspective of religious citizens, the immutable boundary between civil authority and private freedom of religion is justified. Showing that religious reasoning supports the political doctrine of public reason is critical, as Locke acknowledges that "obedience is due in the first place to God, and afterwards to the laws" (FLT: 43). Because "the principal and chief care of every one ought to be of his own soul first, and, in the next place, of the public peace" (FLT: 44 [160]), no reasonable person would respect the public/private boundary, no matter how important for civil peace, if it endangers her soul. However, while the "overlapping consensus" element of Rawlsian public reason is manifestly important to Locke, Jeremy Waldron has demonstrated that Locke cannot be attributed with a "freestanding," *secular*, argument for his political doctrine.[14] On Waldron's careful reading, Locke's very conception of human equality, upon which his political doctrine is based, requires appeal to Christian belief.[15] To take a different but fundamental element, consider the idea of morality, which it is the chief task of the civil magistrate to publicly interpret. For the public realm to be thoroughly secular, it must be the case that full knowledge of the law of nature can be achieved through secular reason alone.[16] But Locke denies this; not only does he think that the common person—"the vulgar"—cannot, from secular premises alone, reason to all the conclusions of morality, but even philosophers fail:

it is too hard a task for unassisted reason to establish morality in all its parts, upon its true foundation, with a clear and convincing light. And it is at least a surer and shorter way, to the apprehensions of the vulgar, and mass of mankind, that one manifestly sent from God, and coming with visible authority from him, should, as a king and law-maker, tell them their

> duties; and require their obedience; than leave it to the long and sometimes intricate deductions of reason, to be made out to them. Such trains of reasoning the greatest part of mankind have neither leisure to weigh; nor, for want of education and use, skill to judge of. We see how unsuccessful in this the attempts of philosophers were before our Saviour's time. How short their several systems came of the perfection of a true and complete morality, is very visible. And if, since that, the christian philosophers have much out-done them: yet we may observe, that the first knowledge of the truths they have added, is owing to revelation: though as soon as they are heard and considered, they are found to be agreeable to reason; and such as can by no means be contradicted.
>
> (RC: 139–40)

And thus

> it is plain, in fact, that human reason unassisted failed men in its great and proper business of morality. It never from unquestionable principles, by clear deductions, made out an entire body of the 'law of nature.' And he that shall collect all the moral rules of the philosophers, and compare them with those contained in the New Testament, will find them to come short of the morality delivered by our Saviour, and taught by his apostles; a college made up, for the most part, of ignorant, but inspired fishermen.
>
> (RC: 140)

Moreover, not only is purely secular reason unable to grasp the full content of morality, but Locke insists that philosophical investigation fails to account for the authority and obligation of morality.

> Did the saying of Aristippus, or Confucius, give it an authority? Was Zeno a law-giver to mankind? If not, what he or any other philosopher delivered, was but a saying of his. Mankind might hearken to it, or reject it, as they pleased; or as it suited their interest, passions, principles or humours. They were under no obligation; the opinion of this or that philosopher was of no authority.... These incoherent apophthegms of philosophers, and wise men, however excellent in themselves, and well intended by them; could never make a morality, whereof the world could be convinced; could never rise to the force of a law, that mankind could with certainty depend on.
>
> (RC: 142–3)

Thus "a body of ethics, proved to be the law of nature, from principles of reason, and teaching all the duties of life... nobody will say the world had before our Saviour's time" (RC: 143). The mistake of the secularist is in thinking of the laws of nature

> that because reason confirms them to us, we had the first certain knowledge of them from thence; and in that clear evidence we now possess them. The contrary is manifest, in the defective morality of the gentiles, before our Saviour's time; and the want of reformation in the principles and measures of it, as well as practice.
>
> (RC: 145–6)

Morality, then, bridges the secular–religious divide (FLT: 41). Without religious conviction a person will have incomplete knowledge of morality and, worse, will not see it as the authoritative command of a lawgiver. Consequently,

> [t]hose are not at all to be tolerated who deny the being of God. Promises, covenants, and oaths, which are the bonds of human society, can have no hold upon an atheist. The taking away of God, though but even in thought, dissolves all.
>
> (FLT: 47 [162])[17]

Without God there cannot be authoritative morality. Manifestly, then, Locke's "freestanding" argument does not stand free of religious belief. But it is a mistake to think—as perhaps does Waldron—that a public reason argument, drawing on shared beliefs to articulate and justify a conception of a common public world, must abstract from all religious argument, or all conceptions of the good.[18] Everything depends on the society to which the account is being addressed. In our twenty-first-century society, where many do not hold religious convictions, an analysis of the public sphere that made necessary an appeal to religion—a justification that only believers could accept—would clearly be inadequate. But in Locke's seventeenth-century England, the supposition of the basic tenants of Christianity could form a common basis for reasoning: the vast majority plausibly accepted premises based on the most general and basic beliefs of Christianity. Just as Rawls draws on common beliefs of a democratic public, Locke could draw on common beliefs of a Christian public. It is fundamental to a public reason view that the nature of the shared, public, beliefs depends on the society being addressed. It is by no means a necessarily secular approach to political justification. The first stage of a Rawlsian public reason argument must abstract from the controversies that divide a society, about which there is deep and continuing reasonable disagreement. In seventeenth-century England the critical dispute was among the divergent religious beliefs distinctive to the followers of the Church of England, a wide array of dissenting Protestants (groups ranging from Quakers and Shakers to Methodists and Presbyterians) and Roman Catholics.[19] It is from these disagreements that a public reason doctrine, structured along the Rawlsian two-staged argumentative strategy, must prescind.

7 Locke's Insulation Thesis and Its Failure

The way in which morality straddles the political/religious divide is not, then, inconsistent with Locke advancing a public reason theory with a Rawlsian two-stage structure (though, of course, it won't have a Rawlsian content): (*i*) the shared argument which stands free of the society's doctrinal disputes and (*ii*) an overlapping consensus justification in which each member of the society affirms the political argument from her own, controversial, religious viewpoint. However, I think it is clear that Locke's insistence that morality depends on religious belief undermines the fundamental claim of his theory: that we can identify a shared reasoning in the public sphere that can be insulated from our disputes about private matters, and in Locke's case, crucially religious disagreement.

For the political doctrine I explicated in Sections 3 and 4 to be viable, there must be a basic shared understanding of the laws of nature and what they call for. Recall that Locke argues that there are limits to the authority of the public umpire, and that there will be a general consensus about when these limits are exceeded. If there is not such a consensus, there will always be significant groups claiming that the umpire has exceeded its authority, that it has strayed outside the bounds of a reasonable interpretation of the laws of nature. In his theory of revolution Locke is especially worried about the charge that individuals will take umbrage and rebel, and his answer is that "the people shall judge" whether the umpire has exceeded its authority (ST: §240 [146]).[20] But this sort of collective decision presupposes a general consensus, and such a consensus arises from a broad consensus about the demands of the laws of nature. For such a broad, general, consensus to persist, the population's beliefs about the laws of nature and their requirements must be relatively insulated from their deep and widespread doctrinal disputes.

I have argued elsewhere that Hobbes insisted that beliefs about political right could not be insulated from religious disputes, and that is why he rejected the idea of a private sphere in which religious groups could freely practice and espouse their doctrines.[21] Locke's insistence that morality presupposes religious belief imperils his own attempt to insulate the political from religious disagreement. Different religions advance vastly different interpretations of the Bible as well as different views of the sources of religions truth. The Fifth Monarchy Men, who arose during the English Revolution, interpreted Daniel's dream (Dan. 7) as indicating that there would be five great legitimate monarchies: the last of which would be that of Christ. They believed that the fourth monarchy, the Roman Empire, had been overturned by the Church of Rome, and so were awaiting the fifth monarchy: the reign of Christ. Consequently, on the basis of their reading of the Bible they denied the legitimacy of all states between the Roman Empire and the Reign of Christ—and so for the time being were anarchists. Less radically, Roman Catholics disagreed with Protestants such as Locke about the source of religious authority, viewing Church tradition as equal in importance to scripture. Catholics pose an especially thorny problem for Locke. In a number of places in his *Letters on Toleration* Locke seems to include Roman Catholics (usually referred to as "papists") in his arguments, as a view of Christianity like others that ought to be tolerated (FLT: 40, 55; SLT: 102, 118; TLT: 147, 219, 229, 231, 280, 301, 322, 400, 528). Yet it is typically thought that Locke was unwilling to extend toleration to Roman Catholics when he writes:

> Another more secret evil, but more dangerous to the commonwealth, is when men arrogate to themselves, and to those of their own sect, some peculiar prerogative covered over with a specious show of deceitful words, but in effect opposite to the civil rights of the community.... What can be the meaning of their asserting that 'kings excommunicated forfeit their crowns and kingdoms?' It is evident that they thereby arrogate unto themselves the power of deposing kings: because they challenge the power of excommunication as the peculiar right of their hierarchy.
> (FLT: 46 [160])

It is hard not to see this as aimed at Roman Catholicism (after all, Pope Paul III excommunicated Henry VIII). In his early nineteenth-century introduction to John Fox's *Book of Protestant Martyrs,* for example, the Reverend John Milner took this passage from Locke as a warning of the "dangerous and *unbounded* influence of the Romish clergy."[22] Overall, it is probably best to read Locke as holding that, as a body of religious doctrine, Roman Catholicism should be tolerated along with other forms of Christianity and Judaism, but not when it claims—as Popes did—an authority to cancel citizens' obligation to civil government.[23] A religion that does not itself respect the insulation of religious belief from political right and obligation, Locke concludes, cannot be tolerated.

And here lies the problem: because Locke insists that civil government concerns the public adjudication of disputes about morality and natural law, and he insists that reason unguided by religious faith cannot discover the full content, and authoritative nature, of morality, religious belief cannot be insulated from the civil sphere. If Christianity is necessary to understand the law of nature, non-Christians will not have a proper understanding of the disputes that the civil magistrate is seeking to adjudicate, and so will not have a proper grasp of the reasonable bounds of these disputes. And presumably Catholics will also fail to have a proper grasp, as their understanding of natural law will be heavily influenced by Church tradition (including decisions of Church councils), a consideration absent from Protestant interpretations. And it is but a short step to conclude that the many Protestant sects, which radically disagree about some key parts of scripture, will also have deep differences about the content of natural law and God's commands (think again of the Fifth Monarchy Men).

It is important to stress that the worry is not simply that we disagree about morality. A strength of Locke's account is that he directly focuses on such disagreement in his theory of public adjudication. The very point of government, we have seen, is that people disagree about natural rights and natural law. Locke, however, focuses on the distortions caused by self-interest in judging in one's own case, not on deep and fundamental disagreements about the content of natural law. Indeed, Locke's liberal theory of public reason, which requires that the umpire only has authority to adjudicate within some reasonable range of disputes, requires a broad consensus among citizens to identify this range. The problem posed by Locke's doctrine that natural reason, shorn of religious belief, cannot reveal the complete content of natural law, is that it dissolves the barrier between civil and religious dispute that his theory of public reason was meant to erect.

8 Conclusion: Locke's Insight and Problem for Liberal Theories of Public Reason

Locke's insulation thesis, I have argued elsewhere, has been absolutely critical to most liberal theories of public reason, including that of John Rawls.[24] Two-staged liberal theories of public reason commence by identifying those political or civil matters about which there is broad agreement, and then construct a theory of justice, or political right, on their basis. We need such a shared basis for thinking about justice, these liberal theorists of public reason insist, because we have such deep and wide disagreement over matters of religion, moral ideals, metaphysical convictions and so on, yet we must forge shared terms on which to live. For this project to succeed, these deep and wide disagreements must not invade the public sphere, for then the broad consensus, upon which such public reason theories depend, would dissolve into the very conflicts they sought to set aside. Thus the need for what I have called the insulation thesis. Locke's great insight—which, alas, was also the undoing of his theory—was that our moral convictions are not freestanding from our broader commitments. Locke's hope, I think, was that there was enough consensus in Christian civilization about these matters that all Christians would agree about the broad contours of the public sphere. Atheists had to be excluded, but that was not terribly significant in the seventeenth century. But the uneasy place of Roman Catholics pointed to the problem. On the one hand Locke sought to include them in the broad Christian consensus, and on strictly theological issues they appeared to qualify for toleration. But then he implies—without explicitly naming them, but identifying the doctrine long associated with Roman Catholicism that the clergy has the authority to deny civil honor (obedience) to the magistrate—Catholics are not due toleration. But that is simply a case where its religious tenets carry over into civil morality. It is not just Catholicism, however, that bridges the public–private divide: Locke has shown that it *must* be bridged.

One might think that Locke could have avoided all of this by simply supposing—as most of his contemporary followers have—that secular reason is complete in itself and needs no supplement from religious belief. But those contemporary followers cannot explain why there should be such consensus on natural rights and law: they often blithely assume it, though most of their fellow political philosophers do not concur. Locke hoped that the broad agreement of Christian civilization could provide the foundation of the consensus while he sought to prevent its deep disagreements from undermining it. The trick, as it were, is to get sufficient consensus in the public sphere to define the limits of public reason while insulating this consensus from private disputes. We should not be hard on Locke for failing: I doubt whether anyone has succeeded.[25]

Notes

1 James E. Rogers Professor of Philosophy, University of Arizona.
2 See Simone Chambers, "Who Shall Judge? Hobbes, Locke and Kant on the Construction of Public Reason," *Ethics and Global Politics* vol. 1(2009): 339–68, at 354.
3 See Robert Nozick, *Anarchy, State and Utopia* (New York: Basic Books, 1974), 10–11.
4 All references to Locke's writings are from *The Works of John Locke in Nine Volumes*, twelfth edition (London: Rivington, 1824). [Page numbers in brackets refer to the Locke selections in this volume—eds.] The following abbreviations are used in the text. FT: *First Treatise of Government* vol. 4 (by section); ST: *Second Treatise of Government*, vol. 4 (by section); FLT: *First Letter on Toleration*, vol. 5 ["A Letter Concerning Toleration," [149–62]—eds.]; SLT: *Second Letter on Toleration*, vol. 5; TLT: *Third Letter on Toleration*, vol. 5; RC: "The Reasonableness of Christianity," vol. 6; TCE: *Some Thoughts Concerning Education*, vol. 8.

5 The most famous of these is, of course, Nozick, *Anarchy, State and Utopia*, Part I. For an overview of positions, see Eric Mack and Gerald Gaus, "Classical Liberalism and Libertarianism: The Liberty Tradition," in *The Handbook of Political Theory*, edited by Gerald Gaus and Chandran Kukathas (London: Sage, 2003): 115–30.
6 See A. John Simmons, *On the Edge of Anarchy: Locke, Consent and the Limits of Society* (Princeton: Princeton University Press, 1993), esp. 260–69.
7 Nozick, *Anarchy, State and Utopia*, 10–11.
8 And:

> To avoid this state of war (wherein there is no appeal but to heaven, and wherein every the least difference is apt to end, where there is no authority to decide between the contenders) is one great reason of men's putting themselves into society, and quitting the state of nature: for where there is an authority, a power on earth, from which relief can be had by appeal, there the continuance of the state of war is excluded, and the controversy is decided by that power.
>
> (ST: §21 [115])

9 As Jeremy Waldron notes, Locke makes this point "again and again." *God, Locke and Equality: Christian Foundations of Locke's Political Thought* (Cambridge: Cambridge University Press, 2002), 65.
10 It is because private judgment must be relied on when citizens ask whether the public authority has stepped beyond its authority, and is no longer performing its designated task, that Jean Hampton insists that Hobbes's contract ends up as a Lockean one. Whereas Hobbes seeks to entirely exclude private judgment, Locke admits that citizens must rely on it in these cases. See her *Hobbes and the Social Contract Tradition* (Cambridge: Cambridge University Press, 1986), chapter 7.
11 John Rawls, *Political Liberalism*, expanded edition (New York: Columbia University Press, 2005), 12, 144, 387. For a sketch of Rawls' argument, see my essay "The Turn to a Political Liberalism," in *The Blackwell Companion to Rawls*, edited by David Reidy and Jon Mandle (New York: Wiley-Blackwell, 2014), 235–50.
12 Rawls, *Political Liberalism*, 387ff.
13 Cf. Chambers, "Who Shall Judge?" 355.
14 Waldron, *God, Locke, and Equality*, esp. 81, 236ff.
15 Recall from our opening sketch, that the state of nature is a condition of

> equality, wherein all the power and jurisdiction is reciprocal, no one having more than another; there being nothing more evident, than that creatures of the same species and rank, promiscuously born to all the same advantages of nature, and the use of the same faculties, should also be equal one amongst another without subordination or subjection.
>
> (ST: §4 [108])

16 As one might well have concluded from the passage from the *Second Treatise* cited above:

> The state of nature has a law of nature to govern it, which obliges every one: and reason, which is that law, teaches all mankind, who will but consult it, that being all equal and independent, no one ought to harm another in his life, health, liberty, or possessions.
>
> (ST: §6 [109])

17 See further Waldron, God, *Locke and Equality*, chapter 8.
18 Ibid., 236–7.
19 I return to Catholics in Sections 7 and 8.
20 See Chambers, "Who Shall Judge?" 354–9.
21 "Hobbes' Challenge to Public Reason Liberalism," in *Hobbes Today: Insights for the 21st Century*, edited by S.A. Lloyd (Cambridge: Cambridge University Press, 2013), 155–77.
22 John Fox, *An Universal History of Christian Martyrdom: Being a Complete and Authentic Account of the Lives, Suffering, and Triumphant Deaths of the Primitive as Well as Protestant Martyrs in All Parts of the World, from the Birth of Our Blessed Savior to the Latest Periods of Pagan and Catholic Persecution Together with a Summary of the Doctrines, Prejudices, Blasphemies, and Superstitions of the Modern Church of Rome* with notes, commentaries by J. Milner (London: B. Crosby and Co, 1807), p. x. Emphasis added.
23 See Waldron, *God, Locke and Equality*, 218–23.
24 "Public Reason Liberalism" in *The Cambridge Companion to Liberalism*, edited by Steve Wall (Cambridge: Cambridge University Press, 2015), 112–40.
25 My thanks to Piers Norris Turner and Luciano Venezia for their comments on an earlier draft of this chapter.

3

JEAN-JACQUES ROUSSEAU (1712–1778)

A Discourse on Political Economy (1755)[1]

The word Economy, or Œconomy, is derived from οἰκός, *a house*, and νόμος, *law*, and meant originally only the wise and legitimate government of the house for the common good of the whole family. The meaning of the term was then extended to the government of that great family, the State. To distinguish these two senses of the word, the latter is called *general* or *political* economy, and the former domestic or particular economy. The first only is discussed in the present discourse.

Even if there were as close an analogy as many authors maintain between the State and the family, it would not follow that the rules of conduct proper for one of these societies would be also proper for the other...

[H]ow could the government of the State be like that of the family, when the basis on which they rest is so different? The father being physically stronger than his children, his paternal authority, as long as they need his protection, may be reasonably said to be established by nature. But in the great family, all the members of which are naturally equal, the political authority, being purely arbitrary as far as its institution is concerned, can be founded only on conventions, and the Magistrate can have no authority over the rest, except by virtue of the laws. The duties of a father are dictated to him by natural feelings, and in a manner that seldom allows him to neglect them. For rulers there is no such principle, and they are really obliged to the people only by what they themselves have promised to do, and the people have therefore a right to require of them...

I must here ask my readers to distinguish also between *public economy*, which is my subject and which I call *government*, and the supreme authority, which I call *Sovereignty*; a distinction which consists in the fact that the latter has the right of legislation, and in certain cases binds the body of the nation itself, while the former has only the right of execution, and is binding only on individuals.

I shall take the liberty of making use of a very common, and in some respects inaccurate, comparison, which will serve to illustrate my meaning.

JEAN-JACQUES ROUSSEAU (1712–1778)

The body politic, taken individually, may be considered as an organised, living body, resembling that of man. The sovereign power represents the head; the laws and customs are the brain, the source of the nerves and seat of the understanding, will and senses, of which the Judges and Magistrates are the organs: commerce, industry, and agriculture are the mouth and stomach which prepare the common subsistence; the public income is the blood, which a prudent *economy*, in performing the functions of the heart, causes to distribute through the whole body nutriment and life: the citizens are the body and the members, which make the machine live, move and work; and no part of this machine can be damaged without the painful impression being at once conveyed to the brain, if the animal is in a state of health.

The life of both bodies is the self common to the whole, the reciprocal sensibility and internal correspondence of all the parts. Where this communication ceases, where the formal unity disappears, and the contiguous parts belong to one another only by juxtaposition, the man is dead, or the State is dissolved.

The body politic, therefore, is also a moral being possessed of a will; and this general will, which tends always to the preservation and welfare of the whole and of every part, and is the source of the laws, constitutes for all the members of the State, in their relations to one another and to it, the rule of what is just or unjust: a truth which shows, by the way, how idly some writers have treated as theft the subtlety prescribed to children at Sparta for obtaining their frugal repasts, as if everything ordained by the law were not lawful.

It is important to observe that this rule of justice, though certain with regard to all citizens, may be defective with regard to foreigners. The reason is clear. The will of the State, though general in relation to its own members, is no longer so in relation to other States and their members, but becomes, for them, a particular and individual will, which has its rule of justice in the law of nature. This, however, enters equally into the principle here laid down; for in such a case, the great city of the world becomes the body politic, whose general will is always the law of nature, and of which the different States and peoples are individual members. From these distinctions, applied to each political society and its members, are derived the most certain and universal rules, by which we can judge whether a government is good or bad, and in general of the morality of all human actions.

Every political society is composed of other smaller societies of different kinds, each of which has its interests and its rules of conduct: but those societies which everybody perceives, because they have an external and authorised form, are not the only ones that actually exist in the State: all individuals who are united by a common interest compose as many others, either transitory or permanent, whose influence is none the less real because it is less apparent, and the proper observation of whose various relations is the true knowledge of public morals and manners. The influence of all these tacit or formal associations causes, by the influence of their will, as many different modifications of the public will. The will of these particular societies has always two relations; for the members of the association, it is a general will; for the great society, it is a particular will; and it is often right with regard to the first object, and wrong as to the second. An individual may be a devout priest, a brave soldier, or a zealous senator, and yet a bad citizen. A particular resolution may be advantageous to the smaller community, but pernicious to the greater. It is true that particular societies being always subordinate to the general society in preference to others, the duty of a citizen takes precedence of that of a senator, and a man's duty of that of a citizen: but unhappily personal interest is always found in inverse ratio to duty, and increases in proportion as the association grows narrower, and the engagement less sacred; which irrefragably proves that the most general will is always the must just also, and that the voice of the people is in fact the voice of God.

It does not follow that the public decisions are always equitable; they may possibly, for reasons which I have given, not be so when they have to do with foreigners. Thus it is not impossible that a Republic, though in itself well governed, should enter upon an unjust war. Nor is it less possible for the Council of a Democracy to pass unjust decrees, and condemn the innocent; but this never happens unless the people is seduced by private interests, which the credit or eloquence of some clever persons substitutes for those of the State: in which case the general will will be one thing, and the result of the public deliberation another. This is not contradicted by the case of the Athenian Democracy; for Athens was in fact not a Democracy, but a very tyrannical Aristocracy, governed by philosophers and orators. Carefully determine what happens in every public deliberation, and it will be seen that the general will is always for the common good; but very often there is a secret division, a tacit confederacy, which, for particular ends, causes the natural disposition of the assembly to be set at nought. In such a case the body of society is really divided into other bodies, the members of which acquire a general will, which is good and just with respect to these new bodies, but unjust and bad with regard to the whole, from which each is thus dismembered.

We see then how easy it is, by the help of these principles, to explain those apparent contradictions, which are noticed in the conduct of many persons who are scrupulously honest in some respects, and cheats and scoundrels in others, who trample under foot the most sacred duties, and yet are faithful to the death to engagements that are often illegitimate. Thus the most depraved of men always pay some sort of homage to public faith; and even robbers, who are the enemies of virtue in the great society, pay some respect to the shadow of it in their secret caves.

JEAN-JACQUES ROUSSEAU (1712–1778)

In establishing the general will as the first principle of public economy, and the fundamental rule of government, I have not thought it necessary to inquire seriously whether the Magistrates belong to the people, or the people to the Magistrates; or whether in public affairs the good of the State should be taken into account, or only that of its rulers. That question indeed has long been decided one way in theory, and another in practice; and in general it would be ridiculous to expect that those who are in fact masters will prefer any other interest to their own. It would not be improper, therefore, further to distinguish public *economy* as popular or tyrannical. The former is that of every State, in which there reigns between the people and the rulers unity of interest and will: the latter will necessarily exist wherever the government and the people have different interests, and, consequently, opposing wills. The rules of the latter are written at length in the archives of history, and in the satires of Macchiavelli. The rules of the former are found only in the writings of those philosophers who venture to proclaim the rights of humanity.

I. The first and most important rule of legitimate or popular government, that is to say, of government whose object is the good of the people, is therefore, as I have observed, to follow in everything the general will. But to follow this will it is necessary to know it, and above all to distinguish it from the particular will, beginning with one's self: this distinction is always very difficult to make, and only the most sublime virtue can afford sufficient illumination for it. As, in order to will, it is necessary to be free, a difficulty no less great than the former arises—that of preserving at once the public liberty and the authority of government. Look into the motives which have induced men, once united by their common needs in a general society, to unite themselves still more intimately by means of civil societies: you will find no other motive than that of assuring the property, life and liberty of each member by the protection of all. But can men be forced to defend the liberty of any one among them, without trespassing on that of others? And how can they provide for the public needs, without alienating the individual property of those who are forced to contribute to them? With whatever sophistry all this may be covered over, it is certain that if any constraint can be laid on my will, I am no longer free, and that I am no longer master of my own property, if any one else can lay a hand on it. This difficulty, which would have seemed insurmountable, has been removed, like the first, by the most sublime of all human institutions, or rather by a divine inspiration, which teaches mankind to imitate here below the unchangeable decrees of the Deity. By what inconceivable art has a means been found of making men free by making them subject; of using in the service of the State the properties, the persons and even the lives of all its members, without constraining and without consulting them; of confining their will by their own admission; of overcoming their refusal by that consent, and forcing them to punish themselves, when they act against their own will? How can it be that all should obey, yet nobody take upon him to command, and that all should serve, and yet have no masters, but be the more free, as, in apparent subjection, each loses no part of his liberty but what might be hurtful to that of another? These wonders are the work of law. It is to law alone that men owe justice and liberty. It is this salutary organ of the will of all which establishes, in civil right, the natural equality between men. It is this celestial voice which dictates to each citizen the precepts of public reason, and teaches him to act according to the rules of his own judgment, and not to behave inconsistently with himself. It is with this voice alone that political rulers should speak when they command; for no sooner does one man, setting aside the law, claim to subject another to his private will, than he departs from the state of civil society, and confronts him face to face in the pure state of nature, in which obedience is prescribed solely by necessity.

The most pressing interest of the ruler, and even his most indispensable duty, therefore, is to watch over the observation of the laws of which he is the minister, and on which his whole authority is founded. At the same time, if he exacts the observance of them from others, he is the more strongly bound to observe them himself, since he enjoys all their favour. For his example is of such force, that even if the people were willing to permit him to release himself from the yoke of the law, he ought to be cautious in availing himself of so dangerous a prerogative, which others might soon claim to usurp in their turn, and often use to his prejudice. At bottom, as all social engagements are mutual in nature, it is impossible for any one to set himself above the law, without renouncing its advantages; for nobody is bound by any obligation to one who claims that he is under no obligations to others. For this reason no exemption from the law will ever be granted, on any ground whatsoever, in a well-regulated government. Those citizens who have deserved well of their country ought to be rewarded with honours, but never with privileges: for the Republic is at the eve of its fall, when any one can think it fine not to obey the laws. If the nobility or the soldiery should ever adopt such a maxim, all would be lost beyond redemption.

The power of the laws depends still more on their own wisdom than on the severity of their administrators, and the public will derives its greatest weight from the reason which has dictated it. Hence Plato looked upon it as a very necessary precaution to place at the head of all edicts a preamble, setting forth their justice and utility. In fact, the first of all laws is to respect the laws: the severity of penalties is only a vain resource, invented by little minds in order to substitute terror for that respect which they have no means of obtaining. It has constantly been observed that in those countries where legal punishments are most severe, they are also most frequent; so that the cruelty of such punishments is a proof only of the multitude of criminals, and, punishing everything with equal severity, induces those who are guilty to commit crimes, in order to escape being punished for their faults.

But though the government be not master of the law, it is much to be its guarantor, and to possess a thousand means of inspiring the love of it. In this alone the talent of reigning consists. With force in one's hands, there is no art required to make the whole world tremble, nor indeed much to gain men's hearts; for experience has long since taught the people to give its rulers great credit for all the evil they abstain from doing it, and to adore them if they do not absolutely hate it. A fool, if he be obeyed, may punish crimes as well as another: but the true statesman is he who knows how to prevent them: it is over the wills, even more than the actions, of his subjects that his honourable rule is extended. If he could secure that every one should act aright, he would no longer have anything to do; and the masterpiece of his labours would be to be able to remain unemployed. It is certain, at least, that the greatest talent a ruler can possess is to disguise his power, in order to render it less odious, and to conduct the State so peaceably as to make it seem to have no need of conductors.

I conclude, therefore, that, as the first duty of the legislator is to make the laws conformable to the general will, the first rule of public *economy* is that the administration of justice should be conformable to the laws. It will even be enough to prevent the State from being ill governed, that the Legislator shall have provided, as he should, for every need of place, climate, soil, custom, neighbourhood, and all the rest of the relations peculiar to the people he had to institute. Not but what there still remains an infinity of details of administration and economy, which are left to the wisdom of the government: but there are two infallible rules for its good conduct on these occasions; one is, that the spirit of the law ought to decide in every particular case that could not be foreseen; the other is that the general will, the source and supplement of all laws, should be consulted wherever they fail. But how, I shall be asked, can the general will be known in cases in which it has not expressed itself? Must the whole nation be assembled together at every unforeseen event? Certainly not. It ought the less to be assembled, because it is by no means certain that its decision would be the expression of the general will; besides, the method would be impracticable in a great people, and is hardly ever necessary where the government is well-intentioned: for the rulers well know that the general will is always on the side which is most favourable to the public interest, that is to say, most equitable; so that it is needful only to act justly, to be certain of following the general will. When this is flouted too openly, it makes itself felt, in spite of the formidable restraint of the public authority...

[T]hat government which confines itself to mere obedience will find difficulty in getting itself obeyed. If it is good to know how to deal with men as they are, it is much better to make them what there is need that they should be. The most absolute authority is that which penetrates into a man's inmost being, and concerns itself no less with his will than with his actions. It is certain that all peoples become in the long run what the government makes them; warriors, citizens, men, when it so pleases; or merely populace and rabble, when it chooses to make them so. Hence every prince who despises his subjects, dishonours himself, in confessing that he does not know how to make them worthy of respect. Make men, therefore, if you would command men: if you would have them obedient to the laws, make them love the laws, and then they will need only to know what is their duty to do it...

II. The second essential rule of public economy is no less important than the first. If you would have the general will accomplished, bring all the particular wills into conformity with it; in other words, as virtue is nothing more than this conformity of the particular wills with the general will, establish the reign of virtue.

If our politicians were less blinded by their ambition, they would see how impossible it is for any establishment whatever to act in the spirit of its institution, unless it is guided in accordance with the law of duty; they would feel that the greatest support of public authority lies in the hearts of the citizens, and that nothing can take the place of morality in the maintenance of government. It is not only upright men who know how to administer the laws; but at bottom only good men know how to obey them...

[W]hen the citizens love their duty, and the guardians of the public authority sincerely apply themselves to the fostering of that love by their own example and assiduity, every difficulty vanishes; and government becomes so easy that it needs none of that art of darkness, whose blackness is its only mystery. Those enterprising spirits, so dangerous and so much admired, all those great ministers, whose glory is inseparable from the miseries of the people, are no longer regretted: public morality supplies what is wanting in the genius of the rulers; and the more virtue reigns, the less need there is for talent. Even ambition is better served by duty than by usurpation: when the people is convinced that its rulers are labouring only for its happiness, its deference saves them the trouble of labouring to strengthen their power: and history shows us, in a thousand cases, that the authority of one who is beloved over those whom he loves is a hundred times more absolute than all the tyranny of usurpers. This does not mean that the government ought to be afraid to make use of its power, but that it ought to make use of it only in a lawful manner. We find in history a thousand examples of pusillanimous or ambitious rulers, who were ruined by their slackness or their pride; not one who suffered for having been strictly just. But we ought not to confound negligence with moderation, or clemency with weakness. To be just, it is necessary to be severe; to permit vice, when one has the right and the power to suppress it, is to be oneself vicious.

It is not enough to say to the citizens, be *good*; they must be taught to be so; and even example, which is in this respect the first lesson, is not the sole means to be employed; patriotism is the most efficacious: for, as I have said already, every man is virtuous when his particular will is in all things conformable to the general will, and we voluntarily will what is willed by those whom we love. It appears that the feeling of humanity evaporates and grows feeble in embracing all mankind, and that we cannot be affected by the calamities of Tartary or Japan, in the same manner as we are by those of European nations. It is necessary in some degree to confine and limit our interest and compassion in order to make it active. Now, as this sentiment can be useful only to those with whom we have to live, it is proper that our humanity should confine itself to our fellow-citizens, and should receive a new force because we are in the habit of seeing them, and by reason of the common interest which unites them. It is certain that the greatest miracles of virtue have been produced by patriotism: this fine and lively feeling, which gives to the force of self-love all the beauty of virtue, lends it an energy which, without disfiguring it, makes it the most heroic of all passions. This it is that produces so many immortal actions, the glory of which dazzles our feeble eyes; and so many great men, whose old-world virtues pass for fables now that patriotism is made mock of. This is not surprising; the transports of susceptible hearts appear altogether fanciful to any one who has never felt them; and the love of one's country, which is a hundred times more lively and delightful than the love of a mistress, cannot be conceived except by experiencing it...

Do we wish men to be virtuous? Then let us begin by making them love their country: but how can they love it, if their country be nothing more to them than to strangers, and afford them nothing but what it can refuse nobody? It would be still worse, if they did not enjoy even the privilege of social security, and if their lives, liberties and property lay at the mercy of persons in power, without their being permitted, or it being possible for them, to get relief from the laws. For in that case, being subjected to the duties of the state of civil society, without enjoying even the common privileges of the state of nature, and without being able to use their strength in their own defence, they would be in the worst condition in which freemen could possibly find themselves, and the word *country* would mean for them something merely odious and ridiculous. It must not be imagined that a man can break or lose an arm, without the pain being conveyed to his head: nor is it any more credible that the general will should consent that any one member of the State, whoever he might be, should wound or destroy another, than it is that the fingers of a man in his senses should wilfully scratch his eyes out. The security of individuals is so intimately connected with the public confederation that, apart from the regard that must be paid to human weakness, that convention would in point of right be dissolved, if in the State a single citizen who might have been relieved were allowed to perish, or if one were wrongfully confined in prison, or if in one case an obviously unjust sentence were given. For the fundamental conventions being broken, it is impossible to conceive of any right or interest that could retain the people in the social union; unless they were restrained by force, which alone causes the dissolution of the state of civil society.

In fact, does not the undertaking entered into by the whole body of the nation bind it to provide for the security of the least of its members with as much care as for that of all the rest? Is the welfare of a single citizen any less the common cause than that of the whole State? It may be said that it is good that one should perish for all. I am ready to admire such a saying when it comes from the lips of a virtuous and worthy patriot, voluntarily and dutifully sacrificing himself for the good of his country: but if we are to understand by it, that it is lawful for the government to sacrifice an innocent man for the good of the multitude, I look upon it as one of the most execrable rules tyranny ever invented, the greatest falsehood that can be advanced, the most dangerous admission that can be made, and a direct contradiction of the fundamental laws of society. So little is it the case that any one person ought to perish for all, that all have pledged their lives and properties for the defence of each, in order that the weakness of individuals may always be protected by the strength of the public, and each member by the whole State. Suppose we take from the whole people one individual after another, and then press the advocates of this rule to explain more exactly what they mean by the *body of the State*, and we shall see that it will at length be reduced to a small number of persons, who are not the people, but the officers of the people, and who, having bound themselves by personal oath to perish for the welfare of the people, would thence infer that the people is to perish for their own.

Need we look for examples of the protection which the State owes to its members, and the respect it owes to their persons? It is only among the most illustrious and courageous nations that they are to be found; it is only among free peoples that the dignity of man is realised...

What is most necessary, and perhaps most difficult, in government, is rigid integrity in doing strict justice to all, and above all in protecting the poor against the tyranny of the rich. The greatest evil has already come about, when there are poor men to be defended, and rich men to be restrained. It is on the middle classes alone that the whole force of the law is exerted; they are equally powerless against the treasures of the rich and the penury of the poor. The first mocks them, the second escapes them. The one breaks the meshes, the other passes through them.

JEAN-JACQUES ROUSSEAU (1712–1778)

It is therefore one of the most important functions of government to prevent extreme inequality of fortunes; not by taking away wealth from its possessors, but by depriving all men of means to accumulate it; not by building hospitals for the poor, but by securing the citizens from becoming poor. The unequal distribution of inhabitants over the territory, when men are crowded together in one place, while other places are depopulated; the encouragement of the arts that minister to luxury and of purely industrial arts at the expense of useful and laborious crafts; the sacrifice of agriculture to commerce; the necessitation of the tax-farmer by the mal-administration of the funds of the State; and in short, venality pushed to such an extreme that even public esteem is reckoned at a cash value, and virtue rated at a market price: these are the most obvious causes of opulence and of poverty, of public interest, of mutual hatred among citizens, of indifference to the common cause, of the corruption of the people, and of the weakening of all the springs of government. Such are the evils, which are with difficulty cured when they make themselves felt, but which a wise administration ought to prevent, if it is to maintain, along with good morals, respect for the laws, patriotism, and the influence of the general will.

But all these precautions will be inadequate, unless rulers go still more to the root of the matter. I conclude this part of public economy where I ought to have begun it. There can be no patriotism without liberty, no liberty without virtue, no virtue without citizens; create citizens, and you have everything you need; without them, you will have nothing but debased slaves, from the rulers of the State downwards. To form citizens is not the work of a day; and in order to have men it is necessary to educate them when they are children. It will be said, perhaps, that whoever has men to govern, ought not to seek, beyond their nature, a perfection of which they are incapable; that he ought not to desire to destroy their passions; and that the execution of such an attempt is no more desirable than it is possible. I will agree, further, that a man without passions would certainly be a bad citizen; but it must be agreed also that, if men are not taught not to love some things, it is impossible to teach them to love one object more than another—to prefer that which is truly beautiful to that which is deformed. If, for example, they were early accustomed to regard their individuality only in its relation to the body of the State, and to be aware, so to speak, of their own existence merely as a part of that of the State, they might at length come to identify themselves in some degree with this greater whole, to feel themselves members of their country, and to love it with that exquisite feeling which no isolated person has save for himself; to lift up their spirits perpetually to this great object, and thus to transform into a sublime virtue that dangerous disposition which gives rise to all our vices. Not only does philosophy demonstrate the possibility of giving feeling these new directions; history furnishes us with a thousand striking examples...

From the first moment of life, men ought to begin learning to deserve to live; and, as at the instant of birth we partake of the rights of citizenship, that instant ought to be the beginning of the exercise of our duty. If there are laws for the age of maturity, there ought to be laws for infancy, teaching obedience to others: and as the reason of each man is not left to be the sole arbiter of his duties, government ought the less indiscriminately to abandon to the intelligence and prejudices of fathers the education of their children, as that education is of still greater importance to the State than to the fathers: for, according to the course of nature, the death of the father often deprives him of the final fruits of education; but his country sooner or later perceives its effects. Families dissolve, but the State remains...

Public education, therefore, under regulations prescribed by the government, and under magistrates established by the Sovereign, is one of the fundamental rules of popular or legitimate government. If children are brought up in common in the bosom of equality; if they are imbued with the laws of the State and the precepts of the general will; if they are taught to respect these above all things; if they are surrounded by examples and objects which constantly remind them of the tender mother who nourishes them, of the love she bears them, of the inestimable benefits they receive from her, and of the return they owe her, we cannot doubt that they will learn to cherish one another mutually as brothers, to will nothing contrary to the will of society, to substitute the actions of men and citizens for the futile and vain babbling of sophists, and to become in time defenders and fathers of the country of which they will have been so long the children...

I know of but three peoples which once practised public education, the Cretans, the Lacedemonians, and the ancient Persians: among all these it was attended with the greatest success, and indeed it did wonders among the two last. Since the world has been divided into nations too great to admit of being well governed, this method has been no longer practicable, and the reader will readily perceive other reasons why such a thing has never been attempted by any modern people...

Wherever men love their country, respect the laws, and live simply, little remains to be done in order to make them happy; and in public administration, where chance has less influence than in the lot of individuals, wisdom is so nearly allied to happiness, that the two objects are confounded.

III. It is not enough to have citizens and to protect them, it is also necessary to consider their subsistence. Provision for the public wants is an obvious inference from the general will, and the third essential duty of government. This duty is not, we should feel, to fill the granaries of individuals and thereby to grant them a dispensation from labour, but to keep plenty so within their reach that labour is always necessary and never useless for its acquisition. It extends also to everything regarding the management of the exchequer, and the expenses of public administration. Having thus treated of general economy with reference to the government of persons, we must now consider it with reference to the administration of property.

This part presents no fewer difficulties to solve, and contradictions to remove, than the preceding. It is certain that the right of property is the most sacred of all the rights of citizenship, and even more important in some respects than liberty itself; either because it more nearly affects the preservation of life, or because, property being more easily usurped and more difficult to defend than life, the law ought to pay a greater attention to what is most easily taken away; or finally, because property is the true foundation of civil society, and the real guarantee of the undertakings of citizens: for if property were not answerable for personal actions, nothing would be easier than to evade duties and laugh at the laws. On the other hand, it is no less certain that the maintenance of the State and the government involves costs and outgoings; and as every one who agrees to the end must acquiesce in the means, it follows that the members of a society ought to contribute from their property to its support. Besides, it is difficult to secure the property of individuals on one side, without attacking it on another; and it is impossible that all the regulations which govern the order of succession, will, contracts, &c. should not lay individuals under some constraint as to the disposition of their goods, and should not consequently restrict the right of property.

But besides what I have said above of the agreement between the authority of law and the liberty of the citizen, there remains to be made, with respect to the disposition of goods, an important observation which removes many difficulties. As Puffendorf has shown, the right of property, by its very nature, does not extend beyond the life of the proprietor, and the moment a man is dead his goods cease to belong to him. Thus, to prescribe the conditions according to which he can dispose of them, is in reality less to alter his right as it appears, than to extend it in fact.

In general, although the institution of the laws which regulate the power of individuals in the disposition of their own goods belongs only to the Sovereign, the spirit of these laws, which the government ought to follow in their application, is that, from father to son, and from relation to relation, the goods of a family should go as little out of it and be as little alienated as possible. There is a sensible reason for this in favour of children, to whom the right of property would be quite useless, if the father left them nothing, and who besides, having often contributed by their labour to the acquisition of their father's wealth, are in their own right associates with him in his right of property. But another reason, more distant, though not less important, is that nothing is more fatal to morality and to the Republic than the continual shifting of rank and fortune among the citizens: such changes are both the proof and the source of a thousand disorders, and overturn and confound everything; for those who were brought up to one thing find themselves destined for another; and neither those who rise nor those who fall are able to assume the rules of conduct, or to possess themselves of the qualifications requisite for their new condition, still less to discharge the duties it entails. I proceed to the object of public finance...

[H]owever small any State may be, civil societies are always too populous to be under the immediate government of all their members. It is necessary that the public money should go through the hands of the rulers, all of whom have, besides the interests of the State, their own individual interests, which are not the last to be listened to. The people, on its side, perceiving rather the cupidity and ridiculous expenditure of its rulers than the public needs, murmurs at seeing itself stripped of necessaries to furnish others with superfluities; and when once these complaints have reached a certain degree of bitterness, the most upright administration will find it impossible to restore confidence. In such a case, voluntary contributions bring in nothing, and forced contributions are illegitimate. This cruel alternative of letting the State perish, or of violating the sacred right of property, which is its support, constitutes the great difficulty of just and prudent economy.

The first step which the founder of a republic ought to take after the establishment of laws, is to settle a sufficient fund for the maintenance of the Magistrates and other Officials, and for other public expenses. This fund, if it consist of money, is called *ærarium* or *fisc*, and *public demesne* if it consist of lands...

Before any use is made of this fund, it should be assigned or accepted by an assembly of the people, or of the estates of the country, which should determine its future use. After this solemnity, which makes such funds inalienable, their very nature is, in a manner, changed, and the revenues become so sacred, that it is not only the most infamous theft, but actual treason, to misapply them or pervert them from the purpose for which they were destined... For when vice is no longer dishonourable, what chiefs will be so scrupulous as to abstain from touching the public revenues that are left to their discretion, and even not in time to impose on themselves, by pretending to confound their own expensive and scandalous dissipations with the glory of the State, and the means of extending their own authority with the means of augmenting its power? It is particularly in this delicate part of the administration that virtue is the only effective instrument, and that the integrity of the Magistrate is the only real check upon his avarice. Books and auditing of accounts, instead of exposing frauds, only conceal them; for prudence is never so ready to conceive new precautions as knavery is to elude them. Never mind, then, about account books and papers; place the management of finance in honest hands: that is the only way to get it faithfully conducted...

But apart from the public demesne, which is of service to the State in proportion to the uprightness of those who govern, any one sufficiently acquainted with the whole force of the general administration, especially when it confines itself to legitimate methods, would be astonished at the resources the rulers can make use of for guarding against public needs, without trespassing on the goods of individuals. As they are masters of the whole commerce of the State, nothing is easier for them than to direct it into such channels as to provide for every need, without appearing to interfere. The distribution of provisions, money, and merchandise in just proportions, according to times and places, is the true secret of finance and the source of wealth, provided those who administer it have foresight enough to suffer a present apparent loss, in order really to obtain immense profits in the future...

If we ask how the needs of a State grow, we shall find they generally arise, like the wants of individuals, less from any real necessity than from the increase of useless desires, and that expenses are often augmented only to give a pretext for raising receipts: so that the State would sometimes gain by not being rich, and apparent wealth is in reality more burdensome than poverty itself would be. Rulers may indeed hope to keep the peoples in stricter dependence, by thus giving them with one hand what they take from them with the other; and this was in fact the policy of Joseph towards the Egyptians: but this political sophistry is the more fatal to the State, as the money never returns into the hands it went out of. Such principles only enrich the idle at the expense of the industrious...

It should be remembered that the foundation of the social compact is property; and its first condition, that every one should be maintained in the peaceful possession of what belongs to him. It is true that, by the same treaty, every one binds himself, at least tacitly, to be assessed toward the public wants: but as this undertaking cannot prejudice the fundamental law, and presupposes that the need is clearly recognised by all who contribute to it, it is plain that such assessment, in order to be lawful, must be voluntary; it must depend, not indeed on a particular will, as if it were necessary to have the consent of each individual, and that he should give no more than just what he pleased, but on a general will, decided by vote of a majority, and on the basis of a proportional rating which leaves nothing arbitrary in the imposition of the tax.

That taxes cannot be legitimately established except by the consent of the people or its representatives, is a truth generally admitted by all philosophers and jurists of any repute on questions of public right, not even excepting Bodin. If any of them have laid down rules which seem to contradict this, their particular motives for doing so may easily be seen; and they introduce so many conditions and restrictions that the argument comes at bottom to the same thing: for whether the people has it in its power to refuse, or the Sovereign ought not to exact, is a matter of indifference with regard to right; and if the point in question concerns only power, it is useless to inquire whether it is legitimate or not. Contributions levied on the people are two kinds; real, levied on commodities, and personal, paid by the head. Both are called taxes or subsidies: when the people fixes the sum to be paid, it is called subsidy; but when it grants the product of an imposition, it is called a tax. We are told in the *Spirit of the Laws* that a capitation tax is most suited to slavery, and a real tax most in accordance with liberty. This would be incontestable, if the circumstances of every person were equal; for otherwise nothing can be more disproportionate than such a tax; and it is in the observations of exact proportions that the spirit of liberty consists. But if a tax by heads were exactly proportioned to the circumstances of individuals, as what is called the capitation tax in France might be, is would be the most equitable and consequently the most proper for free-men.

These proportions appear at first very easy to note, because, being relative to each man's position in the world, their incidence is always public: but proper regard is seldom paid to all the elements that should enter into such a calculation, even apart from deception arising from avarice, fraud and self-interest. In the first place, we have to consider the relation of quantities, according to which, *ceteris paribus*, the person who has ten times the property of another man ought to pay ten times as much to the State. Secondly, the relation of the use made, that is to say, the distinction between necessaries and superfluities. He who possesses only the common necessaries of life should pay nothing at all, while the tax on him who is in possession of superfluities may justly be extended to everything he has over and above mere necessaries. To this he will possibly object that, when his rank is taken into account, what may be superfluous to a man of inferior station is necessary for him. But this is false: for a grandee has two legs just like a cow-herd, and, like him again, but one belly. Besides, these pretended necessaries are really so little necessary to his rank, that if he should renounce them on any worthy occasion, he would only be the more honoured. The populace would be ready to adore a Minister who went to Council on foot, because he had sold off his carriages to supply a pressing need of the State. Lastly, to no man does the law prescribe magnificence; and propriety is no argument against right.

A third relation, which is never taken into account, though it ought to be the chief consideration, is the advantage that every person derives from the social confederacy; for this provides a powerful protection for the immense possessions of the rich, and hardly leaves the poor man in quiet possession of the cottage he builds with his own hands. Are not all the advantages of society for the rich and powerful? Are not all lucrative posts in their hands? Are not all privileges and exemptions reserved for them alone? Is not the public authority always on their side? If a man of eminence robs his creditors, or is guilty of other knaveries, is he not always assured of impunity? Are not the assaults, acts of violence, assassinations, and even murders committed by the great, matters that are hushed up in a few months, and of which nothing more is thought? But if a great man himself is robbed or insulted, the whole police force is immediately in motion, and woe even to innocent persons who chance to be suspected. If he has to pass through any dangerous road, the country is up in arms to escort him. If the axle-tree of his chaise breaks, everybody flies to his assistance. If there is a noise at his door, he speaks but a word, and all is silent. If he is incommoded by the crowd, he waves his hand and every one makes way. If his coach is met on the road by a wagon, his servants are ready to beat the driver's brains out, and fifty honest pedestrians going quietly about their business had better be knocked on the head than an idle jackanapes be delayed in his coach. Yet all this respect costs him not a farthing: it is the rich man's right, and not what he buys with his wealth. How different is the case of the poor man! the more humanity owes him, the more society denies him. Every door is shut against him, even when he has a right to its being opened: and if ever he obtains justice, it is with much greater difficulty than others obtain favours. If the militia is to be raised or the highway to be mended, he is always given the preference; he always bears the burden which his richer neighbour has influence enough to get exempted from. On the least accident that happens to him, everybody avoids him: if his cart be overturned in the road, so far is he from receiving any assistance, that he is lucky if he does not get horse-whipped by the impudent lackeys of some young Duke; in a word, all gratuitous assistance is denied to the poor when they need it, just because they cannot pay for it. I look upon any poor man as totally undone, if he has the misfortune to have an honest heart, a fine daughter, and a powerful neighbour.

Another no less important fact is that the losses of the poor are much harder to repair than those of the rich, and that the difficulty of acquisition is always greater in proportion as there is more need for it. "Nothing comes out of nothing," is as true of life as in physics: money is the seed of money, and the first guinea is sometimes more difficult to acquire than the second million. Add to this that what the poor pay is lost to them for ever, and remains in, or returns to, the hands of the rich: and as, to those who share in the government or to their dependents, the whole produce of the taxes must sooner or later pass, although they pay their share, these persons have always a sensible interest in increasing them.

The terms of the social compact between these two estates of men may be summed up in a few words. "You have need of me, because I am rich and you are poor. We will therefore come to an agreement. I will permit you to have the honour of serving me, on condition that you bestow on me the little you have left, in return for the pains I shall take to command you."

Putting all these considerations carefully together, we shall find that, in order to levy taxes in a truly equitable and proportionate manner, the imposition ought not to be in simple ratio to the property of the contributors, but in compound ratio to the difference of their conditions and the superfluity of their possessions. This very important and difficult operation is daily made by numbers of honest clerks, who know their arithmetic; but a Plato or a Montesquieu would not venture to undertake it without the greatest diffidence, or without praying to Heaven for understanding and integrity...

We may add to all this a very important distinction in matters of political right, to which governments, constantly tenacious of doing everything for themselves, ought to pay great attention. It has been observed that personal taxes and duties on the necessaries of life, as they directly trespass on the right of property, and consequently on the true foundation of political society, are always liable to have dangerous results, if they are not established with the express consent of the people or its representatives. It is not the same with articles the use of which we can deny ourselves; for as the individual is under no absolute necessity to pay, his contribution may count as voluntary. The particular consent of each contributor then takes the place of the general consent of the whole people: for why should a people oppose the imposition of a tax which falls only on those who desire to pay it? It appears to me certain that everything, which is not proscribed by law, or contrary to morality, and yet may be prohibited by the government, may also be permitted on payment of a certain duty. Thus, for example, if the government may prohibit the use of coaches, it may certainly impose a tax on them; and this is a prudent and useful method of censuring their use without absolutely forbidding it. In this case, the tax may be regarded as a sort of fine, the product of which compensates for the abuse it punishes.

It may perhaps be objected that those, whom Bodin calls *impostors*, i.e. those who impose or contrive the taxes, being in the class of the rich, will be far from sparing themselves to relieve the poor. But this is quite beside the point. If, in every nation, those to whom the Sovereign commits the government of the people, were, from their position, its enemies, it would not be worth while to inquire what they ought to do to make the people happy.

Note

1 Rousseau selections are from Jean-Jacques Rousseau, *The Social Contract and Discourses*, translated with introduction by G.D.H. Cole (New York: E.P. Dutton & Co., 1913).

THE SOCIAL CONTRACT
(1762)

BOOK I

I mean to inquire if, in the civil order, there can be any sure and legitimate rule of administration, men being taken as they are and laws as they might be. In this inquiry I shall endeavour always to unite what right sanctions with what is prescribed by interest, in order that justice and utility may in no case be divided.

I enter upon my task without proving the importance of the subject. I shall be asked if I am a prince or a legislator, to write on politics. I answer that I am neither, and that is why I do so. If I were a prince or a legislator, I should not waste time in saying what wants doing; I should do it, or hold my peace.

As I was born a citizen of a free State, and a member of the Sovereign, I feel that, however feeble the influence my voice can have on public affairs, the right of voting on them makes it my duty to study them: and I am happy, when I reflect upon governments, to find my inquiries always furnish me with new reasons for loving that of my own country.

CHAPTER I

Subject of the first book

Man is born free; and everywhere he is in chains. One thinks himself the master of others, and still remains a greater slave than they. How did this change come about? I do not know. What can make it legitimate? That question I think I can answer.

If I took into account only force, and the effects derived from it, I should say: "As long as a people is compelled to obey, and obeys, it does well; as soon as it can shake off the yoke, and shakes it off, it does still better; for, regaining its liberty by the same right as took it away, either it is justified in resuming it, or there was no justification for those who took it away." But the social order is a sacred right which is the basis of all other rights. Nevertheless, this right does not come from nature, and must therefore be founded on conventions. Before coming to that, I have to prove what I have just asserted.

CHAPTER II

The first societies

The most ancient of all societies, and the only one that is natural, is the family: and even so the children remain attached to the father only so long as they need him for their preservation. As soon as this need ceases, the natural bond is dissolved. The children, released from the obedience they owed to the father, and the father, released from the care he owed his children, return equally to independence. If they remain united, they continue so no longer naturally, but voluntarily; and the family itself is then maintained only by convention.

This common liberty results from the nature of man. His first law is to provide for his own preservation, his first cares are those which he owes to himself; and, as soon as he reaches years of discretion, he is the sole judge of the proper means of preserving himself, and consequently becomes his own master.

The family then may be called the first model of political societies: the ruler corresponds to the father, and the people to the children; and all, being born free and equal, alienate their liberty only for their own advantage. The whole difference is that, in the family, the love of the father for his children repays him for the care he takes of them, while, in the State, the pleasure of commanding takes the place of the love which the chief cannot have for the peoples under him.

Grotius denies that all human power is established in favour of the governed, and quotes slavery as an example. His usual method of reasoning is constantly to establish right by fact.[1] It would be possible to employ a more logical method, but none could be more favourable to tyrants.

It is then, according to Grotius, doubtful whether the human race belongs to a hundred men, or that hundred men to the human race: and, throughout his book, he seems to incline to the former alternative, which is also the view of Hobbes. On this showing, the human species is divided into so many herds of cattle, each with its ruler, who keeps guard over them for the purpose of devouring them.

As a shepherd is of a nature superior to that of his flock, the shepherds of men, *i.e.* their rulers, are of a nature superior to that of the peoples under them. Thus, Philo tells us, the Emperor Caligula reasoned, concluding equally well either that kings were gods, or that men were beasts.

The reasoning of Caligula agrees with that of Hobbes and Grotius. Aristotle, before any of them, had said that men are by no means equal naturally, but that some are born for slavery, and others for dominion.

Aristotle was right; but he took the effect for the cause. Nothing can be more certain than that every man born in slavery is born for slavery. Slaves lose everything in their chains, even the desire of escaping from them: they love their servitude, as the comrades of Ulysses loved their brutish condition.[2] If then there are slaves by nature, it is because there have been slaves against nature. Force made the first slaves, and their cowardice perpetuated the condition.

I have said nothing of King Adam, or Emperor Noah, father of the three great monarchs who shared out the universe, like the children of Saturn, whom some scholars have recognised in them. I trust to getting due thanks for my moderation; for, being a direct descendant of one of these princes, perhaps of the eldest branch, how do I know that a verification of titles might not leave me the legitimate king of the human race? In any case, there can be no doubt that Adam was sovereign of the world, as Robinson Crusoe was of his island, as long as he was its only inhabitant; and this empire had the advantage that the monarch, safe on his throne, had no rebellions, wars, or conspirators to fear.

CHAPTER III

The right of the strongest

The strongest is never strong enough to be always the master, unless he transforms strength into right, and obedience into duty. Hence the right of the strongest, which, though to all seeming meant ironically, is really laid down as a fundamental principle. But are we never to have an explanation of this phrase? Force is a physical power, and I fail to see what moral effect it can have. To yield to force is an act of necessity, not of will—at the most, an act of prudence. In what sense can it be a duty?

Suppose for a moment that this so-called "right" exists. I maintain that the sole result is a mass of inexplicable nonsense. For, if force creates right, the effect changes with the cause: every force that is greater than the first succeeds to its right. As soon as it is possible to disobey with impunity, disobedience is legitimate; and, the strongest being always in the right, the only thing that matters is to act so as to become the strongest. But what kind of right is that which perishes when force fails? If we must obey perforce, there is no need to obey because we ought; and if we are not forced to obey, we are under no obligation to do so. Clearly, the word "right" adds nothing to force: in this connection, it means absolutely nothing.

Obey the powers that be. If this means yield to force, it is a good precept, but superfluous: I can answer for its never being violated. All power comes from God, I admit; but so does all sickness: does that mean that we are forbidden to call in the doctor? A brigand surprises me at the edge of a wood: must I not merely surrender my purse on compulsion; but, even if I could withhold it, am I in conscience bound to give it up? For certainly the pistol he holds is also a power.

Let us then admit that force does not create right, and that we are obliged to obey only legitimate powers. In that case, my original question recurs.

CHAPTER IV

Slavery

Since no man has a natural authority over his fellow, and force creates no right, we must conclude that conventions form the basis of all legitimate authority among men.

If an individual, says Grotius, can alienate his liberty and make himself the slave of a master, why could not a whole people do the same and make itself subject to a king? There are in this passage plenty of ambiguous words which would need explaining; but let us confine ourselves to the word *alienate*. To alienate is to give or to sell. Now, a man who becomes the slave of another does not give himself; he sells himself, at the least for his subsistence: but for what does a people sell itself? A king is so far from furnishing his subjects with their subsistence that he gets his own only from them; and, according to Rabelais, kings do not live on nothing. Do subjects then give their persons on condition that the king takes their goods also? I fail to see what they have left to preserve.

It will be said that the despot assures his subjects civil tranquillity. Granted; but what do they gain, if the wars his ambition brings down upon them, his insatiable avidity, and the vexatious conduct of his ministers press harder on them than their own dissensions would have done? What do they gain, if the very tranquillity they enjoy is one of their miseries? Tranquillity is found also in dungeons; but is that enough to make them desirable places to live in? The Greeks imprisoned in the cave of the Cyclops lived there very tranquilly, while they were awaiting their turn to be devoured.

To say that a man gives himself gratuitously, is to say what is absurd and inconceivable; such an act is null and illegitimate, from the mere fact that he who does it is out of his mind. To say the same of a whole people is to suppose a people of madmen; and madness creates no right.

Even if each man could alienate himself, he could not alienate his children: they are born men and free; their liberty belongs to them, and no one but they has the right to dispose of it. Before they come to years of discretion, the father can, in their name, lay down conditions for their preservation and well-being, but he cannot give them irrevocably and without conditions: such a gift is contrary to the ends of nature, and exceeds the rights of paternity. It would therefore be necessary, in order to legitimise an arbitrary government, that in every generation the people should be in a position to accept or reject it; but, were this so, the government would be no longer arbitrary.

To renounce liberty is to renounce being a man, to surrender the rights of humanity and even its duties. For him who renounces everything no indemnity is possible. Such a renunciation is incompatible with man's nature; to remove all liberty from his will is to remove all morality from his acts. Finally, it is an empty and contradictory convention that sets up, on the one side, absolute authority, and, on the other, unlimited obedience. Is it not clear that we can be under no obligation to a person from whom we have the right to exact everything? Does not this condition alone, in the absence of equivalence or exchange, in itself involve the nullity of the act? For what right can my slave have against me, when all that he has belongs to me, and, his right being mine, this right of mine against myself is a phrase devoid of meaning?

Grotius and the rest find in war another origin for the so-called right of slavery. The victor having, as they hold, the right of killing the vanquished, the latter can buy back his life at the price of his liberty; and this convention is the more legitimate because it is to the advantage of both parties.

But it is clear that this supposed right to kill the conquered is by no means deducible from the state of war. Men, from the mere fact that, while they are living in their primitive independence, they have no mutual relations stable enough to constitute either the state of peace or the state of war, cannot be naturally enemies. War is constituted by a relation between things, and not between persons; and, as the state of war cannot arise out of simple personal relations, but only out of real relations, private war, or war of man with man, can exist neither in the state of nature, where there is no constant property, nor in the social state, where everything is under the authority of the laws.

Individual combats, duels and encounters, are acts which cannot constitute a state; while the private wars, authorised by the Establishments of Louis IX, King of France, and suspended by the Peace of God, are abuses of feudalism, in itself an absurd system if ever there was one, and contrary to the principles of natural right and to all good polity.

War then is a relation, not between man and man, but between State and State, and individuals are enemies only accidentally, not as men, nor even as citizens,[3] but as soldiers; not as members of their country, but as its defenders. Finally, each State can have for enemies only other States, and not men; for between things disparate in nature there can be no real relation.

Furthermore, this principle is in conformity with the established rules of all times and the constant practice of all civilised peoples.

Declarations of war are intimations less to powers than to their subjects. The foreigner, whether king, individual, or people, who robs, kills or detains the subjects, without declaring war on the prince, is not an enemy, but a brigand. Even in real war, a just prince, while laying hands, in the enemy's country, on all that belongs to the public, respects the lives and goods of individuals: he respects rights on which his own are founded. The object of the war being the destruction of the hostile State, the other side has a right to kill its defenders, while they are bearing arms; but as soon as they lay them down and surrender, they cease to be enemies or instruments of the enemy, and become once more merely men, whose life no one has any right to take. Sometimes it is possible to kill the State without killing a single one of its members; and war gives no right which is not necessary to the gaining of its object. These principles are not those of Grotius: they are not based on the authority of poets, but derived from the nature of reality and based on reason.

The right of conquest has no foundation other than the right of the strongest. If war does not give the conqueror the right to massacre the conquered peoples, the right to enslave them cannot be based upon a right which does not exist. No one has a right to kill an enemy except when he cannot make him a slave, and the right to enslave him cannot therefore be derived from the right to kill him. It is accordingly an unfair exchange to make him buy at the price of his liberty his life, over which the victor holds no right. Is it not clear that there is a vicious circle in founding the right of life and death on the right of slavery, and the right of slavery on the right of life and death?

Even if we assume this terrible right to kill everybody, I maintain that a slave made in war, or a conquered people, is under no obligation to a master, except to obey him as far as he is compelled to do so. By taking an equivalent for his life, the victor has not done him a favour; instead of killing him without profit, he has killed him usefully. So far then is he from acquiring over him any authority in addition to that of force, that the state of war continues to subsist between them: their mutual relation is the effect of it, and the usage of the right of war does not imply a treaty of peace. A convention has indeed been made; but this convention, so far from destroying the state of war, presupposes its continuance.

So, from whatever aspect we regard the question, the right of slavery is null and void, not only as being illegitimate, but also because it is absurd and meaningless. The words *slave* and *right* contradict each other, and are mutually exclusive. It will always be equally foolish for a man to say to a man or to a people: "I make with you a convention wholly at your expense and wholly to my advantage; I shall keep it as long as I like, and you will keep it as long as I like."

THE SOCIAL CONTRACT (1762)

CHAPTER V

That we must always go back to a first convention

Even if I granted all that I have been refuting, the friends of despotism would be no better off. There will always be a great difference between subduing a multitude and ruling a society. Even if scattered individuals were successively enslaved by one man, however numerous they might be, I still see no more than a master and his slaves, and certainly not a people and its ruler; I see what may be termed an aggregation, but not an association; there is as yet neither public good nor body politic. The man in question, even if he has enslaved half the world, is still only an individual; his interest, apart from that of others, is still a purely private interest. If this same man comes to die, his empire, after him, remains scattered and without unity, as an oak falls and dissolves into a heap of ashes when the fire has consumed it.

A people, says Grotius, can give itself to a king. Then, according to Grotius, a people is a people before it gives itself. The gift is itself a civil act, and implies public deliberation. It would be better, before examining the act by which a people gives itself to a king, to examine that by which it has become a people; for this act, being necessarily prior to the other, is the true foundation of society.

Indeed, if there were no prior convention, where, unless the election were unanimous, would be the obligation on the minority to submit to the choice of the majority? How have a hundred men who wish for a master the right to vote on behalf of ten who do not? The law of majority voting is itself something established by convention, and presupposes unanimity, on one occasion at least.

CHAPTER VI

The social compact

I suppose men to have reached the point at which the obstacles in the way of their preservation in the state of nature show their power of resistance to be greater than the resources at the disposal of each individual for his maintenance in that state. That primitive condition can then subsist no longer; and the human race would perish unless it changed its manner of existence.

But, as men cannot engender new forces, but only unite and direct existing ones, they have no other means of preserving themselves than the formation, by aggregation, of a sum of forces great enough to overcome the resistance. These they have to bring into play by means of a single motive power, and cause to act in concert.

This sum of forces can arise only where several persons come together: but, as the force and liberty of each man are the chief instruments of his self-preservation, how can he pledge them without harming his own interests, and neglecting the care he owes to himself? This difficulty, in its bearing on my present subject, may be stated in the following terms:

"The problem is to find a form of association which will defend and protect with the whole common force the person and goods of each associate, and in which each, while uniting himself with all, may still obey himself alone, and remain as free as before." This is the fundamental problem of which the *Social Contract* provides the solution.

The clauses of this contract are so determined by the nature of the act that the slightest modification would make them vain and ineffective; so that, although they have perhaps never been formally set forth, they are everywhere the same and everywhere tacitly admitted and recognised, until, on the violation of the social compact, each regains his original rights and resumes his natural liberty, while losing the conventional liberty in favour of which he renounced it.

These clauses, properly understood, may be reduced to one—the total alienation of each associate, together with all his rights, to the whole community; for, in the first place, as each gives himself absolutely, the conditions are the same for all; and, this being so, no one has any interest in making them burdensome to others.

Moreover, the alienation being without reserve, the union is as perfect as it can be, and no associate has anything more to demand: for, if the individuals retained certain rights, as there would be no common superior to decide between them and the public, each, being on one point his own judge, would ask to be so on all; the state of nature would thus continue, and the association would necessarily become inoperative or tyrannical.

Finally, each man, in giving himself to all, gives himself to nobody; and as there is no associate over whom he does not acquire the same right as he yields others over himself, he gains an equivalent for everything he loses, and an increase of force for the preservation of what he has.

If then we discard from the social compact what is not of its essence, we shall find that it reduces itself to the following terms:

> "Each of us puts his person and all his power in common under the supreme direction of the general will, and, in our corporate capacity, we receive each member as an indivisible part of the whole."

At once, in place of the individual personality of each contracting party, this act of association creates a moral and collective body, composed of as many members as the assembly contains votes, and receiving from this act its unity, its common identity, its life and its will. This public person, so formed by the union of all other persons formerly took the name of *city*,[4] and now takes that of *Republic* or *body politic*; it is called by its members *State* when passive. *Sovereign* when active, and *Power* when compared with others like itself. Those who are associated in it take collectively the name of *people*, and severally are called *citizens*, as sharing in the sovereign power, and *subjects*, as being under the laws of the State. But these terms are often confused and taken one for another: it is enough to know how to distinguish them when they are being used with precision.

CHAPTER VII

The sovereign

This formula shows us that the act of association comprises a mutual undertaking between the public and the individuals, and that each individual, in making a contract, as we may say, with himself, is bound in a double capacity; as a member of the Sovereign he is bound to the individuals, and as a member of the State to the Sovereign. But the maxim of civil right, that no one is bound by undertakings made to himself, does not apply in this case; for there is a great difference between incurring an obligation to yourself and incurring one to a whole of which you form a part.

Attention must further be called to the fact that public deliberation, while competent to bind all the subjects to the Sovereign, because of the two different capacities in which each of them may be regarded, cannot, for the opposite reason, bind the Sovereign to itself; and that it is consequently against the nature of the body politic for the Sovereign to impose on itself a law which it cannot infringe. Being able to regard itself in only one capacity, it is in the position of an individual who makes a contract with himself; and this makes it clear that there neither is nor can be any kind of fundamental law binding on the body of the people—not even the social contract itself. This does not mean that the body politic cannot enter into undertakings with others, provided the contract is not infringed by them; for in relation to what is external to it, it becomes a simple being, an individual.

But the body politic or the Sovereign, drawing its being wholly from the sanctity of the contract, can never bind itself, even to an outsider, to do anything derogatory to the original act, for instance, to alienate any part of itself, or to submit to another Sovereign. Violation of the act by which it exists would be self-annihilation; and that which is itself nothing can create nothing.

As soon as this multitude is so united in one body, it is impossible to offend against one of the members without attacking the body, and still more to offend against the body without the members resenting it. Duty and interest therefore equally oblige the two contracting parties to give each other help; and the same men should seek to combine, in their double capacity, all the advantages dependent upon that capacity.

Again, the Sovereign, being formed wholly of the individuals who compose it, neither has nor can have any interest contrary to theirs; and consequently the sovereign power need give no guarantee to its subjects, because it is impossible for the body to wish to hurt all its members. We shall also see later on that it cannot hurt any in particular. The Sovereign, merely by virtue of what it is, is always what it should be.

This, however, is not the case with the relation of the subjects to the Sovereign, which, despite the common interest, would have no security that they would fulfil their undertakings, unless it found means to assure itself of their fidelity.

In fact, each individual, as a man, may have a particular will contrary or dissimilar to the general will which he has as a citizen. His particular interest may speak to him quite differently from the common interest: his absolute and naturally independent existence may make him look upon what he owes to the common cause as a gratuitous contribution, the loss of which will do less harm to others than the payment of it is burdensome to himself; and, regarding the moral person which constitutes the State as a *persona ficta*, because not a man, he may wish to enjoy the rights of citizenship without being ready to fulfil the duties of a subject. The continuance of such an injustice could not but prove the undoing of the body politic.

In order then that the social compact may not be an empty formula, it tacitly includes the undertaking, which alone can give force to the rest, that whoever refuses to obey the general will shall be compelled to do so by the whole body. This means nothing less than that he will be forced to be free; for this is the condition which, by giving each citizen to his country, secures him against all personal dependence. In this lies the key to the working of the political machine; this alone legitimises civil undertakings, which, without it, would be absurd, tyrannical, and liable to the most frightful abuses.

CHAPTER VIII

The civil state

The passage from the state of nature to the civil state produces a very remarkable change in man, by substituting justice for instinct in his conduct, and giving his actions the morality they had formerly lacked. Then only, when the voice of duty takes the place of physical impulses and right of appetite, does man, who so far had considered only himself, find that he is forced to act on different principles, and to consult his reason before listening to his inclinations. Although, in this state, he deprives himself of some advantages which he got from nature, he gains in return others so great, his faculties are so stimulated and developed, his ideas so extended, his feelings so ennobled, and his whole soul so uplifted, that, did not the abuses of this new condition often degrade him below that which he left, he would be bound to bless continually the happy moment which took him from it for ever, and, instead of a stupid and unimaginative animal, made him an intelligent being and a man.

Let us draw up the whole account in terms easily commensurable. What man loses by the social contract is his natural liberty and an unlimited right to everything he tries to get and succeeds in getting; what he gains is civil liberty and the proprietorship of all he possesses. If we are to avoid mistake in weighing one against the other, we must clearly distinguish natural liberty, which is bounded only by the strength of the individual, from civil liberty, which is limited by the general will; and possession, which is merely the effect of force or the right of the first occupier, from property, which can be founded only on a positive title.

We might, over and above all this, add, to what man acquires in the civil state, moral liberty, which alone makes him truly master of himself; for the mere impulse of appetite is slavery, while obedience to a law which we prescribe to ourselves is liberty. But I have already said too much on this head, and the philosophical meaning of the word liberty does not now concern us.

CHAPTER IX

Real property

Each member of the community gives himself to it, at the moment of its foundation, just as he is, with all the resources at his command, including the goods he possesses. This act does not make possession, in changing hands, change its nature, and become property in the hands of the Sovereign; but, as the forces of the city are incomparably greater than those of an individual, public possession is also, in fact, stronger and more irrevocable, without being any more legitimate, at any rate from the point of view of foreigners. For the State, in relation to its members, is master of all their goods by the social contract, which, within the State, is the basis of all rights; but, in relation to other powers, it is so only by the right of the first occupier, which it holds from its members.

The right of the first occupier, though more real than the right of the strongest, becomes a real right only when the right of property has already been established. Every man has naturally a right to everything he needs; but the positive act which makes him proprietor of one thing excludes him from everything else. Having his share, he ought to keep to it, and can have no further right against the community. This is why the right of the first occupier, which in the state of nature is so weak, claims the respect of every man in civil society. In this right we are respecting not so much what belongs to another as what does not belong to ourselves.

In general, to establish the right of the first occupier over a plot of ground, the following conditions are necessary: first, the land must not yet be inhabited; secondly, a man must occupy only the amount he needs for his subsistence; and, in the third place, possession must be taken, not by an empty ceremony, but by labour and cultivation, the only sign of proprietorship that should be respected by others, in default of a legal title.

In granting the right of first occupancy to necessity and labour, are we not really stretching it as far as it can go? Is it possible to leave such a right unlimited? Is it to be enough to set foot on a plot of common ground, in order to be able to call yourself at once the master of it? Is it to be enough that a man has the strength to expel others for a moment, in order to establish his right to prevent them from ever returning? How can a man or a people seize an immense territory and keep it from the rest of the world except by a punishable usurpation, since all others are being robbed, by such an act, of the place of habitation and the means of subsistence which nature gave them in common? When Nunez Balboa, standing on the seashore, took possession of the South Seas and the whole of South America in the name of the crown of Castile, was that enough to dispossess all their actual inhabitants, and to shut out from them all the princes of the world? On such a showing, these ceremonies are idly multiplied, and the Catholic King need only take possession all at once, from his apartment, of the whole universe, merely making a subsequent reservation about what was already in the possession of other princes.

We can imagine how the lands of individuals, where they were contiguous and came to be united, became the public territory, and how the right of Sovereignty, extending from the subjects over the lands they held, became at once real and personal. The possessors were thus made more dependent, and the forces at their command used to guarantee their fidelity. The advantage of this does not seem to have been felt by ancient monarchs, who called themselves Kings of the Persians, Scythians, or Macedonians, and seemed to regard themselves more as rulers of men than as masters of a country. Those of the present day more cleverly call themselves Kings of France, Spain, England, etc.: thus holding the land, they are quite confident of holding the inhabitants.

The peculiar fact about this alienation is that, in taking over the goods of individuals, the community, so far from despoiling them, only assures them legitimate possession, and changes usurpation into a true right and enjoyment into proprietorship. Thus the possessors, being regarded as depositaries of the public good, and having their rights respected by all the members of the State and maintained against foreign aggression by all its forces, have, by a cession which benefits both the public and still more themselves, acquired, so to speak, all that they gave up. This paradox may easily be explained by the distinction between the rights which the Sovereign and the proprietor have over the same estate, as we shall see later on.

It may also happen that men begin to unite one with another before they possess anything, and that, subsequently occupying a tract of country which is enough for all, they enjoy it in common, or share it out among themselves, either equally or according to a scale fixed by the Sovereign. However the acquisition be made, the right which each individual has to his own estate is always subordinate to the right which the community has over all: without this, there would be neither stability in the social tie, nor real force in the exercise of Sovereignty.

I shall end this chapter and this book by remarking on a fact on which the whole social system should rest: *i.e.* that, instead of destroying natural inequality, the fundamental compact substitutes, for such physical inequality as nature may have set up between men, an equality that is moral and legitimate, and that men, who may be unequal in strength or intelligence, become every one equal by convention and legal right.[5]

BOOK II

CHAPTER I

That sovereignty is inalienable

The first and most important deduction from the principles we have so far laid down is that the general will alone can direct the State according to the object for which it was instituted, *i.e.* the common good: for if the clashing of particular interests made the establishment of societies necessary, the agreement of these very interests made it possible. The common element in these different interests is what forms the social tie; and, were there no point of agreement between them all, no society could exist. It is solely on the basis of this common interest that every society should be governed.

I hold then that Sovereignty, being nothing less than the exercise of the general will, can never be alienated, and that the Sovereign, who is no less than a collective being, cannot be represented except by himself: the power indeed may be transmitted, but not the will.

In reality, if it is not impossible for a particular will to agree on some point with the general will, it is at least impossible for the agreement to be lasting and constant; for the particular will tends, by its very nature, to partiality, while the general will tends to equality. It is even more impossible to have any guarantee of this agreement; for even if it should always exist, it would be the effect not of art, but of chance. The Sovereign may indeed say: "I now will actually what this man wills, or at least what he says he wills"; but it cannot say: "What he wills tomorrow, I too shall will" because it is absurd for the will to bind itself for the future, nor is it incumbent on any will to consent to anything that is not for the good of the being who wills. If then the people promises simply to obey, by that very act it dissolves itself and loses what makes it a people; the moment a master exists, there is no longer a Sovereign, and from that moment the body politic has ceased to exist.

This does not mean that the commands of the rulers cannot pass for general wills, so long as the Sovereign, being free to oppose them, offers no opposition. In such a case, universal silence is taken to imply the consent of the people. This will be explained later on.

CHAPTER II

That sovereignty is indivisible

Sovereignty, for the same reason as makes it inalienable, is indivisible; for will either is, or is not, general;[6] it is the will either of the body of the people, or only of a part of it. In the first case, the will, when declared, is an act of Sovereignty and constitutes law: in the second, it is merely a particular will, or act of magistracy—at the most a decree.

But our political theorists, unable to divide Sovereignty in principle, divide it according to its object: into force and will; into legislative power and executive power; into rights of taxation, justice and war; into internal administration and power of foreign treaty. Sometimes they confuse all these sections, and sometimes they distinguish them; they turn the Sovereign into a fantastic being composed of several connected pieces: it is as if they were making man of several bodies, one with eyes, one with arms, another with feet, and each with nothing besides. We are told that the jugglers of Japan dismember a child before the eyes of the spectators; then they throw all the members into the air one after another, and the child falls down alive and whole. The conjuring tricks of our political theorists are very like that; they first dismember the Body politic by an illusion worthy of a fair, and then join it together again we know not how.

This error is due to a lack of exact notions concerning the Sovereign authority, and to taking for parts of it what are only emanations from it. Thus, for example, the acts of declaring war and making peace have been regarded as acts of Sovereignty; but this is not the case, as these acts do not constitute law, but merely the application of a law, a particular act which decides how the law applies, as we shall see clearly when the idea attached to the word *law* has been defined.

If we examined the other divisions in the same manner, we should find that, whenever Sovereignty seems to be divided, there is an illusion: the rights which are taken as being part of Sovereignty are really all subordinate, and always imply supreme wills of which they only sanction the execution.

It would be impossible to estimate the obscurity this lack of exactness has thrown over the decisions of writers who have dealt with political right, when they have used the principles laid down by them to pass judgment on the respective rights of kings and peoples. Every one can see, in Chapters III and IV of the First Book of Grotius, how the learned man and his translator, Barbeyrac, entangle and tie themselves up in their own sophistries, for fear of saying too little or too much of what they think, and so offending the interests they have to conciliate. Grotius, a refugee in France, ill-content with his own country, and desirous of paying his court to Louis XIII, to whom his book is dedicated, spares no pains to rob the peoples of all their rights and invest kings with them by every conceivable artifice. This would also have been much to the taste of Barbeyrac, who dedicated his translation to George I of England. But unfortunately the expulsion of James II, which he called his "abdication," compelled him to use all reserve, to shuffle and to tergiversate, in order to avoid making William out a usurper. If these two writers had adopted the true principles, all difficulties would have been removed, and they would have been always consistent; but it would have been a sad truth for them to tell, and would have paid court for them to no one save the people. Moreover, truth is no road to fortune, and the people dispenses neither ambassadorships, nor professorships, nor pensions.

CHAPTER III

Whether the general will is fallible

It follows from what has gone before that the general will is always right and tends to the public advantage; but it does not follow that the deliberations of the people are always equally correct. Our will is always for our own good, but we do not always see what that is; the people is never corrupted, but it is often deceived, and on such occasions only does it seem to will what is bad.

There is often a great deal of difference between the will of all and the general will; the latter considers only the common interest, while the former takes private interest into account, and is no more than a sum of particular wills: but take away from these same wills the pluses and minuses that cancel one another,[7] and the general will remains as the sum of the differences.

If, when the people, being furnished with adequate information, held its deliberations, the citizens had no communication one with another, the grand total of the small differences would always give the general will, and the decision would always be good. But when factions arise, and partial associations are formed at the expense of the great association, the will of each of these associations becomes general in relation to its members, while it remains particular in relation to the State: it may then be said that there are no longer as many votes as there are men, but only as many as there are associations. The differences become less numerous and give a less general result. Lastly, when one of these associations is so great as to prevail over all the rest, the result is no longer a sum of small differences, but a single difference; in this case there is no longer a general will, and the opinion which prevails is purely particular.

It is therefore essential, if the general will is to be able to express itself, that there should be no partial society within the State, and that each citizen should think only his own thoughts:[8] which was indeed the sublime and unique system established by the great Lycurgus. But if there are partial societies, it is best to have as many as possible and to prevent them from being unequal, as was done by Solon, Numa and Servius. These precautions are the only ones that can guarantee that the general will shall be always enlightened, and that the people shall in no way deceive itself.

CHAPTER IV

The limits of sovereign power

If the State is a moral person whose life is in the union of its members, and if the most important of its cares is the care for its own preservation, it must have a universal and compelling force, in order to move and dispose each part as may be most advantageous to the whole. As nature gives each man absolute power over all his members, the social compact gives the body politic absolute power over all its members also; and it is this power which, under the direction of the general will, bears, as I have said, the name of Sovereignty.

But, besides the public person, we have to consider the private persons composing it, whose life and liberty are naturally independent of it. We are bound then to distinguish clearly between the respective rights of the citizens and the Sovereign,[9] and between the duties the former have to fulfil as subjects, and the natural rights they should enjoy as men.

Each man alienates, I admit, by the social compact, only such part of his powers, goods and liberty as it is important for the community to control; but it must also be granted that the Sovereign is sole judge of what is important.

Every service a citizen can render the State he ought to render as soon as the Sovereign demands it; but the Sovereign, for its part, cannot impose upon its subjects any fetters that are useless to the community, nor can it even wish to do so; for no more by the law of reason than by the law of nature can anything occur without a cause.

The undertakings which bind us to the social body are obligatory only because they are mutual; and their nature is such that in fulfilling them we cannot work for others without working for ourselves. Why is it that the general will is always in the right, and that all continually will the happiness of each one, unless it is because there is not a man who does not think of "each" as meaning him, and consider himself in voting for all?

This proves that equality of rights and the idea of justice which such equality creates originate in the preference each man gives to himself, and accordingly in the very nature of man. It proves that the general will, to be really such, must be general in its object as well as its essence; that it must both come from all and apply to all; and that it loses its natural rectitude when it is directed to some particular and determinate object, because in such a case we are judging of something foreign to us, and have no true principle of equity to guide us.

Indeed, as soon as a question of particular fact or right arises on a point not previously regulated by a general convention, the matter becomes contentious. It is a case in which the individuals concerned are one party, and the public the other, but in which I can see neither the law that ought to be followed nor the judge who ought to give the decision. In such a case, it would be absurd to propose to refer the question to an express decision of the general will, which can be only the conclusion reached by one of the parties and in consequence will be, for the other party, merely an external and particular will, inclined on this occasion to injustice and subject to error. Thus, just as a particular will cannot stand for the general will, the general will, in turn, changes its nature, when its object is particular, and, as general, cannot pronounce on a man or a fact. When, for instance, the people of Athens nominated or displaced its rulers, decreed honours to one, and imposed penalties on another, and, by a multitude of particular decrees, exercised all the functions of government indiscriminately, it had in such cases no longer a general will in the strict sense; it was acting no longer as Sovereign, but as magistrate. This will seem contrary to current views; but I must be given time to expound my own.

It should be seen from the foregoing that what makes the will general is less the number of voters than the common interest uniting them; for, under this system, each necessarily submits to the conditions he imposes on others: and this admirable agreement between interest and justice gives to the common deliberations an equitable character which at once vanishes when any particular question is discussed, in the absence of a common interest to unite and identify the ruling of the judge with that of the party.

From whatever side we approach our principle, we reach the same conclusion, that the social compact sets up among the citizens an equality of such a kind, that they all bind themselves to observe the same conditions and should therefore all enjoy the same rights. Thus, from the very nature of the compact, every act of Sovereignty, *i.e.* every authentic act of the general will, binds or favours all the citizens equally; so that the Sovereign recognises only the body of the nation, and draws no distinctions between those of whom it is made up. What, then, strictly speaking, is an act of Sovereignty? It is not a convention between a superior and an inferior, but a convention between the body and each of its members. It is legitimate, because based on the social contract, and equitable, because common to all; useful, because it can have no other object than the general good, and stable, because guaranteed by the public force and the supreme power. So long as the subjects have to submit only to conventions of this sort, they obey no-one but their own will; and to ask how far the respective rights of the Sovereign and the citizens extend, is to ask up to what point the latter can enter into undertakings with themselves, each with all, and all with each.

We can see from this that the sovereign power, absolute, sacred and inviolable as it is, does not and cannot exceed the limits of general conventions, and that every man may dispose at will of such goods and liberty as these conventions leave him; so that the Sovereign never has a right to lay more charges on one subject than on another, because, in that case, the question becomes particular, and ceases to be within its competency.

When these distinctions have once been admitted, it is seen to be so untrue that there is, in the social contract, any real renunciation on the part of the individuals, that the position in which they find themselves as a result of the contract is really preferable to that in which they were before. Instead of a renunciation, they have made an advantageous exchange: instead of an uncertain and precarious way of living they have got one that is better and more secure; instead of natural independence they have got liberty, instead of the power to harm others security for themselves, and instead of their strength, which others might overcome, a right which social union makes invincible. Their very life, which they have devoted to the State, is by it constantly protected; and when they risk it in the State's defence, what more are they doing than giving back what they have received from it? What are they doing that they would not do more often and with greater danger in the state of nature, in which they would inevitably have to fight battles at the peril of their lives in defence of that which is the means of their preservation? All have indeed to fight when their country needs them; but then no one has ever to fight for himself. Do we not gain something by running, on behalf of what gives us our security, only some of the risks we should have to run for ourselves, as soon as we lost it?

CHAPTER V

The Right of Life and Death

The question is often asked how individuals, having no right to dispose of their own lives, can transfer to the Sovereign a right which they do not possess. The difficulty of answering this question seems to me to lie in its being wrongly stated. Every man has a right to risk his own life in order to preserve it. Has it ever been said that a man who throws himself out of the window to escape from a fire is guilty of suicide? Has such a crime ever been laid to the charge of him who perishes in a storm because, when he went on board, he knew of the danger?

The social treaty has for its end the preservation of the contracting parties. He who wills the end wills the means also, and the means must involve some risks, and even some losses. He who wishes to preserve his life at others' expense should also, when it is necessary, be ready to give it up for their sake. Furthermore, the citizen is no longer the judge of the dangers to which the law desires him to expose himself; and when the prince says to him: "It is expedient for the State that you should die," he ought to die, because it is only on that condition that he has been living in security up to the present, and because his life is no longer a mere bounty of nature, but a gift made conditionally by the State.

The death-penalty inflicted upon criminals may be looked on in much the same light: it is in order that we may not fall victims to an assassin that we consent to die if we ourselves turn assassins. In this treaty, so far from disposing of our own lives, we think only of securing them, and it is not to be assumed that any of the parties then expects to get hanged.

Again, every malefactor, by attacking social rights, becomes on forfeit a rebel and a traitor to his country; by violating its laws he ceases to be a member of it; he even makes war upon it. In such a case the preservation of the State is inconsistent with his own, and one or the other must perish; in putting the guilty to death, we slay not so much the citizen as an enemy. The trial and the judgment are the proofs that he has broken the social treaty, and is in consequence no longer a member of the State. Since, then, he has recognised himself to be such by living there, he must be removed by exile as a violator of the compact, or by death as a public enemy; for such an enemy is not a moral person, but merely a man; and in such a case the right of war is to kill the vanquished.

But, it will be said, the condemnation of a criminal is a particular act. I admit it: but such condemnation is not a function of the Sovereign; it is a right the Sovereign can confer without being able itself to exert it. All my ideas are consistent, but I cannot expound them all at once.

We may add that frequent punishments are always a sign of weakness or remissness on the part of the government. There is not a single ill-doer who could not be turned to some good. The State has no right to put to death, even for the sake of making an example, any one whom it can leave alive without danger.

The right of pardoning or exempting the guilty from a penalty imposed by the law and pronounced by the judge belongs only to the authority which is superior to both judge and law, *i.e.* the Sovereign; even its right in this matter is far from clear, and the cases for exercising it are extremely rare. In a well-governed State, there are few punishments, not because there are many pardons, but because criminals are rare; it is when a State is in decay that the multitude of crimes is a guarantee of impunity. Under the Roman Republic, neither the Senate nor the Consuls ever attempted to pardon; even the people never did so, though it sometimes revoked its own decision. Frequent pardons mean that crime will soon need them no longer, and no one can help seeing whither that leads. But I feel my heart protesting and restraining my pen; let us leave these questions to the just man who has never offended, and would himself stand in no need of pardon.

CHAPTER VI

Law

By the social compact we have given the body politic existence and life; we have now by legislation to give it movement and will. For the original act by which the body is formed and united still in no respect determines what it ought to do for its preservation.

What is well and in conformity with order is so by the nature of things and independently of human conventions. All justice comes from God, who is its sole source; but if we knew how to receive so high an inspiration, we should need neither government nor laws. Doubtless, there is a universal justice emanating from reason alone; but this justice, to be admitted among us, must be mutual. Humanly speaking, in default of natural sanctions, the laws of justice are ineffective among men: they merely make for the good of the wicked and the undoing of the just, when the just man observes them towards everybody and nobody observes them towards him. Conventions and laws are therefore needed to join rights to duties and refer justice to its object. In the state of nature, where everything is common, I owe nothing to him whom I have promised nothing; I recognise as belonging to others only what is of no use to me. In the state of society all rights are fixed by law, and the case becomes different.

But what, after all, is a law? As long as we remain satisfied with attaching purely metaphysical ideas to the word, we shall go on arguing without arriving at an understanding; and when we have defined a law of nature, we shall be no nearer the definition of a law of the State.

I have already said that there can be no general will directed to a particular object. Such an object must be either within or outside the State. If outside, a will which is alien to it cannot be, in relation to it, general; if within, it is part of the State, and in that case there arises a relation between whole and part which makes them two separate beings, of which the part is one, and the whole minus the part the other. But the whole minus a part cannot be the whole; and while this relation persists, there can be no whole, but only two unequal parts; and it follows that the will of one is no longer in any respect general in relation to the other.

But when the whole people decrees for the whole people, it is considering only itself; and if a relation is then formed, it is between two aspects of the entire object, without there being any division of the whole. In that case the matter about which the decree is made is, like the decreeing will, general. This act is what I call a law.

When I say that the object of laws is always general, I mean that law considers subjects *en masse* and actions in the abstract, and never a particular person or action. Thus the law may indeed decree that there shall be privileges, but cannot confer them on anybody by name. It may set up several classes of citizens, and even lay down the qualifications for membership of these classes, but it cannot nominate such and such persons as belonging to them; it may establish a monarchical government and hereditary succession, but it cannot choose a king, or nominate a royal family. In a word, no function which has a particular object belongs to the legislative power.

On this view, we at once see that it can no longer be asked whose business it is to make laws, since they are acts of the general will; nor whether the prince is above the law, since he is a member of the State; nor whether the law can be unjust, since no one is unjust to himself; nor how we can be both free and subject to the laws, since they are but registers of our wills.

We see further that, as the law unites universality of will with universality of object, what a man, whoever he be, commands of his own motion cannot be a law; and even what the Sovereign commands with regard to a particular matter is no nearer being a law, but is a decree, an act, not of sovereignty, but of magistracy.

I therefore give the name "Republic" to every State that is governed by laws, no matter what the form of its administration may be: for only in such a case does the public interest govern, and the *res publica* rank as a *reality*. Every legitimate government is republican;[10] what government is I will explain later on.

Laws are, properly speaking, only the conditions of civil association. The people, being subject to the laws, ought to be their author: the conditions of the society ought to be regulated solely by those who come together to form it. But how are they to regulate them? Is it to be by common agreement, by a sudden inspiration? Has the body politic an organ to declare its will? Who can give it the foresight to formulate and announce its acts in advance? Or how is it to announce them in the hour of need? How can a blind multitude, which often does not know what it wills, because it rarely knows what is good for it, carry out for itself so great and difficult an enterprise as a system of legislation? Of itself the people wills always the good, but of itself it by no means always sees it. The general will is always in the right, but the judgment which guides it is not always enlightened. It must be got to see objects as they are, and sometimes as they ought to appear to it; it must be shown the good road it is in search of, secured from the seductive influences of individual wills, taught to see times and spaces as a series, and made to weigh the attractions of present and sensible advantages against the danger of distant and hidden evils. The individuals see the good they reject; the public wills the good it does not see. All stand equally in need of guidance. The former must be compelled to bring their wills into conformity with their reason; the latter must be taught to know what it wills. If that is done, public enlightenment leads to the union of understanding and will in the social body: the parts are made to work exactly together, and the whole is raised to its highest power. This makes a legislator necessary.

CHAPTER VII

The Legislator

In order to discover the rules of society best suited to nations, a superior intelligence beholding all the passions of men without experiencing any of them would be needed. This intelligence would have to be wholly unrelated to our nature, while knowing it through and through; its happiness would have to be independent of us, and yet ready to occupy itself with ours; and lastly, it would have, in the march of time, to look forward to a distant glory, and, working in one century, to be able to enjoy in the next.[11] It would take gods to give men laws.

What Caligula argued from the facts, Plato, in the dialogue called the *Politicus*, argued in defining the civil or kingly man, on the basis of right. But if great princes are rare, how much more so are great legislators? The former have only to follow the pattern which the latter have to lay down. The legislator is the engineer who invents the machine, the prince merely the mechanic who sets it up and makes it go. "At the birth of societies," says Montesquieu, "the rulers of Republics establish institutions, and afterwards the institutions mould the rulers."[12]

He who dares to undertake the making of a people's institutions ought to feel himself capable, so to speak, of changing human nature, of transforming each individual, who is by himself a complete and solitary whole, into part of a greater whole from which he in a manner receives his life and being; of altering man's constitution for the purpose of strengthening it; and of substituting a partial and moral existence for the physical and independent existence nature has conferred on us all. He must, in a word, take away from man his own resources and give him instead new ones alien to him, and incapable of being made use of without the help of other men. The more completely these natural resources are annihilated, the greater and the more lasting are those which he acquires, and the more stable and perfect the new institutions; so that if each citizen is nothing and can do nothing without the rest, and the resources acquired by the whole are equal or superior to the aggregate of the resources of all the individuals, it may be said that legislation is at the highest possible point of perfection.

The legislator occupies in every respect an extraordinary position in the State. If he should do so by reason of his genius, he does so no less by reason of his office, which is neither magistracy, nor Sovereignty. This office, which sets up the Republic, nowhere enters into its constitution; it is an individual and superior function, which has nothing in common with human empire; for if he who holds command over men ought not to have command over the laws, he who has command over the laws ought not any more to have it over men; or else his laws would be the ministers of his passions and would often merely serve to perpetuate his injustices: his private aims would inevitably mar the sanctity of his work.

When Lycurgus gave laws to his country, he began by resigning the throne. It was the custom of most Greek towns to entrust the establishment of their laws to foreigners. The Republics of modern Italy in many cases followed this example; Geneva did the same and profited by it.[13] Rome, when it was most prosperous, suffered a revival of all the crimes of tyranny, and was brought to the verge of destruction, because it put the legislative authority and the sovereign power into the same hands.

Nevertheless, the decemvirs themselves never claimed the right to pass any law merely on their own authority. "Nothing we propose to you," they said to the people, "can pass into law without your consent. Romans, be yourselves the authors of the laws which are to make you happy."

He, therefore, who draws up the laws has, or should have, no right of legislation, and the people cannot, even if it wishes, deprive itself of this incommunicable right, because, according to the fundamental compact, only the general will can bind the individuals, and there can be no assurance that a particular will is in conformity with the general will, until it has been put to the free vote of the people. This I have said already; but it is worth while to repeat it.

Thus in the task of legislation we find together two things which appear to be incompatible: an enterprise too difficult for human powers, and, for its execution, an authority that is no authority.

There is a further difficulty that deserves attention. Wise men, if they try to speak their language to the common herd instead of its own, cannot possibly make themselves understood. There are a thousand kinds of ideas which it is impossible to translate into popular language. Conceptions that are too general and objects that are too remote are equally out of its range: each individual, having no taste for any other plan of government than that which suits his particular interest, finds it difficult to realise the advantages he might hope to draw from the continual privations good laws impose. For a young people to be able to relish sound principles of political theory and follow the fundamental rules of statecraft, the effect would have to become the cause; the social spirit, which should be created by these institutions, would have to preside over their very foundation; and men would have to be before law what they should become by means of law. The legislator therefore, being unable to appeal to either force or reason, must have recourse to an authority of a different order, capable of constraining without violence and persuading without convincing.

This is what has, in all ages, compelled the fathers of nations to have recourse to divine intervention and credit the gods with their own wisdom, in order that the peoples, submitting to the laws of the State as to those of nature, and recognising the same power in the formation of the city as in that of man, might obey freely, and bear with docility the yoke of the public happiness.

This sublime reason, far above the range of the common herd, is that whose decisions the legislator puts into the mouth of the immortals, in order to constrain by divine authority those whom human prudence could not move.[14] But it is not anybody who can make the gods speak, or get himself believed when he proclaims himself their interpreter. The great soul of the legislator is the only miracle that can prove his mission. Any man may grave tablets of stone, or buy an oracle, or feign secret intercourse with some divinity, or train a bird to whisper in his ear, or find other vulgar ways of imposing on the people. He whose knowledge goes no further may perhaps gather round him a band of fools; but he will never found an empire, and his extravagances will quickly perish with him. Idle tricks form a passing tie; only wisdom can make it lasting. The Judaic law, which still subsists, and that of the child of Ishmael, which, for ten centuries, has ruled half the world, still proclaim the great men who laid them down; and, while the pride of philosophy or the blind spirit of faction sees in them no more than lucky impostures, the true political theorist admires, in the institutions they set up, the great and powerful genius which presides over things made to endure.

We should not, with Warburton, conclude from this that politics and religion have among us a common object, but that, in the first periods of nations, the one is used as an instrument for the other.

....

BOOK III

....

CHAPTER IX

The marks of a good government

The question "What absolutely is the best government?" is unanswerable as well as indeterminate; or rather, there are as many good answers as there are possible combinations in the absolute and relative situations of all nations.

But if it is asked by what sign we may know that a given people is well or ill governed, that is another matter, and the question, being one of fact, admits of an answer.

It is not, however, answered, because everyone wants to answer it in his own way. Subjects extol public tranquillity, citizens individual liberty; the one class prefers security of possessions, the other that of person; the one regards as the best government that which is most severe, the other maintains that the mildest is the best; the one wants crimes punished, the other wants them prevented; the one wants the State to be feared by its neighbours, the other prefers that it should be ignored; the one is content if money circulates, the other demands that the people shall have bread. Even if an agreement were come to on these and similar points, should we have got any further? As moral qualities do not admit of exact measurement, agreement about the mark does not mean agreement about the valuation.

For my part, I am continually astonished that a mark so simple is not recognised, or that men are of so bad faith as not to admit it. What is the end of political association? The preservation and prosperity of its members. And what is the surest mark of their preservation and prosperity? Their numbers and population. Seek then nowhere else this mark that is in dispute. The rest being equal, the government under which, without external aids, without naturalisation or colonies, the citizens increase and multiply most, is beyond question the best. The government under which a people wanes and diminishes is the worst. Calculators, it is left for you to count, to measure, to compare.[15]

CHAPTER X

The abuse of government and its tendency to degenerate

As the particular will acts constantly in opposition to the general will, the government continually exerts itself against the Sovereignty. The greater this exertion becomes, the more the constitution changes; and, as there is in this case no other corporate will to create an equilibrium by resisting the will of the prince, sooner or later the prince must inevitably suppress the Sovereign and break the social treaty. This is the unavoidable and inherent defect which, from the very birth of the body politic, tends ceaselessly to destroy it, as age and death end by destroying the human body.

There are two general courses by which government degenerates: *i.e.* when it undergoes contraction, or when the State is dissolved.

Government undergoes contraction when it passes from the many to the few, that is, from democracy to aristocracy, and from aristocracy to royalty. To do so is its natural propensity.[16] If it took the backward course from the few to the many, it could be said that it was relaxed; but this inverse sequence is impossible.

Indeed, governments never change their form except when their energy is exhausted and leaves them too weak to keep what they have. If a government at once extended its sphere and relaxed its stringency, its force would become absolutely nil, and it would persist still less. It is therefore necessary to wind up the spring and tighten the hold as it gives way: or else the State it sustains will come to grief.

The dissolution of the State may come about in either of two ways.

First, when the prince ceases to administer the State in accordance with the laws, and usurps the Sovereign power. A remarkable change then occurs: not the government, but the State, undergoes contraction; I mean that the great State is dissolved, and another is formed within it, composed solely of the members of the government, which becomes for the rest of the people merely master and tyrant. So that the moment the government usurps the Sovereignty, the social compact is broken, and all private citizens recover by right their natural liberty, and are forced, but not bound, to obey.

The same thing happens when the members of the government severally usurp the power they should exercise only as a body; this is as great an infraction of the laws, and results in even greater disorders. There are then, so to speak, as many princes as there are magistrates, and the State, no less divided than the government, either perishes or changes its form.

When the State is dissolved, the abuse of government, whatever it is, bears the common name of *anarchy*. To distinguish, democracy degenerates into *ochlocracy*, and aristocracy into *oligarchy;* and I would add that royalty degenerates into *tyranny;* but this last word is ambiguous and needs explanation.

In vulgar usage, a tyrant is a king who governs violently and without regard for justice and law. In the exact sense, a tyrant is an individual who arrogates to himself the royal authority without having a right to it. This is how the Greeks understood the word "tyrant": they applied it indifferently to good and bad princes whose authority was not legitimate.[17] *Tyrant* and *usurper* are thus perfectly synonymous terms. In order that I may give different things different names, I call him who usurps the royal authority a *tyrant*, and him who usurps the sovereign power a *despot*. The tyrant is he who thrusts himself in contrary to the laws to govern in accordance with the laws; the despot is he who sets himself above the laws themselves. Thus the tyrant cannot be a despot, but the despot is always a tyrant.

CHAPTER XI

The death of the body politic

Such is the natural and inevitable tendency of the best constituted governments. If Sparta and Rome perished, what State can hope to endure for ever? If we would set up a long-lived form of government, let us not even dream of making it eternal. If we are to succeed, we must not attempt the impossible, or flatter ourselves that we are endowing the work of man with a stability of which human conditions do not permit.

The body politic, as well as the human body, begins to die as soon as it is born, and carries in itself the causes of its destruction. But both may have a constitution that is more or less robust and suited to preserve them a longer or a shorter time. The constitution of man is the work of nature; that of the State the work of art. It is not in men's power to prolong their own lives; but it is for them to prolong as much as possible the life of the State, by giving it the best possible constitution. The best constituted State will have an end; but it will end later than any other, unless some unforeseen accident brings about its untimely destruction.

The life-principle of the body politic lies in the sovereign authority. The legislative power is the heart of the State; the executive power is its brain, which causes the movement of all the parts. The brain may become paralysed and the individual still live. A man may remain an imbecile and live; but as soon as the heart ceases to perform its functions, the animal is dead.

The State subsists by means not of the laws, but of the legislative power. Yesterday's law is not binding to-day; but silence is taken for tacit consent, and the Sovereign is held to confirm incessantly the laws it does not abrogate as it might. All that it has once declared itself to will it wills always, unless it revokes its declaration.

Why then is so much respect paid to old laws? For this very reason. We must believe that nothing but the excellence of old acts of will can have preserved them so long: if the Sovereign had not recognised them as throughout salutary, it would have revoked them a thousand times. This is why, so far from growing weak, the laws continually gain new strength in any well constituted State; the precedent of antiquity makes them daily more venerable: while wherever the laws grow weak as they become old, this proves that there is no longer a legislative power, and that the State is dead.

....

CHAPTER XVI

That the institution of government is not a contract

The legislative power once well established, the next thing is to establish similarly the executive power; for this latter, which operates only by particular acts, not being of the essence of the former, is naturally separate from it. Were it possible for the Sovereign, as such, to possess the executive power, right and fact would be so confounded that no one could tell what was law and what was not; and the body politic, thus disfigured, would soon fall a prey to the violence it was instituted to prevent.

As the citizens, by the social contract, are all equal, all can prescribe what all should do, but no one has a right to demand that another shall do what he does not do himself. It is strictly this right, which is indispensable for giving the body politic life and movement, that the Sovereign, in instituting the government, confers upon the prince.

It has been held that this act of establishment was a contract between the people and the rulers it sets over itself,—a contract in which conditions were laid down between the two parties binding the one to command and the other to obey. It will be admitted, I am sure, that this is an odd kind of contract to enter into. But let us see if this view can be upheld.

First, the supreme authority can no more be modified than it can be alienated; to limit it is to destroy it. It is absurd and contradictory for the Sovereign to set a superior over itself; to bind itself to obey a master would be to return to absolute liberty.

Moreover, it is clear that this contract between the people and such and such persons would be a particular act; and from this it follows that it can be neither a law nor an act of Sovereignty, and that consequently it would be illegitimate.

It is plain too that the contracting parties in relation to each other would be under the law of nature alone and wholly without guarantees of their mutual undertakings, a position wholly at variance with the civil state. He who has force at his command being always in a position to control execution, it would come to the same thing if the name "contract" were given to the act of one man who said to another: "I give you all my goods, on condition that you give me back as much of them as you please."

There is only one contract in the State, and that is the act of association, which in itself excludes the existence of a second. It is impossible to conceive of any public contract that would not be a violation of the first.

CHAPTER XVII

The institution of government

Under what general idea then should the act by which government is instituted be conceived as falling? I will begin by stating that the act is complex, as being composed of two others—the establishment of the law and its execution.

By the former, the Sovereign decrees that there shall be a governing body established in this or that form; this act is clearly a law.

By the latter, the people nominates the rulers who are to be entrusted with the government that has been established. This nomination, being a particular act, is clearly not a second law, but merely a consequence of the first and a function of government.

The difficulty is to understand how there can be a governmental act before government exists, and how the people, which is only Sovereign or subject, can, under certain circumstances, become a prince or magistrate.

It is at this point that there is revealed one of the astonishing properties of the body politic, by means of which it reconciles apparently contradictory operations; for this is accomplished by a sudden conversion of Sovereignty into democracy, so that, without sensible change, and merely by virtue of a new relation of all to all, the citizens become magistrates and pass from general to particular acts, from legislation to the execution of the law.

This changed relation is no speculative subtlety without instances in practice: it happens every day in the English Parliament, where, on certain occasions, the Lower House resolves itself into Grand Committee, for the better discussion of affairs, and thus, from being at one moment a sovereign court, becomes at the next a mere commission; so that subsequently it reports to itself, as House of Commons, the result of its proceedings in Grand Committee, and debates over again under one name what it has already settled under another.

It is, indeed, the peculiar advantage of democratic government that it can be established in actuality by a simple act of the general will.

Subsequently, this provisional government remains in power, if this form is adopted, or else establishes in the name of the Sovereign the government that is prescribed by law; and thus the whole proceeding is regular. It is impossible to set up government in any other manner legitimately and in accordance with the principles so far laid down.

CHAPTER XVIII

How to check the usurpations of government

What we have just said confirms Chapter XVI, and makes it clear that the institution of government is not a contract, but a law; that the depositaries of the executive power are not the people's masters, but its officers; that it can set them up and pull them down when it likes; that for them there is no question of contract, but of obedience and that in taking charge of the functions the State imposes on them they are doing no more than fulfilling their duty as citizens, without having the remotest right to argue about the conditions.

When therefore the people sets up an hereditary government, whether it be monarchical and confined to one family, or aristocratic and confined to a class, what it enters into is not an undertaking; the administration is given a provisional form, until the people chooses to order it otherwise.

It is true that such changes are always dangerous, and that the established government should never be touched except when it comes to be incompatible with the public good; but the circumspection this involves is a maxim of policy and not a rule of right, and the State is no more bound to leave civil authority in the hands of its rulers than military authority in the hands of its generals.

It is also true that it is impossible to be too careful to observe, in such cases, all the formalities necessary to distinguish a regular and legitimate act from a seditious tumult, and the will of a whole people from the clamour of a faction. Here above all no further concession should be made to the untoward possibility than cannot, in the strictest logic, be refused it. From this obligation the prince derives a great advantage in preserving his power despite the people, without it being possible to say he has usurped it; for, seeming to avail himself only of his rights, he finds it very easy to extend them, and to prevent, under the pretext of keeping the peace, assemblies that are destined to the re-establishment of order; with the result that he takes advantage of a silence he does not allow to be broken, or of irregularities he causes to be committed, to assume that he has the support of those whom fear prevents from speaking, and to punish those who dare to speak. Thus it was that the decemvirs, first elected for one year and then kept on in office for a second, tried to perpetuate their power by forbidding the comitia to assemble; and by this easy method every government in the world, once clothed with the public power, sooner or later usurps the sovereign authority.

The periodical assemblies of which I have already spoken are designed to prevent or postpone this calamity, above all when they need no formal summoning; for in that case, the prince cannot stop them without openly declaring himself a law-breaker and an enemy of the State.

The opening of these assemblies, whose sole object is the maintenance of the social treaty, should always take the form of putting two propositions that may not be suppressed, which should be voted on separately.

The first is: "Does it please the Sovereign to preserve the present form of government?"

The second is: "Does it please the people to leave its administration in the hands of those who are actually in charge of it?"

I am here assuming what I think I have shown; that there is in the State no fundamental law that cannot be revoked, not excluding the social compact itself; for if all the citizens assembled of one accord to break the compact, it is impossible to doubt that it would be very legitimately broken. Grotius even thinks that each man can renounce his membership of his own State, and recover his natural liberty and his goods on leaving the country.[18] It would be indeed absurd if all the citizens in assembly could not do what each can do by himself.

BOOK IV

CHAPTER I

That the general will is indestructible

As long as several men in assembly regard themselves as a single body, they have only a single will which is concerned with their common preservation and general well-being. In this case, all the springs of the State are vigorous and simple and its rules clear and luminous; there are no embroilments or conflicts of interests; the common good is everywhere clearly apparent, and only good sense is needed to perceive it. Peace, unity and equality are the enemies of political subtleties. Men who are upright and simple are difficult to deceive because of their simplicity; lures and ingenious pretexts fail to impose upon them, and they are not even subtle enough to be dupes. When, among the happiest people in the world, bands of peasants are seen regulating affairs of State under an oak, and always acting wisely, can we help scorning the ingenious methods of other nations, which make themselves illustrious and wretched with so much art and mystery?

A State so governed needs very few laws; and, as it becomes necessary to issue new ones, the necessity is universally seen. The first man to propose them merely says what all have already felt, and there is no question of factions or intrigues or eloquence in order to secure the passage into law of what every one has already decided to do, as soon as he is sure that the rest will act with him.

Theorists are led into error because, seeing only States that have been from the beginning wrongly constituted, they are struck by the impossibility of applying such a policy to them. They make great game of all the absurdities a clever rascal or an insinuating speaker might get the people of Paris or London to believe. They do not know that Cromwell would have been put to "the bells" by the people of Berne, and the Duc de Beaufort on the treadmill by the Genevese.

But when the social bond begins to be relaxed and the State to grow weak, when particular interests begin to make themselves felt and the smaller societies to exercise an influence over the larger, the common interest changes and finds opponents: opinion is no longer unanimous; the general will ceases to be the will of all; contradictory views and debates arise; and the best advice is not taken without question.

Finally, when the State, on the eve of ruin, maintains only a vain, illusory and formal existence, when in every heart the social bond is broken, and the meanest interest brazenly lays hold of the sacred name of "public good," the general will becomes mute: all men, guided by secret motives, no more give their views as citizens than if the State had never been; and iniquitous decrees directed solely to private interest get passed under the name of laws.

Does it follow from this that the general will is exterminated or corrupted? Not at all: it is always constant, unalterable and pure; but it is subordinated to other wills which encroach upon its sphere. Each man, in detaching his interest from the common interest, sees clearly that he cannot entirely separate them; but his share in the public mishaps seems to him negligible beside the exclusive good he aims at making his own. Apart from this particular good, he wills the general good in his own interest, as strongly as any one else. Even in selling his vote for money, he does not extinguish in himself the general will, but only eludes it. The fault he commits is that of changing the state of the question, and answering something different from what he is asked. Instead of saying, by his vote, "It is to the advantage of the State," he says, "It is of advantage to this or that man or party that this or that view should prevail." Thus the law of public order in assemblies is not so much to maintain in them the general will as to secure that the question be always put to it, and the answer always given by it.

I could here set down many reflections on the simple right of voting in every act of Sovereignty—a right which no one can take from the citizens—and also on the right of stating views, making proposals, dividing and discussing, which the government is always most careful to leave solely to its members, but this important subject would need a treatise to itself, and it is impossible to say everything in a single work.

CHAPTER II

Voting

It may be seen, from the last chapter, that the way in which general business is managed may give a clear enough indication of the actual state of morals and the health of the body politic. The more concert reigns in the assemblies, that is, the nearer opinion approaches unanimity, the greater is the dominance of the general will. On the other hand, long debates, dissensions and tumult proclaim the ascendancy of particular interests and the decline of the State.

This seems less clear when two or more orders enter into the constitution, as patricians and plebeians did at Rome; for quarrels between these two orders often disturbed the comitia, even in the best days of the Republic. But the exception is rather apparent than real; for then, through the defect that is inherent in the body politic, there were, so to speak, two States in one, and what is not true of the two together is true of either separately. Indeed, even in the most stormy times, the plebiscita of the people, when the Senate did not interfere with them, always went through quietly and by large majorities. The citizens having but one interest, the people had but a single will.

At the other extremity of the circle, unanimity recurs; this is the case when the citizens, having fallen into servitude, have lost both liberty and will. Fear and flattery then change votes into acclamation; deliberation ceases, and only worship or malediction is left. Such was the vile manner in which the senate expressed its views under the Emperors. It did so sometimes with absurd precautions. Tacitus observes that, under Otho, the senators, while they heaped curses on Vitellius, contrived at the same time to make a deafening noise, in order that, should he ever become their master, he might not know what each of them had said.

On these various considerations depend the rules by which the methods of counting votes and comparing opinions should be regulated, according as the general will is more or less easy to discover, and the State more or less in its decline.

There is but one law which, from its nature, needs unanimous consent. This is the social compact; for civil association is the most voluntary of all acts. Every man being born free and his own master, no one, under any pretext whatsoever, can make any man subject without his consent. To decide that the son of a slave is born a slave is to decide that he is not born a man.

If then there are opponents when the social compact is made, their opposition does not invalidate the contract, but merely prevents them from being included in it. They are foreigners among citizens. When the State is instituted, residence constitutes consent; to dwell within its territory is to submit to the Sovereign.[19]

Apart from this primitive contract, the vote of the majority always binds all the rest. This follows from the contract itself. But it is asked how a man can be both free and forced to conform to wills that are not his own. How are the opponents at once free and subject to laws they have not agreed to?

I retort that the question is wrongly put. The citizen gives his consent to all the laws, including those which are passed in spite of his opposition, and even those which punish him when he dares to break any of them. The constant will of all the members of the State is the general will; by virtue of it they are citizens and free.[20] When in the popular assembly a law is proposed, what the people is asked is not exactly whether it approves or rejects the proposal, but whether it is in conformity with the general will, which is their will. Each man, in giving his vote, states his opinion on that point; and the general will is found by counting votes. When therefore the opinion that is contrary to my own prevails, this proves neither more nor less than that I was mistaken, and that what I thought to be the general will was not so. If my particular opinion had carried the day I should have achieved the opposite of what was my will; and it is in that case that I should not have been free.

This presupposes, indeed, that all the qualities of the general will still reside in the majority: when they cease to do so, whatever side a man may take, liberty is no longer possible.

In my earlier demonstration of how particular wills are substituted for the general will in public deliberation, I have adequately pointed out the practicable methods of avoiding this abuse; and I shall have more to say of them later on. I have also given the principles for determining the proportional number of votes for declaring that will. A difference of one vote destroys equality; a single opponent destroys unanimity; but between equality and unanimity, there are several grades of unequal division, at each of which this proportion may be fixed in accordance with the condition and the needs of the body politic.

There are two general rules that may serve to regulate this relation. First, the more grave and important the questions discussed, the nearer should the opinion that is to prevail approach unanimity. Secondly, the more the matter in hand calls for speed, the smaller the prescribed difference in the numbers of votes may be allowed to become: where an instant decision has to be reached, a majority of one vote should be enough. The first of these two rules seems more in harmony with the laws, and the second with practical affairs. In any case, it is the combination of them that gives the best proportions for determining the majority necessary.

CHAPTER III

Elections

In the elections of the prince and the magistrates, which are, as I have said, complex acts, there are two possible methods of procedure, choice and lot. Both have been employed in various republics, and a highly complicated mixture of the two still survives in the election of the Doge at Venice.

"Election by lot," says Montesquieu, "is democratic in nature." I agree that it is so; but in what sense? "The lot," he goes on, "is a way of making choice that is unfair to nobody; it leaves each citizen a reasonable hope of serving his country." These are not reasons.

If we bear in mind that the election of rulers is a function of government, and not of Sovereignty, we shall see why the lot is the method more natural to democracy, in which the administration is better in proportion as the number of its acts is small.

In every real democracy, magistracy is not an advantage, but a burdensome charge which cannot justly be imposed on one individual rather than another. The law alone can lay the charge on him on whom the lot falls. For, the conditions being then the same for all, and the choice not depending on any human will, there is no particular application to alter the universality of the law.

In an aristocracy, the prince chooses the prince, the government is preserved by itself, and voting is rightly ordered.

The instance of the election of the Doge of Venice confirms, instead of destroying, this distinction; the mixed form suits a mixed government. For it is an error to take the government of Venice for a real aristocracy. If the people has no share in the government, the nobility is itself the people. A host of poor Barnabotes never gets near any magistracy, and its nobility consists merely in the empty title of Excellency, and in the right to sit in the Great Council. As this Great Council is as numerous as our General Council at Geneva, its illustrious members have no more privileges than our plain citizens. It is indisputable that, apart from the extreme disparity between the two republics, the *bourgeoisie* of Geneva is exactly equivalent to the *patriciate* of Venice; our *natives* and *inhabitants* correspond to the *townsmen* and the *people* of Venice; our *peasants* correspond to the *subjects* on the mainland; and, however that republic be regarded, if its size be left out of account, its government is no more aristocratic than our own. The whole difference is that, having no life-ruler, we do not, like Venice, need to use the lot.

Election by lot would have few disadvantages in a real democracy, in which, as equality would everywhere exist in morals and talents as well as in principles and fortunes, it would become almost a matter of indifference who was chosen. But I have already said that a real democracy is only an ideal.

When choice and lot are combined, positions that require special talents, such as military posts, should be filled by the former; the latter does for cases, such as judicial offices, in which good sense, justice, and integrity are enough, because in a State that is well constituted, these qualities are common to all the citizens.

Neither lot nor vote has any place in monarchical government. The monarch being by right sole prince and only magistrate, the choice of his lieutenants belongs to none but him. When the Abbé de Saint-Pierre proposed that the Councils of the King of France should be multiplied, and their members elected by ballot, he did not see that he was proposing to change the form of government.

I should now speak of the methods of giving and counting opinions in the assembly of the people; but perhaps an account of this aspect of the Roman constitution will more forcibly illustrate all the rules I could lay down. It is worth the while of a judicious reader to follow in some detail the working of public and private affairs in a Council consisting of two hundred thousand men.

....

CHAPTER VIII

Civil religion

At first men had no kings save the gods, and no government save theocracy. They reasoned like Caligula, and, at that period, reasoned aright. It takes a long time for feeling so to change that men can make up their minds to take their equals as masters, in the hope that they will profit by doing so.

From the mere fact that God was set over every political society, it followed that there were as many gods as peoples. Two peoples that were strangers the one to the other, and almost always enemies, could not long recognise the same master: two armies giving battle could not obey the same leader. National divisions thus led to polytheism, and this in turn gave rise to theological and civil intolerance, which, as we shall see hereafter, are by nature the same.

The fancy the Greeks had for rediscovering their gods among the barbarians arose from the way they had of regarding themselves as the natural Sovereigns of such peoples. But there is nothing so absurd as the erudition which in our days identifies and confuses gods of different nations. As if Moloch, Saturn, and Chronos could be the same god! As if the Phoenician Baal, the Greek Zeus, and the Latin Jupiter could be the same! As if there could still be anything common to imaginary beings with different names!

If it is asked how in pagan times, where each State had its cult and its gods, there were no wars of religion, I answer that it was precisely because each State, having its own cult as well as its own government, made no distinction between its gods and its laws. Political war was also theological; the provinces of the gods were, so to speak, fixed by the boundaries of nations. The god of one people had no right over another. The gods of the pagans were not jealous gods; they shared among themselves the empire of the world: even Moses and the Hebrews sometimes lent themselves to this view by speaking of the God of Israel. It is true, they regarded as powerless the gods of the Canaanites, a proscribed people condemned to destruction, whose place they were to take; but remember how they spoke of the divisions of the neighbouring peoples they were forbidden to attack! "Is not the possession of what belongs to your god Chamos lawfully your due?" said Jephthah to the Ammonites. "We have the same title to the lands our conquering God has made his own."[21] Here, I think, there is a recognition that the rights of Chamos and those of the God of Israel are of the same nature.

But when the Jews, being subject to the Kings of Babylon, and, subsequently, to those of Syria, still obstinately refused to recognise any god save their own, their refusal was regarded as rebellion against their conqueror, and drew down on them the persecutions we read of in their history, which are without parallel till the coming of Christianity.[22]

Every religion, therefore, being attached solely to the laws of the State which prescribed it, there was no way of converting a people except by enslaving it, and there could be no missionaries save conquerors. The obligation to change cults being the law to which the vanquished yielded, it was necessary to be victorious before suggesting such a change. So far from men fighting for the gods, the gods, as in Homer, fought for men; each asked his god for victory, and repaid him with new altars. The Romans, before taking a city, summoned its gods to quit it; and, in leaving the Tarentines their outraged gods, they regarded them as subject to their own and compelled to do them homage. They left the vanquished their gods as they left them their laws. A wreath to the Jupiter of the Capitol was often the only tribute they imposed.

Finally, when, along with their empire, the Romans had spread their cult and their gods, and had themselves often adopted those of the vanquished, by granting to both alike the rights of the city, the peoples of that vast empire insensibly found themselves with multitudes of gods and cults, everywhere almost the same; and thus paganism throughout the known world finally came to be one and the same religion.

It was in these circumstances that Jesus came to set up on earth a spiritual kingdom, which, by separating the theological from the political system, made the State no longer one, and brought about the internal divisions which have never ceased to trouble Christian peoples. As the new idea of a kingdom of the other world could never have occurred to pagans, they always looked on the Christians as really rebels, who, while feigning to submit, were only waiting for the chance to make themselves independent and their masters, and to usurp by guile the authority they pretended in their weakness to respect. This was the cause of the persecutions.

What the pagans had feared took place. Then everything changed its aspect: the humble Christians changed their language, and soon this so-called kingdom of the other world turned, under a visible leader, into the most violent of earthly despotisms.

However, as there have always been a prince and civil laws, this double power and conflict of jurisdiction have made all good polity impossible in Christian States; and men have never succeeded in finding out whether they were bound to obey the master or the priest.

Several peoples, however, even in Europe and its neighbourhood, have desired without success to preserve or restore the old system: but the spirit of Christianity has everywhere prevailed. The sacred cult has always remained or again become independent of the Sovereign, and there has been no necessary link between it and the body of the State. Mahomet held very sane views, and linked his political system well together; and, as long as the form of his government continued under the caliphs who succeeded him, that government was indeed one, and so far good. But the Arabs, having grown prosperous, lettered, civilised, slack and cowardly, were conquered by barbarians: the division between the two powers began again; and, although it is less apparent among the Mahometans than among the Christians, it none the less exists, especially in the sect of Ali, and there are States, such as Persia, where it is continually making itself felt.

Among us, the Kings of England have made themselves heads of the Church, and the Czars have done the same: but this title has made them less its masters than its ministers; they have gained not so much the right to change it, as the power to maintain it: they are not its legislators, but only its princes. Wherever the clergy is a corporate body,[23] it is master and legislator in its own country. There are thus two powers, two Sovereigns, in England and in Russia, as well as elsewhere.

Of all Christian writers, the philosopher Hobbes alone has seen the evil and how to remedy it, and has dared to propose the reunion of the two heads of the eagle, and the restoration throughout of political unity, without which no State or government will ever be rightly constituted. But he should have seen that the masterful spirit of Christianity is incompatible with his system, and that the priestly interest would always be stronger than that of the State. It is not so much what is false and terrible in his political theory, as what is just and true, that has drawn down hatred on it.[24]

I believe that if the study of history were developed from this point of view, it would be easy to refute the contrary opinions of Bayle and Warburton, one of whom holds that religion can be of no use to the body politic, while the other, on the contrary, maintains that Christianity is its strongest support. We should demonstrate to the former that no State has ever been founded without a religious basis, and to the latter, that the law of Christianity at bottom does more harm by weakening than good by strengthening the constitution of the State. To make myself understood, I have only to make a little more exact the too vague ideas of religion as relating to this subject.

Religion, considered in relation to society, which is either general or particular, may also be divided into two kinds: the religion of man, and that of the citizen. The first, which has neither temples, nor altars, nor rites, and is confined to the purely internal cult of the supreme God and the eternal obligations of morality, is the religion of the Gospel pure and simple, the true theism, what may be called natural divine right or law. The other, which is codified in a single country, gives it its gods, its own tutelary patrons; it has its dogmas, its rites, and its external cult prescribed by law; outside the single nation that follows it, all the world is in its sight infidel, foreign and barbarous; the duties and rights of man extend for it only as far as its own altars. Of this kind were all the religions of early peoples, which we may define as civil or positive divine right or law.

There is a third sort of religion of a more singular kind, which gives men two codes of legislation, two rulers, and two countries, renders them subject to contradictory duties, and makes it impossible for them to be faithful both to religion and to citizenship. Such are the religions of the Lamas and of the Japanese, and such is Roman Christianity, which may be called the religion of the priest. It leads to a sort of mixed and antisocial code which has no name.

In their political aspect, all these three kinds of religion have their defects. The third is so clearly bad, that it is a waste of time to stop to prove it such. All that destroys social unity is worthless; all institutions that set man in contradiction to himself are worthless.

The second is good in that it unites the divine cult with love of the laws, and, making country the object of the citizens' adoration, teaches them that service done to the State is service done to its tutelary god. It is a form of theocracy, in which there can be no pontiff save the prince, and no priests save the magistrates. To die for one's country then becomes martyrdom; violation of its laws, impiety; and to subject one who is guilty to public execration is to condemn him to the anger of the gods: *Sacer estod.*

On the other hand, it is bad in that, being founded on lies and error, it deceives men, makes them credulous and superstitious, and drowns the true cult of the Divinity in empty ceremonial. It is bad, again, when it becomes tyrannous and exclusive, and makes a people bloodthirsty and intolerant, so that it breathes fire and slaughter, and regards as a sacred act the killing of every one who does not believe in its gods. The result is to place such a people in a natural state of war with all others, so that its security is deeply endangered.

There remains therefore the religion of man or Christianity—not the Christianity of to-day, but that of the Gospel, which is entirely different. By means of this holy, sublime, and real religion all men, being children of one God, recognise one another as brothers, and the society that unites them is not dissolved even at death.

But this religion, having no particular relation to the body politic, leaves the laws in possession of the force they have in themselves without making any addition to it; and thus one of the great bonds that unite society considered in severally fails to operate. Nay, more, so far from binding the hearts of the citizens to the State, it has the effect of taking them away from all earthly things. I know of nothing more contrary to the social spirit.

We are told that a people of true Christians would form the most perfect society imaginable. I see in this supposition only one great difficulty: that a society of true Christians would not be a society of men.

I say further that such a society, with all its perfection, would be neither the strongest nor the most lasting: the very fact that it was perfect would rob it of its bond of union; the flaw that would destroy it would lie in its very perfection.

Every one would do his duty; the people would be law-abiding, the rulers just and temperate; the magistrates upright and incorruptible; the soldiers would scorn death; there would be neither vanity nor luxury. So far, so good; but let us hear more.

Christianity as a religion is entirely spiritual, occupied solely with heavenly things; the country of the Christian is not of this world. He does his duty, indeed, but does it with profound indifference to the good or ill success of his cares. Provided he has nothing to reproach himself with, it matters little to him whether things go well or ill here on earth. If the State is prosperous, he hardly dares to share in the public happiness, for fear he may grow proud of his country's glory; if the State is languishing, he blesses the hand of God that is hard upon His people.

For the State to be peaceable and for harmony to be maintained, all the citizens without exception would have to be good Christians; if by ill hap there should be a single self-seeker or hypocrite, a Catiline or a

Cromwell, for instance, he would certainly get the better of his pious compatriots. Christian charity does not readily allow a man to think hardly of his neighbours. As soon as, by some trick, he has discovered the art of imposing on them and getting hold of a share in the public authority, you have a man established in dignity; it is the will of God that he be respected: very soon you have a power; it is God's will that it be obeyed: and if the power is abused by him who wields it, it is the scourge wherewith God punishes His children. There would be scruples about driving out the usurper: public tranquillity would have to be disturbed, violence would have to be employed, and blood spilt; all this accords ill with Christian meekness; and after all, in this vale of sorrows, what does it matter whether we are free men or serfs? The essential thing is to get to heaven, and resignation is only an additional means of doing so.

If war breaks out with another State, the citizens march readily out to battle; not one of them thinks of flight; they do their duty, but they have no passion for victory; they know better how to die than how to conquer. What does it matter whether they win or lose? Does not Providence know better than they what is meet for them? Only think to what account a proud, impetuous and passionate enemy could turn their stoicism! Set over against them those generous peoples who were devoured by ardent love of glory and of their country, imagine your Christian republic face to face with Sparta or Rome: the pious Christians will be beaten, crushed and destroyed, before they know where they are, or will owe their safety only to the contempt their enemy will conceive for them. It was to my mind a fine oath that was taken by the soldiers of Fabius, who swore, not to conquer or die, but to come back victorious—and kept their oath. Christians would never have taken such an oath; they would have looked on it as tempting God.

But I am mistaken in speaking of a Christian republic; the terms are mutually exclusive. Christianity preaches only servitude and dependence. Its spirit is so favourable to tyranny that it always profits by such a *régime*. True Christians are made to be slaves, and they know it and do not much mind: this short life counts for too little in their eyes.

I shall be told that Christian troops are excellent. I deny it. Show me an instance. For my part, I know of no Christian troops. I shall be told of the Crusades. Without disputing the valour of the Crusaders, I answer that, so far from being Christians, they were the priests' soldiery, citizens of the Church. They fought for their spiritual country, which the Church had, somehow or other, made temporal. Well understood, this goes back to paganism: as the Gospel sets up no national religion, a holy war is impossible among Christians.

Under the pagan emperors, the Christian soldiers were brave; every Christian writer affirms it, and I believe it: it was a case of honourable emulation of the pagan troops. As soon as the emperors were Christian, this emulation no longer existed, and, when the Cross had driven out the eagle, Roman valour wholly disappeared.

But, setting aside political considerations, let us come back to what is right, and settle our principles on this important point. The right which the social compact gives the Sovereign over the subjects does not, we have seen, exceed the limits of public expediency.[25] The subjects then owe the Sovereign an account of their opinions only to such an extent as they matter to the community. Now, it matters very much to the community that each citizen should have a religion. That will make him love his duty; but the dogmas of that religion concern the State and its members only so far as they have reference to morality and to the duties which he who professes them is bound to do to others. Each man may have, over and above, what opinions he pleases, without it being the Sovereign's business to take cognisance of them; for, as the Sovereign has no authority in the other world, whatever the lot of its subjects may be in the life to come, that is not its business, provided they are good citizens in this life.

There is therefore a purely civil profession of faith of which the Sovereign should fix the articles, not exactly as religious dogmas, but as social sentiments without which a man cannot be a good citizen or a faithful subject.[26] While it can compel no one to believe them, it can banish from the State whoever does not believe them—it can banish him, not for impiety, but as an anti-social being, incapable of truly loving the laws and justice, and of sacrificing, at need, his life to his duty. If any one, after publicly recognising these dogmas, behaves as if he does not believe them, let him be punished by death: he has committed the worst of all crimes, that of lying before the law.

The dogmas of civil religion ought to be few, simple, and exactly worded, without explanation or commentary. The existence of a mighty, intelligent and beneficent Divinity, possessed of foresight and providence, the life to come, the happiness of the just, the punishment of the wicked, the sanctity of the social contract and the laws: these are its positive dogmas. Its negative dogmas I confine to one, intolerance, which is a part of the cults we have rejected.

Those who distinguish civil from theological intolerance are, to my mind, mistaken. The two forms are inseparable. It is impossible to live at peace with those we regard as damned; to love them would be to hate God who punishes them: we positively must either reclaim or torment them. Wherever theological intolerance is admitted, it must inevitably have some civil effect;[27] and as soon as it has such an effect, the Sovereign is no longer Sovereign even in the temporal sphere: thenceforth priests are the real masters, and kings only their ministers.

Now that there is and can be no longer an exclusive national religion, tolerance should be given to all religions that tolerate others, so long as their dogmas contain nothing contrary to the duties of citizenship.

But whoever dares to say: *Outside the Church is no salvation*, ought to be driven from the State, unless the State is the Church, and the prince the pontiff. Such a dogma is good only in a theocratic government; in any other, it is fatal. The reason for which Henry IV is said to have embraced the Roman religion ought to make every honest man leave it, and still more any prince who knows how to reason.

Notes

1 "Learned inquiries into public right are often only the history of past abuses; and troubling to study them too deeply is a profitless infatuation," (Essay on the Interests of France in Relation to its Neighbours, by the Marquis d'Argenson). This is exactly what Grotius has done.
2 See a short treatise of Plutarch's entitled That Animals Reason.
3 The Romans, who understood and respected the right of war more than any other nation on earth, carried their scruples on this head so far that a citizen was not allowed to serve as a volunteer without engaging himself expressly against the enemy, and against such and such an enemy by name. A legion in which the younger Cato was seeing his first service under Popilius having been reconstructed, the elder Cato wrote to Popilius that, if he wished his son to continue serving under him, he must administer to him a new military oath, because, the first having been annulled, he was no longer able to bear arms against the enemy. The same Cato wrote to his son telling him to take great care not to go into battle before taking this new oath. I know that the siege of Clusium and other isolated events can be quoted against me; but I am citing laws and customs. The Romans are the people that least often transgressed its laws; and no other people has had such good ones.
4 The real meaning of this word has been almost wholly lost in modern times; most people mistake a town for a city, and a townsman for a citizen. They do not know that houses make a town, but citizens a city. The same mistake long ago cost the Carthaginians dear. I have never read of the title of citizens being given to the subjects of any prince, not even the ancient Macedonians or the English of to-day, though they are nearer liberty than anyone else. The French alone everywhere familiarly adopt the name of citizens, because, as can be seen from their dictionaries, they have no idea of its meaning; otherwise they would be guilty in usurping it, of the crime of lèse-majesté: among them, the name expresses a virtue, and not a right. When Bodin spoke of our citizens and townsmen, he fell into a bad blunder in taking the one class for the other. M. d'Alembert has avoided the error, and, in his article on Geneva, has clearly distinguished the four orders of men (or even five, counting mere foreigners) who dwell in our town, of which two only compose the Republic. No other French writer, to my knowledge, has understood the real meaning of the word citizen.
5 Under bad governments, this equality is only apparent and illusory: it serves only to keep the pauper in his poverty and the rich man in the position he has usurped. In fact, laws are always of use to those who possess and harmful to those who have nothing: from which it follows that the social state is advantageous to men only when all have something and none too much.
6 To be general, a will need not always be unanimous; but every vote must be counted: any exclusion is a breach of generality.

7 "Every interest," says the Marquis d'Argenson, "has different principles. The agreement of two particular interests is formed by opposition to a third." He might have added that the agreement of all interests is formed by opposition to that of each. If there were no different interests, the common interest would be barely felt, as it would encounter no obstacle; all would go on of its own accord, and politics would cease to be an art.

8 "In fact," says Machiavelli, "there are some divisions that are harmful to a Republic and some that are advantageous. Those which stir up sects and parties are harmful; those attended by neither are advantageous. Since, then, the founder of a Republic cannot help enmities arising, he ought at least to prevent them from growing into sects," (*History of Florence*, Book vii).

9 Attentive readers, do not, I pray, be in a hurry to charge me with contradicting myself. The terminology made it unavoidable, considering the poverty of the language; but wait and see.

10 I understand by this word, not merely an aristocracy or a democracy, but generally any government directed by the general will, which is the law. To be legitimate, the government must be, not one with the Sovereign, but its minister. In such a case even a monarchy is a Republic. This will be made clearer in the following book.

11 A people becomes famous only when its legislation begins to decline. We do not know for how many centuries the system of Lycurgus made the Spartans happy before the rest of Greece took any notice of it.

12 Montesquieu, *The Greatness and Decadence of the Romans*, chapter i.

13 Those who know Calvin only as a theologian much underestimate the extent of his genius. The codification of our wise edicts, in which he played a large part, does him no less honour than his *Institute*. Whatever revolution time may bring in our religion, so long as the spirit of patriotism and liberty still lives among us, the memory of this great man will be for ever blessed.

14 "In truth," says Machiavelli, "there has never been, in any country, an extraordinary legislator who has not had recourse to God; for otherwise his laws would not have been accepted: there are, in fact, many useful truths of which a wise man may have knowledge without their having in themselves such clear reasons for their being so as to be able to convince others" (*Discourses on Livy*, Book v, chapter xi).

15 On the same principle it should be judged what centuries deserve the preference for human prosperity. Those in which letters and arts have flourished have been too much admired, because the hidden object of their culture has not been fathomed, and their fatal effects not taken into account. "*Idque apud imperitos humanitas vocabatur, cum pars servitutis esset.*" (Fools called "humanity" what was a part of slavery, Tacitus, *Agricola*, 31.) Shall we never see in the maxims books lay down the vulgar interest that makes their writers speak? No, whatever they may say, when, despite its renown, a country is depopulated, it is not true that all is well, and it is not enough that a poet should have an income of 100,000 francs to make his age the best of all. Less attention should be paid to the apparent repose and tranquillity of the rulers than to the well-being of their nations as wholes, and above all of the most numerous States. A hailstorm lays several cantons waste, but it rarely makes a famine. Outbreaks and civil wars give rulers rude shocks, but they are not the real ills of peoples, who may even get a respite, while there is a dispute as to who shall tyrannise over them. Their true prosperity and calamities come from their permanent condition: it is when the whole remains crushed beneath the yoke, that decay sets in, and that the rulers destroy them at will,

and *"ubi solitudinem faciunt, pacem appellant."* (Where they create solitude, they call it peace, Tacitus, *Agricola*, 31.) When the bickerings of the great disturbed the kingdom of France, and the Coadjutor of Paris took a dagger in his pocket to the Parliament, these things did not prevent the people of France from prospering and multiplying in dignity, ease and freedom. Long ago Greece flourished in the midst of the most savage wars; blood ran in torrents, and yet the whole country was covered with inhabitants. It appeared, says Machiavelli, that in the midst of murder, proscription and civil war, our republic only throve: the virtue, morality and independence of the citizens did more to strengthen it than all their dissensions had done to enfeeble it. A little disturbance gives the soul elasticity; what makes the race truly prosperous is not so much peace as liberty.

16 The slow formation and the progress of the Republic of Venice in its lagoons are a notable instance of this sequence; and it is most astonishing that, after more than twelve hundred years' existence, the Venetians seem to be still at the second stage, which they reached with the *Serrar di Consiglio* in 1198. As for the ancient Dukes who are brought up against them, it is proved, whatever the *Squittinio della libertà veneta* may say of them, that they were in no sense sovereigns.

A case certain to be cited against my view is that of the Roman Republic, which, it will be said, followed exactly the opposite course, and passed from monarchy to aristocracy and from aristocracy to democracy. I by no means take this view of it.

What Romulus first set up was a mixed government, which soon deteriorated into despotism. From special causes, the State died an untimely death, as new-born children sometimes perish without reaching manhood. The expulsion of the Tarquins was the real period of the birth of the Republic. But at first it took on no constant form, because, by not abolishing the patriciate, it left half its work undone. For, by this means, hereditary aristocracy, the worst of all legitimate forms of administration, remained in conflict with democracy, and the form of the government, as Machiavelli has proved, was only fixed on the establishment of the tribunate: only then was there a true government and a veritable democracy. In fact, the people was then not only Sovereign, but also magistrate and judge; the senate was only a subordinate tribunal, to temper and concentrate the government, and the consuls themselves, though they were patricians, first magistrates, and absolute generals in war, were in Rome itself no more than presidents of the people.

From that point, the government followed its natural tendency, and inclined strongly to aristocracy. The patriciate, we may say, abolished itself, and the aristocracy was found no longer in the body of patricians as at Venice and Genoa, but in the body of the senate, which was composed of patricians and plebeians, and even in the body of tribunes when they began to usurp an active function: for names do not affect facts, and, when the people has rulers who govern for it, whatever name they bear, the government is an aristocracy.

The abuse of aristocracy led to the civil wars and the triumvirate. Sulla, Julius Cæsar and Augustus became in fact real monarchs; and finally, under the despotism of Tiberius, the State was dissolved. Roman history then confirms, instead of invalidating, the principle I have laid down.

17 *"Omnes enim et habentur et dicuntur tyranni, qui potestate utuntur perpetua in ea civitate quæ libertate usa est"* (Cornelius Nepos, *Life of Miltiades*). (For all those are called and considered tyrants, who hold perpetual power in a State

that has known liberty.) It is true that Aristotle (*Ethics*, Book viii, chapter x) distinguishes the tyrant from the king by the fact that the former governs in his own interest, and the latter only for the good of his subjects; but not only did all Greek authors in general use the word *tyrant* in a different sense, as appears most clearly in Xenophon's *Hiero*, but also it would follow from Aristotle's distinction that, from the very beginning of the world, there has not yet been a single king.

18 Provided, of course, he does not leave to escape his obligations and avoid having to serve his country in the hour of need. Flight in such a case would be criminal and punishable, and would be, not withdrawal, but desertion.

19 This should of course be understood as applying to a free State; for elsewhere family, goods, lack of a refuge, necessity, or violence may detain a man in a country against his will; and then his dwelling there no longer by itself implies his consent to the contract or to its violation.

20 At Genoa, the word *Liberty* may be read over the front of the prisons and on the chains of the galley-slaves. This application of the device is good and just. It is indeed only malefactors of all estates who prevent the citizen from being free. In the country in which all such men were in the galleys, the most perfect liberty would be enjoyed.

21 *Nonne ea quæ possidet Chamos deus tuus, tibi jure debentur?* (Judges, 11:24.) Such is the text in the Vulgate. Father de Carrières translates: "Do you not regard yourselves as having a right to what your god possesses?" I do not know the force of the Hebrew text: but I perceive that, in the Vulgate, Jephthah positively recognises the right of the god Chamos, and that the French translator weakened this admission by inserting an "according to you," which is not in the Latin.

22 It is quite clear that the Phocian War, which was called "the Sacred War," was not a war of religion. Its object was the punishment of acts of sacrilege, and not the conquest of unbelievers.

23 It should be noted that the clergy find their bond of union not so much in formal assemblies, as in the communion of Churches. Communion and excommunication are the social compact of the clergy, a compact which will always make them masters of peoples and kings. All priests who communicate together are fellow citizens, even if they come from opposite ends of the earth. This invention is a masterpiece of statesmanship: there is nothing like it among pagan priests; who have therefore never formed a clerical corporate body.

24 See, for instance, in a letter from Grotius to his brother (April 11, 1643), what that learned man found to praise and to blame in the *De Cive*. It is true that, with a bent for indulgence, he seems to pardon the writer the good for the sake of the bad; but all men are not so forgiving.

25 "In the republic," says the Marquis d'Argenson, "each man is perfectly free in what does not harm others." This is the invariable limitation, which it is impossible to define more exactly. I have not been able to deny myself the pleasure of occasionally quoting from this manuscript, though it is unknown to the public, in order to do honour to the memory of a good and illustrious man, who had kept even in the Ministry the heart of a good citizen, and views on the government of his country that were sane and right.

26 Cæsar, pleading for Catiline, tried to establish the dogma that the soul is mortal: Cato and Cicero, in refutation, did not waste time in philosophising. They were content to show that Cæsar spoke like a bad citizen, and brought forward a doctrine that would have a bad effect on the State. This, in fact, and not a problem of theology, was what the Roman senate had to judge.

27 Marriage, for instance, being a civil contract, has civil effects without which society cannot even subsist. Suppose a body of clergy should claim the sole right of permitting this act, a right which every intolerant religion must of necessity claim, is it not clear that in establishing the authority of the Church in this respect, it will be destroying that of the prince, who will have thenceforth only as many subjects as the clergy choose to allow him? Being in a position to marry or not to marry people according to their acceptance of such and such a doctrine, their admission or rejection of such and such a formula, their greater or less piety, the Church alone, by the exercise of prudence and firmness, will dispose of all inheritances, offices and citizens, and even of the State itself, which could not subsist if it were composed entirely of bastards? But, I shall be told, there will be appeals on the ground of abuse, summonses and decrees; the temporalities will be seized. How sad! The clergy, however little, I will not say courage, but sense it has, will take no notice and go its way: it will quietly allow appeals, summonses, decrees and seizures, and, in the end, will remain the master. It is not, I think, a great sacrifice to give up a part, when one is sure of securing all.

ROUSSEAU ON PUBLIC REASON

Christopher Bertram[1]

1 Introduction

Jean-Jacques Rousseau's best-known contribution to political philosophy is his doctrine of the general will.[2] Specifically, the idea that it is a necessary condition of legitimate sovereignty that the exercise of state power via the law be carried out in accordance with the will of the citizenry as a whole if it is to be exercised in a manner compatible with individual freedom. What exactly this means and whether Rousseau succeeds in his task are matters of deep controversy and some of the issues are discussed below. For Rousseau, the law, in a legitimate state, just is the public reason of the citizenry, expressed in codified form, and any "law" that reflects instead the private reason of individuals is an instrument of tyranny that necessarily oppresses the individuals subject to it. Rousseau's contribution anticipates many modern discussions of public reason both in its general outlines and with respect to particular topics. In contrast to some depictions of Rousseau as "totalitarian," he is alive to the challenges faced by public reason in an age of religious pluralism, and his position on social unity in the face of religious and philosophical diversity anticipates ideas such as John Rawls's overlapping consensus.

The central problem Rousseau sets out to answer in the *Social Contract* is how individual freedom and moral responsibility can be preserved given the need for social and political co-ordination under shared authority. Rousseau's problem, then, is exactly the same problem later explored by *a priori* philosophical anarchists such as Robert Paul Wolff.[3] Unlike Wolff, Rousseau concludes that freedom and authority are compatible, just so long as the authority expresses the will of the individual subject to it so that he,[4] in effect, is not governed by an alien force but rather by his own desire and judgment. Since the law does in actuality preempt and override the private judgment of individuals about what they have reasons to do, the claim that in doing so it somehow corresponds to and implements their will is a bold and surprising one. Rousseau achieves the apparently impossible resolution of this contradiction by making distinctions among the interests and volitions of citizens and by imposing a hierarchical structure on those interests and volitions, such that the law realizes and implements the most important of them when it countermands the subjective and empirical intentions of citizens. This is because Rousseau believes that our deepest interest is in realizing the conditions under which we can coexist under relations of freedom and equality with others, so pursuing interests that undermine those conditions defeats the aim that we have most reason to pursue.

In this chapter, I first explore some general considerations about Rousseau's understanding of public reason, explaining how public reason is always relative to a particular public. Then I go on to discuss the central case of public reason, that of the general will of a state and Rousseau's idea that the general will must both come from all citizens via a process of public decision-making which generates valid laws, and apply to all citizens and be justifiable to each of them. I shall express some skepticism about how successful Rousseau's project is in achieving these aims. Returning to the theme of the relativity of public reason, I then look at Rousseau's use of this idea as he tracks the way in which the collective will of the magistrates comes to dominate over the general will of citizens as the state loses its legitimacy over time. Finally, I look at Rousseau's anticipation of Rawlsian thoughts on overlapping consensus and religious pluralism with his doctrine of civil religion.

2 The Relativity of Public Reason

For Rousseau, reason is public not in an absolute sense, but always relative to a given group of people, whether that group of people is some enduring institutional entity like a state or whether it is an episodic coming together of individuals on some occasion or for some purpose.[5] Most of the time in his discussion of public reason, this relativity is obscured by the fact that he wants to contrast the public reason of the state, as expressed by the general will and the law, with the private reason of individuals centered on their naturally selfish interests. But at times Rousseau also writes of the public reason of the human race as a whole—which can find expression in both morality and international law—and the corporate interest of sub-state groups, a corporate interest that is public relative to the private interest of the constituent members of those groups but private relative to the general will of the sovereign. This nesting of different levels of individual and collective interest and reason is central to his theory of government (as opposed to sovereignty) and also to his explanation of how states tend to become corrupt and to degenerate.

The relativity of public reason stems from the fact that Rousseau understands people as possessing multiple identities, each of which comes packaged with a set of interests and reasons appropriate to it. Individuals find themselves in a permanent state of tension as the wants, impulses and reasons corresponding to these various identities conflict with one another. The more general and abstract the identity, Rousseau thinks, the more closely the related reasons approach what morality requires. The more particular and individual the identity, at least as a generalization, the more disruptive the corresponding volitions are for the peaceful coexistence of people together within society. The great difficulty, however, is that the motivational pull of highly abstract identities—such as that of being a human being as such—is very weak and that of being an individual, with concrete needs, tastes, fears and wants is very strong. The trick of statecraft is to get people to identify to a sufficient degree with a persona that is both general enough to allow people to coexist with one another on terms of freedom, equality and non-domination, whilst being sufficiently concrete to motivate people in ways that overcome their individually selfish impulses. Rousseau believes that the identity or role of "citizen" can mostly bridge this gap between the demands of morality and our natural motivational weakness.

It is important to remember, though, that for Rousseau, these conflicts between individual interest, group identity and morality are products of our social evolution as a species rather than being timeless natural facts about us. The individual, whose consideration of self-interest leads him into conflict with the group or state, or to disregard the demands of conscience and morality, has self-interest with a socially evolved content. The original humans who Rousseau describes in the *Discourse on Inequality* have individual interests and impulses, but these do not lead them into systematic conflict with one another, they simply get on with the business of taking care of their biological needs in parallel with one another, with any episodic and contingent conflict being mitigated by a natural impulse of compassion or pitié. Socially evolved humans, by contrast, cannot solve their problem of subsistence alone, since they have developed needs that can now only be satisfied through social cooperation via a division of labor. Yet the same historical process that requires their co-operation has also made it fraught with difficulty because dependence on others, both psychological and material, opens new possibilities for exploitation, domination, disrespect and individual resentment.[6]

The opening slogan of the *Social Contract*, enjoining us to take "men as they are and laws as they might be" (SC 9; OC3, 351 [201]), expresses Rousseau's position that the general will and law of particular states is the appropriate level of compromise between the demands of universal morality and the shortcomings of evolved human nature. In the *Discourse on Political Economy*, written for Diderot's and d'Alembert's *Encyclopedia*, Rousseau had written of public reason operating on different levels and in different arenas and had argued that the more general ought to take precedence over the particular, the implication being that universal morality should trump the particular interests of states, and that the general will of a people should always take precedence over the particular wills of sub-groups or individuals. This structure is very much congruent with the view that Diderot had endorsed for his own *Encyclopedia* article on "Natural Right,"[7] where Diderot had written of the "general society of the human race," a general society equipped by a kind of cosmopolitan public reason. But by the time Rousseau came to draft the *Social Contract*, he had become much more skeptical about such a possibility on the grounds that such universalist reasoning would be unable to motivate individuals. Instead, in the unpublished second chapter of the Geneva manuscript draft of the *Social Contract*, Rousseau argues that only the pressures of socialization in a polity will shape human nature in such a way as to make just conduct possible. The particular republic, then, is the point of compromise between the possibility of disinterested moral conduct and the private impulses of selfish individuals. People can be brought to identify with and internalize the values of citizenship in a particular community to a degree that disciplines and represses those private impulses, whereas expecting them reliably to act from considerations of reason, morality and universal interest is a vain and unachievable hope.

The arena of the particular state is therefore the one that most commands Rousseau's attention when discussing public reason and the general will. In the next two sections I look at this from two aspects. First, what the general will is and how citizens come to decide on its content together; second, what Rousseau has to say about the justification of those laws to individuals and whether he is correct to say that obedience to the general will ensures their freedom.

3 Public Reason as a Collective Practice: The General Will Comes from All

The literature on public reason and public justification has always been marked by a divide between two different conceptions of what it involves, together with a variety of ingenious attempts to bridge that divide. The divide in question is between a view of public reason as involving the actual collective argument, deliberation and decision of the citizenry on the one hand, and a more objective understanding that stresses the reasons that apply to people, independently of whether those people actually acknowledge the reasons, on the other. Equivocation between those two conceptions and an attempt to blur the distinction between them is also a feature of Rousseau's writings on the subject. One way of making sense of his difficulties on the matter is to see him as committed to a hypothetical and procedural view, such that the general will would indeed emerge from the collective decision-making of the citizens, just in case the right conditions for its emergence were actually in place. However, Rousseau's own delineation of those conditions is far from precise.

That Rousseau does equivocate between these conceptions can be seen from a number of passages in the *Social Contract*. In Book 4 chapter 1, for example, he discusses the case where the state is on the edge of ruin and corrupted by partial societies and writes that though the general will "falls silent" it is not "annihilated or corrupted" but "is always unchanging, incorruptible and pure." (SC 100; OC3, 438 [232]). This suggests a notion of the general will as something that transcends the empirical deliberations and choices of citizens, an objective conception of their common interest that holds true whatever their opinion on the matter happens to be. Yet in earlier discussion, for example in Book 2 chapter 3—"Whether the general will can err"—he discusses a similar case but concludes that then "there is no longer a general will," but also writes that it is necessary to take "precautions" so that the "general will is always enlightened" (SC 33; OC3, 372 [216]), clearly presupposing that at times it is not. This tension between what I have elsewhere called the "transcendent" and "democratic" conceptions of the general will,[8] is a permanent feature of the *Social Contract*. Elsewhere in his writings, for example in the *Discourse on Political Economy*, the general will and public reason take on a far more objective character and the actual decision-making of citizens plays less of a role. But in the *Social Contract* at least, though the tension is never resolved, the suggestion is that under the right conditions, actual citizen choices would converge on what is objectively in the public interest.

Rousseau does most of the important work in chapters 3–6 of Book 2 of the *Social Contract*. In chapter 3, he famously makes a distinction between the general will and the "will of all," though it is important to note that the latter is not a technical term and that in other contexts the exact same phrase is used to denote the general will. Here, however, the contrast is between a collective will that genuinely corresponds to the collective interest of the citizens and one that is merely the aggregation of their private, selfish, wills. In a puzzling reference to the infinitesimal calculus, Rousseau tells us that if we "remove from these same wills the pluses and minuses that cancel each other out,... what is left as the sum of the differences is the general will." (SC 32; OC3, 372 [216]) He tries to clarify this obscure passage by a footnote in which he asserts "agreement between all interests is formed through opposition to the interests of each." (SC 32, OC3, 371n [244n7]). What Rousseau seems to have in mind is the idea that each citizen has both a private interest in exempting himself from socially useful rules that prescribe co-operation and an interest in other people not exempting themselves: once we remove from this calculus all the self-interested exemptions or differences we have a perspective from which each urges universal compliance with these rules or laws.

Rousseau believes this procedure only works if citizens are prevented from forming coalitions with one another. This is because any such coalitions will have a collective interest (and therefore a corporate will) of their own. If they are sufficiently large as a proportion of the citizenry, they can co-ordinate their votes so as to bias the collective decision of the state in ways that shift the benefits and burdens of social co-operation in favor of their own members. If, by contrast, individuals are forced to approve or disapprove of the laws without "communication with one another" (SC 32; OC3, 371 [216]) they are thereby deprived of the opportunity to organize this kind of anti-social conspiracy. Though Rousseau concedes that this isolation of individuals' decisions from one another is probably impractical, it nevertheless gives rise to the rather paradoxical state of affairs that for him public reason reaches its zenith of perfection when decision-making is completely isolated and non-public.

The way in which formal features of the decision-making situation force individuals psychologically to adopt a public point of view is also brought out in a passage in the immediately following chapter, where Rousseau emphasizes the effect that the fact that laws consist of general and impartial rules will have on individual choice:

> Why is the general will always rightful, and why do all continuously wish for the happiness of each, unless it is because there is no one who does not appropriate that word *each*, and who does not think about himself in voting for all. This proves that equal rights, and the notion of justice they produce, derive from the preference that everyone accords to himself: hence, from the nature of man.
>
> (SC 34; OC3, 373 [216])

What we have then is a structure in some ways akin to that of Rawls's original position. Individuals are guided by considerations of self-interest, but they have to do so in a manner that is framed by features of the choice situation that lead them to adopt an impartial perspective despite themselves. If they cannot combine with others to skew the result in their favor and if the general will only approves proposals which are couched in a general form and do not mention particulars, then Rousseau thinks they will endorse a content for the law that is in the public interest.

4 Justification to Individuals: The General Will Applies to All

Formulating the content of the general will and approving it is only part of the business of public justification. Once the law is approved it also needs justification to individuals to explain why they ought to consider it as applying to them. Rousseau has two things to say here, one of which is somewhat more convincing than the other. The first of these is that citizens are authors of the law and that in following the law they are obeying their own will. They are free in the sense that they obey a law that they have given to themselves. The second is that obedience to the law is a condition of republican freedom: it frees individuals from the danger of being subject to the arbitrary will of others, providing a mutual guarantee of non-domination. The first has to do with the particular content of laws, the second with the benefits of living in a law-governed society where negative freedom is reciprocally limited.

Do Citizens Obey Themselves, as Rousseau Claimed?

Rousseau's claim in the *Social Contract* is to have reconciled the authority necessary for social co-ordination with individual freedom, and that citizens subject to the law nevertheless remain as free as before. But he comes to see in Book 4 chapter 2 of the Social Contract that this claim is problematic, for the simple reason that when any vote fails to be unanimous there will then be a minority who obey not themselves but rather a victorious majority. Rousseau's answer to this problem is to conceive of sovereign decision-making as being epistemic in character: it is a method of finding out the facts about where the public interest lies. On this way of thinking about the problem, there is a fact of the matter and citizens are engaged in the collective task of finding out what it is (what the best terms of association are, where justice lies). Before the vote is taken, citizens may have differing private opinions about what the general will will decide. In this they are like members of a team participating in a treasure hunt, each of whom has a different opinion about where the treasure is buried, but all of whom want their team to find the treasure, which they will only do in the place where it is actually buried.[9] Since they all will that the right answer, whatever it turns out to be, is arrived at, those whose opinion turns out to have been mistaken still end up getting what they wanted and so, thinks Rousseau, everyone still ends up both willing and obeying the general will which is theirs.

Needless to say, this strategy is immensely problematic. First, it assumes without argument that there is a fact about where the public interest lies, a fact of the matter that voters are trying to discover. But not all political decisions are of this character. Some of them are merely about the aggregation of wants, none of which may be right or wrong in themselves, and where there is no "right answer" as to which aggregation is the correct one. Second, even if we assume that there is a right answer, Rousseau gives us no reason to believe that virtuous citizens, voting on propositions selected by the magistrates, will reliably discover it. At best, there is a mere hope that they will. Rousseau tells us that citizens will converge on the general will just in case "all the qualities of the general will still reside in the majority" (SC 103; OC3, 441 [234]). Taking this statement to refer to the presuppositions of good decision-making in some extended sense, we can understand Rousseau as asserting that when properly-informed and patriotic citizens decide on the (general and universal) laws against a background of roughly equal social conditions, they will inevitably pick that option, from those presented to them, that corresponds to the general will. But Rousseau gives us no reason to believe that this is true.

Rousseau writes that

> when the opposite opinion to mine prevails, that proves nothing other than that I was mistaken, and that what I considered to be the general will was not. If my particular opinion had prevailed, I should have done something other than what I had willed, and it is then that I should not have been free.
>
> (SC 103; OC3, 441 [234])

We can see that this claim is incorrect. Since Rousseau has not delineated a reliable method whereby an objective truth about the public good will be the result of the voting procedure,[10] there is no reason for citizens who find themselves in the minority to believe that they simply got things wrong. In fact, they may very well have been correct and thus, when they end up being constrained to obey the law, they subject themselves not to their own will on the particular matter, but rather to the will of other people, the majority.

There may, nevertheless, be a residual sense in which, in obeying the law, the minoritarians end up obeying themselves. This is that although they are outvoted on the particular proposition being decided upon, their desires are structured such that they prefer to go along with the majority anyway, because they place a high value on agreed co-operation with their fellows and they recognize the vote as a fair procedure. But that would be a rather different sort of argument to the one that Rousseau actually puts. Some grounds for such a preference, though, are provided by Rousseau's belief that compliance with the general will is necessary for non-domination, as I shall suggest in the next section.

Does Compliance with the General Will Promote Individual Freedom in Other Ways?

Although Rousseau's story about the justification of particular laws to individuals is implausible, he has a different tale to tell about submission to a framework of law in general. In a notorious passage from Book 1 chapter 7 of the *Social Contract*, Rousseau writes:

> in order that the social pact should not be a vain formula, it tacitly incorporates a commitment that alone can give force to all the rest: namely, that whosoever refuses to obey the general will shall be constrained to do so by the whole body. This means nothing other than that he shall be forced to be free. For such is the condition that, by giving each Citizen to the Fatherland, guarantees him against all personal dependence.
>
> (SC 3; OC3, 364 [210])

Rousseau's thought, however colorfully expressed, is that when citizens are subject to a set of laws that equally and reciprocally limit their negative freedom, they nevertheless enjoy freedom in another sense, namely that they are not subject to the arbitrary will of others. In the *Letters from the Mountains* he explicitly endorses such a republican understanding of freedom when he writes

> Liberty consists less in acting upon your wish than in not being subjected to the wish of others; it further consists of not subjecting the wish of others to our own.[11]

The idea then is that in being secured by the law against the personal domination of others, individuals are rendered comparatively free, that is, freer than they would be under any other possible and realizable state of affairs. This seems not implausible, just so long as two further conditions are met. Both of these conditions relate to the previous discussion of the citizen who finds himself in the minority. First, though Rousseau failed to show that the vote of the citizens, even under ideal conditions, would reliably track the public interest, a weaker relationship between democratic choice and outcomes might be enough to make popular sovereignty better from the point of view of republican freedom than are other regimes. The popular vote may fail to track the truth (if there is one) about the public interest, but it may avoid choices that are severely damaging. The fact that citizens, in considering the law, consider its impact on themselves will, at least under conditions of rough equality and similar modes of living, ensure that they reject proposals that are severely detrimental to their negative freedom or well-being. The second condition is that the state is not factionalized into permanent majorities and minorities because then the state would become an instrument of the private wills of a part of the population and the minority would not be free from their arbitrary interference. Rousseau considers this possibility when he writes about the degeneration of the state, but mainly in the form of domination by the rich as a consequence of growing luxury and inequality. Readers might have concerns, though, that there are other bases for social division and factionalism. These might include intrusive moral beliefs about how other people should live their lives, and also sectarian divisions based on religion. Though Rousseau never really considers these problems, he does at least address the question of religious pluralism and social unity, a matter I turn to below.

Justification and the Lawgiver

A final matter needs discussing concerning justification of the law to individuals. Although much of what Rousseau says about framing the choice situation so as to direct self-interest to produce an impartial law might suggest that the private virtue of citizens is a minor matter, other passages tell us that he believed that in order reliably to will the general will, citizens would need to have a strong patriotic sense of their identity as members of the state. Rousseau's anxiety about this is probably the source of one of the oddest features of the *Social Contract*, his insistence in Book 2 chapter 7 of the need for a lawgiver or legislator. His idea is that, as citizens of a new state have not been socialized within one, they will lack the ability reliably to will the general will, they will be too savage, selfish and individualistic. Having the right citizenly virtues is the result of having been formed by the laws and so cannot be their original source. It hardly helps to address this problem to summon up a mysterious figure from nowhere, whose role is to inspire the population by his charismatic authority to act as they would act if only they were virtuous. After all, where does he come from, and how was he socialized in the right way?

The concern here, though, is that Rousseau doesn't give up his requirement that the law must come from the people and apply to the people. Rather he treats laws as authentically coming from the people when they have been inspired by irrational means to give their assent and where they still lack the cognitive and volitional apparatus to evaluate the propositions they are being asked to decide. If the point of tying legitimate authority to public reason depends on a respect for citizens as rational agents, the fable of the lawgiver is a massive failure. Other features of Rousseau's ideal republic, such as the role of the magistrates, also give cause for concern.

5 Government, the Relativity of Public Reason and the Degeneration of the State

The Reason of the Magistrates

Rousseau's view that when reason is public it is relative to some given group, rather than absolute, is central to his explanation of how the state tends to degenerate over time, a process that is outlined in the *Social*

Contract and further explored, with respect to his home city of Geneva, in the *Letters from the Mountains*. To understand this process, it is vital to grasp Rousseau's distinction between sovereignty and government. Sovereignty is the exercise of the public reason of the citizen-body as a whole and finds expression in the general will, which is codified in general and universal laws. These laws come from everybody and apply to everybody (*Social Contract* Book 2, chapter 6). Government, or magistracy, by contrast is a specific function within the state that takes the form of implementing and enforcing the laws in particular cases and managing the day-to-day business of the state in a manner framed by the law and the general will. Whereas sovereignty is the business of the people as a whole and cannot be exercised via deputies or representatives (Book 3, chapter 15), government is carried out by an elected subset of the population, who constitute a kind of elite or aristocracy. Failure to grasp this distinction in Rousseau's thought often leads to him being thought of as an opponent of representative government, but he is not,[12] since government is carried out by magistrates who are the representatives of the people.

Rousseau posits a numerical relationship between the size of the state and the size of the government. Roughly speaking, the idea is that government, as a distinct institution, is needed less in a very small state with a strong sense of civil identity than it is in a very large one. This is coupled with the idea that collective bodies (such as committees) tend to be more capable of resolute and decisive action when they are small, and become less capable as they grow in size. In a very small state, then, there is little for the government to do as the laws are simple and few in number and everyone has a strong sense of being a member of the community and therefore a strong internal motive both to comply with the laws and to express social disapproval of people who step out of line. A small state, then, can approximate communitarian anarchy of the kind discussed by Michael Taylor.[13] A much larger state, by contrast, needs a government that is more forceful and capable of action and this means a government that is smaller *relative to the size of the state* than in a small community.

This is because larger states tend to reproduce the same problem that makes it impossible for people to live together according to abstract and universal principles of morality, namely that the voice of the collective within their own personal deliberations is weak compared to that of their own purely private interest (and perhaps compared to sectional interests, such as family or clan). The individual within a large state experiences his membership of it as more of a formal matter, it does not motivate him as immediately and directly as his private concerns do and it requires reflection and mental effort. Accordingly, the individual takes less interest in what the general will might say and is perennially tempted to ignore the law when it is in his private interest to do so. So rather than, for example, contributing gladly with his neighbors to the provision of some public good for the village, the citizen of a large state is more likely to free ride by evading his taxes. As voluntary compliance diminishes, the need for government to act to overcome that lack of compliance increases, if the state is not to unravel altogether.

This is where the collective reasoning and identity of the magistrates emerges as a problem in its own right. The magistrates are supposedly servants of the public reason of the citizens, but as a group, a public, they also have a public reason of their own which expresses their collective interest. They have a sense of identity and belonging that is no doubt forged in opposition to the people whose trustees they are meant to be. Rousseau's suspicions seem plausible: any group of managers, administrators, or police, faced with a recalcitrant population whom they have the task of getting to behave, is likely to develop its own *ésprit de corps*, its own feelings of mutual trust and comradeship and some tendency to regard the wider population with a mixture of frustration and contempt. True, magistrates are citizens too, and the voice of citizenry speaks to them also, but it is comparatively muted and competes with their identities as magistrates and as private individuals. In addition, the magistrates will also interpret the public interest in a distorted way through the lens of their particular role (in other words the effects are cognitive as well as volitional). Over time this sets the stage for the end of popular sovereignty and the degeneration of the state into an oligarchy governed according to the interests of the magistracy.

Government and Popular Sovereignty

Although Rousseau has long been an inspiration to advocates of various forms of direct, participatory or deliberative democracy, his account suggests a picture of the ideal state where—as we have seen—very little public conversation about politics goes on. Moreover, the selection of political choices for citizens to consider may be confined to a small elite. This, at any rate, seems to be the implication of a curious passage that occurs at the end of Book 4 chapter 1 where Rousseau writes

> the simple right to vote in every act of sovereignty: a right that no one can take away from Citizens. Also... the right of voicing an opinion, proposing, dividing and debating—which the Government always takes great care to confine to its own members.
> (SC 101; OC3, 439 [232–3])

These remarks, which appear to reserve the right of legislative initiative to the magistrates are somewhat ambiguous, since they are expressed in a way that can be read either as a remark about the likely behavior of governments (and hence as indicating tacit disapproval) or as some kind of recommendation on Rousseau's part. Those determined to read Rousseau as a participatory democrat are forced to take the former path.[14] The trouble with such a reading is that it jars with what he writes in other texts such as the *Letters from the Mountains*. These require a little bit of context.

The *Letters from the Mountains* are Rousseau's belated response to the condemnation of the *Social Contract* and *Emile* by the government of Geneva. Though a citizen of Geneva by birth, Rousseau had lost his citizenship when he converted to Catholicism only to reclaim it later in the 1750s and had thenceforward used the title "Citizen of Geneva" with pride as self-description of himself as an author. Geneva had, as Rousseau was well aware, been the site of several bitter conflicts between its oligarchic government and the wider citizenry (themselves only a small subset of the population) over the issue of sovereignty. After the *Social Contract* was condemned, Rousseau's own reaction was to renounce his citizenship for good, but citizens of republican persuasion nevertheless initiated protests on his behalf, protests which met with a polemical rebuttal from the oligarchy in the form of Jean-Robert Tronchin's *Letters from the Country*. Rousseau's reply is notable for its striking depiction of the logic of oligarchy and of the ways in which those who supposedly work for the people can concentrate power in their own hands. But it is also remarkable for his failure to endorse, indeed his rejection of, the idea that the common citizens ought to have the legislative initiative. Instead, he largely endorses the "Règlement" (the de facto constitution) of 1738 as legitimate. This suggests that he does in fact reject as a matter of principle, a conception of public reason as involving the active participation of the citizens in formulating the general will. Rather, they get to choose between options formulated by the magistrates, with the constitutional backstop that they may replace those magistrates with new ones.

We have, then, the combination of two factors which, together, are fatal for popular sovereignty in the long term. First, government is a necessary function in the state, but the government has an inbuilt tendency to detach itself from the public interest and to deliberate from its own perspective rather than that of the state as a whole. Second, though this is a contingent feature of his constitutional preferences and one he might have done well to abandon, Rousseau grants all legislative initiative to a group who are subject to these distortions. The government has, then, both the motive and the means to subvert public decision-making and to impose their own will on the collective.

6 Public Reason and Civil Religion

There is one further point of connection between Rousseau's thought and modern discussions in public reason. For most of the *Social Contract*, Rousseau has little to say about the substantive content of the law as willed by the general will. Rather, that content is left open: the law is whatever the citizens decide that it will be and that is not something that the philosopher or theorist is able to anticipate in abstraction from the culture and traditions of a particular society. But in the final full chapter of the book (Book 4, chapter 8), there is a striking departure from this that anticipates in interesting ways some modern discussions of public reason in a context of religious pluralism.[15]

In the chapter "Of Civil Religion," Rousseau wrestles with the tension between the need for social unity and the fact of religious diversity. This focus is slightly odd in itself, since most of the discussion in the book, though drawing on models from the ancient world (particularly Rome), remains somewhat abstract and ahistorical, a discussion of the legitimate state in general. In this chapter, however, Rousseau engages with modern, post-Reformation societies, riven between Catholics and Protestants (and no doubt containing Jews and other minorities). The chapter is essentially about toleration and its limits and seeks to find a reasonable basis on which different religious believers can coexist without coming into conflict.

The civil religion that Rousseau proposes has five "positive dogmas" and one negative one. The positive ones are: (1) the existence of an omniscient and benign deity; (2) that there is an afterlife; (3) that just people will prosper; (4) that the wicked will be punished; (5) that the social contract and laws are sacred. The negative dogma is that intolerance will not be tolerated. These dogmas, Rousseau tells us are "simple, few in number, enunciated with precision and without explanations or commentaries" (SC 131; OC3, 468 [242]).

The modern reader is apt to read Rousseau's words with alarm and to perceive the civil religion as just another manifestation of Rousseau's supposed "totalitarianism." There is some basis for this. Rousseau writes that though the state cannot force anyone to accept the dogmas, anyone who does not may be exiled on the grounds that he lacks the capacity to do his duty as a citizen. Anyone who, perhaps hesitating at the prospect of exile, signs up for the civil religion but afterwards shows by his actions that he did so insincerely may justly be put to death. Both atheists, who cannot accept the existence of God and the afterlife, and members of intolerant sects, therefore face an unpalatable choice and the prospect of dire punishment. This is certainly an unattractive feature of Rousseau's view and we should not underplay it. However, nor should we ignore the fact that the civil religion is intended to promote mutual tolerance and that it has structural features of great interest from the perspective of public reason.

The simplicity and economy of the dogmas and the fact that they are not given explanations or justifications have the effect of maximizing the extent to which they can be shared and affirmed by citizens who differ from one another in their religious beliefs. To draw on terminology from John Rawls, the dogmas of the civil religion are inside an "overlapping consensus" of "reasonable comprehensive doctrines."[16] Protestants and Catholics may disagree about the precise nature of the deity, the character of the afterlife and on what justifies belief in these features of their religion. But they can all affirm belief in a set of conclusions whilst differing on the underlying explanations, and this shared affirmation provides a basis for mutual trust and social unity. This consensus also excludes the unreasonable; the people who are not prepared to coexist with others on fair terms but who insist that the political realm must be bent to the triumph of their own sectarian viewpoint. Those who say, *"No salvation outside the Church* must be driven from the State" (SC 132; OC3, 469 [243]) because they cannot live with others and others cannot live with them on the basis of freedom and reciprocity.

7 Conclusion

Rousseau's contribution to our thinking about public reason is immense. The idea of the general will and that the law ought to be justifiable to citizens who are themselves its makers is central both to his and to modern discussions. Unsurprisingly, Rousseau failed to solve all the problems (if indeed they are solvable at all) but he has much to say to us about the connection between the public interest and collective decision-making and how the two might be brought together. Ultimately his claim that citizens who are subject to the law, though in a minority, still obey only themselves looks implausible. Yet the idea that a framework of impartial law might be the best means to free citizens from the arbitrary interference of one another rightly endures.

Notes

1. Professor of Social and Political Philosophy, Department of Philosophy, University of Bristol.
2. In-text references to the *Social Contract* are henceforth to Rousseau (2012), given as SC followed by the page number. For references to this and other works I also give the corresponding reference in Rousseau (1959–95) as OC3 (volume 3) followed by the page number. [Page numbers in brackets refer to the corresponding reference in this volume—eds.]
3. Wolff (1970).
4. Rousseau's citizens are all male.
5. See *Discourse on Political Economy* in Rousseau (1997), 7; OC3, 245–6 [185–6].
6. For a general account of Rousseau's views on human moral psychology and its historical development, see Bertram (2003) chapter 2; also Dent (1988), chapters 2–4, and Neuhouser (2008), chapters 1–4.
7. Diderot (1992), 17–21.
8. Bertram (2012).

9 This simile is adapted from Arneson (2004).
10 Some writers have seen in Rousseau's remarks in Book 2 chapter 3 of *Social Contract* an anticipation of Condorcet's jury theorem. If this were so, and there were a fact of the matter about the public interest, and citizens were on average more likely than not to perceive that truth, then Rousseau might have outlined a reliable method. But his remarks are too vague and the historical connection between Rousseau and Condorcet is too implausible to support this conjecture.
11 Eighth letter, from Rousseau (2012), 185 (OC3, 841).
12 As well-argued in Marini (1967).
13 Taylor (1982).
14 Joshua Cohen would be a good example of this, and much of chapter 4 of Cohen (2010) is devoted to rebutting the views of Fralin (1978).
15 In this section, I draw on Bertram (2009).
16 See, for example, Rawls (1993) chapter 4.

Bibliography

Arneson, Richard. 2004. "Democracy Is Not Intrinsically Just." In *Justice and Democracy*, edited by Carole Pateman, Keith Dowding, and Robert E. Goodin, 40–58. Cambridge: Cambridge University Press.

Bertram, Christopher. 2003. *Rousseau and the Social Contract*. London: Routledge.

———. 2009. "Toleration and Pluralism in Rousseau's Civil Religion." In *Rousseau and L'Infâme: Religion, Toleration and Fanaticism in the Age of Enlightenment*, edited by Ourida Mostefai and John T. Scott, 137–52. Amsterdam: Rodopi.

———. 2012. "Rousseau's Legacy in Two Conceptions of the General Will: Democratic and Transcendent." *The Review of Politics* 73 (3): 403–19.

Cohen, Joshua. 2010. *Rousseau: A Free Community of Equals*. Oxford: Oxford University Press.

Dent, N.J.H. 1988. *Rousseau*. Oxford: Blackwell.

Diderot, Denis. 1992. *Diderot: Political Writings*. Edited by Hope Mason and Wokler. Cambridge: Cambridge University Press.

Fralin, Richard. 1978. *Rousseau and Representation*. New York: Columbia.

Marini, Frank. 1967. "Popular Sovereignty but Representative Government: The Other Rousseau." *Midwest Journal of Political Science* 11 (4): 451–70.

Neuhouser, Frederick. 2008. *Rousseau's Theodicy of Self-Love*. Oxford: Oxford University Press.

Rawls, John. 1993. *Political Liberalism*. New York: Columbia.

Rousseau, Jean-Jacques. 1959/1995AD. *Œuvres Complètes*. Edited by B. Gagnebin and M. Raymond. Paris: Gallimard.

———. 1997. *The Social Contract and Other Later Political Writings*. Edited by Victor Gourevitch. Cambridge: Cambridge University Press.

———. 2012. *Of the Social Contract and Other Political Writings*. Edited by Christopher Bertram. Translated by Quintin Hoare. London: Penguin.

Taylor, Michael. 1982. *Community, Anarchy and Liberty*. Cambridge: Cambridge University Press.

Wolff, Robert Paul. 1970. *In Defense of Anarchism*. New York: Harper & Row.

4

IMMANUEL KANT (1724–1804)
The Science of Right (1796)[1]

INTRODUCTION TO THE SCIENCE OF RIGHT

....

C. Universal Principle of Right

'Every Action is right which in itself, or in the maxim on which it proceeds, is such that it can co-exist along with the Freedom of the Will of each and all in action, according to a universal Law.'

If, then, my action or my condition generally can co-exist with the freedom of every other, according to a universal Law, any one does me a wrong who hinders me in the performance of this action, or in the maintenance of this condition. For such a hindrance or obstruction cannot co-exist with Freedom according to universal Laws.

It follows also that it cannot be demanded as a matter of Right, that this universal Principle of all maxims shall itself be adopted as my maxim, that is, that I shall make it the maxim of my actions. For any one may be free, although his Freedom is entirely indifferent to me, or even if I wished in my heart to infringe it, so long as I do not actually violate that freedom by my external action. Ethics, however, as distinguished from Jurisprudence, imposes upon me the obligation to make the fulfilment of Right a maxim of my conduct.

The universal Law of Right may then be expressed, thus: 'Act externally in such a manner that the free exercise of thy Will may be able to co-exist with the Freedom of all others, according to a universal Law.' This is undoubtedly a Law which imposes obligation upon me; but it does not at all imply and still less command that I ought, merely on account of this obligation, to limit my freedom to these very conditions. Reason in this connection says only that it is restricted thus far by its Idea, and may be likewise thus limited in fact by others; and it lays this down as a Postulate which is not capable of further proof. As the object in view is not to teach Virtue, but to explain what Right is, thus far the Law of Right, as thus laid down, may not and should not be represented as a motive-principle of action.

D. *Right is conjoined with the Title or Authority to Compel*

The resistance which is opposed to any hindrance of an effect, is in reality a furtherance of this effect, and is in accordance with its accomplishment. Now, everything that is wrong is a hindrance of freedom, according to universal Laws; and Compulsion or Constraint of any kind is a hindrance or resistance made to Freedom. Consequently, if a certain exercise of Freedom is itself a hindrance of the Freedom that is according to universal Laws, it is wrong; and the compulsion or constraint which is opposed to it is right, as being a hindering of a hindrance of Freedom, and as being in accord with the Freedom which exists in accordance with universal Laws. Hence, according to the logical principle of Contradiction, all Right is accompanied with an implied Title or warrant to bring compulsion to bear on any one who may violate it in fact.

THE SCIENCE OF RIGHT, PART FIRST: PRIVATE RIGHT

....

Transition from the mine and thine in the state of nature to the mine and thine in the juridical state generally

41. Public Justice as related to the Natural and the Civil state

The Juridical state is that relation of men to one another which contains the conditions, under which it is alone possible for every one to obtain the Right that is his due. The formal Principle of the possibility of actually *participating* in such Right, viewed in accordance with the Idea of a universally legislative Will, is PUBLIC JUSTICE. Public Justice may be considered in relation either to the Possibility, or Actuality, or Necessity of the Possession of objects—regarded as the matter of the activity of the Will—according to laws. It may thus be divided into *Protective Justice (justitia testatrix), Commutative Justice (justitia commutativa),* and *Distributive Justice (justitia distributiva).* In the *first* mode of Justice, the Law declares merely what Relation is internally *right* in respect of Form (*lex justi*); in the *second*, it declares what is likewise externally in accord with a Law in respect of the Object, and what Possession is rightful (*lex juridica*); and in the *third*, it declares what is right, and what is *just*, and to what extent, by the Judgment of a Court in any particular case coming under the given Law. In this latter relation, the Public Court is called the *Justice* of the Country; and the question whether there actually is or is not such an administration of Public Justice, may be regarded as the most important of all juridical interests.

The non-juridical state is that condition of Society in which there is no Distributive Justice. It is commonly called the *Natural* state (*status naturalis*), or the state of Nature. It is not the 'Social' State,' as Achenwall puts it, for this may be in itself an *artificial* state (*status artificialis*), that is to be contradistinguished from the 'Natural' state. The opposite of the state of Nature is the *Civil* state (*status civilis*) as the condition of a Society standing under a Distributive Justice. In the state of Nature there may even be juridical forms of Society—such as Marriage, Parental Authority, the Household, and such like. For none of these, however, does any Law *à priori* lay it down as an incumbent obligation, 'Thou *shalt* enter into this state.' But it may be said of the *Juridical* state that 'all men who may even involuntarily come into Relations of Right with one another, *ought* to enter into this state.'

The Natural or non-juridical Social state may be viewed as the sphere of PRIVATE RIGHT, and the Civil state may be specially regarded as the sphere of PUBLIC RIGHT. The latter state contains no more and no other Duties of men towards each other than what may be conceived in connection with the former state; the Matter of Private Right is, in short, the very same in both. The Laws of the Civil state, therefore, only turn upon the juridical Form of the co-existence of men under a common Constitution; and in this respect these Laws must necessarily be regarded and conceived as Public Laws.

The Civil Union (*Unio civilis*) cannot, in the strict sense, be properly called a *Society*; for there is no sociality in common between the Ruler (*imperans*) and the Subject (*subditus*) under a Civil Constitution. They are not co-ordinated as Associates in a Society with each other, but the one is *subordinated* to the other. Those who may be co-ordinated with one another must consider themselves as mutually equal, in so far as they stand under common Laws. The Civil Union may therefore be regarded not so much as *being*, but rather as *making* a Society.

42. The Postulate of Public Right

From the conditions of Private Right in the Natural state, there arises the Postulate of Public Right. It may be thus expressed: 'In the relation of unavoidable co-existence with others, thou shalt pass from the state of Nature into a juridical Union constituted under the condition of a Distributive Justice.' The Principle of this Postulate may be unfolded analytically from the conception of *Right* in the external relation, contradistinguished from mere *Might* as Violence.

No one is under obligation to abstain from interfering with the Possession of others, unless they give him a reciprocal guarantee for the observance of a similar abstention from interference with his Possession. Nor does he require to wait for proof by experience of the need of this guarantee, in view of the antagonistic disposition of others. He is therefore under no obligation to wait till he acquires practical prudence at his own cost; for he can perceive in himself evidence of the natural Inclination of men to play the master over others, and to disregard the claims of the Right of others, when they feel themselves their superiors by Might or Fraud. And thus it is not necessary to wait for the melancholy experience of actual hostility; the individual is from the first entitled to exercise a rightful compulsion towards those who already threaten him by their very nature. *Quilibet præsumitur malus, donec securitatem dederit oppositi.*

So long as the intention to live and continue in this state of externally lawless Freedom prevails, men may be said to do no wrong or injustice at all *to one another*, even when they wage war against each other. For what seems competent as good for the one, is equally valid for the other, as if it were so by mutual agreement. *Uti partes de jure suo disponunt, ita jus est.* But generally they must be considered as being in the highest state of Wrong, as being and willing to be in a condition which is not juridical; and in which, therefore, no one can be secured against Violence, in the possession of his own.

The distinction between what is only *formally* and what is also *materially* wrong and unjust, finds frequent application in the Science of Right. An enemy who, on occupying a besieged fortress, instead of honourably fulfilling the conditions of a Capitulation, maltreats the garrison on marching out, or otherwise violates the agreement, cannot complain of injury or wrong if on another occasion the same treatment is inflicted upon themselves. But, in fact, all such actions fundamentally involve the commission of wrong and injustice, in the highest degree; because they take all validity away from the conception of Right, and give up everything, as it were by law itself, to savage Violence, and thus overthrow the Rights of Men generally.

THE SCIENCE OF RIGHT, PART SECOND: PUBLIC RIGHT

43. Definition and Division of Public Right

PUBLIC RIGHT embraces the whole of the Laws that require to be universally promulgated in order to produce a juridical state of Society. It is therefore a System of those Laws that are requisite for a People as a multitude of men forming a Nation, or for a number of Nations, in their relations to each other. Men and Nations, on account of their mutual influence on one another, require a juridical *Constitution* uniting them under one Will, in order that they may participate in what is right.—This relation of the Individuals of a Nation to each other, constitutes THE CIVIL UNION in the social state; and, viewed as a whole in relation to its constituent members, it forms THE POLITICAL STATE (*Civitas*).

1. The State, as constituted by the common interest of all to live in a juridical union, is called, in view of its form, the COMMONWEALTH or the REPUBLIC in the wider sense of the term (*Res publica latius sic dicta*). The Principles of Right in this sphere, thus constitute the first department of Public Right as the RIGHT OF THE STATE (*jus Civitatis*) or National Right.—2. The State, again, viewed in relation to other peoples, is called a Power (*potentia*), whence arises the idea of Potentates. Viewed in relation to the supposed hereditary unity of the people composing it, the State constitutes a Nation (*gens*). Under the general conception of Public Right, in addition to the Right of the individual State, there thus arises another department of Right, constituting the RIGHT OF NATIONS (*jus gentium*) or International Right.—3. Further, as the surface of the earth is not unlimited in extent, but is circumscribed into a unity, National Right and International Right necessarily culminate in the idea of a UNIVERSAL RIGHT OF MANKIND, which may be called 'Cosmopolitical Right' (*jus cosmopoliticum*). And National, International, and Cosmopolitical Right are so interconnected, that if any one of these three possible forms of the juridical Relation fails to embody the essential Principles that ought to regulate external freedom by law, the structure of Legislation reared by the others will also be undermined, and the whole System would at last fall to pieces.

44. *Origin of the Civil Union and Public Right*

It is not from any Experience prior to the appearance of an external authoritative Legislation, that we learn of the maxim of natural violence among men, and their evil tendency to engage in war with each other. Nor is it assumed here that it is merely some particular historical condition or fact, that makes public legislative constraint necessary; for however well-disposed or favourable to Right men may be considered to be of themselves, the rational Idea of a state of Society not yet regulated by Right, must be taken as our starting-point. This Idea implies that before a legal state of Society can be publicly established, individual Men, Nations and States can never be safe against violence from each other; and this is evident from the consideration that every one of his own Will naturally does *what seems good and right in his own eyes*, entirely independent of the opinion of others. Hence, unless the institution of Right is to be renounced, the first thing incumbent on men is to accept the Principle that it is necessary to leave the state of Nature, in which every one follows his own inclinations, and to form a union of all those who cannot avoid coming into reciprocal communication, and thus subject themselves in common to the external restraint of public compulsory Laws. Men thus enter into a Civil Union, in which every one has it determined by Law what shall be recognised as his; and this is secured to him by a competent external Power distinct from his own individuality. Such is the primary Obligation, on the part of all men, to enter into the relations of a Civil State of Society.

The natural condition of mankind need not, on this ground, be represented as a state of absolute *Injustice*, as if there could have been no other relation originally among men but what was merely determined by force. But this natural condition must be regarded, if it ever existed, as a state of society that was void of regulation by Right (*status justitiæ vacuus*), so that if a matter of Right came to be *in dispute* (*jus controversum*), no competent judge was found to give an authorized legal decision upon it. It is therefore reasonable that any one should constrain another by force, to pass from such a non-juridical state of life and enter within the jurisdiction of a civil state of Society. For, although on the basis of the *ideas of Right* held by individuals as such, external things may be acquired by Occupancy or Contract, yet such acquisition is only *provisory* so long as it has not yet obtained the sanction of a Public Law. Till this sanction is reached, the condition of possession is not determined by any public Distributive Justice, nor is it secured by any Power exercising Public Right.

If men were not disposed to recognise any Acquisition at all as rightful—even in a provisional way—prior to entering into the Civil state, this state of Society would itself be impossible. For the Laws regarding the Mine and Thine in the state of Nature, contain formally the very same thing as they prescribe in the Civil state, when it is viewed merely according to rational conceptions: only that in the forms of the Civil state the conditions are laid down under which the formal prescriptions of the state of Nature attain realization conformable to Distributive Justice.—Were there, then, not even *provisionally*, an external Meum and Tuum in the state of Nature, neither would there be any juridical Duties in relation to them; and, consequently, there would be no obligation to pass out of that state into another.

45. The Form of the State and its Three Powers.

A State (*Civitas*) is the union of a number of men under juridical Laws. These Laws, as such, are to be regarded as necessary à priori,—that is, as following of themselves from the conceptions of external Right generally,—and not as merely established by Statute. The FORM of the

State is thus involved in the *Idea* of the State, viewed as it ought to be according to pure principles of Right; and this ideal Form furnishes the normal criterion of every real union that constitutes a Commonwealth.

Every State contains in itself THREE POWERS, the universal united Will of the People being thus personified in a political triad. These are *the Legislative Power, the Executive Power,* and *the Judiciary Power.*—1. The *Legislative* Power of the Sovereignty in the State, is embodied in the person of the Lawgiver; 2. the Executive Power is embodied in the person of the Ruler who administers the Law; and 3. the Judiciary Power, embodied in the person of the Judge, is the function of assigning every one what is his own, according to the Law (*Potestas legislatoria, rectoria et judiciaria*). These three Powers may be compared to the three propositions in a practical Syllogism:—the Major as the sumption laying down the universal *Law* of a Will, the Minor presenting the *command* applicable to an action according to the Law as the principle of the subsumption, and the Conclusion containing the Sentence or judgment of Right in the particular case under consideration.

Note

1 From the translation by William Hastie in Immanuel Kant, *The Philosophy of Law: An Exposition of the Fundamental Principles of Jurisprudence as the Science of Right* (Edinburgh: Clark, 1887). Many thanks to Oliver Sensen for his guidance on these selections from Kant.

THE PRINCIPLES OF POLITICAL RIGHT CONSIDERED IN CONNECTION WITH THE RELATION OF THEORY TO PRACTICE IN THE RIGHT OF THE STATE (1793)[1]

THE PRINCIPLES OF POLITICAL RIGHT

The establishment of a Civil Constitution in society is one of the most important facts in human history. In the principle on which it is founded this institution differs from all the other forms of social union among mankind. Viewed as a compact, and compared with other modes of compact by which numbers of men are united into one Society, the formation of a Civil Constitution has much in common with all other forms of Social Union in respect of the mode in which it is carried out in practice. But while all such compacts are established for the purpose of promoting in common some chosen End, the Civil Union is essentially distinguished from all others, by the principle on which it is based. In all social contracts we find a union of a number of persons for the purpose of carrying out some one End which they all have in common. But a Union of a multitude of men, viewed as an end in itself that every person ought to carry out, and which consequently is a primary and unconditional duty amid all the external relations of men who cannot help exercising a mutual influence on one another,—is at once peculiar and unique of its kind. Such a Union is only to be found in a Society which, by being formed into a Civil State, constitutes a Commonwealth. Now the End which in such external relations is itself a duty and even the highest formal condition—the *conditio sine quâ non*—of all other external duties, is the realisation of the Rights of Men *under public compulsory Laws*, by which every individual can have what is his own assigned to him, and secured against the encroachments or assaults of others.

The idea of an external Right, however, arises wholly out of the idea of human Freedom or Liberty, in the external relations of men to one another. As such, it has nothing specially to do with the realisation of Happiness as a purpose which all men naturally have, or with prescription of the means of attaining it; and it is absolutely necessary that this End shall not be mixed up with the Laws of Right as their motive. Right in general, may be defined as the limitation of the Freedom of any individual to the extent of its agreement with the freedom of all other individuals, in so far as this is possible by a universal Law. Public Right, again, is the sum of the external Laws which make such a complete agreement of freedom in Society possible. Now as all limitation of freedom by external acts of the will of another, is a mode of *coercion or compulsion*, it follows that the Civil Constitution is a relation of free men who live under coercive Laws, without prejudicing their liberty otherwise in the whole of their connection with others. For, Reason itself wills this. By 'Reason' is here meant the pure innate law-giving, Reason which gives no regard to any End that is derived from experience, such as are all comprehended under the general name of Happiness. In respect of any such End or in what any individual may place it, men may think quite differently, so that their wills could not be brought under any common principle, nor, consequently, under any External Laws that would be compatible with the liberty of all.

The Civil State, then, regarded merely as a social state that is regulated by laws of right, is founded upon the following rational principles:—

1 The Liberty of every Member of the Society as a Man;
2 The Equality of every Member of the Society with every other, as a Subject;
3 The Self-dependency of every Member of the Commonwealth, as a Citizen.

These Principles are not so much Laws given by the State when it is established, as rather fundamental conditions according to which alone the institution of a State is possible, in conformity with the pure rational Principles of external Human Right generally.

....

3. The SELF-DEPENDENCY of a member of the Commonwealth as a citizen, or fellow-legislator, is the third principle or condition of Right in the State. In the matter of the legislation itself, all are to be regarded as free and equal *under* the already existing public Laws; but they are not to be all regarded as equal in relation to the right to give or *enact* these laws. Those who are not capable of this right are, notwithstanding, subjected to the observance of the laws as members of the Commonwealth, and thereby they participate in the protection which is in accordance therewith; they are, however, not to be regarded as *Citizens* but as protected fellow-subjects.—
All right, in fact, depends on the laws. A public law, however, which determines for all what is to be legally allowed or not allowed in their regard, is

the act of a public Will, from which all right proceeds and which therefore itself can do no wrong to anyone. For this, however, there is no other Will competent than that of the *whole* people, as it is only when all determine about all that each one in consequence determines about himself. For it is only to himself that one can do no wrong. But if it be another will that is in question, then the mere will of anyone different from it, could determine nothing for it which might not be wrong; and consequently the law of such a will would require another law to limit its legislation. And thus no particular will can be legislative for a Commonwealth.—Properly speaking, in order to make out this, the ideas of the external Liberty, Equality, and *Unity* of the will of all, are to be taken into account; and for the last of these *Self-dependency* is the condition, since the exercising of a vote is required when the former two ideas are taken along with it. The fundamental law thus indicated, which can only arise out of the universal united will of the people, is what is called the *'Original Contract.'*

....

We have next to consider what follows by way of *Corollary* from the principles thus enunciated. We have before us the idea of an 'Original Contract' as the only condition upon which a civil and, therefore, wholly rightful, constitution can be founded among men, and as the only basis upon which a State can be established. But this fundamental condition—whether called an 'original contract' or a 'social compact'—may be viewed as the coalition of all the private and particular wills of a people into one common and public Will, having a purely juridical legislation as its end. But it is not necessary to presuppose this contract or compact, to have been actually a fact; nor indeed is it possible as a fact. We have not to deal with it as if it had first to be proved from history that a people into whose rights and obligations we have entered as their descendants, did actually on a certain occasion execute such a contract, and that a certain evidence or instrument regarding it of an oral or written kind, must have been transmitted so as to constitute an obligation that shall be binding in any existing civil constitution. In short, this idea is merely *an idea of Reason*; but it has undoubtedly a practical reality. For it ought to bind every legislator by the condition that he shall enact such laws as might have arisen from the united will of a whole people; and it will likewise be binding upon every subject, in so far as he will be a citizen, so that he shall regard the Law as if he had consented to it of his own will. This is the test of the rightfulness of every public law. If the law be of such a nature that it is *impossible* that the whole people could give their assent to it, it is not a just law. An instance of this kind would be a law, enacting that a certain class of subjects should have all the privileges of hereditary rank by mere birth (TP: 8:297 [273]). But if it be merely *possible* that a people could consent to a law, it is a duty to regard it as just, even supposing that the people were at the moment in such a position or mood, that if it were referred to them, their consent to it would probably be refused.[2]

This limitation, however, manifestly applies only to the judgment of the Legislator and not to that of the Subject. If, then, under a certain actual state of the law, a people should conclude that the continuance of that law would probably take away their happiness, what would they have to do? Would it not be a duty to resist the law? The answer can only be that the people should do nothing but obey. For the question here does not turn upon the happiness which the subject may expect from some special institution or mode of administering the Commonwealth, but the primary concern is purely that of the Right which has thus to be secured to every individual. This is the supreme principle from which all the maxims relating to the Commonwealth must proceed; and it cannot be limited by anything else. In regard to the interest of happiness, no principle that could be universally applicable, can be laid down for the guidance of legislation; for not only the circumstances of the time, but the very contradictory and ever-changing opinions which men have of what will constitute happiness, make it impossible to lay down fixed principles regarding it; and so the idea of Happiness, taken by itself, is not available as a principle of legislation. No one can prescribe for another as to what he shall find happiness in. The principle, *salus publica suprema civitatis lex est*, remains undiminished in value and authority; and the public weal, which has first of all to be taken into consideration, is just the maintenance of that legal constitution by which the liberty of all is secured through the laws. Along with this, the individual is left undisturbed in his right to seek his happiness in whatever way may seem to him best, if only he does not infringe the universal liberty secured through the law, by violating the rights of other fellow subjects. When the sovereign Power enacts laws which are directed primarily towards the happiness of the citizens, out of regard to their well-being, the state of the population and such like, this is not done from its being the end for which the civil constitution is established, but merely as a means of securing the state of Right, especially against the external enemies of the people. The Government must be capable of judging, and has alone to judge, whether such legislation belongs to the constitution of the Commonwealth, and whether it is requisite in order to secure its strength and steadfastness, both within itself and against foreign enemies; but this is not to be done as if the aim were to make the people happy even against their will, but only to bring it about that they shall exist as a Commonwealth. In thus judging whether any such measure can be taken prudently or not, the legislator may indeed err. But he does not err in so far as he considers whether the law does or does not agree with a principle of Right.

And in doing so he has an infallible criterion in the idea of the 'original contract,' viewed as an essential idea of reason; and hence he does not require—as would be the case with the principle of happiness—to wait for experience to instruct him about the utility rather than the rightness of his proposed measure. For if it is only not contradictory in itself that a whole people should agree to such a law, however unpleasant may be its results in fact, it would as such be conformable to Right. If a public law be thus conformable to Right, it is irreprehensible, and hence it will give the right to coerce; and, on the other hand, it would involve the prohibition of active resistance to the will of the legislator. The power in the State which gives effect to the law, is likewise irresistible; and no rightful commonwealth exists without such a power to suppress all internal resistance to it. For, such resistance would proceed according to a rule which if made universal would destroy all civil constitutionalism, and would annihilate the only state in which men can live in the actual possession of rights.

Hence it follows that all resistance to the Sovereign Legislative Power, every kind of instigation to bring the discontent of the subjects into active form, and rebellion or insurrection of every degree and kind, constitute the highest and most punishable crimes in the commonwealth; for they would destroy its very foundations. The prohibition of them is therefore absolute; so that even if the Supreme Power, or the Sovereign as its agent, were to violate the original contract, and thereby in the judgment of the subject to lose the right of making the laws, yet as the Government has been empowered to proceed even thus tyrannically, no right of resistance can be allowed to the subject as a power antagonistic to the State. The reason of this is that in the actually existing Civil Constitution the people have no longer the right to determine by their judgment how it is to be administered. For suppose they had such a right, and that it was directly opposed to the judgment of the actual Head of the State, who would there be to decide with which of them the right lay? Evidently neither of them could do this, as it makes them judges in their own cause. There would therefore have to be another sovereign Head above the sovereign Head to decide between it and the people, but this is a contradiction.

Notes

1 From the translation by William Hastie, in Immanuel Kant, *Kant's Principles of Politics, including his essay on Perpetual Peace. A Contribution to Political Science* (Edinburgh: Clark, 1891).
2 If, for example, a proportioned war-tax were imposed on all the subjects, they are not entitled, because it is burdensome, to say that it is unjust because somehow, according to their opinion, the war was unnecessary. For they are not entitled to judge of this; whereas because it is at least always *possible* that the war was inevitable and the tax indispensable, it must be regarded as rightful in the judgment of the subject. If, however, in such a war certain owners of property were to be burdened by imposts, from which others of the same class were spared, it is easily seen that a whole people could not concur in such a law, and it is entitled at the least to make protestation against it, because it could not regard this unequal distribution of the public burdens as just.

PERPETUAL PEACE (1795)[1]

FIRST SUPPLEMENT. OF THE GUARANTEE OF PERPETUAL PEACE

....

1. Even if a people were not compelled by internal discord to submit to the coercion of public laws, War as an external influence would effect this. For, according to the arrangement of nature already indicated, every people finds another pressing upon it in its neighbourhood, and it must form itself internally into a State in order to be equipped as a *Power* so as to defend itself. Now the Republican Constitution is the only one which perfectly corresponds to the Rights of man; but it is at the same time the most difficult to found, and still more so to maintain. So much is this the case that many have asserted that the realisation of a true Republic would be like a State formed by angels, because men with their selfish inclinations are incapable of carrying out a constitution of so sublime a form. In these circumstances, then, nature comes to the aid of the rational and universal will of man, which, however honoured in itself, is impotent in practice; and it does this just by means of these selfish inclinations. Thus it comes that the chief interest turns only upon a good organisation of the State, which is certainly within the power of man, whereby the powers of the human will shall be so directed in relation to each other, that the one will check the destructive effects of the other, or nullify them; and hence the result will be as regards reason the same as if these forces did not exist when their evil effects are thus neutralised; and man, although not possessed of real moral goodness, yet becomes constrained to be a good citizen.

The problem of the institution of a State, however hard it may appear, would not be insoluble even for a race of devils, assuming only that they have intelligence, and it may be put as follows: 'A multitude of rational beings all requiring laws in common for their own preservation, and yet of such a nature that each of them is inclined secretly to except himself from their sway, have to be put under order, and a constitution has to be established among them so that, although they may be antagonistic to one another in their private sentiments, they have yet to be so organised that, in their public relations, their conduct will have the same result as if they had no such bad sentiments.'

Such a problem must be *capable of solution*. For it does not turn directly upon the moral improvement of men, but only upon the mechanism of nature; and the problem is to know how men can use the conditions of nature in order so to regulate the antagonism of the hostile sentiments at work among the people that the individuals composing it shall have to compel each other to submit to common compulsory laws, and that there shall thus be brought about a state of peace in which the laws will have full power.

Note

1 From the translation by William Hastie in Immanuel Kant, *Kant's Principles of Politics, including his essay on Perpetual Peace. A Contribution to Political Science* (Edinburgh: Clark, 1891).

WHAT IS ENLIGHTENMENT? (1784)[1]

Enlightenment is man's release from his self-incurred tutelage. Tutelage is man's inability to make use of his understanding without direction from another. Self-incurred is this tutelage when its cause lies not in lack of reason but in lack of resolution and courage to use it without direction from another. *Sapere aude!* "Have courage to use your own reason!"—that is the motto of enlightenment.

....

For this enlightenment, however, nothing is required but freedom, and indeed the most harmless among all the things to which this term can properly be applied. It is the freedom to make public use of one's reason at every point. But I hear on all sides, "Do not argue!" The Officer says: "Do not argue but drill!" The tax collector: "Do not argue but pay!" The cleric: "Do not argue but believe!" Only one prince in the world says, "Argue as much as you will, and about what you will, but obey!" Everywhere there is restriction on freedom.

Which restriction is an obstacle to enlightenment, and which is not an obstacle but a promoter of it? I answer: The public use of one's reason must always be free, and it alone can bring about enlightenment among men. The private use of reason, on the other hand, may often be very narrowly restricted without particularly hindering the progress of enlightenment. By the public use of one's reason I understand the use which a person makes of it as a scholar before the reading public. Private use I call that which one may make of it in a particular civil post or office which is entrusted to him. Many affairs which are conducted in the interest of the community require a certain mechanism through which some members of the community must passively conduct themselves with an artificial unanimity, so that the government may direct them to public ends, or at least prevent them from destroying those ends. Here argument is certainly not allowed—one must obey. But so far as a part of the mechanism regards himself at the same time as a member of the whole community or of a society of world citizens, and thus in the role of a scholar who addresses the public (in the proper sense of the word) through his writings, he certainly can argue without hurting the affairs for which he is in part responsible as a passive member. Thus it would be ruinous for an officer in service to debate about the suitability or utility of a command given to him by his superior; he must obey. But the right to make remarks on errors in the military service and to lay them before the public for judgment cannot equitably be refused him as a scholar. The citizen cannot refuse to pay the taxes imposed on him; indeed, an impudent complaint at those levied on him can be punished as a scandal (as it could occasion general refractoriness). But the same person nevertheless does not act contrary to his duty as a citizen, when, as a scholar, he publicly expresses his thoughts on the inappropriateness or even the injustices of these levies. Similarly a clergyman is obligated to make his sermon to his pupils in catechism and his congregation conform to the symbol of the church which he serves, for he has been accepted on this condition. But as a scholar he has complete freedom, even the calling, to communicate to the public all his carefully tested and well meaning thoughts on that which is erroneous in the symbol and to make suggestions for the better organization of the religious body and church. In doing this there is nothing that could be laid as a burden on his conscience. For what he teaches as a consequence of his office as a representative of the church, this he considers something about which he has not freedom to teach according to his own lights; it is something which he is appointed to propound at the dictation of and in the name of another. He will say, "Our church teaches this or that; those are the proofs which it adduces." He thus extracts all practical uses for his congregation from statutes to which he himself would not subscribe with full conviction but to the enunciation of which he can very well pledge himself because it is not impossible that truth lies hidden in them, and, in any case, there is at least nothing in them contradictory to inner religion. For if he believed he had found such in them, he could not conscientiously discharge the duties of his office; he would have to give it up. The use, therefore, which an appointed teacher makes of his reason before his congregation is merely private, because this congregation is only a domestic one (even if it be a large gathering); with respect to it, as a priest, he is not free, nor can he be free, because he carries out the orders of another. But as a scholar, whose writings speak to his public, the world, the clergyman in the public use of his reason enjoys an unlimited freedom to use his own reason to speak in his own person. That the guardian of the people (in spiritual things) should themselves be incompetent is an absurdity which amounts to the eternalization of absurdities.

But would not a society of clergymen, perhaps a church conference or a venerable classis (as they call themselves among the Dutch), be justified in obligating itself by oath to a certain unchangeable symbol in order to enjoy an unceasing guardianship over each of its numbers and thereby over the people as a whole, and even to make it eternal? I answer that this is altogether impossible. Such contract, made to shut off all further enlightenment from the human race, is absolutely null and void even if confirmed by the supreme power, by parliaments, and by the most ceremonious of peace treaties. An age cannot bind itself and ordain to put the succeeding one into such a condition that it cannot extend its (at best very occasional) knowledge, purify itself of errors, and progress in general enlightenment. That would be a crime against human nature, the proper destination of which lies precisely in this progress and the descendants would be fully justified in rejecting those decrees as having been made in an unwarranted and malicious manner.

The touchstone of everything that can be concluded as a law for a people lies in the question whether the people could have imposed such a law on itself. Now such religious compact might be possible for a short and definitely limited time, as it were, in expectation of a better. One might let every citizen, and especially the clergyman, in the role of scholar, make his comments freely and publicly, i.e. through writing, on the erroneous aspects of the present institution. The newly introduced order might last until insight into the nature of these things had become so general and widely approved that through uniting their voices (even if not unanimously) they could bring a proposal to the throne to take those congregations under protection which had united into a changed religious organization according to their better ideas without, however, hindering others who wish to remain in the order. But to unite in a permanent religious institution which is not to be subject to doubt before the public even in the lifetime of one man, and thereby to make a period of time fruitless in the progress of mankind toward improvement, thus working to the disadvantage of posterity—that is absolutely forbidden. For himself (and only for a short time) a man may postpone enlightenment in what he ought to know, but to renounce it for posterity is to injure and trample on the rights of mankind. And what a people may not decree for itself can even less be decreed for them by a monarch, for his lawgiving authority rests on his uniting the general public will in his own. If he only sees to it that all true or alleged improvement stands together with civil order, he can leave it to his subjects to do what they find necessary for their spiritual welfare. This is not his concern, though it is incumbent on him to prevent one of them from violently hindering another in determining and promoting this welfare to the best of his ability. To meddle in these matters lowers his own majesty, since by the writings in which his own subjects seek to present their views he may evaluate his own governance. He can do this when, with deepest understanding, he lays upon himself the reproach, *Caesar non est supra grammaticos*.

Far more does he injure his own majesty when he degrades his supreme power by supporting the ecclesiastical despotism of some tyrants in his state over his other subjects.

If we are asked, "Do we now live in an enlightened age?" the answer is, "No," but we do live in an age of enlightenment...

Note

1 From the translation by Lewis White Beck in Immanuel Kant, *On History* (Indianapolis: Bobbs-Merrill, 1963).

KANT ON PUBLIC REASON

Oliver Sensen[1]

1 Introduction

The institutions of a state, as the instruments of a political order, will often frustrate the interests of an individual. A state might, for instance, coerce its members to pay taxes, to undergo certain medical procedures, or fight in wars. What is the legitimacy of this coercion, and how can it be justified to the individual? It is not likely that everyone has the same interests and always agrees on what is right, and people may fail to consent to even what they agree is right. Any form of actual consent, therefore, is unlikely to ground a political order with universal support. But if one does not consent to a political order, how can it possibly be justified?

In this chapter I analyze Kant's views on the significance of private judgment for political justification. Kant does not ground the political order on people's actual desires and interests, but instead he argues that one's reason provides a general standard of what is right. As long as the particular political arrangement does not violate this standard of one's own reason, the individual could consent to the arrangement, even if it goes against his actual desires and interests. In accordance with this, coercion is justified if an individual violates the standard of his own reason. Kant therefore agrees with the basic tenets of what nowadays is called a public reason approach to political philosophy (cf. Rawls 2005; Gaus 2011). Kant shares with this approach the view that coercive state power has to be justifiable to each individual. But he offers a distinctive version of a public reason account.

In this chapter, I first try to spell out how Kant envisions the relation between the laws of a state and the particular judgment of an individual (Section 2), and what form of consent is needed to justify coercion (Section 3). I then specify Kant's proposed understanding of the standard of reason through which public reason could be possible despite individual differences (Section 4), and briefly sketch its justification (Section 5). These sections will pave the way for explaining how Kant himself uses 'public reason' (Section 6), and in a final section I elucidate his puzzling claim that the conscience of the individual cannot err (Section 7). If the conscience of an individual cannot err, why would one be bound by any particular political order?

2 The Political Order

Kant is, of course, aware that people's opinions differ. People have different conceptions of a good life, and their views on happiness, therefore, cannot ground a *universal* order: "the very contradictory and ever-changing opinions which men have of what will constitute happiness, make it impossible to lay down fixed principles regarding it; and so the idea of Happiness, taken by itself, is not available as a principle of legislation" (TP 8:298 [274][2]). But even if people were to agree upon what happiness consists in, this does not by itself create *order*. If, for instance, two men desire the same job, or covet the same woman, this is not the foundation of unity (cf. KpV 5:28). Kant is also aware that people come up with different moral codes: "The Esquimaux, when their parents are decrepit, and no longer capable of working, strangle them; and the old also make preparation for this. But the children do it from true filial love, because in winter they are absent for many weeks out hunting, and during that time the old might starve" (Lectures 29:622). Different societies will come up with different solutions to solve their problems. Kant is aware that reasonable and informed people will disagree on how to govern their lives. Kant can therefore agree to what Rawls called a "reasonable pluralism" (cf. Rawls 2005, xvii).

But Kant also believes that there is a very general principle that reason prescribes in every human being equally. The principle runs: "Act externally in such a manner that the free exercise of thy Will may be able to co-exist with the Freedom of all others, according to a universal Law" (MS 6:231 [264]). A person therefore has a right to his or her freedom in accordance with a universal law: "the individual is left undisturbed in his right to seek his happiness in whatever way may seem to him best, if only he does not infringe the universal liberty secured through the law" (TP 8:298 [274]). In Sections 4 and 5 of this chapter I reflect upon the content, source and justification of this general political principle. In this section I spell out the relation between the general principle, the particular laws that govern a state, and the judgment of an individual.

How can one establish particular coercive laws that are justifiable to each individual member of a state? Kant does not advocate a direct democracy, in which the citizens vote on each particular law. In a direct democracy, there will be winners and losers, and the minority might be oppressed. To establish a just legislation "there is no other Will competent than that of the *whole* people" (TP 8:294 [273]). This "act of a Public will" (TP 8:294 [273]) comes about if the particular laws are formulated by representatives who are guided by the general political principle that the freedom of each can coexist with the freedom of everyone else. Kant argues that only such a public will is incapable of doing wrong to anyone. For "it is only when all determine about all that each one in consequence determines about himself" and "it is only to himself that one can do no wrong" (TP 8:295 [273]). Furthermore, in order to avoid a despotic government, Kant advocates separating the legislative, executive, and judicial functions in a state (cf. MS 6:313 [270]): "no particular will can be legislative for a Commonwealth" (TP 8:295 [273]), "only the united and consenting Will of all the People... ought to have the power of enacting Law in the State" (MS 6:314).

Kant sees the aim of legislation not directly in the happiness of the individual human beings. The happiness of the members of a state is merely a means to "securing the state of Right" (TP 8:298 [274]), and keeping it stable. A legislator can err about which measures will keep the state strong (in terms of the prosperity of its citizens and a healthy birth rate), but Kant holds that the legislator does not err "in so far as he considers whether the law does or does not agree with a principle of Right" (TP 8:299 [274]), for he has in the general political principle "an infallible criterion... as an essential idea of reason; and hence does not require—as would be the case with the principle of happiness—to wait for experience" (TP 8:299 [274f]). In accordance with this standard, the state is justified to use coercion if someone violates its laws. This is because the aim of the law is to further freedom in accordance with universal laws. If someone resists these laws, for example, by driving on the wrong side of the road, it constitutes a hindrance to freedom. Coercion tries to remove this hindrance and is a *"hindering of a hindrance of Freedom"* (MS 6:231 [265]). Therefore, coercion is justified in reference to the principle of political right: "Right and the Title to compel, thus indicate the same thing" (MS 6:232).

This has the further consequence that a rebellion or any use of force in order to defy or overthrow the public order "constitute the highest and most punishable crimes in the commonwealth; for they would destroy its very foundations" (TP 8:299 [275]). More controversially, Kant even holds this in cases where the authority legislates in violation of the highest political principle. Kant's reasoning is that in such a case there is no judge who could arbitrate. If there is such a difference in judgment about what is right, "who would there be to decide with which of them the right lay?" It would need someone higher than the highest state authority, which "is a contradiction" (TP 8:300 [275]). This is a much-discussed topic in the Kant literature. Kantians usually try to soften this stance in light of the unjust regimes of the twentieth century. They argue that living in such a regime amounts to being in the state of nature, and that therefore any such rebellion is not a resistance against a state (cf. Ripstein 2009, 325–52; Byrd and Hruschka 2010, 181–7).

The general political principle is not just a standard of what is right, but it is also connected with the duty to leave the state of nature, and form a civil society. The problem in the state of nature, as Kant sees it, is not that everyone would necessarily fight against everyone else, nor that one would not know what is right: "In the state of Nature there may even be juridical forms of Society" (MS 6:306 [266]). The problem is rather that one's rights "can never be safe" (MS 6:312 [268]). Without a police force one would not be secure against violence, and without a judicial system to solve a dispute about what is right, there would be "no competent judge... to give an authorized legal decision" (MS 6:312 [269]). A state is therefore "a condition... which Reason by a Categorical Imperative makes it obligatory upon us to strive after" (MS 6:318).

The general political principle is therefore the highest normative principle. It commands to form a state, and is the limiting condition for any positive law legislated by the state. This conception is also Kant's solution for the problem of how individuals can consent to laws that override their particular wishes.

3 The Role of Consent

Kant agrees with public reason accounts that coercive state power has to be justifiable to each individual, and he gives consent a central role. Consent is, on his account, the "test of the rightfulness of every public law" (TP 8:297 [273]). But he advocates a distinct conception of consent. As we have seen, positive laws of a state can—without violating the general conception of right—override the interests of an individual. For instance, a particular law to ride on the right side of the road makes the freedom of movement of everyone possible under a general law (to ride on the right side). The law therefore passes the test of the general political principle, and whoever rides on the wrong side of the road, can be coerced to comply. How can it be justified to the individual? The individual can willingly consent to this because his own reason demands compliance with the very general principle of right: "For, Reason itself wills this. By 'Reason' is here meant the pure *a priori* [tra. changed, O.S.] law-giving, Reason which gives no regard to... Happiness" (TP 8:290 [272]). Even if the individual's desires go against the particular law (to ride on the right side), the individual could agree that the demand is in accordance with right, and coercion justified. The individual could willingly consent. What form of consent is this?

The type of consent Kant has in mind is not *actual* consent. The individual might never have actually consented to laws he agrees with and that are in his interests. But even if a law is not in his interest, and he does not consent to it, it might still be consistent with the general political principle. The form of consent Kant advocates is a version of hypothetical consent, or something a person would consent to under special conditions. However, Kant's version of hypothetical consent differs from how it is usually understood. Common forms of hypothetical consent consider what a person would consent to if he were more or fully rational (cf. Van Schoelandt 2015, 1035f), or what one would consent to from an impartial perspective. But under these conditions one might still refuse consent to a particular law. Imagine that you have a deep knowledge of human psychology and social behavior patterns. Based on your expert knowledge, you might conclude that driving on the left side of the road would fit much better with human nature. So even if the person is fully rational and looks at the matter from an impartial perspective, he might not consent to a law to drive on the right side of the road.

But the agent *could* consent if he were presented with a law to drive on the right side of the street, and if he tests it against the general political principle of his own reason. He might not think that the particular law is the best way to regulate traffic, and he can voice his objections, but he can agree that it is a way to make possible the freedom of all in accordance with a universal law (to ride on the right side of the street). It is a form of hypothetical consent under these specific conditions, but in order to distinguish Kant's form of consent from the more common versions of hypothetical consent, one could call it *possible* consent (cf. O'Neill 1989, 105). What is possible consent?

For Kant, what one can possibly consent to is guided by the general political principle. One can possibly consent to a particular law if it is in accordance with this general principle, because it is a command of one's own reason. Conversely, one could not consent to a particular law that violates the general standard, and therefore would be unjust: "if the law be of such a nature that it is *impossible* that the whole people could give their assent to it, it is not a just law. An instance... would be... privileges of hereditary rank by mere birth" (TP 8:297 [273]). Kant's example is a war tax. The tax is just "if it be merely *possible* that a people could consent to a law... even supposing that the people were at the moment in such a position or mood, that if it were referred to them, their consent to it would probably be refused" (TP 8:297 [273f]). His point is not about actual consent, and not about the most popular forms of hypothetical consent— what one would consent to if one were in a different frame of mind. If the war tax is justly distributed, the people cannot refuse it because they feel that the war is unnecessary: "it is at least always *possible* that the war was inevitable" (TP 8:297 n. [275]). But the people could not consent to an *unjust* distribution of the tax: "because it could not regard this unequal distribution of the public burdens as just" (TP 8:297 n. [275]).

What counts as possible consent is determined by what is just. For Kant, consent is therefore not the fundamental right-making feature, but possible consent tracks what the general political principle states as just and right. Kant's version of consent is therefore dependent upon the political principle. It is in this way a form of hypothetical consent in that one can formulate the requirement as saying that what is right is what a person would consent to if it followed the political principle of his own reason. Consent is only a "test," an epistemic criterion, not the standard that makes a particular law right.

In sum: Kant's solution to the problem of public justification is that one's own reason provides a law that determines one's possible consent, and thereby the public order is justifiable to each: "Right in general, may be defined as the limitation of the Freedom of any individual to the extent of its agreement with the freedom of all other individuals, in so far as this is possible by a universal Law" (TP 8:290 [272]). But why should reason come up with this law and not another? How exactly does reason come up with it, on Kant's account, and why should one think that everyone comes up with this law? I shall start with Kant's answer to the second question. If one clarifies what Kant means by locating this law in reason, one also sees why he thinks that it has this content and no other. In Section 5, I shall then address Kant's argument for why one should think that there really is such a law.

4 Reason and the Political Principle

What does it mean to say that the political principle "Act externally in such a manner that the free exercise of thy Will may be able to co-exist with the Freedom of all others, according to a universal Law" (MS 6:231 [264]) is given by one's own reason? In which sense does it belong to everyone's reason, and what exactly is meant by 'reason' in this context? These questions concern the source of the political principle, not yet Kant's distinction between a public and private use of one's reason (see Section 6 below). The questions can be illustrated with an objection that has been raised against public reason accounts in general. If public reason accounts claim that the political order has to be justifiable to each, how can the theory deal with an illiberal objector (cf. Quong 2013; Van Schoelandt 2015)? An illiberal objector, such as a racist or religious militant, might deny a system of rights and freedom for all persons. He might therefore deny that all human beings count, and that certain actions would need to be justifiable to each. It seems that the illiberal objector will not consent to a liberal political order, given his actual desires. But if he does not consent, then the liberal political order does not seem to be justified *to all*, violating its own standard. How does Kant's theory avoid this problem?

Kant's answer is that the liberal political order with the values of freedom, equality, and independence of each individual follow from a principle of *everyone's* reason (cf. TP 8:290). Even an illiberal objector therefore should be under the command to respect all human beings. But how, more specifically, does an illiberal objector possess the general political principle? How is reason the source for this command? For instance, it can be doubted that a racist or religious militant would adopt liberalism under ideal conditions, for example, if he were to reason calmly or even with perfect rational capacities (cf. Van Schoelandt 2015, 1035–7). Instead, what is often ascribed to Kant is one of the following three positions: (1) that reason discovers the political principle as the means to a particular thing everyone wants; (2) that reason discovers the principle as a commitment to wanting anything at all; or (3) that reason discovers an objective reason for adopting the political principle. In detail:

1   There is a plausible case to be made that Kant regards the political principle as a means to something else everyone wants (e.g. peace or security). Similar to Hobbes and Pufendorf before him, Kant might simply say that in a state of nature where everyone fights against everyone else, one would not achieve anything one desires (apart from fighting). The political principle would then be the means to securing one's desires (cf. Pogge 2002). The textual basis for this interpretation is in Kant's essay *Toward Perpetual Peace*. There he famously says that the "problem of the institution of a State… would not be insoluble even for a race of devils, assuming only that they have intelligence" (ZeF 8:366 [276]). This passage seems to affirm that even a multitude of thoroughly selfish human beings could realize that they should govern themselves in accordance with the political principle. If one wants peace and justice, the liberal political principle might be the best prudential way to secure it. The political principle is then prudentially necessary in order to solve a coordination problem of a multitude of finite rational beings when resources are limited (cf. O'Neill 1989, 3–27). The systematic problem for this interpretation is that it presupposes that everyone wants peace and justice. A war-prone illiberal objector might not agree.

    There are also textual reasons to doubt that this interpretation is what Kant had in mind. If one reads on, Kant affirms the very opposite. Kant says explicitly that the political order is not merely based on prudence. First, the requirement to leave the state of nature and form a political order "is not founded upon prudence but upon duty" (ZeF 8:378). But also the political principle itself, which states how one should govern the political order, does not merely have the hypothetical necessity of a means to acquiring certain ends (e.g., peace, security), but has "unconditional necessity" (ZeF 8:377). The reason

Kant talks about a race of devils is not to explain how reason discovers what is right, as a means to desire satisfaction, but how one could be *motivated* to enter a society governed by a principle one's own reason already knows. In short: Kant's claim responds to the charge that human beings are not motivated to comply with reason's commands: "because men with their selfish inclinations are incapable of carrying out a constitution of so sublime a form" (ZeF 8:366 [276]) To this Kant replies that even thoroughly self-interested beings will see that it is in their self-interest to comply with the law of reason. In short: Kant talks about the motivation to enter a political order, not the justification for what the order should look like.

2 The first option was premised on the view that there is something that everyone, including the illiberal objector, wants (e.g., peace, justice). The second option that is often ascribed to Kant is not based on any particular end human beings want, but on the preconditions for wanting anything at all. The general political principle would be based in reason because it is reason by which one discerns what one is committed to. There are several versions of such an argument in the Kant literature. For instance, in acting one might be committed to valuing one's own agency as the means for getting whatever one wants (cf. Gewirth 1980, 48–63). If that is so, then everyone has to value his or her own agency. The systematic challenge for this kind of argument is to bridge the gap from valuing *one's own* capacity of agency to the requirement of valuing the freedom of *others*. This is the case irrespective of whether one argues that the agent values his own agency so strongly that he claims it as a right (cf. Gewirth 1980, 63–103), that the agent does not value his particular agency, but agency as such wherever one finds it (cf. Nagel 1979, 79–89), or that reasons are public (cf. Korsgaard 2009, 188–206). However, it does not seem to be a fact that everyone values agency wherever he finds it, nor does it seem to follow from the requirement that reasons be publicly expressible alone. (For a more elaborate criticism of this kind of argument see Sensen 2011, 69–75.)

3 A third option that is prominently discussed in the Kant literature conceives of human beings as objectively valuable, and as giving each other reasons to respect their freedoms. This value might be a distinct metaphysical property, such as a non-natural property (cf. Langton 2007). Kant does not believe that one can discern such properties by an intellectual intuition (cf. KrV B 798), but one might be able to reason one's way to the view that all human beings really are objectively valuable. This argument can be questioned for systematic reasons (cf. Sensen 2011, 55–69), but also on textual grounds. Kant argues that it is not value that grounds moral requirements, but that it is the requirement that grounds the value: "For nothing

can have a worth other than that which the law determines for it." (GMS 4:436; KpV 5:62f). Kant sets the right prior to the good. For the purpose of this chapter I therefore set options (1)–(3) aside. Kant, as I will try to show, has an even different sense in mind in which the political principle is grounded in reason.

What is this alternative reading I ascribe to Kant? On this view the supreme political principle is a constitutive principle of reason. By this I mean that one's reason brings forth the principle by itself, not prompted by anything else one wants (e.g. peace), and not as an insight at the end of reasoning (e.g. about the preconditions of wanting anything at all). The reason Kant talks about here is not one's empirical reasoning, one's deliberation as it is accessible in introspection. Rather, Kant argues that the political principle is part of one's *pure* reason, and describes how one's reason necessarily functions. It is as if this principle is innate. Independently of how one deliberates, one's pure reason holds up the political principle—somewhat like what one would call a guilty conscience. As such this account is different from options (1)–(3) sketched above. The source of the political principle is not (1) means–ends reasoning about something one wants (e.g. peace), since the principle is not based in one's wants; but it is also not (2) the result of what one is committed to in wanting anything at all, because one could perfectly will an immoral action without invoking the principle; nor (3) is the principle the result of acknowledging an independent reason out there in the world (the value of other human beings). This interpretation can be supported with references to Kant's texts.

In the previous discussion surrounding the nation of devils, Kant said that the political principle is not conditioned upon something else one wants, but has "unconditional necessity" (ZeF 8:377). Necessity, Kant argues, cannot be gained by experience but must have its origin a priori. This is because experience only shows that something is the case, but not that it is necessarily so. Therefore: "Necessity and strict universality are... secure indications of an *a priori* cognition" (KrV B4). Furthermore, it is not an a priori insight about means–ends relationships or the existence of properties. Rather, the political principle is an "a priori proposition that is not based on any intuition, either pure or empirical" (KrV 5:31). As such the law is something "our own cognitive faculty... provides out of itself" (KrV B2), independently of anything one wants. Accordingly, "reason does not give in to those grounds which are empirically given, but with complete spontaneity it makes its own order according to ideas... according to which it even declares actions to be necessary" (KrV A548/B576). So, an a priori principle is not something one reasons oneself to in deliberation, but something that is directly given in virtue of one's pure reason: "Pure reason... gives (to the human being) a universal law" (KpV 5:31).

Kant, therefore, conceives of the political principle as something that is similar to an innate principle, however, he does not think that the necessary law is innate. For if the law would be innate, say: implanted by a creator, or learned in the process of evolution, it would also lack the unconditional necessity. The creator could have given a different law, or under different circumstances, another law would have been innate. So, any innate principle would really "lack the necessity that is essential to their concept." They would merely have a "subjective necessity, arbitrarily implanted in us" (KrV B168), but not the unconditional necessity of the highest political principle. In contrast, Kant regards absolutely necessary principles as created spontaneously by one's pure reason. This means that if one reasons about the right political constitution, one's reason spontaneously brings forth the principle out of itself (cf. KpV 5:29).

The source of the law, that reason gives rise to it "with complete spontaneity," Kant calls "autonomy." Autonomy is the "law-giving of human reason" (Lectures 27:499). The political principle is a constitutive principle of reason similar to the way in which Kant proposes these principles in his theoretical philosophy: So "the understanding is the one that contains the **constitutive** principles *a priori* for the **faculty of cognition**...; for the **feeling of pleasure and displeasure** it is the power of judgment...; for the **faculty of desire** it is reason, which is practical without the mediation of any sort of pleasure" (KU 5:196f). Kant's argument is that only such a source could ground an unconditional necessity. Any other principle would only yield heteronomy: "If the will seeks the law that is to determine it *anywhere else* than in the fitness of its maxims for its own giving of universal laws... *heteronomy* always results." (GMS 4:441) The problem with heteronomy is that it only generates conditional necessity: "Wherever an object of the will has to be laid down as the basis for prescribing the rule that determines the will, there the rule is none other than heteronomy; the imperative is conditional, namely: *if* or *because* one wills this object, one ought to act in such or such a way; hence it can never command... categorically" (GMS 4:444).

The idea is roughly that if a moral command were to come from the outside—such as an arbitrary divine command or a demand of society—one would still need a desire (not to be punished or to be rewarded) in order for this law to be binding. But also if one were to try to ground the political law on a desire the agent has, it would only be binding as long as this desire is overriding. However, desires are relative and contingent, and cannot ground a universal and necessary law (cf. GMS 4:441–5). More controversially, this thought also applies against attempts to ground obligation on metaphysically real properties. Kant holds that any knowledge begins with the senses (cf. KrV B1). If one needed to discern and be bound by a metaphysical value property, one would need to discern it with one's senses. If the property is supposed to be a nonnatural property, the only sense that is left would be a feeling of pleasure (cf. KpV 5:26). Pleasure is relative and contingent, and cannot ground a necessary law. If, against Kant's own views (cf. KrV B798), one postulates that one can discern this property with an intellectual intuition, then still the discovery would be based on experience, and experience cannot give necessity. (For a longer defense of this argument, see Sensen 2011, 14–27.)

So far I have given textual evidence from different sources for Kant's view that a principle with unconditional necessity must be an a priori law of pure reason. Now I want to give the evidence that the political principle is also such an a priori law. The political principle too aims to express an unconditional necessity, or obligation. The political law is "a Law which imposes obligation upon me" (MS 6:231 [264]). Therefore a particular law that is "Right is founded, no doubt, upon the consciousness of the Obligation of every individual according to the Law" (MS 6:232). Obligation, or to "be bound to something" (Lectures 27:493), expresses "an *ought* or a *necessitation*." (Lectures 27:488) The necessitation Kant has in mind here is of course not a making necessary by laws of nature, but by motives or "representations of the understanding, and of reason" (Lectures 29:611). There are two kinds of motives, according to Kant, depending on whether the representations relate to our well-being, in which case they are contingent, or to universality given by reason (cf. GMS 4:427). Kant calls the first kind "pragmatic," and the second kind "moral motives" (Lectures 29:612). Pragmatic motives necessitate only conditionally, while moral motives do so unconditionally. Kant reserves "obligation" for moral necessitation: "*Necessitatio moralis* is *obligatio*." (Lectures 29:612) All sources that are not grounded in pure reason, Kant has argued, yield heteronomy, and heteronomy cannot yield obligation: "*heteronomy* of choice, on the other hand, not only does not ground any obligation at all but is instead opposed to the principle of obligation" (KpV 5:33).

Of course, Kant conceives of a difference between political obligation and moral obligation more narrowly construed. Law and politics, on the one hand, are merely concerned with the outward performance of actions. The police checks that one stop at a red traffic light, it is not concerned with whether one did so out of a motive of duty or self-interested motivations, for example, to avoid a ticket. Morality, on the other hand, also cares about the inner motives or maxim from which one acts: "The conformity of an Action to the Law of Duty constitutes its *Legality*; the conformity of the Maxim of the Action with the Law constitutes its *Morality*." (MS 6:225; cf. 6:232) But content-wise and in their ultimate justification, the political principle of the first part of the *Metaphysics of Morals* as well as the moral principle of the second part are the same:

"The following Conceptions are common to Jurisprudence and Ethics as the two main Divisions of *the Metaphysic of Morals*. *Obligation* is the Necessity of a free Action when viewed in relation to a Categorical Imperative of Reason." (MS 6:222) There is one a priori law from which one can later derive legal/political and moral laws: "Within this universal moral law are comprehended both legal and ethical laws" (Lectures 27:526; cf. 524).

If a legislator lays down a particular law, for example, to stop at red traffic lights, this is obligatory only under this further natural law: "a previous Natural Law must be presupposed to establish the authority of the Lawgiver" (MS 6:224). Notice the similarity between Kant's political and ethical principle. The former runs: "Act externally in such a manner that the free exercise of thy Will may be able to co-exist with the Freedom of all others, according to a universal Law" (MS 6:231 [264]). The ethical principle demands: *"act only in accordance with that maxim through which you can at the same time will that it become a universal law."* (GMS 4:421) But when Kant speaks more loosely, he gives both principles the same content: "'Act so that thou canst will that thy maxim shall become a universal Law whatever may be its End'..., as a principle of right, it has unconditional necessity" (ZeF 8:377).

In sum: Kant solves the problem of reasonable pluralism by identifying a highest political principle that is spontaneously but necessarily dictated by everyone's own reason. Even an illiberal objector is under this principle, and the political order can be justified to him. But why should one think that there really is such a general political principle coming from everyone's reason, and why should one think that reason gives this law and no other?

5 The Content and Justification of the Political Principle

Kant's view offers a solution to the tension between reasonable pluralism and the requirement of universal justifiability. But so far this is just a possibility. Why should one believe that there really is such a law of reason that binds everyone? Kant does not believe that one can empirically examine one's reason and demonstrate that there is this law: "all human insight is at an end as soon as we have arrived at basic powers" (KpV 5:46). However, he argues that there is an indirect way of demonstrating the existence of the supreme moral principle: "We can become aware of pure practical laws just as we are aware of pure theoretical principles, by attending to the necessity with which reason prescribes them to us" (KpV 5:30). Necessity, he has argued (cf. again KrV B3f), cannot be gained by experience, but must be a priori instead. If one can show that the supreme principle is necessary, it must originate in reason. But in which sense could the principle be said to be necessary?

Kant tries to demonstrate that one is aware of this principle, and that it is not conditioned upon any desires one has. In order to make that case, Kant gives the example of a prince who demands of you to give false testimony against an honorable and innocent man. If you refuse, the prince will find another to make the accusation and execute you at the gallows (cf. KpV 5:30). The example is to be construed in such a way that no desire speaks in favor of refusing: Imagine that you love your life, and your position at court; you do not see any good coming out of your punishment, and you have no particular desire to be moral. Nonetheless, Kant alleges, you would judge the false accusation to be unjust and morally wrong. Inasmuch as one judges an action—any example will do—to be unjust and morally wrong even though no desire speaks for this action, the judgment of wrongness is not based on a desire. As such it is not conditioned by any desire and in this sense is necessary. It does not arise out of desires, as far as one knows, and therefore must have its origin somewhere else. Kant gave an argument according to which the principle is not learned over the process of evolution or otherwise innate (see above), and so it must arise from reason.

But even if one follows Kant this far, why should one believe that the law of reason has the particular content of universality? Kant's reasoning is very similar independently of whether one follows the gallows example or his account of obligation. The point of the gallows example is not to affirm universal moral intuitions about what is right, but rather to warrant the belief in *freedom* as the power to act independently of desires. Even if one does not know whether one would refuse to give false testimony, and even if afterwards one could not know whether one did not secretly refuse from a hidden desire, the moral ought warrants that one believes in the possibility of refusing: "He judges, therefore, that he can do something because he is aware that he ought to do it and cognizes freedom within" (KpV 5:30). Kant uses our moral intuitions in the gallows example as an *epistemic* access to freedom, and then argues that freedom *metaphysically* grounds the existence of the moral law (cf. KpV 5:4 note). Kant conceives of freedom as the power to be a first cause or an unmoved mover. He further believes with Hume that every form of causality involves laws: "the concept of causality brings with it that of laws" (GMS 4:446). If acting freely—as a form of causality—involves laws, but—in virtue of being free—excludes all desires, then only the form of a law (universality) remains: "what, then, can freedom of the will be other than autonomy, that is... to act on no other maxim than that which can also have as object itself as universal law" (GMS 4:446f; cf. 402; KpV 5:29)?

The content of Kant's highest political principle can also be derived from his views on obligation sketched above. In virtue of being obligatory, the political principle should be binding independently of what the agent wants. Since the desires of individuals differ, the political principle cannot be grounded in any particular desire or content. However, if one abstracts from the content of a principle, only its form remains. The only obligatory requirement Kant finds, therefore, restricts the freedom of an agent to laws that could be willed as universal. This also explains Kant's specific expression 'public use of reason' to which I shall now turn.

6 Autonomy and Public Reason

Kant shares the essential elements of a contemporary public reason account. He also uses a similar expression, 'the public use of reason,' most notably in his earlier essay "What is Enlightenment?" However, there he makes a slightly different point. His emphasis is not that the source of political justification must lie in one's own reason (autonomy), but that one's empirical reasoning can be conditioned by one's role in society (private use), or the general political principle (public use).

The context in which Kant talks about the public use of one's reason is the attempt to clarify the concept of enlightenment. He defines enlightenment as "man's release from his self-incurred tutelage" (WE 8:35 [278]). Kant specifies the self-incurred nature of the tutelage as a lack of courage to use one's own reason without the direction from another. The slogan for finding enlightenment is therefore: "Have courage to use your own reason!" (WE 8:35 [278]) Courage is the remedy on the part of the individual. But it is also necessary for institutions to allow their members the freedom of the pen, or the "freedom to make public use of one's reason at every point" (WE 8:36 [278]).

What, then, is a public use of reason? Kant's distinction between a public and a private use of reason is not marked by the size of an audience. A military officer, a public official or clergyman might address a large audience, but still Kant would count this reasoning as private. The reasoning is private because in these roles one is not free to teach according to one's own light. Rather in these roles one "is appointed to propound at the dictation of and in the name of another" (WE 8:38 [279]). In contrast, one makes a public use of one's reason if one's reasoning is not conditioned by one's appointment, but if one addresses the public as a member of society at large or a world citizen. As a tax official, for instance, a person has to enforce the tax laws, but the same person should be allowed to criticize these taxes as unjust or inappropriate as a scholar (cf. WE 8:37 [279]). The important difference, therefore, between a private and public use of one's reason is whether one's reasoning is conditioned by one's role, or whether it is unconditioned and free (cf. O'Neill 1989, 28–50).

The public use of reason, accordingly, has similarities with Kant's account of autonomy. Both are unconditioned; however, they operate at slightly different levels. Autonomy, as we have seen, is Kant's doctrine that in order to have unconditional obligation, the moral law must originate in one's own pure reason. This is one's reason, as it is constituted prior to one's awareness. The public use of reason, in contrast, is located on the level of one's empirical reasoning and deliberation. As such, the public use of reason is an analogue to pure autonomy.

In the context of the question: 'What is Enlightenment?' Kant is not explicitly concerned with the justification for why the public use of reason should be allowed. He spells out a necessary condition for enlightenment to come about, and he argues that the claim that the professionals in the military, state, and church should be incompetent would be an "absurdity" (WE 8:38 [279]). However, the real reason for the public use of reason must again be the general political principle. Everyone has it in virtue of his or her own reason, and can determine which particular laws are in accordance with right. Rather, Kant's concern in the essay is how the private use of reason can be justified. His argument is that many community affairs require that their leaders act "with an artificial unanimity, so that the government may direct them to public ends" (WE 8:37 [278]). However, if any of these experts use the freedom of the pen to criticize unjust or inefficient practices as a scholar, "there is nothing that could be laid as a burden on his conscience" (WE 8:38 [279]).

7 Conscience

Kant places great weight on the judgment and conscience of the individual. What is more, he famously says that the conscience of the individual cannot err: "an *erring* conscience is an absurdity" (MS 6:401). But this gives rise to a new problem. If an individual's conscience cannot err, and if people's reasonable judgment differs, how can there be a unified public order? If one's conscience is against the public order, and one's conscience is right, why not follow one's inner judge rather than the public order (cf. Gaus 2015)?

However, Kant's claim that one's conscience cannot err does not necessarily lead to the same problem of public disobedience. For we have already seen that Kant argues against any right of rebellion. Even if one would disagree with the particular public order, this does not mean that one should resist that order (see Section 2). But there is a further reason why Kant's views do not give rise to the tension between conscience and public order, and this lies in his notion of conscience itself. Kant does not understand conscience to be an immediate sense of what is right and wrong. This judgment is the task of reason, not conscience:

"it is understanding, not conscience, which judges whether an action is in general right or wrong" (Religion 6:186). Conscience, on the other hand, checks whether one reached a moral conclusion with due diligence (cf. Hill 2002, 348). In German, the term for conscience, *Gewissen*, is the noun to *gewiss*—to be certain. Conscience is therefore a second-order reflection on whether one is sure about one's moral judgments: "here reason judges itself, whether it has actually undertaken, with all diligence, that examination of actions (whether they are right or wrong)" (Religion 6:186). The demand of conscience is therefore to be sure in one's judgment. "With respect to the action that *I* want to undertake, however, I must not only judge, and be of the opinion, that it is right; I must also be *certain* that it is. And this is a requirement of conscience" (Religion 6:186).

When Kant therefore says that conscience cannot err, he does not mean that we can never be wrong in our moral judgments. Rather the claim amounts to saying that we can never be uncertain whether we are certain about something. But he qualifies even the infallibility of conscience. For he acknowledges several ways in which one's conscience can go wrong after all, for example, one's conscience could be misdirected by plaguing the owner about matters of prudence rather than morality (cf. Lectures 27:352). Similarly, the conscience is too strong if it is tyrannical, always suspecting that one is at fault (cf. Lectures 27:357). Or one's conscience could turn trivial matters into severe faults. Kant's example is, interestingly enough—given his strict stance against lying—the question of whether one could lie on April Fools' Day (cf. Lectures 27:356).

8 Conclusion

Kant agrees with the basic premises of contemporary public reason approaches. Coercive laws have to be justifiable to each individual member of a state, but people differ widely in their views about what is right. On Kant's account, this tension dissolves because each individual is under the same general political law given by his or her own reason. If a particular law does not violate the general political law, it is justifiable to an individual. Since each individual has the same general law, the particular law will be justifiable to each.[3]

Notes

1 Associate Professor, Department of Philosophy, Tulane University.
2 Page numbers in brackets refer to the Kant selections in this volume.
3 I want to thank Piers Turner and Chad Van Schoelandt for their excellent comments on an earlier draft.

Bibliography

Kant Editions

GMS: *Groundwork of the Metaphysics of Morals*, in *Practical Philosophy*, ed. M. Gregor, Cambridge: Cambridge University Press, 1996.
KpV: *Critique of Practical Reason* in *Practical Philosophy*, ed. M. Gregor, Cambridge: Cambridge University Press, 1996.
KrV: *Critique of Pure Reason*, ed. P. Guyer and A. Wood, Cambridge: Cambridge University Press, 1998.
KU: *Critique of the Power of Judgement*, ed. P. Guyer, Cambridge: Cambridge University Press, 2000.
Lectures: *Lectures on Ethics*, ed. P. Heath and J.B. Schneewind, Cambridge: Cambridge University Press, 1997.
MS: *Philosophy of Law*, trans. W. Hastie. Available online at http://oll.libertyfund.org/titles/359 (accessed August 1, 2015).
Religion: *Religion within the Boundaries of Mere Reason*, in *Religion and Rational Theology*, ed. A. Wood and G. di Giovanni, Cambridge: Cambridge University Press, 1996.
TP: *The Principle of Political Right Considered in Connection with the Relation of Theory to Practice in the Right of the State*, trans. W. Hastie. Available online at http://oll.libertyfund.org/titles/358 (accessed August 1, 2015).
WE: *What Is Enlightenment?* trans. L.W. Beck. Available online at https://en.wikisource.org/wiki/What_is_Enlightenment%3F (accessed August 1, 2015).
ZeF: *Perpetual Peace*, trans. W. Hastie. Available online at http://oll.libertyfund.org/titles/358 (accessed August 1, 2015).
All page references cite Volume:Page *of the Prussian Academy Edition of* Kant's Gesammelte Schriften, *de Gruyter*, 1902ff.

Secondary Literature

Byrd, Sharon and Joachim Hruschka. 2010. *Kant's Doctrine of Right. A Commentary*. Cambridge: Cambridge University Press.
Gaus, Gerald. 2011. *The Order of Public Reason*. Cambridge: Cambridge University Press.
———. 2015. "Private and Public Conscience (Or, Is the Sanctity of Conscience a Liberal Commitment, or an Anarchical Fallacy?)" In *Reason, Value, and Respect*, edited by Mark Timmons and Robert Johnson, 135–56. Oxford: Oxford University Press.
Gewirth, Alan. 1980. *Reason and Morality*. Chicago: University of Chicago Press.
Hill, Thomas. 2002. *Human Welfare and Moral Worth*. Oxford: Oxford University Press.
Korsgaard, Christine. 2009. *Self-Constitution*. Oxford: Oxford University Press.
Langton, Rae. 2007. "Objective and Unconditioned Value." *Philosophical Review* 116: 157–85.

Nagel, Thomas. 1979. *The Possibility of Altruism*. Princeton, NJ: Princeton University Press.

O'Neill, Onora. 1989. *Constructions of Reason*. Cambridge: Cambridge University Press.

Pogge, Thomas. 2002. "Is Kant's Rechtslehre a 'Comprehensive Liberalism'?" In *Kant's Metaphysics of Morals*, edited by Mark Timmons, 133–58. Oxford: Oxford University Press.

Quong, Jonathan. 2014. "What Is the Point of Public Reason?" *Philosophical Studies* 170: 545–53.

Rawls, John. 2005. *Political Liberalism*. New York: Columbia University Press.

Ripstein, Arthur. 2009. *Force and Freedom*. Cambridge, MA: Harvard University Press.

Sensen, Oliver. 2011. *Kant on Human Dignity*, Berlin: de Gruyter.

Van Schoelandt, Chad. 2015. "Justification, Coercion, and the Place of Public Reason" *Philosophical Studies* 172: 1031–50.

Part II

PUBLIC REASON IN BROADER HISTORICAL CONTEXT

5

HUME'S THEORY OF PUBLIC REASON[1]

Geoffrey Sayre-McCord[2]

1 Introduction

Public reason theories—however they are developed—embrace the idea that principles, rules, or institutions have authority only if those who fall within their scope have independent reason to accept them.[3] On such views two claims are crucial. The first is that the *authority* of a principle, rule, or institution requires that those who fall within its scope have independent reason to accept and conform to it. Where such reasons are lacking the principle, rule, or institution, may have an impact on what reasons people have, but will not itself be a source of reasons agents would not otherwise have. The second is that the *shape and substance* of the principles, rules, and institutions that do have authority is sensitive these differences among people and their reasons make a difference to which principles, rules, and institutions they might have reason to accept and conform to. According to public reason theorists, these differences among people and their reasons make a difference to what can legitimately be demanded of them and so to which principles, rules, and institutions have authority for them.

Against this background, our public reasons are the reasons we share with others, thanks to there being principles, rules, or institutions that have authority for us in virtue of our each having a (potentially different) reason to accept and conform to them. And, public reason theorists usually argue, these public reasons reflect our respect for each other as free and equal, properly subject to demands only when we could in the appropriate way, accept those demands.

Needless to say, different public reason theories play out against a variety of views concerning the nature of the original, independent, reasons that matter. Regardless of whether they are reasons of self-interest, or of religious conviction, or of moral outlook, and whether they are practical, or moral, or theoretical reasons, the common theme is that a respect for those who differ, or an appreciation of their autonomy, or a recognition of their standing as equals, requires seeing their reasons, no less than one's own, as shaping what we all have reason in common to accept as authoritative.

"Public Reason" as a label for this view is due to John Rawls' seminal work on the nature of justice.[4] His concern in that work was specifically with justice in a society in which one finds simultaneously the opportunity for cooperative ventures that offer mutual advantage and reasonable disagreement among its members about how such ventures should be structured. The basic idea, though, finds important expression in the history of political philosophy, going back to Glaucon's characterization of the nature and origin of justice in the *Republic*, figuring centrally in Hobbes' *Leviathan*, and running through the enlightenment and beyond.

David Hume is sometimes mentioned in passing in discussions of public reason. But he rarely figures prominently.[5] This is understandable. Yet leaving Hume to one side represents an important opportunity missed. After briefly highlighting why Hume rarely figures in discussions of public reason, I will turn to exploiting the missed opportunity.

2 Why Hume so Rarely Figures in Discussions of Public Reason

Without pausing to go into detail, I'll mention several aspects of Hume's moral theory that help to explain why appeals to public reason might seem to fit uncomfortably with Hume's views.

To start with, Hume pretty clearly eschews any appeal to autonomy or to respect or to equality. Unlike Rousseau, he is not at all haunted by the observation that *"Man is born free, and everywhere he is in chains,"* nor does he set himself the task of articulating a moral theory that assumes our standing as free and equal.[6]

Indeed, Hume steers clear of moral principles more generally, working primarily to explain our moral thoughts and practices, not to justify them. As a result, Hume does not so much offer a substantive moral theory as explain the context within which such theories find their point and place. He wants to make sense of when and why we think in moral terms, not to justify thinking in one particular way rather than another.[7] That Hume's aim is primarily explanatory and not justificatory puts him at odds, or at least out of kilter with, public reason theories across the board, all of which are aimed at identifying normative constraints on authority and then spelling out the implications of those constraints when it comes to identifying authoritative principles, rules, or institutions.[8]

Moreover, Hume explicitly takes up and rejects the idea that the legitimacy of government depends on the sort of social contract (or agreement, or promise) that figures so prominently in the literature on public reason.[9] Such a contract, he argues, is neither necessary nor even helpful in establishing the authority of a government.

As Hume points out, a social contract's authorizing power needs as much justification as government's. Just as we might wonder why we have a duty to obey a particular government, so too we might equally wonder why we have a duty to comply with some contract we have made. The nature of the challenge in the one case is so similar to that in the other, Hume argues, that whatever might work to explain when and why contracts establish duties to comply will work directly, unmediated by contract, to establish a duty to obey government. The heart of such an explanation, Hume maintains, is found in an appeal to utility (specifically the utility of having and enforcing a practice of promising, by contract or otherwise, and of having and enforcing expectations of allegiance to a government). Exactly how this (expected) utility works to explain our duties—whether duties to keep our promises (or comply with our contracts) or duties to show allegiance to our government—turns out to be a complex and interesting story (more about which, below).[10] The key point here is that Hume explicitly rejects as inadequate an appeal to a social contract as a means of establishing the authority of a government. Understandably, that contributes to the thought that Hume's own allegiance is not with public reason.

Finally, Hume famously holds reason—public or otherwise—in low regard, as being at most a handmaiden to the passions in practical matters. Reason's role, he claims, is to serve as the slave of the passions, charged simply with determining effective means to the ends set by our passions, not with setting ends or establishing the legitimacy of anything, let alone standards for evaluating principles or institutions. Hume's general views concerning reason strike many as almost trivially implying that he would see any candidate conception of public reason as nothing more than passions dressed in elegant robes but lacking any distinctive claim to reign.

Each of these considerations—and especially all of them taken together—makes Hume's absence from the public reason literature more than understandable. They suggest that any defense of public reason as a standard of authority will be worlds away from anything Hume would defend or embrace.

Yet, as I argue below, to follow this suggestion is to be led far afield. Hume's account of justice (which covers the virtues of respect for property, fidelity to promises, and allegiance to government) is, at its heart, an account *of* public reason. This is true, I will argue, even though (importantly) his is not an account that appeals in the first instance *to* public reason. Hume offers a theory of public reason, which is not, itself, a public reason theory.

Hume does not begin with a commitment to people being autonomous or free and equal, nor does he offer a substantive normative argument for any specific principles or institutions as authoritative, nor does he appeal directly to anything he would recognize as reason, public or otherwise. Rather, what Hume provides is an account of moral judgment that makes sense of why appeals to autonomy, freedom, and equality play the central roles they do in moral deliberation and argument. The explanation Hume offers of our judgments of justice concerning property, of the obligation to keep one's promises, and of civic obligations, invokes an explanatory architecture that provides a natural home for the substantive normative views public reason theories advance. This architecture has it that the substantive principles, rules, and institutions that emerge as moral, and so as having authority over those who are subject to them, are all properly shaped and constrained by the reasons each has to accept them.

Still, the concerns that animate public reason theories have their impact only indirectly. They stand not as the grounds offered by Hume for a particular moral view, but as crucial aspects of moral thought that need to be accommodated by any adequate explanation of what we are doing in thinking morally. Thus, Hume does not defend the concerns. What he does is offer an explanation of our moral judgments that makes sense of those concerns having an impact on our judgments regarding our duties of justice, fidelity to promises, and allegiance to government.[11]

Significantly, the impact of these concerns is not restricted to respect for property, fidelity to promises and allegiance to government, all of which Hume saw as "artificial virtues" that depend on conventions. Far from it. Hume's account of the standard that informs all of our moral judgments, not just those regarding the artificial virtues but of all the others as well, is isomorphic to his account of our judgments of the artificial virtues—to such a degree (I'll argue) that Hume's explanation of the general standard of moral judgment itself underwrites public reason's core commitment to the idea that the authority of a principle, rule, or institution depends on whether those subject to it have reason to accept it.

Hume sees not just the artificial virtues, but the practice of making moral judgments *tout court*, as a solution to a shared practical problem—a solution that has a claim on our allegiance when, but only when, and then because, we each have reason to embrace its guidance. And the authority of the standard that practice embodies depends on it itself meeting that standard.[12]

To make the case, I will begin with a description of Hume's general account of the virtues, natural and artificial alike. Along the way, though, I will be especially concerned to bring out the extent to which, in the case of the artificial virtues, Hume

   i first characterizes the salient shared problem that gives the virtues their point,
  ii then argues that an appreciation of the problem predictably leads people (often, but not necessarily, consciously) to establish certain conventions,
 iii all while maintaining that if but only if these conventions meet certain conditions—including solving the shared problem for those who

fall under the convention—will complying with the convention itself secure moral approval and, in light of that, provide new (shared) reasons to act in accord with the conventions, reasons that are over and above those (convention-independent) reasons people would otherwise have.

This last aspect of Hume's view in effect allows that the standards of the convention may be authoritative, but only if complying with the convention works for each to solve a problem that each would otherwise face. What matters to the authority of the convention is that those who are subject to it have reason (in light of the problems solved by it) to accept its requirements.

Against that background, I will turn to the standard of moral judgment on which Hume relies to account for all the virtues and argue that his explanation of that standard mirrors precisely the structure and point of his earlier account of the artificial virtues. Hume in effect argues that the disposition to regulate one's actions and decisions by the standard of morality is an artificial virtue. And, as with all the artificial virtues, he holds that the authority of the standard depends on all who fall within its scope having reason (in light of the problems it solves and the opportunities it affords) to accept it, since only then will it secure its own endorsement.

3 The Virtues

Hume's moral theory plays out against the observation that the moral standing of an action depends on why it was performed—that the very same behavior might be virtuous or vicious depending on the agent's motive:

> Tis evident, that when we praise any actions, we regard only the motives that produced them, and consider the actions as signs or indications of certain principles in the mind and temper. The external performance has no merit. We must look within to find the moral quality.
> (*Treatise*, 3.2.1.2, SBN 477)

So the question Hume treats as central is "What explains the difference between virtuous and vicious motives?" His answer to this question, in broad outline, is that the virtuous motives are those that would secure our approval were we to take up what he calls the "General Point of View" (*Treatise* 3.3.1.15–16, SBN 581–2), from which we are suitably informed and appropriately impartial, whereas the vicious motives are those that would secure our disapproval were we to take up that point of view. Just which motives secure this approval (or disapproval) turns, Hume argues, on whether acting on them is *"useful or agreeable to the person himself or to others."*[13] In taking up the General Point of View we leave behind our own particular interests and limit ourselves to the feelings of approbation or disapprobation caused by our sympathy with the pleasures and pains caused by the motives in question. As a result, on thinking of the usefulness or agreeableness of certain actions, we find ourselves (thanks to sympathy with those affected) approving of the motives that produce those actions. (Similarly, and as a result of the same mechanism, we find ourselves disapproving of the motives that lead to dis-utile or disagreeable actions.)[14]

Hume ends up using his account to explain a broad range of virtues. Just to mention a few: beneficence, charity, generosity, clemency, moderation, and equity are all among those that are useful to others (*Treatise* 3.3.1.11, SBN 578–9), while prudence, temperance, frugality, industry, assiduity, enterprise, and dexterity are primarily useful to those who possess them (*Treatise* 3.3.1.24, SBN 587–8), and good humor, wit, and eloquence all tend to be immediately agreeable either to those who have them or to others (*Treatise* 3.3.4.8, SBN 611).

For all of these virtues Hume thinks it is easy both (i) to identify the motives characteristic of people with these traits and (ii) to explain why those motives secure approval from the General Point of View and so count as virtuous.[15] The relevant motives as well as our approval of those motives from the General Point of View, are, he maintains "entirely natural, and have no dependance on the artifice and contrivance of men" (*Treatise*, 3.3.1.1, SBN 574). Consequently, Hume thinks of them as "natural virtues."

These virtues stand in sharp contrast, Hume maintains, with (what he calls) the artificial virtues of justice, which include respect for property, fidelity to promises, and allegiance to government: the relevant motives of those who have these traits, as well as our approval of them from the General Point of View, are entirely dependent "on the artifice and contrivance of men." The dependence on artifice is two-fold:

First, the motives distinctive of those who have the artificial virtues cannot even be identified without appeal to the presence of an appropriate artifice or contrivance—specifically a convention. It is only once conventions are in place, Hume holds, that we can even identify actions as instances of respecting the property of others, or of keeping one's promise, or of showing allegiance to one's country. Absent the conventions, people have no property to respect, no promises to keep, and no countries to which to give their allegiance. The very possibility of performing the relevant virtuous actions depends, on Hume's view, on the existence of conventions.[16] When does "mixing your labor" with something make it yours? How might you transfer ownership of what is yours to someone else? By what act or form of words do you commit yourself to some future performance (as opposed, say, merely to predicting that performance)? What counts as a country to which one might give allegiance? In each case, Hume maintains, there is no answer unless relevant conventions are in place.

Second, the artificial virtues depend on "artifice and the contrivances of men"—that is, on conventions—even once the relevant motives and corresponding actions can be identified since their usefulness, which is what garners them approval from the General Point of View, is "somewhat singular" in that it can be understood only by seeing their place within the conventions that make them possible:

> A single act of justice is frequently contrary to *public interest*; and were it to stand alone, without being followed by other acts, may, in itself, be very prejudicial to society... Nor is every single act of justice, considered apart, more conducive to private interest, than to public... But however single acts of justice may be contrary, either to public or private interest, it is certain, that the whole plan or scheme is highly conducive, or indeed absolutely requisite, both to the support of society, and the well-being of every individual.
> (*Treatise* 3.2.2.22, SBN 497–8)

That the usefulness of the acts turns on the whole plan or scheme—that is, on the convention—of which they are a part means that their role in the plan or scheme is crucial to our approval (from the General Point of View) of the motives that give rise to them. In thinking about the motives of those with these virtues Hume argues that we will miss the target entirely unless and until we appreciate the conventions within which people with the virtues are acting.

With this all in mind, Hume offers a lovely explanation of how conventions concerning property could emerge spontaneously, and be sustained, without coercion or deception.

Hume starts his explanation by highlighting all the problems we would face, and all the opportunities we would forego, if we had no shared understanding of property (of who owned what and how that ownership might be transferred) or if we exercised no restraint concerning the taking of what we understood to belong to others. To appreciate these problems and opportunities, he points out, is to recognize that we would all be better off if only we were to coordinate around an appropriate understanding of what counts as whose property and restrain ourselves accordingly. Once this "common sense of interest is mutually express'd, and is known...," Hume observes, "it produces a suitable resolution and behaviour" (*Treatise*, 3.2.2.10, SBN 490). We will each, on the condition that others will as well, establish rules of property and resolve to abstain from taking what (in light of those rules) belongs to others.[17]

Hume offers an analogous story for the emergence of conventions that allow us to make promises, and to count on each other to keep them. We of course might not have such conventions. But in their absence we would all be worse off than if we made promising possible. To appreciate this is to recognize that we could all be better off if only we were to coordinate around an appropriate understanding of what counts as giving a promise and then act so as to keep promises made, resisting opportunities to profit from breaking them. And once this "common sense of interest is mutually express'd, and is known...," Hume observes, "it produces a suitable resolution and behaviour." We will each, on the condition that others will as well, settle on ways of making commitments to each other and resolve subsequently to act to keep them.

So, too, on Hume's account, for all the other artificial virtues. In each case there are salient shared problems that could be effectively addressed if only we had in place certain conventions. And it is no surprise that for each case it would be possible for conventions that solve the shared problems to arise spontaneously, without coercion or deception. In each case, the recognition of mutual interest can, even absent a concern for the interest of others, lead intelligent people to put such conventions in place.

That is not to say that the relevant problems are always addressed without coercion or deception. As Hume knows well, plenty of conventions concerning property, promise, etc. emerge and are sustained only thanks to coercion and deception. But the conventions that matter to the artificial virtues are, on Hume's view, restricted to those that at least could in principle emerge and be sustained without recourse to either. That possibility indicates that the convention in question is one with which all have independent reason to comply. (Compliance with a convention that can only be maintained by force or deception is not, on Hume's account, required by justice. It may still be virtuous to comply with such a convention, though, since proper regard to one's own interest, and to the interests of others, are virtuous. But acting from these motives reflects the virtues of prudence or benevolence, not justice.)

Even when the appropriate conventions are in place, of course, all sorts of motives lead people to perform the actions required by the conventions in question, not always ones that are distinctive of the artificial virtue in question. It is one thing to refrain from theft from a fear of punishment, quite another to do so for the motive that would animate a person who respects property. Similarly, it is one thing to keep one's promise out of a concern for a future reward, quite another to do so for the motive that animates a person who is true to her word. So too, whether we are considering property or promises, it is one thing to act from an admittedly virtuous concern for overall welfare, another to act from the motives that animate those who are just or true to their word.

Self-interest, a concern for one's family, and general benevolence, Hume recognizes, do often lead people to act in the ways people with the artificial virtues would act. And these motives play an essential role in establishing the relevant conventions in the first place and, in many cases, in helping to sustain them. But, Hume argues, they are not the motives characteristic of a just person, of a person who is good for her word, or of a person loyal to her government. Indeed, he maintains that no natural motive—no motive people might have absent a relevant convention—qualifies as motives characteristic of such people.

Yet, Hume holds, in order for us to understand these artificial virtues as distinctive virtues, we need to identify the motives characteristic of those who have them and explain why those motives would be approved of from the General Point of View.

What are the relevant motives, if not self-interest, limited benevolence, or general benevolence? One candidate Hume considers is the motive of duty or, as he sometimes puts it, "a regard to the virtue of the action" (*Treatise*, 3.2.1.4, SBN 478). To act from a sense of duty is indeed virtuous, Hume acknowledges. And this is a motive that might well often cause people to act justly, or to keep their word, or to obey their government, in a way that is markedly different from being moved by self-interest, or a concern for one's family, or even general benevolence.[18]

Yet, Hume argues, the motive of duty or "a regard to the virtue" of an action cannot be the motive in light of which the artificial virtues count as virtues. This is because some action counts as our duty (on Hume's account) only if some motive for it would secure approval from the General Point of View. So there needs to be some such "original" or "first" motive for that kind of action before we could then be moved by the recognition that acting on *that* motive would secure approval.[19]

> To suppose, that the mere regard to the virtue of the action, may be the first motive, which produc'd the action, and render'd it virtuous, is to reason in a circle. Before we can have such a regard, the action must be really virtuous; and this virtue must be deriv'd from some virtuous motive: And consequently the virtuous motive must be different from the regard to the virtue of the action.
>
> (*Treatise*, 3.2.1.4, SBN 478)[20]

When we are talking about the natural virtues, finding that "first motive" is no challenge; nature has provided it.[21] But we are talking about the artificial virtues here and we are trying to identify the motive on which those with the relevant virtue would be acting in performing the action that we (and they) might, then, recognize as their duty. The sense of duty, or a regard to the virtue of the action, Hume maintains, cannot play that role.

Strikingly, Hume seems never to identify explicitly the particular motives that do play this role for the artificial virtues. Given the importance he places on the existence of a first virtuous motive for each kind of virtuous action, this is surprising, to say the least.

Predictably, a number of suggestions have been made. According to some, Hume identifies no first virtuous motive because there is no such motive, which shows (they argue) either that Hume's actual view is that the artificial virtues are not really virtues at all (because there is no first virtuous motive) or that he abandoned the idea that the status of actions as virtuous depends on there being a virtuous motive to prompt them.[22] Others have held that Hume does in fact identify the virtuous motive and that it is the motive—enlightened self-interest—which he highlights in his accounts of the origin of the conventions that make the artificial virtues possible.[23] Still others, though, reject self-interest, enlightened or otherwise, as not plausibly motives of justice (for the reasons Hume himself seems to identify) and have argued that the relevant motives depend on which conventions are in place and involve the recognition of the actions as required by the relevant conventions.[24] There is a fair amount that can be said on behalf of each of these interpretations.

My own view is that the last is the closest to the truth. But its defense and development calls for some care, not least because, put the way I have put it, the proposal risks mis-identifying as a virtue what is really a vice—fetishizing conventions, as if the fact that a convention requires something by itself justifies doing what it requires. This sort of convention-fetishism, which involves taking "that is how things are done" reasoning as sufficient, is no part of Hume's view.

Not just any convention that establishes property, or creates a way to make a promise to others, or defines what allegiance requires, works, on Hume's view, to make conformity with the convention a virtue. To respect property, for instance, without regard to whether and how coercion or deception figures in the maintenance of the convention, is no virtue.[25] Hume is clear that the relevant conventions must offer the prospect of advantage, through cooperation, to all who fall within their compass, and do so without recourse to coercion or deception. Where those conditions are not met, Hume thinks the conventions that are in place do not work to define the virtue of justice, and justice does not demand what they require.[26]

The artificial virtues are, on Hume's view, essentially reciprocal, reflecting what people owe to each other in light of their mutually restricting what they willingly do in light of others similarly imposing such restrictions on themselves.[27] Central to Hume's account of the artificial virtues is that they involve a *conditional* willingness to comply with the relevant conventions, where the conditions involved concern (i) whether the convention provides the prospect of mutual advantage without coercion or deception and (ii) others being similarly conditionally willing to comply. Only when these conditions are met will the convention be solving the relevant problems appropriately—that is, in a way that means *being motivated by the recognition that the convention requires one to perform an action* will secure approval from the General Point of View.

Crucially, a proper understanding of the relevant problems involves seeing that a convention might adequately solve them only if it involves the willing participation of those subject to the convention, where their willingness does not depend on coercion or deception. From the General Point of View, it is the recognition that the convention does solve a salient shared problem that leads to approval of those who are willing (conditionally) to act in accord with the convention.

Needless to say, relevant conventions are not always in place. When they are not, those concerned with an artificial virtue find themselves at a loss when it comes to determining what the virtue requires. Other times, there may be conventions in place, but bad ones that do not work well to solve the relevant problems.[28] In this case too, Hume thinks, those concerned with an artificial virtue find themselves at a loss when it comes to determining what the virtue requires. The bad conventions may shape expectations and direct action, but to the extent that they do not address well the relevant problems, compliance with them will not secure approval from the General Point of View as a useful way to address the problems that give rise to a concern for justice.[29] It is only in contexts where there are established and effective conventions, well designed to address the relevant problems, that the artificial virtues find a home as virtues. And when they do, the shape they take turns critically on the specific conventions, which in turn reflect what each has reason to embrace (given what others have reason to embrace).

That others show a like restraint is crucial, according to Hume. The *conditional* willingness to comply with a mutually advantageous convention, in a context where others are similarly willing, offers tremendous advantages, both in avoiding otherwise inevitable conflicts and in offering beneficial opportunities that otherwise are simply not available. Yet it is important that the willingness be just conditional, and specifically conditional on others likewise being willing, since the important benefits from one person complying with the convention depend on others complying with it as well. As a result, Hume notes, if a just person should fall among thieves "his particular regard to justice being no longer of use to his own safety or that of others, he must consult the dictates of self-preservation alone, without concern for those who no longer merit his care and attention" (*Enquiry*, SBN 187). An unconditional willingness to comply with a convention specifying the demands of justice would simply set one up as a "cully" of one's integrity and would not secure approval from the General Point of View.[30]

Importantly, a general conditional willingness to comply with a mutually advantageous convention, free of coercion and deception, taken alone, provides no motive to do anything in particular. Until there is a convention in place, and so a specified way to act in order to comply, there is nothing in particular for a person who is conditionally willing to comply to do. She will have no motive to act at all, despite being primed to have one. When it comes to the artificial virtues, the relevant conditional willingness turns into an effective motive only in contexts where, in fact, conventions are in place to settle how one is to act when the conditions are met.

The original or first virtuous motives of the artificial virtues are, on this understanding of Hume's account, the motives that those with the conditional willingness to comply with appropriate conventions have, when they find themselves in a context where the conditions are met. These people act as they do *because the convention requires it* but only given that the convention in question offers the prospect of mutual advantage free of coercion and deception, and only given that others too are willing to comply if they do.

The story of the emergence of the required conventions will be a story of people acting on *other* motives, not the motives distinctive of the virtue the convention makes possible. In general, Hume suggests, self-interest plays this role, providing the initial motives for people to establish and then conform to conventions. Yet other natural motives (e.g. a concern for others, the desire for approval, fear of punishment), as well as mindless imitation and habit, all have their roles to play in getting conventions up and running and then in sustaining them. It is only once the conventions are in place that an appropriately conditional willingness to comply with a convention, if others will similarly comply, will provide a motive to act in any particular way.

While the original reasons for establishing the relevant conventions that make respecting property, keeping your promise, showing allegiance, possible, are found in the interests of each that might be served, the range and scope of the duty those reasons put in place are, Hume holds, determined by an appropriate convention, which itself establishes what is one's fair share of the burden that comes with trying, together, to satisfy those interests.

Central to Hume's view is that the relevant conventions offer the prospect of *mutual advantage* (however the people involved might measure advantage); the conventions that help to constitute the virtues are restricted to those of which it is true that each stands to gain and so has reason to comply.[31] This is a serious and substantive restriction, though what its implications are depends crucially on what the world is like, both in terms of what our individual interests happen to be and what opportunities we might have for beneficial cooperation.

As interests and opportunities shift across populations or through time, so too will the rules of the conventions that count as mutually advantageous, and so too will the actions of a person concerned with justice. The demands of justice, and so a just person's actions, will vary in response to which conventions are in place, and in response to whether those conventions are such that the people subject to them have reason to comply with the conventions in question.

We can, in an abstract way, say what the conditions are under which a just person will be motivated to act, and so the conditions under which an action will count as just. But without knowing which conventions are in place, there is no saying what the specific motives of a person with an artificial virtue will be. It is fair enough here to note that she will be motivated by a concern for justice—for doing her share within a convention or practice, assuming both that others are too and that the convention or practice offers the prospect of benefit to all expected to comply, absent coercion or deception. But there is no fact of the matter about what that will involve unless and until a convention is in place.

It is worth noting the difference between asking whether compliance with a convention offers you advantages, and whether compliance with it is a virtue or a duty (or is even allowed by virtue or duty). The first may well get a positive answer even when the second gets a negative one. Or the first may get a negative answer even when the second gets a positive answer. But, when it comes to the artificial virtues, a positive answer to the second depends on the convention being one that has offered you and others advantages and with which others have willingly complied.

As Hume emphasizes, while *the relevant conventions* must promise mutual advantage, complying with their demands, and so with the demands of virtue, can be individually costly. The benefits on offer, the prospect of which lead to approval from the General Point of View, come not from the particular actions one might be required to perform, but from the convention that requires them. Moreover, from the General Point of View what matters is that the conventions are well suited to solving the problems that give them point and purpose. Their success on this front is not a matter of whether they promise the best consequences overall, but in whether and for whom they offer a solution. What secures approval from the General Point of View, and so counts as virtuous, is willingly playing one's part in an existing convention that has provided (or promises to provide) one with benefits thanks to the willing cooperation of others. The benefits that matter to approval from the General Point of View are the benefits to each that the conventions make possible.

The prospective benefits in play, it is worth noting, are to be measured (Hume emphasizes) by the interests of each. But this is in a context in which (Hume also emphasizes) people regularly have interests that reach far beyond themselves.[32] While justice is a "cautious, jealous virtue" (*Enquiry*, SBN 183–4) those who are just are often cautious about the welfare of others and jealous of actions that put those they care about at a disadvantage.

Although a concern for others is among the interests Hume recognizes as a central aspect of humanity, it is important to mark the deep difference, as Hume sees it, between benevolence and justice. Consider a case in which we are all concerned with the welfare of some group of people and decide to work together to meet their needs, with the understanding that by each playing a role we will together achieve our shared end. Benevolence has us focused on the needs of others. Yet in a context where some, but not others, might end up contributing, a concern for justice finds its place. The end is a benevolent one; yet the concern of justice is not with that end, but with whether people are doing their share in their pursuit of it. The concern with justice stands even if, as things turn out, the needs of those in the group we hope to help are met unfairly by some contributing more. The benevolent person cares that the end is achieved. Just people care not (simply) that the end is achieved but that people have done their share (assuming others too are doing theirs) in pursuing that end.

Hume's focus on actual conventions being in place as a condition for justice goes with his side-lining the discussion of ideal conditions, except to note that certain ideal conditions—of say unlimited benevolence or super-abundance—would render certain conventions (say concerning property) pointless.[33] This is not because he thinks actual conventions are uncriticizable, but because (on his view) substantive claims of justice depend on the nature of the conventions actually in place. These might be conventions that, if changed, would make at least some people better off, perhaps dramatically. If so, that would count as moral grounds to work for a change.[34] Yet unless and until the change is made, the legitimate claims of justice, made by, on behalf of, or of, people willingly participating in the convention do not reflect those (as yet merely) possible improvements.[35]

Given this, it is complicated to say just how conservative the view is. On the one hand, claims of justice have their content determined by existing conventions (when those conventions satisfy the relevant conditions). On the other hand, such conventions may allow internal critiques that would fund the claim that aspects of the existing convention are unjust and the conventions will in any case be open to moral evaluation and criticism on other grounds, all of which exert pressure for change.

One crucial element of Hume's view is that the content of authoritative standards of justice are not just sensitive to, but are determined by, what the people subject to them can willingly, absent coercion, embrace. Another is that participating willingly in certain conventions and practices creates reciprocal obligations towards others who do so as well. These reciprocal obligations, it is worth highlighting, reach beyond—and may actually oppose—the interests that provided reason to participate in the convention in the first place. Moreover, they remain even in the face of, though often not withstanding, moral objections to the convention in question.

With this last point in mind, consider a slave-owning society in which the slave owners cooperate together, to their mutual benefit, in order to exploit successfully those they treat as property. In such societies, it is clear that on Hume's view the slaves have no moral duty whatsoever of restraint or cooperation with respect to those who exploit them.[36] Respecting property in their society is no virtue for them. The situation with regard to those who have benefited from the convention, though, is made more complicated, I think, by their recognition that the benefits they have enjoyed depended on the willing cooperation of their fellow slave-holders in enforcing the convention. For them, there is sense to be made of owing something to those people, in light of their compliance with the convention. This is true even though other moral considerations tell decisively against the reprehensible convention and in favor of destroying it. Similarly, Hume is well placed to make sense of honor among thieves as a real possibility and a (limited) virtue, despite it being in the service of (mutually embraced but) immoral ends.

The key point, for our purposes, though, is that on Hume's account our obligations of justice exist only if the conventions in place are such that we, and others who are subject to them, have reason to accept them. If and when that is true, those who willingly participate, absent coercion and deception, acquire new, and distinctively moral, reasons to comply with the convention's rules, principles, or institutions—reasons provided by the reciprocal obligations to others that their willing and un-coerced participation in a mutually advantageous convention creates. This means that public reason's core commitment, as articulated at the beginning, finds a place at the heart of Hume's account of which standards of justice we judge authoritative and why we make those judgments, albeit absent any appeal to the substantive moral commitments to mutual respect, freedom, or equality that figure in standard public reason theories.

At the same time, though, those substantive moral commitments articulate well what might be said, morally, in defense of the standards Hume's theory says would emerge as, by our lights, authoritative. In particular, if Hume is right about the conditions under which we see certain standards as authoritative for people, it will be natural to see those judgments and standards as embodying and respecting the substantive moral commitments, precisely because they are conditioned on the thought that the standards, and the obligations they establish (when they do), depend on those subject to them being able willingly, and without coercion, to accept them. That is, after all, the constraint those public reason theorists see as the proper expression of mutual respect, freedom, and equality. In Hume, though, the constraint emerges from his *explanation* of why we count complying with certain conventions as virtuous, not as a substantive premise in defense of such conventions.

In evaluating Hume's account of the artificial virtues, three questions loom large: does it fit the phenomena? Are the resources it relies on legitimate? Does it expand our understanding of, or insight into, the phenomena? Needless to say, with respect to each question there is plenty to say about what exactly is being asked and also about what the right answers might be. My aim here, though, is not to offer an evaluation of Hume's account, but to bring out the ways in which it makes sense of why our moral judgments are so often well articulated by the considerations that figure prominently in the public reason literature, so I will be leaving these questions aside.

Still, it is worth noting with respect to the first question, that Hume's account implies that all disputes concerning justice, as Hume understands it, are disputes either about what the relevant existing conventions require and allow, or about whether the conventions in place satisfy the conditions required in order to succeed in establishing (reciprocal) obligations. Arguments about which possible conventions would be better, morally or otherwise, are often, Hume is prepared to acknowledge, deeply important; answers to them properly shape efforts at reform and, potentially, offer grounds for revolution. Yet, he is committed to holding, they are not arguments about what our (reciprocal) obligations of justice actually are.[37]

4 The Standard of Morality

So far the focus has been on the ways in which Hume's account of the artificial virtues provides a framework within which to understand how the substantive moral commitments of public reason would naturally emerge. That is enough, I think, to make the case that a crucial part of Hume's theory fits comfortably with, and provides the underpinnings for, public reason theory. There are, of course, all of the obstacles mentioned at the beginning, to which I will return towards the end. For now, though, let me say that if none of them constitute arguments against the reading of Hume I have offered (and I don't think they do) neither do they tell against understanding Hume as offering an account *of* public reason, even if not an account that appeals *to* public reason.

Yet this restricted focus underplays, to a dramatic degree, the extent to which Hume's overall account of moral judgment, not just his account of our judgments of the artificial virtues, harmonizes with public reason theory. To appreciate this, the important thing is to see the extent to which Hume's account of the General Point of View, which sets the standard for all the virtues, is modeled directly on his account of the artificial virtues.

So, for instance, Hume's explanation of the General Point View plays out against an appreciation of the problems we would face and the opportunities we would forgo were we to lack a shared standard for moral judgment. Absent such a standard, people faced with conflicting interests and variable feelings (specifically though not solely of approbation and disapprobation), would have no way, through reflection and discussion, to pursue effectively a shared view of how to act in, and react to, the world in which they found themselves.

Hobbes famously highlighted the downsides of this situation with his description of the state of nature, in which (as he saw it) people would inevitably be at war, "every man against every man" with predictable results.[38] His view is that nothing shy of setting up an absolute political power, a Leviathan, to settle disputes and enforce peace, could possibly address the problem. Hume embraces a less draconian picture of what life would be like in the state of nature, not least because he thought people's "humanity" would render the situation more tractable. But he shares Hobbes' view that peoples' different and often conflicting interests, and their variable affective responses, predictably and, indeed, inevitably, generate conflicts. According to Hume, "every particular man has a peculiar position with regard to others; and 'tis impossible we cou'd ever converse together on any reasonable terms, were each of us to consider characters and persons, only as they appear from his peculiar point of view" (*Treatise*, 3.3.1.15, SBN 581–2). Fortunately, he thinks, we have found a solution:

> In order, therefore, to prevent those continual *contradictions*, and arrive at a more *stable* judgment of things, we fix on some *steady* and *general* points of view; and always, in our thoughts, place ourselves in them, whatever may be our present situation.
> (*Treatise*, 3.3.1.15, SBN 581–2)

In contrast with Hobbes, Hume thinks that a significant amount of the problem can be, and indeed has been, addressed by adding moral concepts to our intellectual repertoire. Being able to think and talk about virtue and vice, and not simply about what we happen to like or dislike, changes the situation dramatically, especially if the results of moral deliberation and discussion can be counted on to engage the heart. As Hume sees things, in regulating what we think and say about virtue and vice (at least implicitly, but quite reliably) by considering what we would approve of from the General Point of View (that is, the reactions of a suitably informed, appropriately impartial, observer) and then (often) setting ourselves to act accordingly, we avoid the need for a Hobbesian Leviathan.

This solution turns crucially on our participating in a convention that has us regulating our thoughts and actions in light of moral considerations, assuming others will as well. The details of the story Hume offers of this convention, and of the moral concepts that figure centrally in it, matter in a number of ways.

For instance, an appropriate standard for those concepts—one that will actually address the shared problems we would otherwise face—must be one that we can all, at least to a great degree, access. A standard for moral judgment that was inaccessible, say because it requires perfect information, or a set of reactions we can neither conceive, nor experience, would likely leave us with just as much disagreement and conflict as if we had no standard at all. Moreover, it must be a standard that works to deliver more or less the same results when appealed to by different people, since, again, a failure to do so would likely leave us with the sort of disagreement and conflict an appeal to them is meant to resolve.

We have crafted such a standard, Hume argues, by doing two things. The first is relying on a standard that appeals to (familiar) feelings of approbation and disapprobation that are available to all who might deliberate and act in light of moral considerations. But of course differences among us in what we find ourselves approving of are one source of the conflict that moral concepts are supposed to help address. So we come to the second thing we have done, according to Hume: we have restricted our attention to approbation and disapprobation that would be felt under circumstances that abstract away from our differences in a way that leaves the results accessible to each of us, but that fixes our attention in a way that holds the prospect of a fruitful consensus. This is accomplished, Hume argues, by restricting the approbation that counts as setting the standard for moral judgment to approbation that results from sympathy (rather than from self-interest, which would simply let the conflicts we are hoping to resolve reverberate), and then by restricting who all, under what circumstances, we are to sympathize with.

> One may, perhaps, be surpriz'd, that amidst all these interests and pleasures, we shou'd forget our own, which touch us so nearly on every other occasion. But we shall easily satisfy ourselves on this head, when we consider, that every particular person's pleasure and interest being different, 'tis impossible men cou'd ever agree in their sentiments and judgments, unless they chose some common point of view, from which they might survey their object, and which might cause it to appear the same to all of them. Now, in judging of characters, the only interest

or pleasure, which appears the same to every spectator, is that of the person himself, whose character is examin'd; or that of persons, who have a connexion with him. And tho' such interests and pleasures touch us more faintly than our own, yet being more constant and universal, they counter-ballance the latter even in practice, and are alone admitted in speculation as the standard of virtue and morality.
(*Treatise* 3.3.1.30, SBN 590–91)

Just which people, under which circumstances, are to be considered when taking up the common point of view varies, on Hume's account, as different shared problems are considered. In each case, the underlying idea is that we focus, from the general point of view, on a set of standard conditions that capture the elements of the circumstances that generate the problems and then reflect on what motives would be such that having them would be (a part of) a solution to the problem under those circumstances. Motives that would secure approbation when thus considered count as virtuous, those that would secure disapprobation count as vicious.

As Hume points out, even when we restrict ourselves to sympathy, leaving aside the impact of self-interest on our feelings of approval and disapproval, we discover our reactions are hugely variable thanks to a range of factors, including "our acquaintance or connexion with the persons, or even by an eloquent recital of the case" (*Enquiry*, 230). Our moral judgments, in contrast, and fortunately, treat these differences as irrelevant. Thus we judge (or at least suppose we should judge) people equally virtuous who have the same character, without regard to their connection to us or to how vividly one person's character happens to be in our mind. "Our servant, if diligent and faithful," Hume observes, "may excite stronger sentiments of love and kindness than *Marcus Brutus*, as represented in history; but we say not upon that account, that the former character is more laudable than the latter" (*Treatise*, 3.3.1.16, SBN 582). In taking up the General Point of View, Hume argues, we are supposed to leave aside, or at least control for, the differences that have to do with their connection to us or our ability to sympathize with the particular people involved.[39]

For similar reasons, Hume argues, what matters from the General Point of View are not the actual effects of the particular motives. "Virtue in rags is still virtue," Hume observes, "and the love, which it procures, attends a man into a dungeon or desert, where the virtue can no longer be exerted in action, and is lost to all the world" (*Treatise*, 3.3.1.19, SBN 584).[40] Taking up the General Point of View involves looking at the effects *that kind of* motive has *under standard conditions, on those in (what Hume calls) the "narrow circle,"* not looking at all the actual effects a particular person's motive happens to have in the circumstances in which she finds herself.[41, 42] That this is true, Hume argues, is crucial to the General Point of View working to solve the problems a good standard of moral judgment must solve. In particular, it is only by considering the usual effects of motives under standard conditions, that we might all understand in the same way, that there is hope for our sympathetic responses to align. Were we to rely, for instance, on each person's estimate of what the actual effects would be of a particular person's action, we would regularly find ourselves mired in disagreement. Fixing instead on standard conditions (that we might all understand in the same way) and on a specific set of people who are usually, and more or less directly, affected by the kind of motive in question (those in the "narrow circle") works to reduce disagreements dramatically by giving people a common understanding of what to focus on.

Needless to say, disagreement is not totally eliminated, most especially because there is room to argue about just what the standard conditions are, and who all falls within the "narrow circle." Similarly, having a suitably structured legal system with courts to adjudicate disputes works to decrease conflicts significantly even though it does not come close to eliminating them entirely. That a legal system can greatly reduce them is enough to recommend having one. So too, Hume thinks, with a suitably structured system of moral evaluation.

The whole package, Hume argues, works as well as anything might to address conflicts of interest and attitude, while avoiding force, abuse, and the other dangers that would come with setting up a Hobbesian Leviathan. Yet Hume knows that moral reflection, deliberation, and discussion is no panacea. Indeed, he is vividly aware of the ways in which moral zealots can wreak havoc on individuals and across societies. Nonetheless, he holds, having the capacity to think and talk in moral terms that are governed by the General Point of View, and requiring that people act according to the results, is dramatically better than the alternatives, assuming others do so as well. If we did not already have such a practice, we would each have ample reason, grounded in our own interests, to establish it together. As Hume notes

> Mankind is an inventive species; and where an invention is obvious and absolutely necessary, it may as properly be said to be natural as any thing that proceeds immediately from original principles, without the intervention of thought or reflection. Tho' the rules of justice be *artificial*, they are not *arbitrary*. Nor is the expression improper to call them *Laws of Nature*; if by natural we understand what is common to any species, or even if we confine it to mean what is inseparable from the species.
> (*Treatise*, 3.2.1.19, SBN 484)

This holds as well for the invention of moral concepts, and the standards we rely on in deploying them, as for the rules of justice. Though they be artificial (that is, a human contrivance) they are not arbitrary.

5 Conclusion

In effect, then, on Hume's view moral thought, like thought about property, promises, or allegiance, is artificial; its existence depends on a convention, and specifically, a convention that, if well designed, can work to address problems that we all would otherwise face. As with conventions concerning property, promises, and allegiance, Hume is well aware that not all moral concepts are created equal: only some will have a claim to authority, while many will not.

In particular, Hume holds that "[c]elibacy, fasting, penance, mortification, self-denial, humility, silence, solitude, and the whole train of monkish virtues" all fail this requirement (*Enquiry* 9.3, SBN 270). The concepts used to characterize the "monkish virtues," he argues, all fail to address any relevant problem and they fail to be useful, or agreeable, either to the possessor or others, in the way that is required to secure approval from the General Point of View.[43]

Other concepts, though, do meet this requirement and have authority for us. They pick out traits that work to solve salient shared problems in ways that make those traits useful or agreeable to those who have them, and thereby secure approval from the General Point of View. What these concepts, in their application, require of us, we have moral reason to do. (Whereas we have no moral reason to do what other moral concepts, in their application, would require of us.)

In drawing this distinction among candidate virtues, and the concepts we might use to pick them out, Hume is relying, crucially, on a standard—provided by the General Point of View—that itself has authority for us only because we each have reason, absent coercion and deception, to rely on moral thought and talk to regulate our actions, assuming others are likewise willing. Only then does the General Point of View secure its own approval and thereby meet the standard of authority it sets. This feature of the General Point of View introduces internal resources for moral criticisms of what is, at any particular time, taken to constitute the relevant standard circumstances and the relevant "narrow circle." As our actual circumstances change, so too, on Hume's view, will the criteria for particular virtues and also for the virtue of relying on moral concepts to regulate our actions.

Thinking back to the reasons people may have had for seeing Hume and public reason theory as worlds apart, it is worth noting that, if I am right about how Hume's theory works, there is no appeal to mutual respect, freedom, or equality, nor to any general moral principles, nor to the authorizing power of consent or contract, nor to an august faculty of reason. Peoples' willing participation in conventions, absent coercion and deception, does play a crucial role in Hume's explanation of our moral judgments, but that role is as setting the conditions under which certain kinds of problems might count as solved, not as themselves an expression of substantive moral requirements.

At the same time, though, once the structure of Hume's account of our moral judgments is laid out, it both provides an explanatory structure that makes good sense of why public reason's distinctive values and constraints would emerge as central to our moral view and articulates a standard of moral judgments that serves those values and satisfies those constraints.

My hope, here, is to have said enough about Hume's moral theory to make the case that those interested in public reason will, perhaps to their surprise, find it a hospitable home.

Notes

1 I am extremely grateful for detailed and thoughtful comments by Piers Turner on an earlier version of this chapter.
2 Morehead-Cain Alumni Distinguished Professor, Department of Philosophy, University of North Carolina at Chapel Hill.
3 Here and throughout, the idea is not just that there is *some* reason for people to accept them but that there is *sufficient* reason, given the alternatives.
4 The fundamental ideas run through *A Theory of Justice*, especially in the role given to (what he calls) the condition of publicity, but find explicit articulation in terms of public reason starting with his *Political Liberalism*.
5 John Rawls appeals to "the circumstances of justice"—an idea that he explicitly takes from Hume—highlighting that certain moral principles have their place and point in contexts that offer opportunities for mutual advantage (*A Theory of Justice*, 127–30). But Rawls quickly leaves behind Hume's own account of the nature of such principles. Gerald Gaus, meanwhile, cites Hume only once in his *The Order of Public Reason*, despite sharing Hume's view that the principles of justice are rightly seen as tools well suited to solving certain practical problems rather than as abstract entities to be identified or discovered. An exception, on this front, is Gerald Postema, who has taken seriously the idea that Hume might be a public reason theorist. See his "Public Practical Reason: An Archeology" *Social Philosophy and Policy*, vol. 12 (1995), 43–86 and his "Public Practical Reason: Political Practice," in *Theory and Practice*, edited by Ian Shapiro and Judith DeCew (New York: New York University Press, 1996), 345–85.
6 Hume does offer an influential compatibilist theory of free will, according to which people are properly seen as free as long as, and to the extent that, they are able to do what they decide to do. (That their decisions—and the desires and beliefs that give rise to them—are determined by forces not under their control is, on his view, not a threat to freedom.) But Hume never turns this account to significant moral purpose as a fundamental value in light of which particular moral principles are to be evaluated. This is true even though he does, pretty clearly, value people having the power to do as they decide.

7 Of course Hume's success on this front depends on capturing our moral thinking accurately. This has implications I will be exploiting later in connecting Hume to public reason. But for now the important point is that Hume's efforts are primarily explanatory, not justificatory.
8 The relevant differences among different approaches to public reason have to do with (i) the sorts of reasons—epistemic, practical, religious—that are embraced as relevant, (ii) why they are taken to be relevant—as a way of acknowledging reasonable disagreement (say because of the so-called burdens of judgment), or inevitable differences among interests that might be served, or the importance of religious freedom—and finally (iii) the domain over which the principles or institutions are taken to have authority, if they are appropriately supported by the reasons the various parties have.
9 See his "Of the Original Contract" in *Essays: Moral, Political and Literary*, edited by Eugene F. Miller, (Indianapolis: Liberty Classics, 1985), 465–87.
10 By way of foreshadowing though: It is the expectation of advantage for each, given the cooperation of others, that underwrites the duty to keep one's promises and the authority of a state. Where there is no expectation of mutual advantage from a practice of giving and keeping one's word, or an established government, there is no duty and no authority. Thus, when a practice of giving and keeping one's word is predictably and consistently exploited by others to one's disadvantage, or government provides no expected benefit to its citizens, the corresponding duties evaporate. Needless to say, risk of exploitation is always present. The question is whether that risk, combined with its expected cost when it happens, outweighs the benefits of being able to rely generally on the advantages of having a practice of making and keeping promises and a government in place.
11 It is no accident that when Hume is referred to in the public reason literature, his account of justice and the circumstances that give rise to our interest in it and shape its demands is what gets attention.
12 This is a non-trivial requirement since any particular standard that we might be relying on in making moral judgments might well fail to meet the standard it sets. In the case of moral judgments, Hume takes such a failure as decisive grounds for revising the standard.
13 *Enquiry*, SBN 268–9 and also SBN 276–8. Hume offers a careful explanation of why such actions, and not others, would secure the relevant approval. Some of the details will be important to understanding the way in which the General Point of View speaks to, and reflects, the concerns animating public reason, as will become clear later.
14 Hume offers a detailed account of how it is that sympathy works to transform the idea of someone's pleasure or pain into corresponding feelings of approval or disapproval of those who are taken to be causes of those pleasures and pains. There are a lot of complexities to his story; one of its signal virtues is that it makes room for the idea that approbation and disapprobation are responsive to considerations that serve as grounds for the person feeling as she does. But these details can, for our purposes, be left to one side.
15 Some of these motives (e.g. benevolence) are approvable however strong they might be, while others (e.g. self-interest) are virtuous only in limited supply.
16 In advancing this view he is rejecting the idea that there are laws of nature in light of which, for instance, the land is all the property of the king or people own whatever they happen to be able to control.
17 The importance of which rules might be put in place pales, he thinks, in comparison to the importance of getting some rules or others: none of the

benefits are available to anyone until specific rules are in place and mutually recognized. In "Of the Rules Which Determine Property," in the *Treatise*, Hume maintains that just which rules will play the required role turns largely on custom and imagination, not on any sort of calculated determination of utility.

18 Significantly, although the motive of duty is different from these others, all of them, Hume recognizes, may be such that a person might perform the actions a person with those motives would perform, but do so from duty rather than from the virtuous motive in question (*Treatise*, 3.2.1.8, SBN 479). The one virtue the motive of duty is characteristic of is the virtue of dutifulness, which is not, in Hume's view, a free-standing virtue, but instead a virtue, when it is one, that is parasitic on there being others.

19 For a detailed discussion of this argument see my "Hume on the Artificial Virtues," in the *Oxford Handbook of David Hume*, edited by Paul Russell (Oxford: Oxford University Press, 2016), 435–69.

20 Hume is here supposing that in acting on the motive of duty, at least when doing so is virtuous, we are right that acting in this way is our duty. Otherwise, it would be possible for there to be no original motive that would secure the appropriate approval, even though acting on the thought that there were such a motive did secure that approval.

21 Thus it is easy to make sense of someone who feels no concern for the welfare of others nonetheless giving to charity (that is, performing a benevolent action) from a sense of duty. The recognition of giving to charity as a duty is the recognition that those who act from the motive of benevolence are acting on a motive that would secure approval from the general point of view, in a context where failing to act in that way would garner disapproval.

22 Marcia Baron, "Hume's Noble Lie: An Account of His Artificial Virtues." *Canadian Journal of Philosophy* 12(3/September 1982), 539–55; Rachel Cohon, "Hume's Difficulty with the Virtue of Justice." *Hume Studies* 23(1/1997), 91–112; *Hume's Morality: Feeling and Fabrication*. (Oxford: Oxford University Press, 2008).

23 David Gauthier, "Artificial Virtues and the Sensible Knave." *Hume Studies* 18(2/November, 1992), 401–28.

24 Stephen Darwall, *The British Moralists and the Internal "Ought."* (Cambridge: Cambridge University Press, 1995); Don Garrett, "The First Motive to Justice: Hume's Circle Argument Squared." *Hume Studies* 33(2/2007), 257–88. That Hume never explicitly identifies a single motive of justice might, on this view, be explained by noting that the relevant motives vary with the conventions.

25 Whether and how it might matter that coercion or deception figured in the establishment of the convention turns on whether that history has an impact on the reasons those currently subject to the convention have for complying. If, for instance, complying now, with, say, a coercively established convention, would introduce incentives to future exploitation that outweigh the benefits expected from complying, then that history matters. But if, alternatively, all still have reason, absent coercion and deception, to comply now, then the history of coercion will not, on Hume's account, undermine the authority of the convention established.

26 Of course, self-interest or benevolence might still demand doing as the convention requires, when so acting is in one's interest or in the interest of others.

27 As Hume recognizes, not all conventions involve restraint. But the conventions that are central to solving the problems that give place and point to the artificial virtues all do, even as they sometime prompt behavior (say, keeping

one's promise) where there is no particular temptation otherwise that needs to be restrained.
28 Conventions count as being bad, in this context, by failing to solve the problems they are meant to solve.
29 Hume emphasizes that his point is not that absent the conventions injustice is not a vice: in claiming "that in the state of nature, or that imaginary state, which preceded society, there be neither justice nor injustice," he is not claiming "that it was allowable, in such a state, to violate the property of others" but rather "that there was no such thing as property; and consequently could be no such thing as justice or injustice" (*Treatise* 3.2.2.28, SBN 501).
30 *Treatise*, 3.2.7.3, SBN 535. It might be that so acting, for the benefit of one's compatriots, might secure approval, if that is why one was doing it, but as benevolent, not as just.
31 *Treatise* 3.2.5.10, SBN 521–2 and 3.2.10.16, SBN 563–4. That the conventions could emerge without coercion or deception is a mark, for Hume, that mutual advantage is available.
32 Hume is especially clear about this in his Appendix on Self-Love, but it shows up throughout the *Treatise* and the *Enquiry*.
33 He maintains that "if men were supplied with every thing in the same abundance, or if *every one* had the same affection and tender regard for *every one* as for himself; justice and injustice would be equally unknown among mankind" (*Treatise*, 3.2.2.17, SBN 495).
34 Hume gives no space to considering either the process of negotiation nor the relevance of what the possible results might be, except as the processes actually occur and the results are in hand, in which case their impact is as direct and substantial as the resulting changes the negotiation brings.
35 Of course, if the conventions in place fail to meet appropriate conditions altogether (as opposed to meeting them, but being such that we can imagine better), then the demands of justice do not apply. So, for instance, if the convention in place fails to be advantageous for part of the population subject to them, as seems often to be the case when it comes to rules of property, that convention's requirements will not be authoritative with respect to them.
36 As Hume notes, "as government is a mere human invention for mutual advantage and security, it no longer imposes any obligation, either natural or moral, when once it ceases to have that tendency" *Treatise* 3.2.10.16, SBN 563–4.
37 I mention this in particular because Hume's conception of the full reach of concerns of justice, specifically, is narrower, I think, than that of many people now. At the same time, though, I suspect that once the full resources of his moral theory are appreciated, it becomes clear it has a place for the concerns at issue, even if not distinctively as concerns of justice.
38 *Leviathan*, XIII, 8.
39 For discussion of Hume's account of moral thought as transcendence to the common, see also Gerald J. Postema, "Public Practical Reason: An Archeology." *Social Philosophy & Policy* 12 (1/1995), 43–86.
40 Appreciating this plays a crucial role in accounting for the fact that in judging of actions we recognize that even vicious motives (and the resulting actions) sometimes have good effects and that virtuous ones the reverse. Any adequate explanation of our judgments needs to respect, and account for, this fact.
41 In much the same way, Hume points out, in evaluating the comfort of a home, we consider not how comfortable it has actually been (no one may ever have

lived in it) but instead whether, were it to be used by the people for whom it was designed, it would be comfortable.
42 For a discussion of this aspect of Hume's theory, see my "Hume and the Bauhaus Theory of Ethics" in *Midwest Studies in Philosophy*, vol. 20. University of Notre Dame Press, 280–98.
43 Of course, were our circumstances to be radically different than they are, Hume is committed to thinking that some of the monkish virtues might really be virtues. But it would take the circumstances being such that they would actually be useful or agreeable to the possessor or others.

Bibliography

Baron, Marcia. 1982. "Hume's Noble Lie: An Account of His Artificial Virtues." *Canadian Journal of Philosophy* 12: 539–55.

Cohon, Rachel. 1997. "Hume's Difficulty with the Virtue of Justice." *Hume Studies* 23: 91–112.

———. 2008. *Hume's Morality: Feeling and Fabrication*. Oxford: Oxford University Press.

Darwall, Stephen. 1995. *The British Moralists and the Internal 'Ought.'* Cambridge: Cambridge University Press.

Garrett, Don. 2007. "The First Motive to Justice; Hume's Circle Argument Squared." *Hume Studies* 33: 257–88.

Gaus, Gerald. 2011. *The Order of Public Reason*. New York: Cambridge University Press.

Gauthier, David. 1992. "Artificial Virtues and the Sensible Knave." *Hume Studies* 18: 401–28.

Hobbes, Thomas. 1994. *Leviathan*. Indianapolis: Hackett Publishing Company.

Hume, David. 1985. "Of the Original Contract." In *Essays: Moral, Political and Literary*, edited by Eugene F. Miller, 465–87. Indianapolis: Liberty Classics.

———. 1998. *Enquiry Concerning the Principles of Morals*. Edited by Tom L. Beauchamp. Oxford and New York: Oxford University Press.

———. 2000. *A Treatise of Human Nature*. Edited by D.F. Norton & M.J. Norton. Oxford: Oxford University Press.

Plato. 1992. *The Republic*. Translated and edited by G.M.A. Grube, revised by C.D.C. Reeve. Indianapolis: Hackett.

Postema, Gerald J. 1995. "Public Practical Reason: An Archeology." *Social Philosophy & Policy* 12: 43–86.

———. 1996. "Public Practical Reason: Political Practice." In *Theory and Practice*, edited by Ian Shapiro and Judith DeCew, 345–85. New York: New York University Press.

Rawls, John. 1971. *A Theory of Justice*. Cambridge: Harvard University Press.

———. 1993. *Political Liberalism*. New York: Columbia University Press.

Sayre-McCord, Geoffrey. 1994. "On Why Hume's General Point of View Isn't Ideal—and Shouldn't Be." *Social Philosophy & Policy* 11: 202–28.

———. 1996. "Hume and the Bauhaus Theory of Ethics." *Midwest Studies in Philosophy* 20: 280–98.

———. 2016. "Hume on the Artificial Virtues." In the *Oxford Handbook of David Hume*, edited by Paul Russell, 435–69. Oxford: Oxford University Press.

Abbreviations of Works Cited

Enquiry: *Enquiry Concerning the Principles of Morals*. Edited by Tom L. Beauchamp. Oxford & New York: Oxford University Press, 1998.

SBN: Formerly standard editions of Hume's works edited by L.A. Selby-Bigge, revised by P.H. Nidditch: *A Treatise of Human Nature*. Oxford: Clarendon Press, 1978; *Enquiry Concerning the Principles of Morals*. Oxford: Clarendon Press, 1975.

Treatise: *A Treatise of Human Nature*. Edited by D.F. Norton & M.J. Norton. Oxford: Oxford University Press, 2000.

6

THE CENTRALITY OF PUBLIC REASON IN HEGEL'S MORAL PHILOSOPHY

Kenneth R. Westphal[1]

FOR BARBARA HERMAN, PHILOSOPHE KANTIENNE

1 Introduction

Liberty, Republicanism, and Public Reason

Recently "public reason" has become an express topic in political philosophy, which may indicate how urgently we need to re-examine and renew our appreciation of reasoning in public, by the public, and for the entire *res publica*. Democracy can avoid tyranny of the majority—or of the sly or zealous minority—only by ardent republican inclusion of all eligible citizens, where eligibility extends to *all* competent adults, regardless of color, creed, gender (Gouge 1791; Sojourner Truth 1851), rank, social station, or wealth. "Deliberative" theories of democracy are important, though belated indicators that republicanism and civic virtues are fundamental to political legitimacy and to any tolerably healthy polity. Democratic republicanism is demanding both in theory and in practice. Understanding, accepting, and addressing those demands within any *res publica* require a broadly shared, well-founded conviction that we citizens *are* all involved collectively in self-governance. This conviction requires reasoning publicly and cogently about how citizens can reason publicly with one another, especially when addressing issues concerning (directly or indirectly) the character and content of a proper, decent, good, or legally permissible life, policy, or action. This conviction requires well-grounded, pervasive constitutional faith, as Levinson (1988) titled it. Public reason and public reasoning have a long, if checkered, history—as checkered as the history of political liberty. For example, public reason was exercised and promoted, and public reasoning was profoundly refashioned, by Lincoln's justly famous 1863 address at Gettysburg, in ways illuminated especially by Wills (1992) and Fletcher (2001). Public reason was well known, if not by that name, to Renaissance and to "Modern" (17–19th C. CE) European authors from the classics of Roman oratory and the ancient republican tradition. Such knowledge was not confined to Europe; it was forefront in the minds of those remarkable delegates to the 1787 constitutional convention in Philadelphia (McDonald 1985). And if the US Constitution they forged was a racist compromise, damned in its infamous 3/5 clause (Article 1: §2, ¶3), many delegates knew that and proposed and promoted various measures to end human bondage in what had proclaimed itself to be the land of liberty.[2]

Yet the phenomenon and cardinal importance of public reason is much older still: it is central, for example, to Thucydides's *History of the Peloponnesian War*, to Pericles' funeral oration reported therein (II:35–46), and to Sophocles' *Antigone*, not only within the play's content (e.g. the chorus credits both Creon and Haemon with speaking well, and recommends they learn from each other; v. 724–5; cf. Nussbaum 1986, 51–70), but also in Sophocles' use of the theater, as had already become custom, to comment upon contemporary social and political affairs (Athens's ostracism of Themistocles). Public reason and public reasoning were vitally important to Athenian democracy (Woodruff 2005); Aristotle accordingly advocated public regulations for adequate education (Curren 2000).

Such observations may be unexpected when examining the centrality of public reason in Hegel's moral philosophy, but public reason belongs to the history of reason and to the historical development of our discovery, understanding, use, and institutionalization of cogent methods, standards, and practices of rational justification: *the* central theme of Hegel's philosophy. These observations underscore that moral philosophy concerns how we live and how we ought to live, as individuals *and* together as members of our polities. In view of our history and practices, we must be prepared, willing, and able to discuss—frankly, cogently, publicly, and constructively—inconvenient or discomfiting truths and redress them properly. Too often and too easily "politesse" is used by theorists, public figures, and "the public" to evade responsibility (cf. Davidson 2004). Hegel understood that history is a slaughter house (*GW* 18:157), which obligates us to improve the justice of our lives and our polities so that those of our predecessors who have sacrificed, and those who have been sacrificed, for the sake of our liberty, freedom, and justice need not have so suffered in vain.

Philosophy, Taxonomy, and Obfuscation

Much moral philosophy and much public reasoning presume a series of dichotomies, including for example: moral realism *versus* moral anti-realism, moral realism *versus* moral conventionalism, individualism *versus* collectivism, consequentialism *versus* deontology, ethics *versus* justice, moral rationalism *versus* moral empiricism, foundationalist *versus* coherentist models of justification, reason *versus* tradition, and philosophy *versus* history of philosophy. Also prevalent is the individualist and internalist presumption that justifying any normative principle requires justifying it *to* some particular agent *on the basis of* his or her commitments (of whatever sort). This presumption is symptomatic of the default empiricism of most contemporary moral philosophy (see below, §2.1). The relations between justifying reasons and motivation are important, but they are not to be settled by philosophical fiat: they are a decisive moral result of proper child rearing, education, and conscientious judgment (Green 1999; Herman 2007, 130–53; Westphal 2012). It is not incidental that Hegel's (1853, 1854) philosophical reflections upon education fill three stout volumes; over 1,300 pages! By striking contrast, most philosophers earn their livelihoods as educators, though only a tiny fraction (even of moral philosophers) consider seriously philosophy of education.

These dichotomies and presumptions simplify intellectual life, but neglect Einstein's (2000, 314) vital qualification to Ockham's razor: "Everything must be made as simple as possible—but not any simpler." Because conceptual analysis can only provide improved knowledge of classificatory content (intension), whereas solving any substantive philosophical perplexity requires conceptual explication, *within* actual contexts of significant use, responsible philosophy must be both systematic and historical, because (as Sellars, too, realized) the relevant issues are so easily obscured or distorted by incautious formulation; even if we reformulate our issues in the formal mode of speech, we must carefully consider how the many and the wise have discussed and formulated these issues, in order better to understand and assess our own and others' formulations presently, and in the future. This, Hegel knew, is central to the pragmatic, social, and historical character of reconsidering, refining, improving and, so far as we now (at any historical juncture) can: *justifying* rationally our locutions, principles, analyses, and judgments about whatever substantive issue we address (Westphal 2010–2011).

Since the Enlightenment it has been common, also amongst philosophers, to contradistinguish reason to tradition, supposing that reason must be independent of tradition, if it is to assess traditions (Will 1988, 1997). Hegel's pragmatic realism and his development of Natural Law Constructivism (see §3) show that reason and tradition are fundamentally interdependent, and have been ever since societies began to grapple, implicitly or explicitly, with reconciling the unwritten standards of justice with human, institutional justice and law—a theme Hegel recognized as central to *Antigone*. Hegel shows that, and how, strictly objective basic moral standards can be identified and justified regarding any human society, while remaining strictly *neutral* regarding moral (ir)realism. He further shows how those standards may be variously instituted, observed, or also violated within specific historical societies. That is a singularly important achievement, within which the fundamentally public character of reason and reasoning are central. Hegel's Natural Law Constructivism builds upon its rudiments in Hume's theory of justice and its further developments by Rousseau and Kant. The very possibility of such a Natural Law Constructivism has been unjustly neglected by the simplifying presumptions and dichotomies just mentioned.

Plan of Discussion

This examination of public reason within Hegel's moral philosophy is underwritten by an interpretation of his *Philosophical Outlines of Justice*—to render idiomatically Hegel's title: *Grundlinien der Philosophie des Rechts*—detailed previously, which cannot be summarized here.[3] Here I highlight how Hegel's solution to the Pyrrhonian Dilemma of the Criterion further develops Kant's Critical insight into the fundamentally public character of justificatory reasoning (§2). Hegel used those insights to further develop a distinctive, powerful method for identifying and justifying basic moral norms, which I call 'Natural Law Constructivism' (§3). Public reason performs important roles within Hegel's account of civil society, highlighting how Hegel shares with Scots political economy the dual concerns of permitting and facilitating individual decision and innovation to develop social (including economic) practices, whilst monitoring and as needed redressing those unintended consequences of social practices (including markets) which jeopardize the citizenship and liberty of those least well off within society (§4). Hegel proposes to institutionalize public reason and public reasoning within the very public functions and functioning of government (§5). I conclude with some observations on inequality, justice, rational justification, and public reason (§6).

2 Justice, Unwritten Law, and the Pyrrhonian Dilemma of the Criterion

Justice and Justification

Sophocles' *Antigone* contains one of the very earliest surviving records of appeal to "unwritten law" (*agraphos nomos*) as a standard of justice by which to assess the justice of human legislation (v. 450–60; Ostwald 1973). That desideratum is vital, Hegel noted, yet the contest between the two lead characters, Antigone and Creon, also reveals a fatal social and rational failing: both characters are dogmatists; neither can nor do *justify* their respective claims by appeal to any (remotely) cogent reasons which contribute to demonstrating that either's claim about justice is indeed just.

The demand and the rational requirement to justify standards of justice quickly raise the most profound difficulty for reasoning cogently about justice, justification, and criteria for either justice or justification: the

Pyrrhonian Dilemma of the Criterion. Sextus Empiricus states this Dilemma thus:

> [I]n order to decide the dispute which has arisen about the criterion [of truth], we must possess an accepted criterion by which we shall be able to judge the dispute; and in order to possess an accepted criterion, the dispute about the criterion must first be decided. And when the argument thus reduces itself to a form of circular reasoning the discovery of the criterion becomes impracticable, since we do not allow [those who make knowledge claims] to adopt a criterion by assumption, while if they offer to judge the criterion by a criterion we force them to a regress *ad infinitum*. And furthermore, since demonstration requires a demonstrated criterion, while the criterion requires an approved demonstration, they are forced into circular reasoning.
> (Sextus Empiricus, *PH* 2:20; cf. 1:116–7; Bury, tr.)

Stated regarding criteria of truth, this Dilemma holds equally for criteria of justification. It cannot be solved by foundationalist or coherence theories of justification, and it is far more challenging than the various "Problems" regarding criteria often mistaken today for the Pyrrhonian original (Westphal 1998, 2013a). The Pyrrhonian Dilemma raises the issue of how (and how well) to justify any first-order claim, how (and how well) to justify one's criteria of justification for those first-order claims, *and* how (and how well) to justify one's meta-theory of justification for one's criteria of justification for those first-order claims. This Dilemma can be neither solved nor avoided by the many varieties of constructivism now popular with moral philosophers, because these all appeal to some sort of subjective factors, for example, validity claims, desires, passions, intuitions, or affective responses. Any theoretical construction based upon such elements can only justify principles for and to whomever shares sufficiently in those (allegedly basic) elements; to whomever denies, disowns, or genuinely lacks those elements, that construction can justify nothing.[4]

Hegel restates the Pyrrhonian Dilemma of the Criterion in the middle of the Introduction to his *Phenomenology of Spirit* (1807; *GW* 9:58.12–22/¶81), and shows that it can be solved by a sophisticated account of the possibility of constructive self-criticism (Westphal 1998). Because we are very finite semi-rational creatures, actually exercising constructive self-criticism, and successfully discriminating more from less effective self-critical assessment, requires that we engage cogently and critically with others' critical assessments of our own reasons, reasoning, and judgments (Westphal 2013b). Hegel's analysis of rational, justificatory judgment and our fallible rational competence shows that we can each *be* maximally rational and actually *justify* our best judgment rationally, only insofar as we recognize our mutual interdependence for the critical assessment of our own best judgments and their grounds. Our *being* rational, so far as we are able, requires us to be public reasoners: reasoners who justify their most considered judgments on principles, grounds, and evidence which can be communicated to, understood by, assessed, and adopted by all concerned (i.e. all affected) parties. This finding raises challenging questions about how and how accurately to distinguish between critical assessment and dogmatism, defective judgment, insufficient competence, or outright deception—Wright's (1992) issues of "cognitive command." No *theory* or *method* of justification can dissolve such problems; they belong to the human condition. Identifying whether or when defective reasoning occurs, and properly assessing it and its redress, itself requires exercising critical self-assessment, including careful consideration of others' critical assessments of the circumstances in question, and of one's assessment of them.

Justification and Public Reason

In these regards, Hegel's analysis of rational justification further develops Kant's Critical account of the social dimensions of rational judgment, which Onora O'Neill (1992, 2004, 2015) has rightly emphasized in connection with public reason, including the modality involved in Kant's universalization tests, which is fundamental not only to Kant's moral philosophy, but throughout his Critical methodology. At the end of "What Does It Mean to Orient Oneself in Thinking?" (1786), Kant responds to skeptical attacks upon reason, which prefigure much of today's post-modern, neo-pragmatist, skeptical or sometimes cynical cant. Concerned about imposition of state censorship (censorship was a problem, e.g. for Humboldt's liberalism in 1792[5]), Kant observes:

> Of course it is said that the freedom to *speak* or to *write* could be taken from us by a superior power, though the freedom to *think* cannot. Yet how much and how correctly would we *think* if we did not think as it were in community with others to whom we *communicate* our thoughts, and who communicate theirs with us! Thus one can very well say that this external power which wrenches away people's freedom publicly to *communicate* their thoughts also takes from them the freedom to *think*.
> (*GS* 8:144; Wood, tr.)

The close interdependence of thinking and public communication Kant highlights may not be self-evident, but consider that whatever cognitive capacities are innate, we each develop and learn to use only through education—both formal and informal—by others who provide information, skills, methods, practice, and critical assessment (Green 1999; Herman 2007, 130–53; Westphal 2012). To "communication" belong all publications and social sources of information, including one's education, without which one cannot at all become a competent thinker or agent. Kant further stresses that thinking cogently (*mit welcher Richtigkeit*; "how accurately") requires more than just thinking: for us fallible, limited human cognizers, distinguishing between genuinely cogent and merely apparently cogent thinking is vital, and requires communicating with others. Communicating with others is required to assess whether our thoughts, as we happen to have formulated and integrated them into judgments which we affirm or deny, are formulated and integrated by us as they *ought* to form a proper, accurate, rationally justifiable judgment (*KdrV* A261-3/B317-9).

Whereas Kant's modal universalizability stresses the positive requirement to judge and to act only on the basis of sufficient justifying grounds which *can* be addressed to and adopted by all others (consistent with one's own judgment and action on that, and on any such relevant occasion), Hegel highlights the complementary requirement that we must each listen to and seriously consider the grounds, justifications, and conclusions others provide us. In "The Animal Kingdom of the Spirit and Humbug, or that which most matters" (*Das geistige Tierreich und der Betrug, oder die Sache selbst*; *GW* 9:216–28/¶¶397–417), Hegel draws the devastating *reductio ad absurdum* within the intellectual realm (specifically the literary realm of self-styled romantic geniuses), parallel to Hobbes' state of nature.

Hobbes' Fundamental Social Coordination Problems

The most important problems Hobbes posed do not concern motivation (greed or malice); they concern simple natural *ignorance* of what belongs to whom within the non-governmental state of nature. That simple ignorance suffices—in conditions of relative population density, Rousseau adds—to generate total, fatal mutual interference. Any possible solution to this problem must be social and public. Indeed, Hume added, it requires publicly acknowledged principles and titles to acquire, possess, use, and exchange things and promised actions, together with sufficient social recourse to make known these principles and titles, to monitor compliance with them, and to make proper and no more than sufficient redress of any infractions (Westphal 2016a, esp. §§4–11, 44).

Hegel's Complement to Kant's Principle of Universal Communication

Hegel's "spiritual" parallel to Hobbes's state of nature skewers Romantic—though likewise cynical or egoistic—self-infatuation which leads individuals to declare that whatever most concerns him- or herself is *the* most important concern for any- and everyone, while consequently neglecting their comparable declarations. No communication, no significant expression can *possibly* be made under such presumptions. Accuracy and cogency are the first casualties of this verbal melé, just as Kant anticipated. Public reason requires much more than merely divulging one's thinking, including one's justifying reasons, publicly. Public reason requires justifying one's assessment on grounds, evidence, and principles which *all* others can understand, assess, adopt, and use—consistently with one's own judgment and action on that (and any such relevant) occasion. This does not require that others in fact do so; it requires that they can do so, and that they pay attention to others' reasons and reasoning. That is the operative modality in Kant's and in Hegel's analysis of this social *conditio sine qua non* of rational justification (in non-formal, substantive domains). This *conditio sine qua non* does not (typically) suffice for rational justification, but typically it suffices to rule out inaccurate, poorly reasoned, self-serving, immoral, or illicit judgments or rationales. That is quite a lot from a universalizability test!

3 Justice, the Euthyphro Question, and Natural Law Constructivism

Edict, Justification, and Fallibilism

Though Antigone and Creon are both dogmatists, in *Antigone* Sophocles develops a devastating internal critique of Creon's ruling principles. Creon's name means 'ruler'; ultimately he retrenches his key ruling principle to consist in edict which (putatively) declares what justice is, thus proclaiming dogmatically to *constitute* justice itself by mere edict. That is the death of justice in any responsive, inclusive, considerate, indeed any tenable sense. This is symbolized dramatically by his wife the queen, Eurydice, whose name means 'broad justice,' who condemns Creon as a multiple murderer and thereupon commits suicide.

Creon reaches his final retrenchment (edict = justice) as the third of three stages. Sophocles' *Antigone* is a direct literary precedent for Hegel's phenomenological dialectic in the *Phenomenology of Spirit*, which uses strictly internal critique of the key principles of views Hegel rejects (and replaces), taken in connection with their intended domains (Westphal 2003, §§3–8). Hegel realized (by 1802) that Kant's Transcendental Idealism is subject to a devastating, strictly internal critique (Westphal 2009b). By re-examining the Pyrrhonian Dilemma of the Criterion, *Antigone*, and Kant's Critical methodology and transcendental principles of cognitive judgment (Westphal 2015d), Hegel developed a sophisticated, robustly pragmatic realism (Westphal 2009a, 2015a, 2015b). Like Kant,

Hegel developed sophisticated fallibilist accounts of rational justification: within his philosophical method and principles, within his substantive philosophical views, and thus within his accounts of our empirical and moral knowledge. Fallibilist accounts of rational justification are fundamentally historical and social, yet such accounts *can*, Hegel recognized, justify realism about the objects of empirical knowledge and strict objectivity about basic moral norms—without taking any stand on issues of moral (ir)realism or motivation.

Infallibilist standards of justification pertain only to strictly formal domains; in all non-formal, substantive domains, rational justification is in principle fallibilist (Westphal 2013b, 2016b). According to any tenable fallibilism, a judgment, claim, or statement is justified insofar and so long as (1) it is more adequate to its tasks than any alternative statement, (2) it is adequate to its designated range of phenomena, and (3) it remains adequate to its domain(s) as its use is renewed upon new, relevant occasions, which may include changed circumstances, information, or context. These results Hegel demonstrates in the *Phenomenology of Spirit* (Westphal 2009a, 2013b); he develops his systematic philosophy in detailed critical consideration of relevant empirical phenomena in history and in the natural and social sciences (political economy).

The Euthyphro Question and Hume's Juridical Insight

Socrates queried Euthyphro whether the pious is pious because the gods love it, or whether the gods love it because it is (unto itself) the pious (Plato, *Euthyphro* 10de). This question permutes regarding all variety of putative normative standards, and suggests the common divide between conventionalism and realism (of whatever forms). Responding to Hobbes' fundamental social coordination problems, Hume (T 3.2.1.19) was the first to recognize that the most basic laws of justice can be literally artificial, our artifacts, and yet *not* be arbitrary, because certain basic principles and practices constituting and regulating acquisition, possession, use, and exchange of goods and promises, together with their authoritative publication, monitoring, and enforcement, are utterly non-optional for us very finite, mutually interdependent beings (above, §2.3).

One key to developing a sound moral constructivism which can identify and justify strictly objective, basic, universal moral principles is to consider basic physiological *facts* about our very finite, mutually interdependent form of semi-rational agency. These are not moral facts, yet they are morally relevant facts because we can do so much to exploit, respect, or minister to them. The second key is the universality requirement of Kant's Critical methodology (above, §§2.2, 2.4). The third key is Rousseau's *conditio sine qua non* for the legitimacy of any social arrangements: To respect in theory and in practice the civil and moral independence of *each* and hence *every* member of society (Westphal 2013c). These three keys form the methodological core of 'Natural Law Constructivism' (Westphal 2016a, 2017). The independence requirement entails that social and political institutions are to be so arranged that no one has the kind or extent of power or wealth to command unilaterally the choice and action of anyone else. Put positively, each member of society deserves sufficient economic, political, and financial security to be independent of the unilateral demands of other individuals. (None are exempted from the demands of justice, nor of legitimate public legislation.)

Hegel's analysis of the character and scope of rational justification and its social and historical dimensions diverges significantly from other approaches to justification within moral philosophy, including other accounts of public reason. Let their advocates solve the Pyrrhonian Dilemma of the Criterion before objecting to Hegel's analysis: consensus as such is neither the goal nor the ground of legitimate public policy; *credible* consensus is, but that is much more demanding. Contemporary forms of moral constructivism strongly tend to conventionalism; these have significantly impoverished the public space of reasons (Westphal 2015c). Hegel's account accommodates sincere, devout religious faith (Houlgate 2005, 242–75), including, for example, conscientious objection to military service (*Rph* §270R, n.2), yet underscores that state authority cannot bow to sectarian demands. Living religious faith is no social problem; dogmatism, intolerance, and zealotry are.

4 Justice, Civil Society, and Public Reason

Justice in the Abstract: Basic Individual Rights and Duties

Omitting details, Hegel's analysis and justification of rights to acquire, possess, use, and exchange goods or services (whether directly or by promise or contract), follows and augments Hume's and Kant's. All three recognize that juridical principles and their institutionalization as law are fundamental *enabling conditions* for a vast range of otherwise impossible, though vitally necessary individual actions and joint activities. Some rightful possession and use of goods is necessary to individual human life, both for nutrition and maintenance, *and* to exercise and develop one's free rational agency (*Rph* §45). Hence everyone is entitled to own some property (*Rph* §49), an implication Hegel stressed in lecture[6]—and a brilliant inversion of the traditional property requirement for suffrage. Children are entitled to a proper upbringing within the family and to education sufficient to prepare them for effective and potentially rewarding adult life, including public life (*Rph* §§158–80). The principles and practices of acquisition, possession, rightful use, exchange, and contract, and the principles of their authoritative juridical review and enforcement,

Hegel develops in "Justice in the Abstract" (*Das abstrakte Recht*; *Rph* §§41–103) as necessary enabling conditions for free individual actions, centrally (in this section) those actions required to produce, acquire, exchange, use, and when need be recover or compensate the necessities of life (or their theft). As principles governing free, legitimate individual *actions*, these must be understood and followed by individual agents, who of course would be much more able and willing to behave justly if they understand the justice of these principles, *and* if they understand that others share this understanding. Hence moral reflection is necessary to any possible system of just principles and actions, and to free, autonomous rational action (cf. §4.2).

Realizing Freedom

In this regard and throughout his *Philosophical Outlines of Justice*, Hegel adopts a key term and issue from Kant and Tetens (1775, 48, cf. 60–1, 80–1), who coined this usage: To "realize" (*realisieren*) a concept is to show that some actual instances of it can be located and identified by us. This task is required to show that we can accurately and justifiedly use any *a priori* concepts we may possess. Hegel uses this term in this sense throughout his corpus (Westphal 2015a, 2015b, 2016c); it is central to his pragmatic realism.[7] In moral philosophy the key concept to be "realized" is the concept "freedom" (cf. *Rph* §§141, 127–8). Realizing the concept of freedom requires agents to act freely by bringing something about. We human beings can only execute actions by transfiguring something in our surroundings (*Rph* §§51Z, 106); even if we only move ourselves corporeally, our comportment requires space, time, air, nutrition, and non-interference with or by others. To realize one's freedom requires successful action; successful action requires abiding by the requirements of justice—otherwise one is subject to just restriction, restitution, or punishment. To realize one's freedom requires acting autonomously; this requires deciding how to act, deciding on what principle(s) to act, and electing to fulfill one's obligations *because* they are one's obligations.[8] Otherwise one is subject either to unreflective, naturally or perhaps sociologically given impulses, or to the legitimate restrictions of, or redress by, others. These requirements are, obviously, extremely abstract. Though the commandment, "above all, do no harm," is fundamental, these strictures of justice provide no positive guidance.

Moral Theory, a Priori *Principles, and Practical Anthropology*

An important difference between Hegel's and Kant's moral theories is this: the proper scope of Kant's Critical *Metaphysics of Morals* is the fundamental *a priori* principles of justice and virtue. Throughout his moral philosophy Kant recognized that these principles, by themselves, specify no specific moral injunctions; specifying any of our duties and rights *also* requires "practical anthropology," which specifies basic features of our finite form of rational agency and very general conditions of our action on Earth. Kant regarded this practical anthropology as only a "proper appendix" to his *Metaphysics of Morals* (*TL* §45, *GS* 6:469.8–12), not an integral part of it, despite the fact that his *Metaphysics of Morals* "must often consider" the specific nature of human beings (*MdS*, Einl. §II; *GS* 6:216–7) and "must" be applied to "specific cases" (*TL* §45, *GS* 6:464). Kant's contorted taxonomy Hegel rejects. Hegel's infamous charge of "empty formalism" is directed against self-proclaimed Kantians, though expressly *not* against Kant.[9] The threat of "empty formalism" restates Kant's own view of his *a priori* principles of morals, in abstraction from practical anthropology. Directly in this connection, after extolling Kant's analysis of freedom as autonomy of the will, which is the sole and proper basis of moral law (*Rph* §§133, 135R, cf. §4), Hegel assumes the task to *avoid* the threat of "empty formalism" and to *preserve* and further develop Kant's moral principles by developing his very detailed practical anthropology (as it were), titled "*Sittlichkeit*" or "ethical life" (Westphal 2009c).

Customs, Customizing Human Nature, and Freedom of Action

In this connection Hegel exploits an important feature of customs and the development of customary social practices, including economic practices (by which "custom" was transmuted into "customer"): customs are not merely habitual, but are intelligent activities; when aggregated across groups they often have important unintended consequences for such social phenomena as the distribution and division of labor, land use, law, public regulations, and the common wealth—whether weal or woe—of the commonwealth (*res publica*). Not only are these activities often intelligent, they also typically serve to specify and to realize individual freedom, including individual innovations, which may become adopted by others. The development and the individual adoption of social customs literally *customize* whatever needs, ends, or motives are due to our natural human psychophysiology. Social custom thus marks, Hegel stresses, a decisive advance in human freedom, both collectively and individually. "Realizing" freedom in individual action should be understood both in Tetens' and in our commonsense senses. Whenever we consider how to act, what to do, we avail ourselves of conceptual and material resources, together with a variety of permissions, entitlements, and prohibitions. All of these are socially constituted, as is our knowledge and understanding of these provisions and how properly to use them.

Hegel's Moderate Collectivism

Unlike social determinists, holists, and atomistic individualists, Hegel recognized that individuals and the group(s) to which they belong are mutually *inter*dependent for their existence and characteristics. Social practices exist only in and through individuals who participate in, perpetuate, or *modify* them as occasion, need, and inventiveness allow and require (Hegel 1994; Westphal 2003, §§32–7; 2014). Hegel's social ontology may be called 'moderate collectivism.'

Custom, Justice, and Natural Law Constructivism

The centrality of social practices, including the economy, to Hegel's moral philosophy may suggest that he espouses historicist relativism, communitarianism, conventionalism, or reform conservatism.[10] Instead, Hegel's moral philosophy combines these concerns about free individual action, social custom, and political economy with the principles of Natural Law Constructivism (Westphal 2007). This is why Hegel's book is a normative theory of justice, a philosophy of moral law: both ethics and jurisprudence, which integrates both natural law and political science, as advertised in his sub-title, *oder Naturrecht und Staatswissenschaft im Grundrisse*. In Hegel's uniquely powerful combination of these resources, public reason is central, indeed precisely because its exercise is fundamental yet decentralized. The core principles of right action, moral freedom, and political liberty identified and justified by Natural Law Constructivism are human necessities and trans-social standards of justice, yet they can be satisfied, specified, and institutionalized in a wide range of social practices, suited to the geographical, historical, technological, and economic conditions of a society.

5 Justice, Republican Government, and Public Reason

Corporative Individualism, Markets, and Republican Liberty

Hegel's moderate collectivism (above, §4.5) and his appeal to Scots political economy undergird his advocacy of his version of Montesquieu's and de Tocqueville's "corporative individualism" (George 1922)—a view shared by T.H. Green (1883) and by Dewey (1922, 1930). Information transmitted *via* markets is important, but only concerns select features of economic production, consumption, and distribution. Production, consumption, and distribution also produce non-market benefits and burdens, including, for example, employment patterns; household weal or woe for employees, employers and managers at all levels; as also waste, habitat destruction, pollution, and human dislocation as labor distributions and production technologies change. Liberal forms of moderate collectivism recognize the vital roles of proper government, law, and non-governmental agencies within civil society to monitor, facilitate, protect, publicize, ameliorate, or correct good or ill effects of economic activities, as classical Scots political economists recognized (Ferguson 1787; Sidgwick 1883, 1903; Devas 1901; J.N. Keynes 1904).

Hegel's Republicanism in Practice

These views were institutionalized by Johan Vilhelm Snellman (1806–1881), an Hegelian who contributed centrally to founding and developing modern Finland, whose liberal, moderately collective republicanism is fundamental to Finnish politics, society, and culture, and typifies the political and social policies and practices of Nordic and Scandinavian republics.[11] Snellman's statue sits before the entrance to the National Bank of Finland; his portrait graced the 100 Markkaa banknote until Finland adopted the Euro in 1999. The Scandinavian and Nordic countries are splendid examples that justice—including far higher levels of social justice—can be achieved, consistent with an excellent standard of living and ample rewards for enterprising, responsible entrepreneurs. They are also splendid empirical examples of Schultz's (2001) theoretical demonstration that economic efficiency can only be achieved within moral constraints—a welcome corroboration of the classical understanding of political economy as a moral science, not merely a human science, but a *normative* discipline. I mention these points to suggest what cannot be detailed here about Hegel's very specific, strongly normative institutional analysis of civil society and government.[12]

Law, Legitimacy, and Freedom

Legitimate statute law, Hegel argues, codifies and protects those social practices, especially economic practices, required to facilitate and protect individual security, freedom of action, and prospects of earning one's livelihood (*Rph* §§209–12, 218, 219; cf. §§187R, 249). Hegel's Administration of Justice (*Rechtspflege*) is charged with monitoring the effectiveness of statute law and proposing revised legislation as needed to better serve and protect individual freedom and prospects of welfare through successful, legitimate individual actions (*Rph* §§298, 299R). Hegel expressly follows Montesquieu's view that positive laws are justified by these functional, systematic interconnections within present social circumstances (*Rph* §§3R, 212), adding that promulgating codified law contributes to informing people about the structure of their social context of action, so that they may deliberate, decide, and act accordingly (*Rph* §§132R,

209, 211R, 215; cf. 228R). Hence law must be codified and publicized in the national language (*Rph* §216) and judicial proceedings must be public (*Rph* §§224, 228R). All of these are institutional contributions to public reason: to publicly acknowledged reasoning about how and how well our legal code and institutions serve justice, individual liberty, and prosperity.

Political Economy, Legislation, and Political Representation

Because legislation is so fundamental to politics and because the economy is so fundamental to legislation, Hegel advocates an unusual form of political representation, not by geographical district, but by corporate representation. The 'corporations' Hegel advocates are for each sector of the economy and each segment of civil society (Heiman 1971). Towns and churches are incorporated. Commercial corporations include both labor and management in all firms engaged in one branch of the economy. Corporate representatives enter the lower chamber of Hegel's Estates Assembly. Hegel expects corporate representatives to be chosen in view of their demonstrated expertise and competence within their respective corporations, and to serve (*inter alia*) as conduits of information, both from their corporate membership to the rest of society *via* public debate in the Assembly, and conversely from the rest of society *via* assembly debate back to their corporate members. In this way the various activities of government, including a rich array of social services provided by Hegel's Public Authority (*Polizei*), all performed on behalf of the public, are also performed *under their purview* so that they may know and monitor how and how well these essential juridical and social provisions for their own liberty, freedom, security, and prosperity are executed, and can advise on needed modifications. In this crucial regard, Hegel's system of representation is designed to facilitate, secure, and indeed maximize individual rational autonomy, freedom of action, prospects for one's own sufficient prosperity, *and* political liberty. Within modern commercial societies, individual autonomy requires public reason in all of these regards.

Civil Independence, Moral Freedom, and Republican Liberty

The *conditio sine qua non* of political legitimacy and social justice according to Hegel, following Rousseau and Kant, is the requirement of moral, civil, and financial independence (*Rph* §§124R, 230, 241–2, 244–5). Because modern nation states with their commercial economies occupy contiguous bounded territories, and have undermined and replaced subsistence production by families (*Rph* §§181, 217, 241–2), nation states are obligated to secure and facilitate for each and every citizen the opportunity to obtain sufficient livelihood *and* social recognition as a citizen in good standing (*Rph* §§241, 244, cf. §§238Z, 244Z). Though Hegel recognized women could acquire education (*Rph* §166Z), he did not transcend traditional patriarchy. He did, however, insist that citizenship is a human right, regardless of religion, nationality, or ethnicity (*Rph* §209R); in this Hegel was ahead of his time. Hegel's principles and institutional provisions provide very well for rectifying his chauvinist misjudgment (cf. Hoy 2009). As for moral and civil independence, and good standing of each citizen, Hegel was crystal clear: poverty is an injustice to one class (*Klasse*) committed by another (*Rph* §§243-5), and must be rectified. He addressed but did not solve this problem, though his reference to Scotland's blue shirts (*Rph* §245R) is significant (Waszek 1984). Hegel's principles and institutions lend themselves very well to J.M. Keynes' policy of government expansion of public works during economic contraction (and contraction of public works during economic expansion).

Poverty and the Res Publica

Hegel's discussion of poverty is significant to public reason in this regard. Hegel stresses that poverty is not only an economic, but also a social status. Those least well off economically within society must nevertheless be *in society*, not merely within its territory, as recognized, contributing members of society—that is, as citizens in good standing. Hegel's minimum for good standing is expressly relative within each society (*Rph* §244), not to some bare subsistence minimum. Whether an economy happens to achieve Pareto-optimality does not settle whether those least well off in that economy are, or are not, contributing members of society in good standing, and are recognized as such members, insofar as they are morally, civilly, and financially independent to the extent that in practice as well as in theory they are at liberty to agree to cooperate with others, or not, as they choose. That, as a matter of statistical fact, some individuals would abuse such liberty is no ground for denying to anyone these basic opportunities to attain and to retain recognized good standing as a citizen. Once the territory is closed and access to self-subsistence denied, societies owe to *all* members the rights, opportunities and privileges, as well as the duties and responsibilities, of citizenship.

Understanding this, and acting on this understanding both institutionally and individually, is a basic requirement of justice, which requires public reason as well as public reasoning to institute effectively and properly. It is part of what constitutes any legitimate constitutional faith within any modern commercial *res publica*: that every adult be honored equally as a citizen.

6 Conclusions

Inequality and the Republican Commonwealth

Conservatives may protest that such measures for effective republican citizenship place excessive burdens upon the earnings of those who are well off in society. In most prosperous societies on Earth, those high earnings are in part reaped from labor markets that violate Hegel's basic provisions of social justice. To that extent and in that regard, those earnings are themselves unjust and so unjustifiable. Only within a society and economy in which those materially least well off are in fact at liberty not to work under unfavorable terms and conditions can labor markets approximate minimum standards of justice. This is one of many points at which issues about public reason and various group interests and ideology cross vexatiously. That, however, is no excuse for neglecting issues about what principles and which institutions and practices can be justified rationally, which requires providing *all* others with sufficient principles and justifying reasons, such that they *can* understand, assess, adopt, and use them, in theory and in practice, consistently with one's own judgment and action on that, and on any such relevant occasion. Others may not do so; that is a further consideration. Others who refuse so to do are yet another matter: it is nonetheless incumbent upon them to justify such refusal to all others for sufficient justifying reasons. Taxes sufficient to maintain the principles and institutions of justice are (at a minimum) rents on earnings, which are, themselves, only made within a society and its economy (cf. Murphy and Nagel 2002).

Justice, Rational Justification, and Public Reason

Hegel thought through the problems, character, and scope of rational justification in non-formal domains—including the entirety of both empirical knowledge and morals—far more insightfully than anyone. In so doing he solved the Pyrrhonian Dilemma of the Criterion, and by solving it showed how public reason is fundamental to rational justification in all non-formal domains. Either we abide by the requirements of public reason and the dictates of justice, or we condemn ourselves to social strife and class war, whether domestically or internationally (or both). This is a stark choice, fundamental to our recognizing and acting effectively upon our individual and collective obligations, to improve the justice of our lives and our polities so that those of our predecessors who have sacrificed, and those who have been sacrificed, for the sake of our liberty, freedom, and justice need not have so suffered in vain. If conservatives wish to disprove or dispense with views they castigate as "socialist," let them work constructively, effectively, and publicly for social justice within our republics.

Through constructive self-criticism and mutual critical assessment we *can* improve our understanding of the most basic requirements of justice, what they require of us, and towards whom we are obligated by justice; indeed, only these forms of cogent self-criticism—individual and social—can resolve the Pyrrhonian Dilemma of the Criterion and avoid *petitio principii*, in theory and in practice. All this is central to our moral literacy: to improve our moral principles and practices, when need be, even through improvisation.[13] This, too, is centrally a matter of public reason, of reason as a public, social, and historical phenomenon and activity. Due to our finitude we human beings cannot descry within the unchartable domain of all logical possibilities exactly those necessities which (supposedly) are the necessary fundamentals of justice. Due to our finitude, we must and can only reason publicly about justice, its requirements, its observance, and about the rectification of injustices, so far as is humanly possible.

Our recognition of this obligation and our capacities to act on it effectively and constructively have for the past century been obscured by a quirk of Anglophone philosophical history which (ca. 1910) reconfigured the genus "moral philosophy" to make "ethics" (or even "meta-ethics") primary, to the widespread demotion or neglect of justice (Westphal 2016a, §41). Natural Law Constructivism shows that the traditional taxonomy of moral philosophy is correct. Moral philosophy is the genus with two proper, coordinate species: justice and ethics. Reasoning on the basis of a false taxonomy (or presuming any of the false dichotomies noted above, §1.2) is a failure of public reason. We must, we can, and we are morally obligated to do much better. Hegel's account of public reason can help us understand how.[14]

Notes

1 Professor, Department of Philosophy, Boğaziçi Üniversitesi (İstanbul).
2 Not for a moment do I pretend that anything—least of all: justice—permitted any liberty to the USA to expand its border at the expense of indigenous peoples; see Black Elk (1932), Matthiessen (1992), Williams (2005).
3 See Westphal (1993, 2007, 2009c, 2010, 2016a). The following reflections depart widely from the "Hegel mythology" (Stewart 1996), much of which results from willful misunderstanding or ideological oversimplifications (Westphal 2013d), and from disregard of Hegel's sophisticated methods for articulating and justifying his philosophical views—neglect which has led fans and foes alike to assimilate their misunderstandings of Hegel's alleged views to philosophical options (several of which are listed in §1.2). Hegel had criticized, rejected, and superceded by further developing Kant's Critical methodological innovations, whilst dispensing with Transcendental Idealism (and its ilk; Westphal 2009a, 2009b, 2015b, 2015c).
4 I detail these problems more fully in Westphal (2013c), §2, and thoroughly in Westphal (2015a).

5 Humboldt's *Limits of State Action* (1851/1969) was composed in 1792; the editor notes (*v–viii*) his problems with government censors.
6 *Rph* §49Z; *VRph* (1819–20), 18.106–7, 18.120–131; *VRph* (1824–25), 177.14–18.
7 Hegel's usage and its derivation from Tetens and Kant has been widely neglected, which leads to the presumption that Hegel's concepts and principles are supposed to "realize" themselves into determinate existence *and* sequence out of ... absolutely nothing. So silly Hegel was not.
8 The "self-legislation" fundamental to Kant's account of autonomy is our self-legislation of our own *obligation* to act as morality requires. We authorize our own moral obligation, we do not invent the basic rules of morality! Kant is quite clear about this in his texts. On the earlier distinction between a normative rule of action and the actual obligation to comply, to which Kant responds, see Haackonssen (2002).
9 Between Kant's publication of the *Groundwork* (1785) and his *Doctrine of Justice* (1797), a plethora of "Kantian" theories of justice appeared, none of which were remotely adequate, nor were they genuinely Kantian, as Bouterwek (1797) observed in his review of Kant (1797). Hegel's editors cite Fichte (*GW* 14.3: 1140–1) as speaking of "duty for duty's sake" without specifying what any such duty may be. They also cite Kant's texts in this connection, though they (too) neglect Kant's persistent, consistent insistence upon practical anthropology for identifying any of our human duties and rights. Hegel knew—and did—much better than that; his extensive notes on Kant's doctrine of justice were, very unfortunately, lost.
10 I borrow Epstein's (1966, 13) useful taxonomy of forms of conservatism.
11 Snellman was not, of course, the first republican in Northern Europe; see Velema (2007).
12 For concise discussion of Hegel's institutional analysis, see Westphal (1993, 2002, 2010); the first diagrams Hegel's social institutions.
13 Cf. Will (1988, 1997), 105–92; Singer (1998); Wallace (1998); Tiles (1998); Herman (2007), 276–99.
14 I gratefully acknowledge yet again that I would never have understood Hegel's issues and analyses without guidance from the last great pragmatic realist, Fred Will (1988, 1997). On Hegel's account of ampliative reasoning, see Stoval (forthcoming). None whose work is cited herein is responsible for the author's views. I am very grateful to the editors for their kind invitation to compose these Hegelian thoughts on this most fundamental issue. The present research was generously supported by the Boğaziçi Üniversitesi Research Fund (BAP; grant code: 9761).

References

Black Elk. 1932. *Black Elk Speaks: Being the Life Story of a Holy Man of the Ogalala Sioux*, as told to John G. Neihardt (Flaming Rainbow), illustrated by Standing Bear. New York: W. Morrow & Co.

Bouterwek, Friedrich. 1797, 1799. Reviews of I. Kant, *Metaphysical Foundations of Justice*, trans. with notes by K.R. Westphal. *Kant Studies Online* (2014): 210–31.

Curren, Randall. 2000. *Aristotle on the Necessity of Public Education*. Lanham, MD: Rowman & Littlefield.

Davidson, Jenny. 2004. *Hypocrisy and the Politics of Politeness: Manners and Moral from Locke to Austen*. Cambridge: Cambridge University Press.

Devas, Charles. 1901. *Political Economy*, 2nd rev. ed. London: Longmans, Green & Co.

Dewey, John. 1922. *Human Nature and Conduct: An Introduction to Social Psychology*. New York: Holt & Co.

———. 1930. *Individualism, Old and New*. New York: Minton, Balch & Co.

Einstein, Albert. 2000. *The Expanded Quotable Einstein*, edited by Alice Calaprice. Princeton, NJ: Princeton University Press.

Epstein, Klaus. 1966. *The Genesis of German Conservatism*. Princeton, NJ: Princeton University Press.

Ferguson, Adam. 1787. *An Essay on the History of Civil Society*, 5th ed. London: Cadell; Edinburgh: Creech & Bell; critical ed. by Fania Oz-Salzberger; Cambridge: Cambridge University Press, 1995.

Fletcher, George. 2001. *Our Secret Constitution: How Lincoln Redefined American Democracy*. New York: Oxford University Press.

George, William Henry. 1922. "Montesquieu and De Tocqueville and Corporative Individualism." *American Political Science Review* 16 (1): 10–21; doi:10.2307/1943884.

Gouge, Olympe de. 1791. "Déclaration des droits de la femme et de la citoyenne." Paris: (n.p.). Available online at http://www.philo5.com/Mes%20lectures/GougesOlympeDe-DeclarationDroitsFemme.htm (accessed October 4, 2015).

Green, Thomas F. 1999. *Voices: The Educational Formation of Conscience*. Notre Dame, IN: University of Notre Dame Press.

Green, Thomas Hill, 1883. *Prolegomena to Ethics*, edited by A.C. Bradley, fourth ed. Oxford, The Clarendon Press.

Haackonssen, Knud. 2002. "The Moral Conservatism of Natural Rights." In *Natural Law and Civil Sovereignty: Moral Right and State Authority in Early Modern Political Thought*, edited by Ian Hunter and David Saunders, 27–42. London: Palgrave.

Hegel, G.W.F. 1807. *Phänomenologie des Geistes*. Bamberg & Würzburg: Goephard; Wolfgang Bonsiepen and Reinhardt Heede, eds., in *GW* 9.

———. 1821. *Grundlinien der Philosophie des Rechts oder Naturrecht und Staatswissenschaft im Grundrisse*. Berlin: Nicolai; abbreviated '*Rph*,' cited by main sections (§) or by Hegel's published Remarks (§*n*R); *GW* 14.

———. 1853, 1854. *Hegel's Ansichten über Erziehung und Unterricht*, 3 vols. Edited by Gustav Thaulow. Kiel: Akademische Buchhandlung.

———. 1973. Philosophie des Rechts nach der Vorlesungsnachschrift K.G. v. Griesheims 1824/25. In *Vorlesungen über Rechtsphilosophie 1818–1831*, 6 vols. edited by Karl-Heinz Ilting, 4: 75–752. frommann-holzoog: Stuttgart-Bad Canstadt; cited as 'VRph (1824–25)' by page, line numbers.

———. 1983. *Philosophie des Rechts. Die Vorlesung von 1819/20 in einer Nachschrift*. Edited by Dieter Henrich. Frankfurt am Main: Suhrkamp; cited as '*VRph* (1819–20)' by page, line numbers.

———. 1986–2016. *Gesammelte Werke*, 31 vols., issued by the Deutsche Forschungsgemeinschaft, with the Hegel-Kommission der Rheinisch-Westfälischen Akademie der Wissenschaften and the Hegel-Archiv der Ruhr-Universität Bochum. Hamburg: Meiner; cited as '*GW*' by volume, page, line numbers. Individual works are indicated by their German initials. These references are used in all recent, reliable translations.

———. 1991. *Elements of the Philosophy of Right*, edited by Allen Wood, trans. By H.B. Nisbet. Cambridge: Cambridge University Press; abbreviated '*Rph*,' cited by main sections (§), by Hegel's published Remarks (§*n*R) or very occasionally by lecture notes (§*n*Z) ('Z' for, *Zusatz*'); *GW* 14.

———. 1994. "Community as the Basis of Free Individual Action." Translation and annotation of excerpts from Hegel's *Phenomenology of Spirit* by K.R. Westphal. In *Communitarianism*, edited by Markate Daly, 36–40. Belmont, CA: Wadsworth.

———. 2011. *Lectures on the Philosophy of World History* 1: Manuscripts of the Introductions and the Lectures of 1822–23. Edited and translated by Robert F. Brown and Peter C. Hodgson, with William G. Geuss; cited as *GW* 18: 121–207, 27.

———. forthcoming. *The Phenomenology of Spirit*, trans. by Terry Pinkard, Draft bi-lingual translation in PDF format; cited by paragraph (¶) numbers correctly provided by the translator corresponding to *GW* 9.

Heiman, G. 1971. "The Sources and Significance of Hegel's Corporate Doctrine." In *Hegel's Political Philosophy*, edited by Z.A. Pelczynski, 111–35. Cambridge: Cambridge University Press.

Herman, Barbara. 2007. *Moral Literacy*. Cambridge, MA: Harvard University Press.

Houlgate, Stephen. 2005. *Introduction to Hegel: Freedom, Truth and History*, 2nd ed. Oxford: Blackwell.

Hoy, Jocelyn B. 2009. "Hegel, *Antigone*, and Feminist Critique: The Spirit of Ancient Greece." In *The Blackwell Guide to Hegel's Phenomenology of Spirit*, edited by Kenneth R. Westphal, 172–89. Oxford: Wiley-Blackwell.

Humboldt, Wilhelm von. 1851. *Ideen zu einem Versuch, die Gränzen der Wirksamkiet des Staats zu Bestimmen*. Breslau: Trewendt.

———. 1969. *The Limits of State Action*, trans. by J.W. Burrow. London: Cambridge University Press.

Kant, Immanuel. 1786. "What Does it Mean to Orient Oneself in Thinking?" in *Religion and Rational Theology*, translated/edited by A. Wood and G. di Giovanni, 1–18. Cambridge: Cambridge University Press, 1996.

———. 1902. *Kants Gesammelte Schriften*, edited by the Könniglich Preussische, now Berlin-Brandenburgische Akademie der Wissenschaften. Berlin: Reimer, now deGruyter; cited by the initials of Kant's titles (or occasionally as '*GS*') and volume: page numbers.

———. 1992–2015. *The Cambridge Edition of the Works of Immanuel Kant in English Translation*, 18 vols. Edited by Paul Guyer and Allen Wood. Cambridge: Cambridge University Press; provides volume:page numbers of *GS*.

Keynes, John Neville. 1904. *The Scope and Method of Political Economy*, 3rd rev. ed. London and New York: Macmillan.

Levinson, Sanford. 1988. *Constitutional Faith*. Princeton, NJ: Princeton University Press.

McDonald, Forrest. 1985. *Novus Ordo Seclorum: The Intellectual Origins of the Constitution*. Kansas City: University Press of Kansas.

Matthiessen, Peter. 1992. *In the Spirit of Crazy Horse*. New York: Penguin.

Murphy, Liam, and Thomas Nagel. 2002. *The Myth of Ownership: Taxes and Justice*. Oxford: Oxford University Press.

Nussbaum, Martha. 1986. *The Fragility of Goodness.* Cambridge: Cambridge University Press.

O'Neill, Onora. 1992. "Vindicating Reason." In *The Cambridge Companion to Kant*, edited by Paul Guyer, 280–308. Cambridge: Cambridge University Press.

———. 2004. "Autonomy, Plurality and Public Reason." In *New Essays on the History of Autonomy*, edited by Natalie Brender and Larry Krasnoff, 181–94. Cambridge: Cambridge University Press.

———. 2015. "Autonomy and Public Reason in Kant." In *Reason, Value, and Respect: Kantian Themes from the Philosophy of Thomas E. Hill*, Jr., edited by Mark Timmons and Robert Johnson, 119–31. Oxford: Oxford University Press.

Ostwald, M. 1973. "Was There a Concept of *agraphos nomos* in Classical Greece?" In *Exegesis and Argument*, edited by E.N. Lee, et al., 70–104. *Phronesis*, Supp. Vol. I, Assen.

Schultz, Walter, 2001. *The Moral Conditions of Economic Efficiency.* Cambridge: Cambridge University Press.

Sextus Empiricus. 1933. *Outlines of Pyrrhonism*, trans. by R.G. Bury. Cambridge, MA: Harvard University Press; cited as '*PH*' by book:¶ numbers.

Sidgwick, Henry. 1883. *The Principles of Political Economy.* London: Macmillan; rpt. 1887, 1901.

———. 1903. *The Development of European Polity.* Edited by E.M. Sidgwick. London: Macmillan.

Singer, Marcus G. 1998. "Some Comments on the Later Philosophy of Frederick L. Will." In *Pragmatism, Reason and Norms*, edited by Kenneth R. Westphal, 185–91. New York: Fordham University Press.

Sophocles. 2001. *Antigone*, trans. by Paul Woodruff. Cambridge, MA: Hackett Publishing Co.

Stewart, Jon. ed., 1996. *The Hegel Myths and Legends.* Evanston, IL: Northwestern University Press.

Stovall, Preston. forthcoming. "Syllogistic Reasoning as the Ground of the Content of Judgment: A Line of Thought from Kant through Hegel to Peirce." *European Journal of Philosophy.*

Tetens, Johann N., 1775. *Über die allgemeine speculativische Philosophie.* Bützow & Wismar, Boedner.

Truth, Sojourner. 1851. Speech to the Akron Suffragist Convention; http://www.suffragist.com/docs.htm.

Velema, Wyger. ed., 2007. *Republicans: Essays on Eighteenth-Century Dutch Political Thought.* Leiden: Brill.

Wallace, James. 1988. "The Spirit of the Enterprise." In *Pragmatism, Reason and Norms*, edited by Kenneth R. Westphal, 243–64. New York: Fordham University Press.

Waszek, Norbert. 1984. "Hegels Schottische Bettler." *Hegel-Studien* 19: 311–16.

Westphal, Kenneth R. 1993. "The Basic Context and Structure of Hegel's *Philosophy of Right*." In *The Cambridge Companion to Hegel*, edited by Frederick C. Beiser, 234–69. Cambridge: Cambridge University Press.

———. 1998. "Hegel's Solution to the Dilemma of the Criterion." In *The Phenomenology of Spirit Reader: A Collection of Critical and Interpretive Essays*, edited by Jon Steward, 76–91. Albany: SUNY Press.

———. 2002. "Hegel's Standards of Political Legitimacy." *Jahrbuch für Recht and Ethik/Annual Review of Law and Ethics* 10: 307–20.

———. 2003. *Hegel's Epistemology: A Philosophical Introduction to the Phenomenology of Spirit*. Cambridge, MA: Hackett Publishing Co.

———. 2007. "Normative Constructivism: Hegel's Radical Social Philosophy." *SATS—Nordic Journal of Philosophy* 8 (2): 7–41.

———. 2009a. "Hegel's Phenomenological Method and Analysis of Consciousness." In *The Blackwell Guide to Hegel's Phenomenology of Spirit*, edited by Kenneth R. Westphal, 1–36. Oxford: Wiley-Blackwell.

———. 2009b. "Does Kant's *Opus Postumum* Anticipate Hegel's Absolute Idealism?" In *Kants Philosophie der Natur. Ihre Entwicklung bis zum Opus postumum und Nachwirkung*, edited by Ernst-Otto Onnasch, 357–83. Berlin: deGruyter.

———. 2009c. "Kant, Hegel and Determining Our Duties." In *G.W.F. Hegel*, edited by Dudley Knowles, 337–56. Aldershot: Ashgate.

———. 2010. "Hegel." In *The Routledge Companion to Ethics*, edited by John Skorupski, 168–80. London: Routledge.

———. 2010–2011. "Analytic Philosophy and the Long Tail of *Scientia*: Hegel and the Historicity of Philosophy." *The Owl of Minerva* 42 (1–2): 1–18.

———. 2012. "Norm Acquisition, Rational Judgment and Moral Particularism." *Theory and Research in Education* 10 (1): 3–25.

———. 2013a. "Proof, Justification, Refutation." In *The Bloomsbury Companion to Hegel*, edited by Allegra deLaurentiis and Jeffrey Edwards, 289–302. London: Bloomsbury Publishing.

———. 2013b. "Rational Justification and Mutual Recognition in Substantive Domains." *Dialogue: Canadian Journal of Philosophy/Revue canadienne de philosophie* 52: 1–40.

———. 2013c. "Natural Law, Social Contract and Moral Objectivity: Rousseau's Natural Law Constructivism." *Jurisprudence* 4 (1): 48–75.

———. 2013d. "Substantive Philosophy, Infallibilism and the Critique of Metaphysics: Hegel and the Historicity of Philosophical Reason." In *Hegel's Thought in Europe: Currents, Cross-Currents and Undercurrents*, edited by Lisa Herzog, 192–220. Basingstoke: Palgrave-Macmillan.

———. 2014. "Autonomy, Freedom and Embodiment: Hegel's Critique of Contemporary Biologism." *Hegel Bulletin* 35 (1): 56–83.

———. 2015a. "Hegel's Pragmatic Critique and Reconstruction of Kant's System of Principles in the 1807 *Phenomenology of Spirit*." *Hegel Bulletin* 36 (2): 159–86.

———. 2015b. "Hegel's Pragmatic Critique and Reconstruction of Kant's System of Principles in the *Logic and Encyclopaedia*." *Dialogue: Canadian Journal of Philosophy/Revue canadienne de philosophie* 54 (2): 333–69.

———. 2015c. "Conventionalism and the Impoverishment of the Space of Reasons: Carnap, Quine and Sellars." *Journal for the History of Analytic Philosophy* 3 (8): 1–67.

———. 2015d. "Kant: Vernunftkritik, Konstruktivismus and Besitzrecht." In *Kant's Theory of Law*, edited by Alexandre Travesonni-Gomez and Jean-Christophe Merle, 57–100. *Archiv für Rechts-und Sozialphilosophie*, Beiheft 143.

———. 2016a. *How Hume and Kant Reconstruct Natural Law: Justifying Strict Objectivity without Debating Moral Realism*. Oxford: Clarendon Press.

———. 2017. "Hegel's Natural Law Constructivism: Progress in Principle and in Practice." In *Hegel's Political Philosophy: On the Normative Significance of Method and System*, edited by Sebastian Stein and Thom Brooks, 253–79. Oxford: Oxford University Press.

———. 2016b. "Mind, Language and Behaviour: Kant's Critical Cautions contra Contemporary Internalism and Causal Naturalism." In *Method in Philosophy*, edited by Saffet Babür, 109–49. İstanbul: Yeditepe Üniversitesi Press.

———. 2016c. "Cognitive Psychology, Intelligence and the Realisation of the Concept in Hegel's Anti-Cartesian Epistemology." In *Hegel's Philosophical Psychology*, edited by Susanne Herrmann-Sinai and Lisa Ziglioli, 191–213. New York and London: Routledge.

Will, Frederick L. 1988. *Beyond Deduction: Ampliative Aspects of Philosophical Reflection*. London: Routledge.

———. 1997. *Pragmatism and Realism*, edited by Kenneth R. Westphal, with a Foreword by Alasdair MacIntyre. Lanham, MD: Rowman & Littlefield.

Williams, Robert A. Jr., 2005. *Like a Loaded Weapon: The Rehnquist Court, Indian Rights, and the Legal History of Racism in America*. Minneapolis: University of Minnesota Press.

Wills, Gary. 1992. *Lincoln at Gettysburg: Words that Remade America*. New York: Simon & Schuster.

Woodruff, Paul. 2005. *First Democracy: The Challenge of an Ancient Idea*. Oxford: Oxford University Press.

Wright, Crispin. 1992. *Truth and Objectivity*. Cambridge, MA: Harvard University Press.

7

JEREMY BENTHAM: THEORIST OF PUBLICITY

Gerald J. Postema[1]

Publicity is a pervasive theme running through Bentham's moral, political, and legal theory. Publicity is foundational to his thought. Bentham was one of the first theorists of publicity of the modern era, and surely its most thorough. He knitted together a systematic theory of (what we would now call) public reason, integrating utility and law into a complex framework for public reasoning, with a detailed architecture of public spaces, articulating key institutions and incentives for public accountability and public deliberation. However, despite its fundamental role in Bentham's thought, publicity has rarely been the focus of critical discussion of his work. This may be due to the fact that Bentham highlighted publicity only relatively late in his career and much of his early work in which publicity plays a critical role is as yet unpublished. In this chapter, I will document Bentham's reliance on the idea of publicity throughout his career and demonstrate its centrality to his moral, legal, and political thought.[2]

1 Utility as Public Reason

Bentham maintained resolutely throughout his life that the principle of utility is the foundation of all moral judgment, the principle by which every action, practice, law, institution, code, and constitution is to be judged. This *ruler* and *decider* of all things (UC 96.73) sets the only right and proper (ultimate) end of government,[3] underwrites and guides the analysis and construction of law (LPBJ 224), and provides the sole measure of moral right and wrong.[4] It "furnishes us with that *reason*, which alone depends not upon any higher reason, but which is itself the sole and all-sufficient reason for every point of practice whatsoever" (FG 448, author's emphasis).

Bentham recognized that this "principium generalissimum" (UC 96.75) cannot be defended directly, but he frequently offered a telling indirect argument for it (IPML ch. 2). He observed, to begin, that moral judgments express the sentiments of approbation or disapprobation (B viii, 93) of persons making the judgments, just as empirical judgments express beliefs. But moral judgments are not "mere averment[s] of one's unfounded sentiments" (IPML 14), or "mere opinion of men self-constituted into Legislators" (UC 69.190); rather, they purport to direct attention to something beyond the sentiment or opinion of the appraiser. Appraisers disapprove of some act or object, "conceiving at the same time that it will be alike disapproved of by most others," because they appreciate or respond to the same judgment-independent ground. They appeal beyond the sentiment of the appraiser to "something that is fixed and certain, and that all men are agreed about, and that it could be told by certain indications independent of opinion, whether a given course of conduct was reasonable [good, right, or ought to be done] or otherwise" (CoC 159). Moral judgments claim to be appraiser-transcendent and point to something in the world on which the appraiser's judgment rests, something others could access and assess. In the absence of such appraiser-transcending grounds, expressions of sentiments of approbation and disapprobation are arbitrary, a matter of the appraiser's whim or caprice, which could only be either "despotical" (because one imposes one's idiosyncratic sentiments on everyone else without allowing them the same privilege) or "anarchical" (allowing as many standards as there are appraisers) (IPML 11, 14, 15).

In the absence of such appraiser-transcendent grounds, moral justification of actions would be impossible, for, on Bentham's view, justification has a public, discursive dimension: justification is a matter of "a person addressing himself to the community" (IPML 28n) with *reasons* that can be communicated to and assessable by others (FG 492). Principles typically offered in justification failed to make good on this promise, Bentham argued. Appeals to "reason," "natural law," "natural rights," "moral sense" and the like fail to offer anything beyond themselves as grounds for their assertions, he maintained;[5] they back their assertions, opinions, or judgments by nothing more than *ipse dixit*: it is so, because I say it is (TSA 24, 26, 304–5; LW 255).

However, Bentham insisted that the principle of utility provides just what the public character of moral judgments demands. "Pains and pleasures... are the only clear sources of ideas in morals. These ideas may be rendered familiar to all the world" (B i, 163). Had theorists appealed to utility, rather than "reason" or "natural law," they "would have said something. [They] would have referred us for a foundation of our judgment, to something distinct from that judgment itself" (CoC 199). The principle of utility rests every dispute on matters of fact (FG 491); those to whom a moral judgment is addressed are directed to matters of fact publicly available, matters of common experience:

> in morals, as in legislation, the *principle of utility* is that which holds up to view, as the only sources and tests of right and

wrong, human suffering and enjoyment—pain and pleasure. It is by experience, and by that alone, that the tendency of human conduct, in all its modifications, to give birth to pain and pleasure, is brought to view: it is by reference to experience, and to that standard alone, that the tendency of any such modifications to produce more pleasure than pain, and consequently to be *right*—or more pain than pleasure, and consequently to be *wrong*—is made known and demonstrated. In this view of the matter, morality, as well as policy, is a matter of account.

(B vi, 238–9)[6]

Shaped by the principle of utility, expressing and sharing moral judgments engage us in the business of publicly offering reasons and arguments. Disagreement is still possible, of course, but it is genuine. Controversy does not immediately disintegrate into "childish altercation," but disputing parties "have a plain and open road... to present reconcilement: at worst to an intelligible and explicit issue" and some reasonable hope for agreement in the future (FG 492).

Reading the passages above, Philip Schofield concludes that Bentham's view was that the principle of utility alone met an essential ontological condition of moral judgments, viz., that they be anchored to "real entities" in the physical world.[7] However, I think Bentham's philosophical motivations were different. He did not offer his analysis of moral language or his critique of "the principle of sympathy and antipathy" as a contribution to the metaphysics of morals; his fundamental concern was publicity not ontology, rational public discourse not metaphysics. His forays into logical and metaphysical analysis, including his analysis of "real" and "fictitious entities," were meant to serve the overarching aim to "rear the fabric of felicity by the hands of reason and law" (IPML 11). Thus, it is the unique capability (as Bentham saw it) of the language of utility to answer to the demands for public argument and justification that recommends it as the sole rational ground of moral and political judgments and the sole ultimate end of government and law.

Moreover, he argued, this necessary public function of the principle determines its general shape: publicity necessitates impartiality with regard to the happiness of all those in the community. "On what ground, in the eyes of a common guardian, can any one man's happiness be shown to have any stronger or less strong claim to regard than any others?" (LW 250). No case for partiality to some individual or subgroup can succeed if it must be made to each member of the community. Thus, only the "Greatest Happiness Principle" answers to the demands of impartiality and hence publicity. "In the eyes of every impartial arbiter... having exactly the same regard for the happiness of every member of the community in question as for that of every other, the greatest happiness of the greatest number of the members of that same community can not but be recognized in the character of the right and proper, and sole right and proper, end of government" (FP 235).

2 The Limits of Utility

Utility—understood as the composite of the pleasures and pains of all members of the community impartially considered—recommended itself to Bentham because of its public accessibility. The utility-effects of actions, policies, or institutions were matters of common knowledge, because matters of common experience. Bentham never abandoned this familiar characterization of utility, but early on he recognized its limitations, especially limits of the public accessibility of the empirical facts regarding these experiences.

First, he acknowledged that, although the duration or extent of pleasures or pains can be measured, the quality or intensity of pleasures are not "ponderable or measureable": "weight, extent, heat, light,—for quantities of these articles, we have perceptible and expressible measures: unhappily or happily, for quantities of pleasure or pain, we have no such measures" (LW 253). Moreover, while each person has direct access to his or her own pleasurable or painful experiences, "to no man, can the quality of sensibility in the breast of any other man be made known by anything like equally probative and unfallacious evidence" (D 131). Interpersonal access and comparison of such sensibilities, thus, is limited. And individuals face a like problem regarding *their own* future selves (D 195). The immediate felt quality of a pleasurable experience is present to one's mind, but when pleasures are considered in prospect, one's access is more akin to that of an observer: "Like a third person his future contingent individual pleasure and pain can not be judged of by him otherwise than from the species it belongs to" (D 195). The discrete felt qualities of pleasures and pains are largely inaccessible (across persons and across time), so to make practical judgments of utility we are forced to take a more public point of view, to look to sensibilities or experiences "in their species," that is, those we tend to share with others and come to know through participating with others in daily life.

This refinement gave Bentham's notion of utility-relevant pleasures and pains a more public dimension, which in his view was especially important for public decision-makers, judges, for example. The primary utility focus for judges in a legal dispute, Bentham insisted, must be on expectations of the parties to the lawsuit and expectations of the public.[8] So, for example, property title should go to the party whose expectation, seconded by the expectations of the public, is greatest (and thus for whom the pain of disappointment would be greatest) (UC 69.238; OAM 353–7). However, there is no reliable direct means for determining such expectations, and parties often have an incentive to exaggerate their disappointment when explicitly asked. The only reliable method for doing so, Bentham conceded, is for the judge to put himself in the place of both parties and of the public and to observe from that perspective where the balance of expectations lies.[9] The judge does not seek to uncover the idiosyncratic disappointment-sensibility of the parties affected, not because they are in principle inaccessible to the intuition of the judge, but because it would not be possible for the judge to communicate effectively to the public the ground of his assessment.

> The reasons which a man could find for supposing one man's temperament more sanguine than another's must be founded on ocular inspection, or at least in presence, and that in a variety of situations and for a length of time. Such reasons are in their nature uncommunicable in words... These appearances then being indescribable, the Judge could have no means of satisfying the public of the existence of them.
> (UC 69.238–9)

The problem is not fundamentally ontological—that there is no fact of the matter regarding a person's particular sensibility—nor is it narrowly epistemic—that judges cannot in principle know where the expectations, and hence balance of utilities, lie—but rather the problem is that judges are not able to make the grounds of their decisions fully public. On Bentham's understanding of the nature of moral judgments, the public accessibility of the grounds of decision is of decisive importance.

Later in his career, Bentham's favored articulation of his notion of utility took on an even more prominent public character: in place of happiness or pleasure, which still may have provided the psychic ("real entity") anchor of the notion (TSA 5–7, 76, 98–9), Bentham tended to focus on interests.[10] "Interest" identified a publicly accessible species of utility. Individuals, in Bentham's understanding, tend to have a special stake in the objects of their interests, yet those objects tend to be widely recognizable and interests in them are widely shared. Talk of interests allows us to bracket the immediate quality of the experience and focus attention on the objects of people's interests and to think about how they fit together with other objects into intelligible and publicly recognizable packages.

Moreover, the language of interests allowed Bentham to articulate a notion of the aggregate good or welfare of the community as a whole. The principle of utility called on policymakers, legislators, officials, and individuals alike to promote the "universal interest"—"that interest which is common to [oneself] and every other member of the community" (B ix, 127, see FP 234). While Bentham often speaks of the universal interest as the "aggregate of individual interests" (FP 133, 192), he may have had in mind the convergence or intersection of such interests, rather than their universal sum. The universal interest is defined in opposition to and excludes the "private" or "sinister" interests of individuals and groups.[11] It embraces the most pressing and important interests of each member, interests that converge with the interests of all the others. An *individual's* public interest is his or her share in the common interest of the community as a whole (B ii, 475; Col 290). *The* public interest—or universal interest—is that set of interests held in common by all members of the community in the realization of which each member has a distinct and positive share (FP 192; Col 290). These interests typically involve projects in which one can reasonably hope to enlist the community at large. "Each separate and sinister interest, finds a bar, and that an insuperable one, in every other separate and sinister interest," Bentham argues, "but each man's share in the universal interest finds an ally and coadjutor in every other man's share in the universal interest" (SM 266; see also SM 56).

The most important of these interests are those served by what Bentham identified as the four immediately subordinate ends of utility: security, subsistence, abundance, and equality (Civ Code 301–13). These goods are the most fundamental constituents of the universal interest—they are, we might say, primary, public goods that promote the good of all and of each. Utility so understood seems to meet the demands of publicity to which the principle of utility was said uniquely to answer.

3 Law: Security, Sovereignty and System

Securing Expectations

The only proper end of government, according to Bentham, is the greatest happiness of all members of the community (FP 232) or the "universal interest" (B iii, 453; FP 234), but *security*, the immediate subordinate end and primary component of the universal interest, is "the unrivalled work of law," the principle object of law in general and in every branch (UC 69.44, B ix, 11; see BCLT 168–75). Law's task is to secure the community against the arbitrary power ("misrule") of officials and fellow citizens, and to secure expectations by respecting and protecting existing expectations and by focusing and fixing new expectations. While "penal law" is primarily responsible for directing and regulating behavior and protecting existing expectations, "distributive law" (civil and constitutional law) is responsible for fixing expectations. Law organizes and structures social and political institutions, it defines and constitutes social relations of all sorts. Indeed, in Bentham's view, the constitutive or "civil" aspect of law was more fundamental than its regulative or "penal" aspect (BCLT 175–83).

Law pursues this complex task by addressing directive and constitutive norms to the community as a whole. For this purpose, Bentham recognized, it is important that individual members are able to grasp the import of the norms for their behavior, but it is equally important that they are assured that others in the community with whom they interact also grasp them and are likely to follow them.

The importance of this public dimension of regulative and constitutive norms was evident to Bentham already early in his career. In an early manuscript, he argued that in novel cases, although judges must ultimately decide in accord with the dictates of utility (including both "original" and "expectation-utilities"), judges should base their decisions on analogies to established rules and past decisions, rather than on direct appeal to utility. The reason for this counsel of indirection was that analogy "is more easily agreed upon" than utility:

> to judge whether such a rule which is proposed as being like another rule, is so, a man has but to compare the rules themselves. To judge whether it be in itself right, he has a variety of other circumstances to consider, which presenting themselves in different numbers and differently upon different persons... make this a task much more difficult.
>
> (UC 63.49)

The problem is not that judges are likely to get the utility calculations wrong, but that their determinations could not be anticipated with sufficient confidence by members of the community at large (UC 63.49). The rules which were to govern their interactions and hence the determinations of judges assessing those interactions would not be sufficiently public. Analogies drawn from established rules and past decisions, Bentham argued (at this point in his career), were more likely to focus expectations on a recognizable pattern of behavior than direct appeals to utility. As we shall see shortly, Bentham's assessment of the publicity promise of practical reasoning by analogy—the heart of common-law reasoning—changed, but his commitment to the basic premise of this argument never wavered.

Bentham relied on a similar argument in his critique of Blackstone's natural law and social contract accounts of the limits of obedience to law (FG 483–4; see BCLT 244–50). Neither natural law nor social contract provides a sufficiently public standard by which individual citizens can judge when disobedience and resistance to existing law is justified. The principle of utility promises such a standard, but utility also is inadequate for this purpose, not because appeals to utility are empty or do not point beyond themselves to accessible facts, but because each individual's persuasion regarding the balance of utilities cannot serve the purpose of coordinating their actions with others, which is necessary for successful, utility-serving resistance. The principle of utility can define for each man in particular the limit of his obedience (FG 484), but the point at which resistance is justified must not only be accessible to each; it must be public, available to all. An "express convention" regarding the limits of ruling authority, however, can provide the necessary "common signal alike conspicuous and perceptible to all" (FG 484). Constitutional conventions—*leges in principem* Bentham called them—provide the needed common signal (LPBJ 38, 85–93).

Bentham's view, forged early in his career, was that law can successfully secure the community against all forms of depredation and can structure social and political relations only if its norms can themselves focus the expectations, and hence the deliberations and actions, of members of the community. Only a system of publicly authenticated, publicly articulated and publicly acknowledged norms can do this job. In contrast, the form of law practiced and praised in Bentham's England was radically unsuited for law's primary task: "As a system of general [and public] rules, the Common Law is a thing merely imaginary," he boldly charged (CoC 119).

Common law, Bentham argued, was radically uncertain and unpredictable, dependent on the arbitrary and unaccountable judgment of judges. According to common-law theory, judges are authorized to decide particular cases, but all formulations of rules grounding their decisions, including those offered by deciding judges themselves, are open to challenge and reformulation. Something akin to rules may emerge from this practice; lawyers may be able to construct rules that "appear to be the just expression of the judicial practice in like cases" (UC 100.98). Indeed, judicial decisions, "in virtue of the more extensive interpretation which the people are disposed to put upon them, have somewhat the effect of general laws" (LPBJ 161). However, such customary rules cannot do the fundamental work of law: "From a set of *data* like these, a law is to be extracted by every man who can fancy that he is able: by each man, perhaps a different law: and these, then, are the *monades* which, meeting together, constitute rules which, taken together, constitute... the common or customary law" (LPBJ 195). Common law turns individuals in the community loose "into the wilds of perpetual conjecture" (CoC 95). Common law rules are nothing more than "the idea that *you* have formed of the act in question, the idea that *I* have formed of it, the idea that *Titus* has formed of it"(UC 69.151). They are nothing but "inferential entities," private conjectures, which converge only by accident and cannot provide "common standard[s] which all men acknowledge, and all men are ready to resort to" (UC 69.188). They cannot serve *as law,* because they lack the law's necessary public character.

Law and the Problem of the Privacy of Reason

We can better appreciate the role Bentham assigns to publicity in his jurisprudence by first considering Hobbes's familiar conception of law.

The fundamental problem at the heart of Hobbes' political and legal theory is that, in the state of nature, absent a common power, there are no common standards to which human beings can regiment their judgments of good and evil, right and wrong, or by which they can order their social interactions. "Right reason" and the language of moral judgments call for public standards, but no such standards are naturally available.[12] Individual rational agents are forced to rely solely on their private judgments; and private reason, rather than uniting human beings, puts them in deadly opposition. We might call this the problem of the privacy of reason. The only solution, according to Hobbes, is for contending parties to "set up for right Reason, the Reason of some Arbitrator, or Judge," which, "though his Reason be but the Reason of one Man, yet it is set up to supply the place of... Universal Reason."[13] The practical reason and judgment of each individual must be supplanted, replaced with the reason and judgment of a sovereign expressed in and through law.

Law plays a critical role in Hobbes's solution to the problem of the privacy of judgment. And he was naturally drawn to the age-old *thetic* conception of law.[14] The defining property of law, on this view is not (cannot be), *wisdom*, which is open to assessment and challenge, but *authority*.[15] Law consists of the commands of one to whom others are antecedently obligated to obey, declaring publicly what one may or must do or forbear to do.[16] The judgment and will of the sovereign displaces the judgment of the law subject, *stet pro rationis voluntas*. Sovereign commands must take the form of law, for the root problem of the state of nature—the problem of the privacy of judgment—lies in the absence of common public standards, not merely the absence of centralized power. "Law is all the Right Reason we have,"[17] and *law*, not merely the will of the sovereign, constitutes right—i.e. public—reason. Thus, if law is to serve its fundamental purpose, it must be general, clearly and publicly declared, intelligible and manifestly authentic (carrying the marks of the sovereign's authority).[18]

Like Hobbes, and for similar reasons, Bentham found the *thetic* model of law initially attractive; the statute, not rules inferred or constructed from judicial decision, was the paradigm. When he found it necessary, Bentham typically defined *a law* in familiar terms of the expression of will of someone related to persons addressed via power or authority.[19] But the thetic model required more of law than that it be a (general) command of someone in authority. Most importantly, the command must be articulated in canonical, public language[20] and formally "authentic," expressing the "will of the accustomed law-giver or law-givers [and] expressed with the accustomed formalities" (UC 69.87; see UC 70a.51). The requirement of formal authentication insured that the rules would be publicly articulated and publicly validated. In contrast with the alleged rules of common law, laws on this thetic model promised to meet the demands of publicity, shaping and focusing expectations even better than conventions, although conventions supplied the "accustomed formalities" and authorized the "accustomed law-giver."

Bentham called the community-wide practice underlying the formalities, the "habit of obedience" of the members of political community; however, it is clear that this "habit" was not the bare disposition of the members severally to respond to commands from certain discrete sources.[21] Rather, Bentham conceived it as a convention-like interactive practice (BCLT 220–30). Likewise, the "obedience" Bentham had in mind was not merely passive or reactive; it always had an active, and critical public dimension. The limits of this habit of obedience, viewed from one perspective, might be seen as a matter of political fact: a disposition of the people only to comply with laws regarding certain matters issuing from certain authorities (LPBJ 42–3 and nn). But these dispositions were shaped by common understandings of the proper limits of the authority and the point at which non-compliance and even resistance could be justified (FG 484; LPBJ 88–9, 92). While citizens were bound to "obey promptly," Bentham urged them also to "censure freely" (FG 399–400). The two activities were interdependent. The critical dimension of his notion of the habit of obedience, nascent in his early jurisprudential writing, became increasingly prominent in his constitutional and political writings later in his career, culminating, as we shall see in the next section, in the central role he assigned to the "Public Opinion Tribunal"—the "tribunal of free criticism" (LW 98).

Stretching the Thetic Model of Law

Although Bentham never abandoned the metaphor of command as a convenient model for thinking about law, almost immediately after offering his definition of law as expression of will of a sovereign in his signal work of analytical jurisprudence, *Of the Limits of the Penal Branch of Jurisprudence*, he began to knead, stretch, and reshape it, and in later work he pushed his revisions further. I will mention several such extensions or revisions that indicate the nature and importance of the idea of publicity in Bentham's jurisprudence.

Following Hobbes (and a long tradition before him[22]), Bentham used the command as a model of law, but he departed from Hobbes's understanding of law in several respects. First, "expressions of will" might include not only imperatives but also permissions and countermands. More generally, Bentham argued that much of law is not immediately *directive*, but rather is *constitutive*, defining and structuring private, public, and political relations. This law is not best understood on the model of commands, although Bentham stretched and pulled the model to fit law somewhat, conceiving of this vast body of constitutive law as shared and presupposed *parts* of a variety of "penal" laws.

Second, even with respect to commands, he resisted the view that law's commands entail coercive sanctions. Lawmakers typically and prudently attach sanctions to their directives, but they are not properly understood as *likely consequences* of non-compliance. Rather, sanctions are consequences that *ought by law* to occur.[23] This *normative* relationship between the directive and the sanction is grounded in secondary legal norms, directives addressed to officials to *see to it* that the primary laws are enforced; these directives in turn rest on more "remote" directives to other officials backing up the proximate one, etc. (LPBJ 151–2). Ultimately, this series of subsidiary laws bottoms out in the judgments of the public, which holds officials to their legal responsibilities (LPBJ 86–92). Thus, on Bentham's view, coercion plays an important role in law, but as one part of multi-part institutional-cum-informal structure for securing the effectiveness of the law's system of norms as a whole. Moreover, lawmakers may decide not to attach, or may find it impossible to attach, legal sanctions to some directives. Constitutional limits on ruling power were typically of the latter kind, in Bentham's view, enforced not in courts of law, but in the court of public opinion (the Public Opinion Tribunal), exercising the "moral sanction."

Third, in an important break with the Hobbesian conception of law, Bentham rejected the view that laws are meant to be *peremptory*. Hobbes wrote that "command is when a man saith do this or do not do this yet without expecting any other reason than the will of him that sayes it."[24] This model equipped law well for the task that Hobbes assigned to it—it displaced judgment from the law-subject to the commanding sovereign. But Bentham was clear from the outset that law requires submission of conduct, but not submission of judgment (CoC 346). Law does not require law-subjects to abandon their critical and deliberative powers, or only to engage them off-line, as it were. Any attempt to do so would amount to intolerable manipulation of will by will, in his view; rather, law must seek to direct understanding by understanding (UC 126.1; B iv, 539). Law inevitably and unavoidably limits liberty and offers primarily negative incentives to comply (as a complement to their directives), but it is meant to address, and can only function properly when it addresses, the understanding and not (only) the will of law-subjects.

Fourth, Bentham stretched the idea of commands, or expressions of will, to incorporate what he took to be law's essential *systemic* character. A law "is a command," that is to say, is a practically determinate directive for action, only "when it is entire" (PF 217), Bentham wrote. But,

> The idea of a law, meaning one single but entire law, is in a manner inseparably connected with that of a compleat body of laws; so that what is a law and what are the contents of a compleat body of the laws are questions of which neither can well be answer'd

without the other. A body of laws is a vast and complicated piece of mechanism of which no part can be fully explained without the rest.

(LPBJ 21)

The law, on Bentham's view, is not merely an aggregate of discrete and individual *laws*, all traceable to a common source, but an interconnected *system* of laws, each of which is individuated, not by being traced to some discrete, observable public event (some expression of volition), but by locating it in the system. What is *a law*—a complete, whole, "entire but single law" (IPML 299)—is determined by examining a complete system of law and identifying the individual practically determinate directives in it. Thus, at bottom, Bentham's concept of law is of a complex rational entity, not merely an empirical one, although it is ultimately tethered to empirical facts ("real entities"). It is, in one sense of the word, an ideal concept. His researches in *Limits of the Penal Branch of Jurisprudence* were meant to uncover and articulate "the logical, ideal, the intellectual whole, not the physical one: the *law* not the *statute*" (IPML 301). "Law—[is] abstract, statute [is] concrete... Statutes are such as we find them, laws are such as we may conceive them" (UC 96.85).

At the core of Bentham's model of a complete law is the idea of a directive for action that includes in it everything necessary for adequate public guidance of behavior, including all the qualifications, limitations, elaborations that apply to it, and all the institutional and procedural conditions of its implementation and enforcement (LPBJ §16). Of course, none of this expository, elaborative and qualificative material is uniquely tied to a single (complete) law; indeed, a vast amount of it will be shared by a large number of laws. A law is complete, then, when all its necessary elements are linked and this is made explicit by "juxtaposition" or "reference" (LPBJ 171–2).

Thus, laws are systematically interconnected, not only in their logical relations, but also in their shared substance. This implies that the idea of a complete law presupposes the idea of a complete body of law. To explicate the concept of law, we must explicate the notion of *a* (complete) *law*, but that is not possible without recognizing, and putting at the center of our explication, the *substantive* relationships that inevitably exist among laws. This insight, which structured all of Bentham's vast writings on universal jurisprudence, follows from his conviction that law by its nature directs and informs actions of rational agents and it can do so only if it is public and accessible. For Bentham, the systematically ordered code of law—the "pannomion"—was designed to serve publicity. Publicity not only demands clear marks of the authenticity of laws, but also demands that all directives are clearly articulated, and that all the material that qualifies and limits a simple directive is accessible as well. That puts any given legal directive in a complex network of relations of substance with much of the rest of the law bearing these same marks of authenticity.

Manifested Reasonableness

Further, Bentham insisted that added to formal authenticity and completeness must be the *manifested reasonableness* of the law's systematically structured directives (LW 121 n.a, 141, 168). Reasons address the understanding, he argued, but bare commands without manifested reasons address only the will. Both are essential if law is to operate in its characteristic mode (LW 100–01, 143–4; B i, 159–60). On Bentham's view, the manifested reasonableness of the law is a requirement of good law: "The greatest advantage" of the manifested reasonableness of the law "is that which results from conciliating the approbation of all minds, by satisfying the public judgment" (B i, 161). But more importantly, it is a condition of law doing its core job of fixing and securing expectations by means of public norms. If law subjects are to apply authoritative directives to their specific circumstances, mindful of the likely reason-governed actions of others with whom they must interact, they must exercise intelligent judgment (a product of "the understanding"); without manifest reasons of the directives to guide them, they cannot proceed with confidence (B i, 160–61; LW 45–6). To do this, the law must offer reasons that are publicly accessible: "the catechism of reasons is worthless, if it cannot be the catechism of the people" (B i, 163). And, as we have learned above, the only catechism of the people, the only language of reasons fit to do the work, is the language of utility (that is, public interests). "To give a reason for a law, is to show that it is conformable to the principle of utility" (B i, 163; see LW 101, 121). Thus, unlike Hobbes, Bentham held that the mode of public reason offered by law itself depends on its manifested reasonableness, where that reasonableness is articulated in terms of universal, public interests of members of the community. Publicly articulated and authenticated law and the public language of utility complement each other.

In Bentham's system, the reasonableness of law is manifested primarily in two ways. First, the law is systematically ordered on a principle of "natural arrangement" (FG 415–8; LPBJ 224; B i, 171–2). A natural arrangement "takes such properties to characterize [the laws] by, as men in general are, by common construction of man's nature, disposed to attend to" (FG 415). A natural arrangement of the laws is "best adapted for the generality of the people" (B iii, 161), one that *"naturally,* that is readily, engage[s], and firmly fix[es] the attention of any one" who examined it (IPML 272). The structure of the law, following the principle of natural arrangement, directly "points out the reason of the law" (FG 416–7; see IPML 273–4), reasons of public utility. Bentham's pannomion was designed to focus attention on publicly salient social harms and threats to the universal interest, and organize its directives around such "offences" (see IPML chapter 16). For Bentham, the "notoriety" or "cognoscibility" of law, its "being present to the mind" (LW 8), depends on its textual clarity, on careful legislative drafting, but his insistence on "natural arrangement" of the law reflects his understanding that genuine clarity of language is possible only if it achieves what John Gardner calls "moral clarity."[25] Law achieves moral clarity when it uses distinctions and terms that reflect the public meanings of actions and engage the public's moral imagination. Bentham's "natural arrangement" sought to do just that. It defined categories and distinctions relying on the language of universal public interests, because that language had the best chance of being a public moral language, available to each member severally and to the public collectively.

Bentham's second device to secure the manifest reasonableness of the law was the "perpetual commentary of reasons" drawn from the principle of utility which, in Bentham's plan, was to accompany the publicly articulated code of law.[26] Moreover, he insisted that the reasons themselves must be manifestly interconnected, thereby underwriting the systemic character of the body of law.

> An isolated reason is a mere trifle: the reasons for the laws, if they are good, are so connected, that unless they have been prepared for the whole body, they cannot with certainty be given for any part. Hence, in order to present in the most advantageous manner the reason for a single law, it is necessary that the plan of a system of reasons for all the laws should have been formed.
> (B i, 163)

Bentham went even further and insisted that the commentary of reasons be interwoven into the text of the publicly promulgated law. "There must be therefore not one system only, but two parallel and connected systems, running on together, the one of legislative provisions, the other of political reasons, each affording to the other correction and support" (IPML 9). He showed how to do it in his *Constitutional Code* of 1830 (LW 257 and CC generally).

The commentary of reasons enables lawmakers or judges to justify their exercise of ruling power to the public (LW 45, 141ff). This is not just shrewd ruling practice; for Bentham it was critical to law's performing its proper function. *Reasons* "alone are addresses from understanding to understanding. *Ordinances* without reasons are but manifestations of will,—of the will of the mighty, exacting obedience from the helpless" (LW 100). Without the accompanying commentary of reasons, the exercise of law-making power is nothing more than an expression of will, a bare exercise of political power, not an attempt to address the understanding of law subjects (LW 7–8, 78–9, 143; B i, 161). Law designed according to these principles promised three additional key benefits, Bentham argued.

First, interpretations of the law, by officials and citizens alike, are directed to a publicly accessible and publicly meaningful source (LW 141, 248; B i, 160–61). Bentham realized that the need for interpretation is inevitable, but, he argued, the systematically articulated code, drafted in readily accessible terms, accompanied by a matching systematic account of its underlying principles, provides a guide for and a limitation on "liberal interpretation" of judges and officials (LPBJ 174–5, 228–9). It also provides a common source of understanding for citizens and hence a basis for anticipating the interpretations of the laws by officials and fellow citizens.

Second, this "rationalized" pannomion supplies a "bridle" with which the public can control "constituted authorities." The rationale provides "a preservative" against "blind routine" and "a restraint to everything arbitrary." Under a "rationalized body of law... the reign of arbitrary power will be at an end."[27] The system of law, to which all officials must appeal to demonstrate warrant for and justification of their actions, provides a "torch" exposing all official acts of oppression to the critical scrutiny of the Public Opinion Tribunal (SM 121). "In his capacity as censor, every citizen will be enabled to act, ... calling to account this or that member of the legislative body, in respect of the code" (LW 270).

Third, it provides a focus for criticism of the law (LW 10–11). "By rendering the law a fully known and comprehensible entity," Lieberman writes, "the *Pannomion* stood exposed to public comment and criticism. This made the Code a fully public resource: an institution of power that utilized methods which enabled the public to monitor and critique the exercise of that power."[28] This, in turn, offered a more general framework of public debate and deliberation. In the early 1780s, Bentham tentatively expressed a hope that giving power to courts to review legislation would provide a framework and discipline for "a public and authorized debate on the propriety of law... The artillery of the tongue is [thereby] played off against the law under the cover of the law itself" (FG 488 n.1). In the 1820s Bentham gave the Public Opinion Tribunal a major role in control of governing power. His publicly articulated and authenticated, reasons-manifesting pannomion promised a public framework for such general criticism.

4 The Political Role of Publicity

The principle of utility, properly refined and focused, promised to provide a language of public reason; law, properly structured and focused, promised the same. Neither, Bentham came to realize, could do so on its own, but in partnership they could make good on their promises. Bentham saw them as complementary, mutually supportive, the strengths of each answering the limitations of the other (LW 78–9, 143). Law was not, as in Hobbes's view, a surrogate for the practical reason of individuals, but rather an essential supplement, a means by which individual practical reason was focused, facilitated, and enhanced. At the same time, Bentham regarded law as a joint product of authority and reason, of authentically public norms integrated into a rationally compelling systematic structure, the reasons for which are manifest.

To this partnership Bentham added an essential third party: an informed, empowered, and active public. Although already implicit in his early jurisprudential work (especially in his reliance on the "moral sanction" at the foundations of law), the political role of publicity became central to his political and constitutional work in his last two decades. Since the sole ultimate aim of government is the greatest happiness, or universal interest, of the community, the fundamental task of the engineer of political arrangements, he argued, is to define and distribute ruling power so as to achieve this goal. This involves securing the "moral, intellectual, and active aptitude" of all political functionaries, and, most importantly, preventing the "sinister sacrifice" of the universal interest to the private interest of those wielding political power. The first task, then, was to define, structure, and fund devices for "security against misrule." To this end, Bentham rejected the familiar liberal devices of imposing legal limits on the exercise of power through entrenching "natural rights" in some fundamental law or separating powers and putting them in competition (SM 23–4n). Rather, he insisted on "constant responsibility," "the strictest and most absolute dependence" on the public (B ix, 62; see B iv, 362). "Maximum publicity" is not just "a necessary condition to the maximum appropriate attitude" (OAM 26), it is the only effective means to this end.[29] Bentham argued that popular control must never be limited to the exercise of the "locative" and "dislocative" power of the electorate. It must be continuous, not episodic. For this, publicity was essential.

The demand for publicity took two interrelated forms: a demand for *transparency*, which mobilizes public discipline, and a demand for *reasons*, which mobilizes public deliberation. First, "sinister interest and evil in every shape," Bentham argued, breeds "in the darkness of secrecy" (CC(B) 493). Publicity's harsh light exposes oppression and misrule to searching public scrutiny. In a variety of works, Bentham designed an extraordinary array of formal and informal devices to secure transparency of all governmental activities. He designed public institutions, public buildings, and public spaces in which officials could be observed, interrogated, and judged by members of the Public Opinion Tribunal. These devices exposed official actions to scrutiny and they enabled, encouraged and educated the public's exercise of governmental oversight. Bentham's aim was to subject official actions to the public's "superintendence" via its exercise of the "moral sanction."[30] Bentham thought that the moral sanction exerts control primarily through officials' concern for their reputations or esteem in the community (UC 57.9). "The eye of the public makes the statesman virtuous" (B x, 145). When opportunities to serve sinister interests are limited, concern for the good opinion of others will motivate most officials to behave in accord with common standards—that is, with perceived universal interests.

Bentham realized that the public has an even more powerful weapon in its disciplinary arsenal: withdrawal of obedience and even active resistance (SM 123). Bentham held that resistance was justified not only at the extreme limit of government dysfunction, but as a regular "disposition" of the public, which should be encouraged by explicit constitutional arrangements. Free governments should "cherish the disposition to eventual resistance," and take steps to keep "the national mind... in a state of appropriate preparation... for eventual resistance" (B ii, 287). Key to such preparation, Bentham argued, was a vigorous free press.

Second, Bentham argued that publicity enables and empowers public *accountability*, an effective demand on officials to give reasons to the public for their actions and policies. In his *Fragment on Government*, Bentham equated "the responsibility of governors" with "the right which a subject has of having the reasons publicly assigned and canvassed of every act of power that is exerted over him" (FG 485); likewise, later he tied "superintendency of the public" to the official's "obligation of assigning reasons for his acts" (B v, 556), reasons appealing to the legal or political principles warranting them and the political goals driving them.[31] Publicity not only exposes an unjust action to public view, but it makes its injustice manifest (B ii, 141, 147); similarly, the manner in which just actions serve universal interests is manifested.

In this way, the evaluation and censure of, and possible resistance to, governmental misrule over time is increasingly better informed and more likely to be articulate and securely focused on the universal interest. The public "may err," but, freed from the distorting influences of the "aristocratical class," and participating in public discussion, "it continually tends to become enlightened" (PT 29). "In proportion as [the public] becomes more and more mature, [it] becomes more and more favorable to the universal interest" (CC(B) 45, see 158). Thus, when subject to the demands of publicity and the institutional structures that seek to meet them, law and its administration provide a *school* for public political morality.[32] By observing the giving and assessing of reasons by officials in public, and eventually participating in the process themselves, citizens, "impressed with their own sense of dignity," (B ii, 127) come to develop "a habit of reasoning and discussion" that focuses more on their common or universal interests than on their particular sinister interest, and their "passions, accustomed to a public struggle, will learn reciprocally to restrain themselves" (PT 31; CC(B) 100). The order of debate and deliberation which the public can observe when the business of a community's political assemblies are fully open to view, will "form by imitation the national spirit," which order, in turn, "will be reproduced in clubs and inferior assemblies" (PT 31). Through participation in debates at the local level, members of the community come to recognize the public dimensions of their concern to secure themselves against depredation or oppression and their individual part in that universal interest, and at the same time come to understand the difficulty of enlisting the cooperation of others to advance their private, "sinister" interests. This more informed and disciplined practice of small-scale public discussion enables the community more articulately and effectively to exercise control over government officials and the larger public assemblies.

Of course, Bentham realized that not everyone in this school earns high marks, and blinkered views of the facts, particular passions, and narrowly focused interests can still influence public opinion (CC(B) 42). Nevertheless, he put his faith in publicity: the only ultimately effective remedy for the defects of publicity is more publicity, more public involvement in public assessment of and debate over the actions and policies of government and the laws which determine the boundaries and directions of the exercise of political power.

Bentham's optimism rested ultimately on his faith in the educative capacity of the continued and widest spread of public discussion in which members of the Public Opinion Tribunal were actively engaged. They were not, on his model, merely passive observers, mobilized when needed to punish governmental misrule; rather, officials addressed to them arguments for laws, policies and official actions, engaging them in the assessment of those reasons, forming and giving expression to judgments, and acting on them (SM 61). Their capacities were developed, resourced, and enriched in this "tribunal of free criticism." Bentham's "public sphere" was meant to be richly deliberative.

5 Conclusion

Bentham's work on publicity integrated utility and law into a complex framework for public reasoning and constructed a network of key institutions and incentives for public accountability and public deliberation. He designed these institutions to secure the transparency of every exercise of ruling power and to encourage, educate, and empower the public in their critical task of holding officials to their responsibilities under the law. The law itself was designed to provide fully public—accessible, assessable, and manifestly reasonable—standards for public as well as private actions. This required, on Bentham's account, explicitly articulated, formally enacted, and fully authenticated legal norms that are internally and systematically related according to a plan that made content of the norms and their reasonableness manifest to all members of the political community, thereby providing guidance to all, and hence to each, that addressed their understanding rather than manipulated their wills. The ultimate principle that secured this public reasonableness was, for Bentham, the principle of utility, the only principle, in his view, that met the fundamental demand in the moral as well as political domain for a truly public, rational basis for judgment and action.

Notes

1 Cary C. Boshamer Distinguished Professor of Philosophy and Professor of Law, University of North Carolina at Chapel Hill.
2 Bentham also offers an account of the infrastructure of the rule of law; Gerald J. Postema, "The Soul of Justice: Bentham on Publicity, Law, and the Rule of Law," in *Bentham's Theory of Law and Public Opinion*, X. Zhai and M. Quinn, eds. (Cambridge: Cambridge University Press, 2014), 40–62.
3 FP, 3, 234–5; CC 136; CC(B), 5; PF, 211.
4 FG, 393, 440n, 446n; IPML, 13; B vi, 238.
5 Appeals to "natural law," Bentham argued, are "from first to last nothing but [one's] own private opinion in disguise" (UC 69.102).

> To say that a thing ought not to be done because there is a law of nature against its being done, is an obscure and roundabout way of saying one of two things. "It ought not to be done, because it would be mischievous or dangerous to the community"; or else 2ndly. "It ought not to be done, because I say it ought not." The grand mischief of the expression is that most commonly when examined into, the only meaning which it is found to cover is the latter.
>
> (UC 69.106)

See also UC 127.483-4; RRR 186-7; SM 23-4n.
6 Nearly forty years earlier Bentham wrote that, when I appeal to utility,

> I put in issue a set of facts, and call in experience to witness. I allege the existence of certain pains and pleasures... pains and pleasures such as men have felt in themselves, or recognized in others... pains and pleasure felt... by the old stock of senses, such as all men have, and all men know of. Of this sort are a man's *reasons*, if he has any.
>
> (UC 69. 72–3 n. i)

7 Philip Schofield, *Utility and Democracy*, 28, 47; Schofield, "A Defense of Jeremy Bentham's Critique of Natural Rights," in *Bentham's Theory of Law and Public Opinion*, 216–7.
8 For Bentham's notion of expectation utilities, see UC 70a.20, UC 96.74, UC 72.1, CoC 231; for the special weight and importance Bentham assigns to expectations, see UC 69.239; UC 70a.20; *Civ Code* 308. See Gerald J. Postema, *Bentham and the Common Law Tradition* [BCLT] (Oxford: Clarendon Press, 1986/9), 151–2, 160–2.
9 CoC, 197 n.c; UC 69.238; OAM 355; B iii, 212; B iv, 312, 388. UC 86.39; UC 81.124-5; UC 114.222, 236.

10 For a general defense of the thesis of this paragraph see Gerald J. Postema, "Interests, Universal and Particular: Bentham's Utilitarian Theory of Value," *Utilitas* 18 (2006), 109–33.
11 The universal interest and rival particular interests stand in a relationship of "implacable hostility" (OAM 43; see SM 252–3; FP 192; *Col* 290).
12 Thomas Hobbes, *Dialogue between a Philosopher and a Student of the Common Laws of England*, Alan Cromartie, ed. (Oxford: Clarendon Press, 2005), 26; *On the Citizen*, Richard Tuck and Michael Silverthorne, eds. and trans. (Cambridge: Cambridge University Press, 1998), 163.
13 Thomas Hobbes, *Leviathan*, Richard Tuck, ed. (Cambridge: Cambridge University Press, 1998), 32–3; *Dialogue*, 26.
14 By *"thetic"* I refer to that family of conceptions of law that understand law as explicitly and intentionally made and imposed on law subjects, the ruling metaphor of which is command. See Gerald J. Postema, "Legal Positivism—Early Foundations," in *Routledge Companion to the Philosophy of Law*, Andrei Marmor, ed. (New York: Routledge, 2012), 32.
15 *Dialogue* 10, 29.
16 *Leviathan* 183; *Dialogue* 31.
17 *Questions regarding Liberty and Necessity* in **English Works of Thomas Hobbes**, William Molesworth, ed. (1841), vol. v, 194.
18 *Leviathan* 187–9, 239–40, 246.
19 Early on, Bentham wrote boldly, "law is a command" (UC 69. 71), but a little later, when he more carefully articulated his definition of law, he used broader language of "expression of will" (LPBJ 24; Chr 205n.).
20 Law, Bentham insisted, must always be "a [piece of] discourse—conceived mostly in *general*, and always in *determinate* words" (Chr 205n, author's emphasis). See also CoC 259 n.a; B vi, 552.
21 As Austin (on Hart's interpretation) portrayed it; see H.L.A. Hart, *The Concept of Law*, third edition (Oxford: Clarendon Press, 2012), chapter 4.
22 Including natural-law theorists (e.g. Suarez) and even committed common-law jurists (e.g. Matthew Hale); see "Legal Positivism—Early Foundations."
23 On Bentham's view, every law consists of a "directive" and a "sanctional" part, the former "bids" the latter "prophecies" or "predicts"; however, that prediction is underwritten by a "subsidiary" which bids others (primarily judges) to fulfill the prediction (CoC 72; LPBJ 146, 150).
24 *Leviathan* 176.
25 John Gardner, *Offences and Defences: Selected Essays in the Philosophy of Criminal Law* (Oxford: Oxford University Press, 2007), 45–7.

26 In a body of law… it being in its fabric *reasonable*, the *reasonableness* is manifested by a correspondent and perpetual accompaniment of *reasons*, these reasons being deduced from the universally prevalent and universally recognized principles of human nature… [which] will of themselves help to lodge, and serve to keep, in the mind those portions of the matter of law, of which the *Main Text* will require to be composed.

(LW 121 n.a, author's emphasis)

See also LW 7–8, 45–6, 79, 101, 248–50, 260; B i, 160–61.
27 LW 269, 248–9, B i, 161; UC 80.36. See also LW 141.
28 David Lieberman, "Bentham's Jurisprudence and Democratic Theory: An Alternative to Hart's Approach," in *Bentham's Theory of Law and Public Opinion*, 139.
29 SM 125; UC 51(b), 378; B iv, 310, 317–18; RRR 202; PT 37; B ii, 8; FP 241.

30 PT 29–30; CC 24; CC(B) 50–51, 151–2; B ii, 31.
31 B ii, 141–2, 147; CC(B) 535, 555; B vi, 356.
32 B vi, 355, 360; B ii, 127, 143, 148, 149–50; PT 31.

References to Bentham's Works

[B] *The Works of Jeremy Bentham* (11 vols.), J. Bowring (ed.), Edinburgh: William Tait, 1838–43.
[CC] *Constitutional Code*, vol. 1, F. Rosen and J.H. Burns (eds.), Oxford: Clarendon Press, 1983.
[CC(B)] Bentham, *Constitutional Code* in B ix.
[Chr] *Chrestomathia*, M.J. Smith and W.H. Burston (eds.), Oxford: Clarendon Press, 1983.
[Civ Code] Principles of Civil Code in B i, 297–364.
[Col] *Colonies, Commerce and Constitutional Law: Rid Yourselves of Ultramaria and Other Writings on Spain and Spanish America*, P. Schofield (ed.), Oxford: Clarendon Press, 1995.
[CoC] *Comment on the Commentaries* in *Comment on the Commentaries and a Fragment on Government*, J.H. Burns and H.L.A. Hart (eds.), London: Athlone Press, 1977.
[D] *Deontology*, in *Deontology Together with a Table of the Springs of Action and Article on Utilitarianism*, A. Goldworth (ed.), Oxford: Clarendon Press, 1983.
[FG] *A Fragment on Government*, in *Comment on the Commentaries and A Fragment on Government*, J.H. Burns and H.L.A. Hart (eds.), London: Athlone Press, 1977.
[FP] *First Principles Preparatory to a Constitutional Code*, P. Schofield (ed.), Oxford: Clarendon Press, 1989.
[IPML]. *An Introduction to the Principles of Morals and Legislation*, F. Rosen (ed.), Oxford: Clarendon Press, 1996.
[LPBJ] *The Limits of the Penal Branch of Jurisprudence*, P. Schofield (ed.), Oxford: Clarendon Press, 2010.
[LW] *Legislator of the World: Writings on Codification, Law, and Education*, P. Schofield and J. Harris (eds.), Oxford: Clarendon Press, 1998.
[OAM] *Official Aptitude Maximized, Expense Minimized*, P. Schofield (ed.), Oxford: Clarendon Press, 1993.
[PF] *Pannomial Fragments* in B iii, 211–30.
[PT] *Political Tactics*, M. James, C. Blamires, and C. Pease-Watkin (eds.), Oxford: Clarendon Press, 1999.
[RRR] *Rights, Representation, and Reform: Nonsense upon Stilts and other Writings on the French Revolution*, P. Schofield (ed.), Oxford: Clarendon Press, 2002.
[SM] *Securities against Misrule and Other Constitutional Writings for Tripoli and Greece*, P. Schofield (ed.), Oxford: Clarendon Press, 1990.
[TSA] *A Table of the Springs of Action*, in *Deontology together with A Table of the Springs of Action and Article on Utilitarianism*, A. Goldworth (ed.) Oxford: Clarendon Press, 1983.
[UC] Bentham MSS, University College London (reference to box, folio number).

8

SOCIAL MORALITY IN MILL

Piers Norris Turner[1]

1 Introduction

A leading classical utilitarian, John Stuart Mill is an unlikely contributor to the public reason tradition in political philosophy. To hold that social rules or political institutions are justified by their contribution to overall happiness is to deny that they are justified by their being the object of consensus or convergence among all those holding qualified moral or political viewpoints. For the utilitarian, the existence of consensus or convergence might be evidence of a tendency to overall happiness and help to establish conditions of security and coordination necessary for it, but it does not constitute the fundamental choiceworthiness of the rules or institutions. In this chapter, I do not mean to challenge that baseline utilitarian understanding of Mill's moral and political framework. But I do want to explore the surprising ways in which he nevertheless works to accommodate the problems and insights of the public reason tradition, and the extent to which he makes arguments that can help those working within that tradition. This is important not only for a richer understanding of Mill's utilitarian ethics and how consequentialists might address themselves to the public reason project, but also for those interested in the ongoing significance of Mill's liberal principles after the turn to public reason in the work of Rawls, Larmore, Gaus, and others.

In what follows I try to show how Mill's utilitarian theory incorporates the claim that the demands of social life require a publicly accepted set of normative expectations to govern judgments about when one has met one's obligations and, relatedly, about the appropriateness of blame or punishment. For Mill, such a social morality properly regulates these judgments even if it is not ideal, that is, even if it is not the set of rules the adoption of which would collectively maximize utility. Importantly, however, social morality is not static. It shapes our collective existence by defining the proper bounds of our practices of accountability even as it evolves over time. And, as we shall see, Mill identifies principles of public reason that he believes should guide the development of social morality.

Ultimately, I believe, Mill's account of social morality remains consistent with his act utilitarian commitment that what makes actions fundamentally choiceworthy is their expediency or contribution to overall happiness (whether or not they are blameworthy). But seeing how Mill's discussion of social morality fits within his overall ethical theory helps to resolve debates about passages in which he seems to endorse an account of moral right and wrong at odds with act utilitarianism. With this unified account of Mill's ethical theory on the table, we can explore the extent to which it allows him to offer arguments about the shape of our social practices and political institutions in the spirit of public reason liberalism, and not always by direct appeal to the principle of utility.

In Section 2, I begin to examine those places where Mill expresses the need for social morality—publicly recognized social rules by which we appropriately hold each other accountable—and addresses what is required to maintain its integrity as it develops over time. It is hard to imagine anyone denying the value of such a social morality, but that is partly the point. Because act utilitarianism is commonly caricatured as failing to respect social rules as the appropriate governors of our actions, it is worth seeing how they are treated in a fully developed "sophisticated" act utilitarian system such as Mill's.[2] In fact, he makes a great deal of the fact that maintaining the integrity of publicly recognized social rules is necessary for cooperative society to exist at all.[3] This justifies a general commitment, on one hand, to restrain our own actions in accordance with those social rules and, on the other, to appeal to them in assigning blame or punishment to others. Mill not only explores the historical circumstances necessary for stable social rules to persist—most interestingly, in a non-despotic, liberal system—but also argues that, except in exceptional cases, individuals' practical deliberation and judgments of holding each other accountable should extend no further than those social rules.[4]

2 Expediency and Blameworthiness

It is important to appreciate a complication for interpreting Mill's overall ethical theory: that he sometimes uses the terms "morality," "moral," and the like to refer to the utilitarian standard of what makes actions fundamentally choiceworthy (namely, their *expediency* or actual contribution to overall happiness) and other times uses those same terms to refer to a standard of *blameworthiness* that does not involve direct appeal to the principle of utility (but rather to whether a person has met social expectations in deciding to act). There are numerous examples of the first sense of "morality" in Mill's work. In chapter 2 of *Utilitarianism* he summarizes his moral theory this way:

> According to the Greatest Happiness Principle... the ultimate end, with reference to and for the sake of which all other things are desirable (whether we are considering our own good or that of other people), is an existence exempt as far as possible from pain, and as rich as possible in enjoyments, both in point of quantity and quality... *This, being, according to the utilitarian opinion, the end of human action, is necessarily also the standard of morality*; which may accordingly be defined, the rules and precepts for human conduct, by the observance of which an existence such as has been described might be, to the greatest extent possible, secured to all mankind; and not to them only, but, so far as the nature of things admits, to the whole sentient creation.
> (CW X.214; emphasis added)

In other passages he similarly refers to "the principle of utility—which is a theory of right and wrong" ("Sedgwick's Discourse" (1835), CW X.71) or notes in passing that "right means productive of happiness, and wrong productive of misery" ("An Examination of Sir William Hamilton's Philosophy" [*Hamilton*] (1865), CW IX.456). In a summary of the argument of chapter 2 of *Utilitarianism* he writes, "The only true or definite rule of conduct or standard of morality is the greatest happiness" (Diary (1854), CW XXVII.663).

These and related passages place Mill within familiar utilitarian territory, according to which (ignoring some intramural disputes) actions are morally right insofar as they maximize overall utility, and wrong to the extent that they fail to do so.

But Mill then goes on to make rather different claims, appealing to a second sense of "morality" that is specifically about moral *obligation* or *duty*. He argues that moral duty is defined by those standards of conduct to which competent individuals are appropriately held accountable in any given state of society, even if reasons of expediency or overall utility speak against actually holding someone accountable in a particular case. To fail to fulfill one's moral duties in this sense is to make oneself the appropriate target of blame or punishment:

> No case can be pointed out in which we consider anything as a duty, and any act or omission as immoral or wrong, without regarding the person who commits the wrong and violates the duty as a fit object of punishment... even if there are preponderant reasons of another kind against inflicting the suffering.
> (*James Mill's Analysis of the Phenomena of the Human Mind* [*Analysis*] (1869), CW XXXI.241–2)

> We do not call anything wrong, unless we mean to imply that a person ought to be punished in some way or other for doing it; if not by law, by the opinion of his fellow creatures; if not by opinion, by the reproaches of his own conscience. This seems to be the real turning point of the distinction between morality and simple expediency... *Reasons of prudence, or the interest of other people, may militate against actually exacting it; but the person himself, it is clearly understood, would not be entitled to complain.* There are other things, on the contrary, which we wish that people should do, which we like or admire them for doing, perhaps dislike or despise them for not doing, but yet admit that they are not bound to do; it is not a case of moral obligation; we do not blame them, that is, we do not think that they are proper objects of punishment.
> (*Utilitarianism* (1861), CW X.246; emphasis added)

In these passages, moral wrongness is identified with blameworthiness, that is, with the failure to do that for which the agent is appropriately held accountable. Mill here seems to reject the utilitarian standard of moral wrongness because, surely, one is not always a fit object of blame or punishment for failing to maximize utility. Though some have wondered whether he thereby gives up his utilitarianism or holds two conflicting standards of moral rightness, I believe the difficulty here is merely verbal. We should not get hung up on Mill's use of "moral," but rather accept that he has identified two non-conflicting categories of evaluation that are both always relevant and important to the assessment of any action. In the first category, we evaluate actions according to whether they are expedient or conducive to overall happiness. In the second, we evaluate actions according to whether they meet or exceed the expectations we have of each other (whatever happens to be expedient), which we may enforce against each other through practices of blame or other punishment.[5] This is the standard of social morality, the shared set of normative expectations among competent persons in a given state of society.[6] These shared normative expectations comprise those "acts which the general experience of life... warrant us in counting upon" (*Analysis*, CW XXXI.241) and define our moral duties. For most cases, they are encapsulated by general practical rules.

I want to emphasize three features of making this distinction between expediency on one hand, and social morality or duty or blameworthiness on the other. First, for Mill, the failure to perform an action that maximizes utility need not count as a failure of moral duty. An action might be inexpedient yet still not open someone to censure, given current social expectations. Conversely, one might fail one's moral duty even when one has maximized utility. One might act rashly or otherwise fail to meet social expectations, yet perform the expedient action.[7]

Second, the distinction allows for a domain of supererogatory action in which an individual exceeds shared normative expectations. These actions Mill calls "meritorious," and are part of a "region of positive worthiness" in which "there is an unlimited range of moral worth, up to the most exalted heroism, which should be fostered by every positive encouragement, though not converted into an obligation" (*Auguste Comte and Positivism* (1865), CW X.337, 339).

Third, for Mill, a person's blameworthiness is not a matter of whether it would be *expedient to blame* that person in the particular case. As he indicates in both passages quoted above, a person can be blameworthy even if reasons of expediency or prudence ultimately tell against holding the person accountable. What matters is that the person is a "fit" object of punishment and "would not be entitled to complain" if he or she were held to account.[8] For Mill, our deserving blame or punishment comes down to "our knowledge that punishment will be just: that by such conduct we shall place ourselves in the position in which our fellow creatures, or the Deity, or both, will naturally, and may justly, inflict punishment upon us" (*Hamilton*, CW IX.461). Mill emphasizes that the word "justly" here does not refer directly to what is expedient or *right*, but (as I read him) to the idea that others may *rightfully* decide this matter. It is true that, for Mill, any allocation of rightful authority over certain matters will ultimately be justified by expediency. But with respect to blameworthiness, his point is that others may rightfully judge a member of the community in light of shared normative expectations. Within those limits it is under others' discretion whether to blame or otherwise punish that person. Thus, even if they hold that person accountable when doing so would not be expedient, it remains the case that their holding him or her to account was rightful.

One thought justifying this claim about our rightful authority to hold each other accountable is that any person "must recognise it as not unjust that others should protect themselves against any disposition on his part to infringe their rights" (ibid.). Social morality is constituted in part by the shared standards that define rights and their corresponding obligations, and we are well placed to hold others accountable for violations of our own rights even if we might choose not to do so in certain cases and even if doing so might be inexpedient in certain cases.

In a passage unpublished in his lifetime, Mill makes the point that if there were no need to enforce shared expectations, there would be no need for "morality" in the second sense—of social morality.[9] Writing to Harriet, his future wife and collaborator, and praising her "higher nature," he remarks that:

> If all persons were like these [i.e. had higher natures], or even would be guided by these, morality might be very different from

> what it must now be; *or rather it would not exist at all as morality, since morality and inclination would coincide.* If all resembled you, my lovely friend, it would be idle to prescribe rules for them. By following their own impulses under the guidance of their own judgment, they would find more happiness, and would confer more, than by obeying any moral principles or maxims whatever... Where there exists a genuine and strong desire to do that which is most for the happiness of all, general rules are merely aids to prudence, in the choice of means; not peremptory obligations.
>
> ...All the difficulties of morality in any of its branches, grow out of the conflict which continually arises between the highest morality and even the best popular morality which the degree of development yet attained by average human nature, will allow to exist.
>
> ("On Marriage," CW XXI.39; emphasis added)

Note that in the imagined case, in the absence of practices of blame and punishment, the principle of utility would still provide a standard by which to praise our inclinations and decisions.

The rest of this chapter grapples with those passages in Mill that bear on the need for social morality, how it changes, and its place within his overall ethical theory. I do not claim to provide a complete account of this part of Mill's ethical theory, but I hope to introduce the main features of it and (given the aims of the present volume) highlight a variety of his writings that are not often given their due. Why do we need social morality? Is it, in any interesting sense, independent of the principle of utility? What should I do when social morality conflicts with my understanding of what utility requires? In trying to answer these questions, I hope to show that Mill demonstrates a remarkable sensitivity to the demands of public reason.

3 Private Conflict and a "Common System of Opinions"

We have already noted that the rules of social morality are relative to a given "state of society." This is due in part to the fact that states of society differ in the prevailing beliefs, including moral beliefs, of those living in them:

> What is called a state of society, is the simultaneous state of all the greater social facts or phenomena. Such are, the degree of knowledge, and *of intellectual and moral culture, existing in the community*, and in every class of it; the state of industry, of wealth and its distribution; the habitual occupations of the community; their division into classes, and the relations of those

classes to one another; *the common beliefs which they entertain on all the subjects most important to mankind, and the degree of assurance with which those beliefs are held*; their tastes, and the character and degree of their aesthetic development; their form of government, and the more important of their laws and customs. The condition of all these things, and of many more which will readily suggest themselves, constitute the state of society or the state of civilization at any given time.

(A System of Logic [Logic] (1843),
CW VIII.911–12; emphasis added)

For Mill, then, the rules of social morality vary not only with different economic and political circumstances, but also according to what the people in a given time and place commonly value and believe. This is important because Mill believes that, if society is to exist at all and to persist over time, it requires a widely accepted set of opinions to serve as a public standard.

The problem, as Mill sees it, starts with a Hobbesian state of nature marked by "private conflict" and devoid of the cooperative benefits that social morality and law allow:

> A rude people though in some degree alive to the benefits of civilized society, may be unable to practice the forbearances which it demands: their passions may be too violent, or their personal pride too exacting, to forgo private conflict, and leave to the laws the avenging of their real or supposed wrongs.
>
> (Considerations on Representative
Government [CRG] (1861), CW XIX.377)[10]

In Mill's account of social development, the path to "civilized" society—that is, to a cooperative society within which most individuals are motivated to compromise and to engage in joint endeavors[11]—is uncertain. In fact, again echoing Hobbes, he suspects that cooperative society cannot get a foothold without the help of some external power, such as a powerful despot, to begin to train individuals to work together:

> a people in a state of savage independence, in which every one lives for himself, exempt, unless by fits, from any external control, is practically incapable of making any progress in civilization until it has learnt to obey. The indispensable virtue, therefore, in a government which establishes itself over a people of this sort is, that it make itself obeyed. To enable it to do this, the constitution of the government must be nearly, or quite, despotic.
>
> (Ibid., 394)

Individuals, he suggests, must initially be forced to cooperate in order to overcome "the difficulty of inducing a brave and warlike race to submit their individual *arbitrium* to any common umpire" (*Logic*, CW VIII.921).

Part of the significance of these passages is that Mill seems to accept the basic Hobbesian point that the state of nature is the worst state. Even living under a despot is better, because at the very least it lays the groundwork for future possible improvements ("Civilization," CW XVIII.120). Unlike Hobbes, however, Mill argues that eventually individuals who have developed cooperative tendencies will no longer require a despot to force cooperation. At that point, the despot should make way for democracy and the vision of liberal society defended in *On Liberty* and *The Subjection of Women*. But the need for a public standard or "common umpire" will always remain:

> [S]ocial existence is only possible by a disciplining of those more powerful propensities, which consists in subordinating them to a common system of opinions. The degree of this subordination is the measure of the completeness of the social union, and the nature of the common opinions determines its kind. But in order that mankind should conform their actions to any set of opinions, these opinions must exist, must be believed by them. And thus, the state of the speculative faculties, the character of the propositions assented to by the intellect, essentially determines the moral and political state of the community.
>
> (*Logic*, CW VIII.926)

Without recognized general rules of social morality, we would be left with "perpetual quarrelling" (Letter to Grote (1862), CW XV.762) and the threat of social dissolution: "The people for whom the form of government is intended must be willing to accept it; or at least not so unwilling, as to oppose an insurmountable obstacle to its establishment" (*CRG*, CW XIX.376).[12]

Consistent with significant variations among social moralities and legal institutions in this social development, Mill identifies three general historical requisites for any "society that has maintained a collective existence" (*Logic*, CW VIII.920), each of which concerns the dispositions and beliefs of the people living in those societies. The first requisite he identifies is a "system of education" that, among other things, is able to carry on training each person in "restraining discipline," i.e. "that habit... of subordinating his personal impulses and aims, to what were considered the ends of society" according to some shared or public standard (ibid., 921). It calls for compromise and deference to a common umpire in the form of recognized social or political rules and authorities. This is a negative requisite insofar as it involves mainly *forbearance* on the part of each individual.

The second requisite for social stability is more positive, namely, the existence of some unifying principle or object that grounds a "feeling of allegiance, or loyalty." This may be generated by different things, such as a charismatic leader or national identity. In developed, non-despotic societies Mill hopes that this loyalty could "attach itself to the principles of freedom and political and social equality, as realized in institutions which as yet exist nowhere..." (ibid., 922). This suggestion expresses an idea at the very core of liberalism, that what could unite a people is equal respect for each other's individuality.

The third general requisite for social stability is, he writes, "a principle of sympathy... a feeling of common interest among those who live under the same government" (ibid., 923). This is not the same as the feeling of allegiance to a leader or ideal. It is the feeling of solidarity to *each other*, "that they are one people, that their lot is cast together" (ibid., 923). It supports community and mutual concern, and opposes both invidious distinctions and free-riding. This is what Mill elsewhere seems to mean by "sociality" (Letter to Ward (1859), CW XV.650).

None of these conditions, alone, is sufficient for social stability; remove any of them and the problem of conflicting propensities and judgments re-emerges. But together these conditions allow for the existence of "public authorities" in the form of stable laws or social rules, functioning tribunals, and "an organized force of some sort to execute their decisions" (ibid., 920). Undoubtedly, there will still be disagreements, but these will occur against a backdrop that allows for a stable collective existence grounded in shared feelings, ideals, and procedures.

Not surprisingly, Mill also argues that the development of social morality and legal institutions will require taking account of people's happiness. But the present point is that the three requisites make possible a kind of "fellow-feeling" around a shared set of beliefs and values, which—because of that very fellow-feeling or coming together—constitute the standard by which we may hold others accountable:

> I feel conscious that if I violate certain laws, other people must necessarily or naturally desire that I shd be punished for the violation. I also feel that I shd desire them to be punished if they violated the same laws towards me. From these feelings & from my sociality of nature I place myself in their situation, & sympathize in their desire that I shd be punished; & (even apart from benevolence) the painfulness of not being in union with them makes me shrink from pursuing a line of conduct which would make my ends, wishes, & purposes habitually conflict with theirs.
> (Letter to Ward, CW XV.650)

In his own way, then, Mill introduces some of the basic elements of the public reason tradition: that people each have an interest in submitting their private judgments to a social morality (or other public authority); that a certain discipline of habit and thought is required to maintain that social morality; and that social morality appropriately governs our practices of holding each other accountable.

It will be wondered what Mill would say about a social morality that is not optimal from the utilitarian perspective. Consider a case in which a different a set of normative expectations, if widely accepted, would in fact be more expedient (and are known by some to be so) than the current social morality, taking people as they are. As I understand the picture, Mill is committed to the view that the less optimal social morality, if it is in place, must nevertheless provide the basis for our practices of holding each other accountable. This is because the function of social morality is to solve the problem of private conflict. Without a solution to this problem, there would be no stable society at all. And to solve it, social morality must be publicly accessible and widely shared.[13]

Social morality grants individuals the right to enforce (through practices of blame or punishment) the expectations contained in the common set of opinions. Others may enforce those rules against you (and vice versa), and whether to do so is left to their discretion ultimately because they have a right to self-protection. As noted before, they might err in the sense that exacting a punishment might not be expedient in a given case, but so long as they are enforcing social morality you would not be entitled to complain. Whether punishment is fitting—whether you have done something "wrong" in that sense—is only a matter of whether others may *rightfully* blame or otherwise punish you, given social morality.[14] If the expectations licensing these judgments were not widely shared, they would neither solve private conflict nor maintain social stability.

The reliance on common opinion does not mean, however, that the existing social morality is beyond criticism: "...bad as well as good institutions create moral obligations; but to erect these into a moral argument against changing the institutions, is as bad morality as it is bad reasoning" ("Newman's Political Economy" [*Newman*] (1851), CW V.445). One important theme in Mill's work is that the progressiveness of social morality depends on the availability of some external standard by which to criticize prevailing social morality. Following Bentham, this is one of his main arguments for utilitarianism and against the intuitionism of Whewell and others. Although intuitionists might be able to offer a social morality, they cannot provide a standard—at least not a publicly accessible one—by which to revise social morality: "The contest between the morality which appeals to an external standard, and that which grounds itself on internal conviction, is the contest of progressive morality against stationary—of reason and argument against the deification of mere opinion and habit" ("Whewell on Moral Philosophy" [*Whewell*] (1852), CW X. 179). He argues in similar terms that the feelings associated with social morality, such as guilt and resentment, should be shaped over time by the principle of utility:

> We are as much for conscience, duty, rectitude, as Dr. Whewell. The terms, and all the feelings connected with them, are as much a part of the ethics of utility as of that of intuition. The point in dispute is, what acts are the proper objects of those feelings; whether we ought to take the feelings as we find them, as accident or design has made them, or whether the tendency of actions to promote happiness affords a test to which the feelings of morality should conform.
> (*Whewell*, CW X.172)

In appealing to the principle of utility, then, Mill the reformer advocates for changes to the social morality he shares with others. But he does not believe that blameworthiness—and moral "wrongness" in that sense—can be divorced from social morality. Rather, those judgments must evolve with social morality over time:

> [I]nasmuch as every one, who avails himself of the advantages of society, leads others to expect from him all such positive good offices and disinterested services as the moral improvement attained by mankind has rendered customary, he deserves moral blame if, without just cause, he disappoints that expectation. Through this principle the domain of moral duty, in an improving society, is always widening. *When what once was uncommon virtue becomes common virtue, it comes to be numbered among obligations*, while a degree exceeding what has grown common, remains simply meritorious.
> (*Auguste Comte and Positivism*, CW X.338; emphasis added)

Here is perhaps Mill's clearest statement that moral duty develops over time with changes in shared social expectations. In an "improving society" we can expect more of each other, if we educate our habits and thoughts at the same time that we work to reform our rules and institutions.

Three clarifications are called for before we consider Mill's account of the way we should engage each other within social morality. First, although Mill believes (following Bentham) that one advantage of the principle of utility itself is its public accessibility, he also recognizes that it is controversial. As we shall see, he therefore introduces mid-level principles that he believes can win support not just from those who share his views, but also from anyone who is sensitive to the main lessons of history.

Second, although I have sometimes referred to social morality as a system of rules, the shared normative expectations need not all be captured by rules. For Mill, the rules of social morality are *general* rules not expected to cover every circumstance. Rather, he emphasizes that there are cases in which individuals are rightly held accountable for failing to *violate* a general rule, and the individual "cannot discharge himself from moral responsibility by pleading that he had the general rule in his favor" ("Taylor's Statesman," CW XIX.640):

> What should we say to a physician, who communicated an agonising piece of family intelligence, in reply to the inquiry of our sick friend, at a moment when the slightest aggravation of malady threatened to place him beyond all hope of recovery? In a case like this, surely there is no man of common sense or virtue, who would think for a moment of sheltering himself under the inexorable law of veracity, and refusing to entertain any thought of the irreparable specific mischief on the other side.
>
> (Ibid.)

Some thorny cases involve conflicting general rules, but sometimes they involve only "peculiarities of circumstances" (*Utilitarianism*, CW X.225). In what follows, I will sometimes refer to social morality as a set of rules, but it should be understood that for Mill the rules of social morality might have exceptions that are also part of our shared expectations.

Third, the social rules might themselves express normative expectations that vary for individuals according to differences in position, influence, or capacity:

> There are times when the grandest results for the human race depend on the public assertion of one's convictions at the risk of death by torture. When this is the case martyrdom may be a duty; & in cases when it does not become the duty of all it may be an admirable act of virtue in whoever does it, & a duty in those who as leaders or teachers are bound to set an example of virtue to others, & to do more for the common faith or cause than a simple believer.
>
> (Letter to Young (1867), CW XVI.1328)

The fact of shared normative expectations does not imply that the expectations for each of us are, in all ways, the same. Unfortunately, Mill does not develop this point in detail. In general, then, the moral or social reformer has two projects: first, to propose new general rules of social morality for individuals as they are currently constituted; and second, to help educate individuals to become capable of inhabiting an even better social world.

As we shall see, Mill argues that the first reform project must begin by critically evaluating prevailing social morality. The main practical consideration is not where we start, but whether we have the means to progress from where we are. Above all, Mill argues, in a civilized society, the social conditions allowing for criticism and learning through experience must be protected against interference: "the source of everything respectable in man either as an intellectual or as a moral being," he writes, "[is] that his errors are corrigible. He is capable of rectifying his mistakes, by discussion and experience" (*On Liberty* (1859), CW XVIII.231). Because revising our beliefs is "predominant, and almost paramount, among the agents of social progression," Mill concludes that "the order of human progression in all respects will mainly depend on the order of progression in the intellectual convictions of mankind" (*Logic*, CW VIII.926, 927). Ensuring the conditions for moral improvement through "discussion and experience" thus becomes the leading theme of his moral and political philosophy, and shapes his account of the practice of public reason.

4 The Practice of Public Reason

So far, then, we have seen that Mill regards social morality as more than a merely sociological or descriptive phenomenon. Social morality must govern much of our moral decision-making, specifically our holding each other accountable. Mill accepts a version of the practical problem that animates the public reason tradition, the problem of conflicting private judgments, and the corresponding need to establish a publicly justified standard or procedure by which to regulate our social and political lives together.

But how are we supposed to accommodate disagreement about what social morality should be, and how can we revise social morality, while maintaining its integrity? This is the question of the practice of public reason, in which social morality is an ongoing construction project for a community.[15] It is particularly important for Mill because he argues that we are never justified in believing that our current social morality—even if it is unanimously accepted—is the best it could be.[16]

As I suggested at the end of the last section, Mill's approach to the practice of public reason begins with the observation that at any given time and place there are certain "received opinions."[17] These, he seems to say, must be our starting points. But what emerges from his discussion of public reasoning is that he is less concerned with the specific content of prevailing beliefs than he is with preserving the conditions necessary for the effective criticism of those beliefs. Unlike some public reason views, for Mill it is not problematic in itself that the prevailing beliefs are controversial, so long as they can be, and are, sincerely held open to revision.[18] The continued openness to discussion and social experimentation is what keeps social morality and legal institutions within reason—what makes them reasonable—on Mill's view. Call this Mill's *legitimacy constraint*. A prevailing social morality violates that constraint by removing itself from those processes of public reasoning that might lead it is own revision.[19] This is why he criticizes the French Assembly in 1848 for placing restrictions on the press.

> It denies them free discussion. It says they shall not be suffered to bring their opinions to the touchstone of the public reason and conscience. It refuses them the chance which every sincere opinion can justly claim, of triumphing in a fair field. It fights them with weapons which can as easily be used to put down the most valuable truth as the most pernicious error.
> ("The French Law Against the Press" (1848), CW XXV.1118)

A good government, then, puts freedom of discussion first: "In government, perfect freedom of discussion in all its modes—speaking, writing, and printing—in law and in fact is the first requisite of good because the first condition of popular intelligence and mental progress. All else is secondary" (Diary (1854), CW XXVII.661). A prevailing morality might be controversial in many ways, but it is not illegitimate as long as it is sincerely held open to the processes of criticism and social experimentation that could lead to its improvement.

In full view, Mill's defense of the legitimacy constraint is grounded in his account of what is required for social improvement, and our never being in a position to say *here progress ends*.[20] As early as the age of eighteen, he criticizes the *Edinburgh Review* for seeming to argue

> that morality will never be better understood than at present; that morality will never be better practised than at present; that mankind will never be more prudent than they now are; that vigour of intellect and sound views of human affairs are oftener found and better listened to at this moment, than they are likely to be at any future period.
> ("Periodical Literature: Edinburgh Review" (1824), CW I.318)

This constant refrain in his work culminates in his "assumption of infallibility" argument in *On Liberty* and the claim that the power to silence discussion is "illegitimate": "The best government has no more title to it than the worst" (CW XVIII.229). Mill argues that, to the extent that a government undermines free discussion, it removes itself from the means of criticism and intellectual improvement that allow for its own future decision-making to improve. Insofar as it does this, it takes up a position of epistemic superiority toward posterity which it is not entitled to adopt—as if its decisions could not be improved upon (Turner 2013a). In a characteristic passage, he concludes:

> Until... somebody else can point out any existing state of society which it is desirable to have stereotyped for perpetual use, we must regard as an evil, all restraint put upon the spirit which never yet since society existed has been in excess—that which bids us "try all things" as the only means by which with knowledge and assurance we can "hold fast to that which is good."
> (*Newman*, CW V.457; but see 454–7)

As individuals, then, our participation in the practice of public reason is exhibited fundamentally by our ongoing support for the social conditions required for free, critical discussion and associated experiments of living on a fair field of play. Call this Mill's *basic norm of public reason*. The practice of public reason is one in which we may propose any idea we like so long as it remains open to criticism, and collectively we may adopt any new set of institutions so long as they are consistent with, and responsive to, the ongoing critical enterprise. The core public reason commitment is just to maintaining those (liberal) practices and institutions that facilitate that enterprise. In this way, social and political arrangements are made consistent with the possibility of progress, and ensure that any future "permanence" in those arrangements "will be the effect of reason and free choice, not of irrevocable engagements" (ibid., 456).[21]

Undoubtedly, we will need formal mechanisms for settling disputes, and in *Considerations on Representative Government* and related writings Mill designs a set of democratic institutions to do just that. But the crucial thing for our purposes is understanding that those institutional designs must be consistent with his underlying commitment to preserving the conditions that allow for public criticism, reasoned decision-making, and progress.

What the basic norm of public reason entails in practice for particular individuals is expressed nicely by some of Mill's writings on education, particularly those concerning the spirit in which a teacher should present controversial material and the intellectual discipline that should then shape the classroom discussion. In these passages, he emphasizes that controversial views are not problematic as long as the material is taught in a way that is meant to engage and develop students' critical capacities:

> It is true mankind differ widely on religion; so widely that [it] is impossible for them to agree in recommending any set of opinions. But they also differ on moral philosophy, metaphysics, politics, political economy, and even medicine; all of which are

admitted to be as proper subjects as any others for a national course of instruction. The falsest ideas have been, and still are, prevalent on these subjects, as well as on religion. But it is the portion of us all, to imbibe the received opinions first, and start from these to acquire better ones. All that is necessary to render religion as unexceptionable a subject of national teaching as any of the other subjects which we have enumerated, is, that it should be taught in the manner in which all rational persons are agreed that every other subject should be taught—in an inquiring, not a dogmatic spirit—so as to call forth, not so as to supersede, the freedom of the individual mind. We should most strongly object to giving instruction on any disputed subject, in schools or universities, if it were done by inculcating any particular set of opinions.

...Let the teaching be in this spirit, and it scarcely matters what are the opinions of the teacher: and it is for their capacity to teach thus, and not for the opinions they hold, that teachers ought to be chosen.

("Lord Brougham's Defence of the Church Establishment," CW VI.228)

The principle itself of dogmatic religion, dogmatic morality, dogmatic philosophy, is what requires to be rooted out; not any particular manifestation of that principle.

...the object is to call forth the greatest possible quantity of intellectual power, and to inspire the intensest love of truth: and this without a particle of regard to the results to which the exercise of that power may lead, even though it should conduct the pupil to opinions diametrically opposite to those of his teachers. We say this, not because we think opinions unimportant, but because of the immense importance which we attach to them...

...We are not so absurd as to propose that the teacher should not set forth his own opinions as the true ones, and exert his utmost powers to exhibit their truth in the strongest light... As a general rule, the most distinguished teacher is selected, whatever be his particular views, and he consequently teaches in the spirit of free inquiry, not of dogmatic imposition.

("Civilization," CW XVIII.144)

In *On Liberty* and other writings, Mill goes on to articulate a "real morality of public discussion," emphasizing candor, openness, and "giving merited honour to every one, whatever opinion he may hold" (*On Liberty*, CW XVIII.259), while condemning intolerance, exaggeration, "casuistry and imposture," and "hypocrisy" ("Perfectibility" (1828), CW XXVI.433). If we could imagine a community of public reasoners engaging each other in this spirit—each with their own beliefs and values, but also fundamentally committed to the practice of free inquiry—we would go a long way toward appreciating his vision of how social morality might improve over time without undermining (and perhaps reinforcing) the requisites of social stability addressed above.

5 Justifying Interference

To this point, I have tried to show, first, that Mill solves a version of the problem of private conflict by appealing to the idea of social morality, and that he introduces a legitimacy constraint and basic norm of public reason that are justified by the need to revise social morality over time. In this section I want to examine three practical principles that Mill argues should enjoy public support and shape revisions to social morality: the presumption in favor of individual liberty, the presumption in favor of equality, and the liberty principle.[22] Consistent with his own utilitarian commitments, but not dependent on them, he recommends these principles to the public conscience as the fruits of common human experience.

If in the last section we glimpsed how Mill handles controversy within public reason, here the question is the extent to which people can come to agree on certain principles. In an early essay, Mill is very optimistic that there could be significant convergence on social rules, despite foundational differences:

> The grand consideration is, not what any person regards as the ultimate end of human conduct, but through what intermediate ends he holds that his ultimate end is attainable, and should be pursued: and in these there is a nearer agreement between some who differ, than between some who agree, in their conception of the ultimate end. When disputes arise as to any of the secondary maxims, they can be decided, it is true, only by an appeal to first principles; but the necessity of this appeal may be avoided far oftener than is commonly believed; it is surprising how few, in comparison, of the disputed questions of practical morals, require for their determination any premises but such as are common to all philosophic sects.
> ("Blakey's History of Moral Science"
> (1833) CW X.29)

We might wonder what overlap of "intermediate ends" Mill has in mind—what are the "secondary maxims" that allow for a relatively stable social morality? Obvious candidates include general rules such as those against taking innocent life and arbitrary violence, or in favor of truth-telling and tending to the sick. Surely such widely accepted rules would be part of any social morality. But Mill also spent much of his career addressing issues on which there was vigorous disagreement, including (just to name some of his preoccupations) women's rights, slavery, domestic violence, free trade, and population control, some of which promised to cause significant social strife.

In the rest of this section, I argue that Mill introduces three main public principles to help us navigate disagreement. This is not to ignore Mill's own utilitarian arguments for various practical conclusions, but to highlight the principles he thought could help us find common ground. Two of them are stated in the following passage:

> The *à priori* presumption is in favour of freedom and impartiality. It is held that there should be no restraint not required by the general good, and that the law should be no respecter of persons, but should treat all alike, save where dissimilarity of treatment is required by positive reasons, either of justice or of policy.
> (*The Subjection of Women* [*Subjection*] (1869), CW XXI.262)

The first principle expressed here, the "presumption in favor of liberty,"[23] is a general "non-interference" principle according to which "the onus of making out a case always lies on the defenders of legal prohibitions" (*Principles of Political Economy* [*Principles*] (1848), CW III.936, 938). In the context of free discussion and social experimentation, the presumption in favor of liberty can help us choose among candidate social rules and legal arrangements. It is justified, he argues, by at least two widely accepted considerations. First, the freedom to live one's life as one sees fit—at least in many respects—is a good felt by most or all individuals: "He who would rightly appreciate the worth of personal independence as an element of happiness, should consider the value he himself puts upon it as an ingredient of his own" (*Subjection*, CW XXI.336–7). Whether a utilitarian or not, our commonly felt irritation at being interfered with reveals that we all care about preserving a range of personal freedom. Second, Mill believes history has shown that leaving activities to the voluntary action of individuals usually leads to better outcomes than placing them under the control of government or social authority: "… freedom of individual choice is now known to be the only thing which procures the adoption of the best processes, and throws each operation into the hands of those who are best qualified for it" (ibid., 273). Mill's own social and political conclusions show that the presumption in favor of liberty can be overcome in a great many cases, but he considers it an important guidepost in considering revisions to social morality.

An important extension of the presumption in favor of liberty is Mill's claim that coercive (what he calls "authoritative") interference requires more justification than non-coercive interference. The upshot of this extension is that social authority should be aware of when a non-coercive measure—one that merely provides us options or encourages us to do something—would obviate the need for an authoritative measure that constrains our options: "When a government provides means for fulfilling a certain end, leaving individuals free to avail themselves of different means if in their opinion preferable, there is no infringement of liberty, no irksome or degrading restraint. One of the principal objections to government interference is then absent" (*Principles*, CW III.938–9). The hope is that non-coercive measures could be widely accepted as a path toward social reform, even if the content of those reforms is otherwise controversial. Recently, this has been revived and developed as a public principle in the libertarian paternalism of Thaler and Sunstein (2008), which seeks to "nudge" us, instead of coerce us, to make better choices for ourselves.

The second public principle expressed in the above passage is the presumption in favor of equality. What Mill calls "impartiality" is the principle that social morality and the law should not make distinctions among persons except where there is good reason for it. This is a central theme, for instance, in his rejection of women's inequality:

> the course of history, and the tendencies of progressive human society, afford not only no presumption in favour of this system of inequality of rights, but a strong one against it; and that, so far as the whole course of human improvement up to the time, the whole stream of modern tendencies, warrants any inference on the subject, it is, that this relic of the past is discordant with the future, and must necessarily disappear.
>
> (*Subjection*, CW XXI.272)

The new default for all groups, Mill argues, should be a presumption of equality—it is inequalities that require justification. He is aware of the motivated reasoning keeping certain prejudices in place, but he argues that as social morality has developed, and whatever concrete rules we might endorse concerning particular matters, it has increasingly been understood to embody respect among equals:

> [C]ommand and obedience are but unfortunate necessities of human life: society in equality is its normal state. Already in modern life, and more and more as it progressively improves, command and obedience become exceptional facts in life, equal association its general rule. The morality of the first ages rested

on the obligation to submit to power; that of the ages next following, on the right of the weak to the forbearance and protection of the strong. How much longer is one form of society and life to content itself with the morality made for another? We have had the morality of submission, and the morality of chivalry and generosity; the time is now come for the morality of justice. Whenever, in former ages, any approach has been made to society in equality, Justice has asserted its claims as the foundation of virtue.
(*Subjection*, CW XXI.293–4)

In his clearest expression of an ideal of social morality—though, again, consistent with varying social rules—Mill argues that complete equality offers something of an end-point:

[T]he true virtue of human beings is fitness to live together as equals; claiming nothing for themselves but what they as freely concede to every one else; regarding command of any kind as an exceptional necessity, and in all cases a temporary one; and preferring, whenever possible, the society of those with whom leading and following can be alternate and reciprocal.
(*Subjection*, CW XXI.294)

At the very least, Mill rejects authoritarian arrangements and inequalities based on race, ethnicity, religion, and gender, and he calls instead for respect for each other as free and equal citizens, in a way that is characteristic of the public reason tradition. He suggests a picture of holding each other accountable that respects the logic of reciprocity. Educating a community capable of sustaining a social morality in this way would be a great achievement.

Mill's third public principle, the most famous of them, is the liberty principle (aka the harm principle). It introduces a strict anti-paternalism constraint on "authoritative" interference with competent individuals, according to which "the only purpose for which power can be rightfully exercised over any member of a civilized community, against his will, is to prevent harm to others" (*On Liberty*, CW XVIII.223). While the presumption in favor of liberty is quite broad and defeasible, the liberty principle is much narrower and absolute. Properly understood, it does not make a claim about when social interference is justified, but about the scope of society's rightful authority: coercive interference may not even be considered by some social or governmental authority except to protect others from harm. To the extent that the actions of competent adults concern only themselves, they are "sovereign" and should be left free from authoritative interference.

The justification of this principle is disputed territory, but I think it is important to see that Mill offers it up, at least in part, as a principle of public reason to help direct our revision of social morality in other respects. Gaus has argued that Mill's strategy to justify this and other liberal principles is to appeal to a "wide array of citizens' beliefs and values" (2008, 84; see also Rawls 2007, 284–91). My view is that the liberty principle is justified primarily by a shared interest in competent decision-making, and by evidence that individuals are the best judges of their own good (Turner 2013b). However it is justified, the liberty principle has been an incredibly influential public principle, shaping our notions of the appropriate limits of government and social interference with personal choices—including, most notably, sexual morality.

Each of these three principles plays a significant part in Mill's thinking, yet accepting them does not require taking up the utilitarian perspective. Rather, they demonstrate the extent to which he believes that we can collectively learn from experience and adopt principles to help us fashion an ever-improving social morality that maintains its integrity over time, despite ongoing disagreement on concrete matters.

6 Conclusion: The Connection to Utility

I have tried to show that Mill recognizes both the problem of private conflict and the need for social morality to solve it, that he articulates a practice of public reason to revise social morality over time, and that he introduces certain public principles that he believes can enjoy broad public support to shape that process. Despite this, Mill's basic commitments undoubtedly remain utilitarian. Social morality may define our moral obligations, but he also writes of "moral obligation, which in itself, and independently of the purposes for which it exists, cannot be accounted a good" (*Newman*, CW V.455). In this last section, then, I want to sketch how Mill's commitment to social morality fits within his utilitarianism and, in particular, what sort of independence it has as a guide for individual moral agents.

Although Mill rejects rule utilitarianism (or so I have argued in Turner 2015a), his account of social morality shares with it the thought that a practice could be justified on utilitarian grounds and that subsequent decisions *within* that practice should then generally proceed without direct reference to the principle of utility (see Rawls 1955). Unlike the rule utilitarian, Mill expects us to appeal directly to utility in exceptional cases.[24] But he argues that our commitment to social morality—to abiding by a shared set of normative expectations—is itself justified by the principle of utility and that the integrity of social morality over time requires us to form a habit of deference, a sense of allegiance, and fellow-feeling. Moreover, because he believes that the state of nature is the worst state, keeping our commitment to social morality outweighs most any other utilitarian consideration. This is, I think, the significance of the following passage:

> Scarcely any degree of utility, short of absolute necessity, will justify a prohibitory regulation, unless it can also be made to recommend itself to the general conscience; unless persons of ordinary good intentions either believe already, or can be induced to believe, that the thing prohibited is a thing which they ought not to wish to do.
>
> (*Principles*, CW III.938)

New coercive measures that risk social unrest, and so the dissolution of social morality, can be justified only in extreme circumstances. The effect of this is to give great weight to maintaining our shared normative expectations. It means generally following the rules widely recognized in society, and being aware of when an exception to those rules would also be expected. In some cases, violating a social expectation might be justified—but it is important that doing so would not threaten the general practice of conforming to social morality. Certainly, at least in the great majority of circumstances, it entails a rejection of revolutionary attempts at reform. Thus, despite endorsing socialist ideas, Mill strongly objects to the "revolutionary Socialists" of the nineteenth century:

> [T]hose who would play this game on the strength of their own private opinion, unconfirmed as yet by any experimental verification—who would forcibly deprive all who have now a comfortable physical existence of their only present means of preserving it, and would brave the frightful bloodshed and misery that would ensue if the attempt was resisted—must have a serene confidence in their own wisdom on the one hand and a recklessness of other people's sufferings on the other.
>
> (*Chapters on Socialism*, CW V.737)

One way to consider the place of social morality in Mill's overall ethical theory is to think of his utilitarianism being applied stepwise. In the first step, it justifies the move from the state of nature to a state of society. And because it is hard to imagine that a return to the state of nature could be justified, Mill's basic commitment to utility is expressed practically by our support for the social morality that keeps us out of the state of nature. We might accept *some* risk of return, but Mill argues that the consequences of that would be so dire that we normally do better keeping to social morality and to piecemeal reform efforts through the practice of public reason.

In the second step, then, Mill's commitment to utility is extended as a practical matter to the basic norm of public reason required for the rational revision of social morality. This is part of the force of his claim in *On Liberty* that "I regard utility as the ultimate appeal on all ethical questions: but it must be utility in the largest sense, grounded on the permanent interests of man as a progressive being" (CW VIII.224). Mill does not have in mind a fully formed, ideal social morality that would allow us to reverse engineer social reforms. We can concentrate our attention on "the *immediate* impediment to progress" (*CRG*, CW XIX.396; emphasis added), but beyond that the key objective is to defend the free discussion and social experimentation that alone give us hope of learning from experience and the assurance that future changes to social morality will constitute improvements.

It bears repeating that, at any given point in time, social morality is unlikely to be optimal from the perspective of any particular person. But it provides what Gaus calls a "moral constitution"—a public standard that each of us has sufficient reason to endorse even though, like our legal constitution, it is "not to be equated with any specific moral perspective, with its particular understanding of values, rightness, and the morally relevant nature of the social world" (Gaus 2016, 179). On the view I have been defending, Mill accepts this basic picture and then emphasizes that the moral constitution, like a legal constitution, must allow for its own revision through free discussion and social experimentation. This latter thought animates his vision of the practice of public reason.[25]

Notes

1 Associate Professor of Philosophy and (by courtesy) Political Science, Ohio State University.
2 Peter Railton (1984) introduced the label "sophisticated" for consequentialist moral theories that distinguish between the standard of correctness and the appropriate decision procedure for human conduct.
3 For elaboration of this point, see Turner (2015a), 728ff.
4 See his discussion in "Taylor's Statesman" (1837), CW XIX.640, co-authored with George Grote. Mill citations marked by "CW [volume #.page #]" refer to the *Collected Works*.
5 Peter Railton (1988, 2005) makes a similar distinction between what is expedient and what social morality requires, and similarly argues that both categories of evaluation are always applicable. For Railton, the fundamental level of evaluation for acts, practices or institutions is their contribution to the overall good, which he calls *fortunateness* instead of expediency. He then introduces another standard:

> The concept of "moral rightness" comes to the consequentialist already well-embedded in our moral thought and practice. If "morally right" meant "optimal from a moral point of view," "morally wrong" would naturally be "less than optimal from a moral point of view". But moral wrongness goes with notions of blameworthiness, condemnation,

resentment, and guilt, and we do not typically dispense these for mere suboptimality.

(2005, 495)

This standard, of social morality, is relative to social expectations in a given place and time.

6 For the articulation and defense of social morality as shared normative expectations, see Gaus (2011, 2015, 2016).
7 For discussion of these points, see Turner (2015a).
8 To my mind, Mill's clarification that a person may be a fit object of punishment "even if there are preponderant reasons of another kind against inflicting the suffering" tells decisively against the indirect "sanction utilitarianism" reading of his account of the rightness of actions. Mill gives us two direct standards.
9 My reading does not depend on this passage. But, following Robson, who included this piece in the *Collected Works*, I believe we can treat it as providing some clue to Mill's thinking, when viewed in light of other evidence.
10 For Mill's Hobbesian moments: "Civilization" (1836), CW XVIII.117–47; *Chapters on Socialism* (1879), CW V.749; and "Use and Abuse of Political Terms" (1832), CW XVIII.10–11.
11 A "civilized" society is marked by: (1) "a dense population, therefore, dwelling in fixed habitations," (2) "agriculture, commerce, and manufactures," (3) "human beings acting together for common purposes in large bodies, and enjoying the pleasures of social intercourse," and (4) "the arrangements of society, for protecting the persons and property of its members, are sufficiently perfect... to induce the bulk of the community to rely for their security mainly upon social arrangements" ("Civilization," CW XVIII.120).
12 In some passages, Mill speaks directly to the need for social morality, and in others he speaks to the need for law or government. For our purposes, I am glossing over that distinction because he distinguishes them mainly in the *means* they employ and not in their basic justification. This, one might note, is true also of Mill's liberty principle, which applies to both government and social authority, and concerns both "legal penalties" and "the moral coercion of public opinion" (CW VIII.223). I, here, leave aside the question of which social expectations should be enforced through formal mechanisms and which not.
13 I will address this issue at greater length in the final section.
14 There will of course be disagreements about the content of social morality, its interpretation, and about the efficiency of each of us enforcing it and what enforcement measures are justified. These problems give us reason to introduce systems of adjudication and enforcement associated with what H.L.A. Hart called "secondary rules."
15 For a partly Mill-inspired approach to morality along these lines, see Kitcher (2011).
16 This is the basic point of his "assumption of infallibility" argument in chapter 2 of *On Liberty*.
17 See extended quotation later in this section from "Lord Brougham's Defence of the Church Establishment" (1834), CW VI.228.
18 See Eric MacGilvray (2004) for development of this important thought.
19 This might happen in more or less significant ways. But to become separated from those processes is to make the prevailing social morality a matter simply of the preferences of the dominant group. This will undermine its tendency

toward improvement and, relatedly, its claim to offer a fair field of play to those who disagree.
20 For examples, see Turner (2013a, section 3).
21 Gaus has claimed that Mill's "master argument" in *On Liberty* is the broadly social epistemic argument for open society that helps to justify what I call his legitimacy constraint and his basic norm of public reason. Gaus argues that, despite differences in values and beliefs, openness to discussion and social experimentation is a value shared "among all citizens who think that some ways of living are better, that we have an interest in finding out which they are, and that we can have justified beliefs about what they are" (Gaus 2008, 100; see also Turner 2017, 576–9). After Mill, perhaps the most prominent versions of this argument are in Dewey (1927, 1939) and Popper (1945, 2008).
22 My discussion in this section is indebted to Gaus (2008).
23 See Gaus (2008, 91–2).
24 For example, "Thornton on Labour and its Claims" (1869), CW V.659. For other relevant passages, see Turner (2015a).
25 For discussion of earlier versions of these ideas, I am especially grateful to Gerald Gaus, Eric MacGilvray, Christopher Macleod, Dale Miller, Amanda Greene, David Estlund and Scott Harkema. It benefited from criticism from graduate students in my seminar at Ohio State on Mill's moral and political philosophy, as well as from audiences at the 14th Conference of the International Society for Utilitarian Studies, at Lille Catholic University, and the Dubrovnik Analytic Philosophy Conference on "Beyond Contractarianism?" at the Dubrovnik Inter-University Center.

Bibliography

Dewey, John. 1927. *The Public and Its Problems*. New York: Henry Holt and Company.

———. 1939. "Science and Free Culture." In *The Political Writings*, edited by Debra Morris and Ian Shapiro, 48–58. Indianapolis: Hackett Publishing.

Gaus, Gerald F. 2008. "State Neutrality and Controversial Values in On Liberty." In *Mill's On Liberty: A Critical Guide*, edited by C.L. Ten, 83–104. Cambridge: Cambridge University Press.

———. 2011. *The Order of Public Reason: A Theory of Freedom and Morality in a Diverse and Bounded World*. Cambridge, MA: Cambridge University Press.

———. 2015. "On Being Inside Social Morality and Seeing It." *Criminal Law and Philosophy* 9: 141–53.

———. 2016. *The Tyranny of the Ideal: Justice in a Diverse Society*. Princeton, NJ: Princeton University Press.

Kitcher, Philip. 2011. *The Ethical Project*. Cambridge, MA: Harvard University Press.

MacGilvray, Eric. 2004. *Reconstructing Public Reason*. Cambridge, MA: Harvard University Press.

Mill, John Stuart. *The Collected Works of John Stuart Mill*. Edited by J.M. Robson. 33 vols. Toronto: University of Toronto Press; London: Routledge and Kegan Paul, 1963–1991.

Popper, Karl. 1945. *The Open Society and Its Enemies*. Princeton, NJ: Princeton University Press.

———. 2008. *After* The Open Society: *Selected Social and Political Writings*. Edited by Jeremy Shearmur and Piers Norris Turner. New York: Routledge Press.
Railton, Peter. 1984. "Alienation, Consequentialism, and the Demands of Morality." *Philosophy & Public Affairs* 13: 134–71.
———. 1988. "How Thinking about Character and Utilitarianism Might Lead to Rethinking the Character of Utilitarianism." *Midwest Studies in Philosophy* 13: 398–416.
———. 2005. "Reply to Ben Eggleston." *Philosophical Studies* 126: 491–9.
Rawls, John. 1955. "Two Concepts of Rules." *The Philosophical Review* 64: 3–32.
———. 2005. *Political Liberalism*, Expanded Edition. New York: Columbia University Press.
———. 2007. *Lectures on the History of Political Philosophy*. Cambridge, MA: Harvard University Press.
Thaler, Richard H., and Cass R. Sunstein. 2008. *Nudge: Improving Decisions about Health, Wealth, and Happiness*. New Haven, CT: Yale University Press.
Turner, Piers Norris. 2013a. "Authority, Progress, and the 'Assumption of Infallibility' in On Liberty." *Journal of the History of Philosophy* 51: 93–117.
———. 2013b. "The Absolutism Problem in *On Liberty*." *Canadian Journal of Philosophy* 43: 322–40.
———. 2015a. "Rules and Right in Mill." *Journal of the History of Philosophy* 53: 723–45.
———. 2015b. "Punishment and Discretion in Mill's *Utilitarianism*." *Utilitas* 27: 165–78.
———. 2017. "Mill and Modern Liberalism." In *A Companion to Mill*, edited by Christopher Macleod and Dale Miller, 567–81. Malden, MA: Wiley-Blackwell.

INDEX

Abel (biblical) 121
Abraham (biblical) 13, 121
Achenwall, G. 266
Adam (biblical) 65, 73, 75, 115–16, 119, 136, 203
Alexander (the Great) 50
Apollos 79
Aquinas, Thomas 105n26
Aristippus 176
Aristotle 28, 32–3, 43, 78, 202–3, 245n17, 331
Arneson, Richard 263n9
Augustus 245n16
Austin, J. 373n21

Baal 237
Balboa, Nunez 212
Barbeyrac 215
Baron, Marcia 326n22
Bayle, P. 239
Beck, Lewis White 278–81
Bentham, Jeremy 2, 4–5, 354–74
Bertram, Christopher 3, 4, 248–63
Black Elk 347n2
Blackstone, William 360
Blakey, R. 391
Bodin, J. 197, 243n4
Brougham, Lord Henry 390, 398n17
Brutus, Marcus 321
Byrd, Sharon 285

Cain (biblical) 111, 121
Caligula (Emperor) 202, 222, 236
Calvin, J. 244n13
Catiline 246n26
Cato the Elder 128, 243n3
Cato the Younger 243n3, 246n26
Cephas 79; *see also* Peter, St

Chambers, Simone 181n2, 182n13, 183n20
Chamos 237
Christ *see* Jesus Christ
Chronos 236
Cicero 43, 76, 246n26
Cohen, Joshua 263n14
Cohon, Rachel 326n22
Coke, Sir Edward 24, 48
Comte, August 385
Condorcet (Marquis) 263n10
Confucius 176
Cromartie, Alan 373n12
Cromwell 232
Curley, Edwin 83n1
Curren, Randall 331

d'Alembert, M. 243n4, 250
Daniel (biblical) 179
d'Argenson (Marquis) 243n1, 244n7, 246n25
Darwall, Stephen 326n24
David (biblical) 42, 65, 116
Davidson, Jenny 331
de Beaufort (Duc) 232
de Carriès (Father) 246n21
DeCew, Judith 324n5
de la Vega, Garcilasso 112
Dent, N.J.H. 262n6
Devas, Charles 343
Dewey, John 342, 399n21
Diderot, D. 250–1, 262n7

Einstein, Albert 332
Elizabeth I, queen of England 79
Empiricus, Sextus 334
Epstein, Klaus 348n10
Esau (biblical) 121

INDEX

Eurydice 337
Euthyphro 338

Ferguson, Adam 343
Fichte, J.G. 348n9
Fletcher, George 330
Fox, John 179
Fralin, Richard 263n14

Gardner, John 367, 373n25
Garrett, Don 326n24
Gaus, Gerald 1–5, 3, 4, 163–83, 282, 296, 324n5, 375, 395, 397, 398n6, 399n21–399n23
Gauthier, David 326n23
George, William Henry 342
George I, king of England 215
Gewirth, Alan 289
Glaucon 304
God 11, 12–14, 20–4, 35, 41–2, 53, 57, 59–60, 62–80, 86, 95, 97–101, 103, 105n20, 106n42, 106n46, 107n50, 109–12, 115–19, 133–4, 137, 142, 147, 148n2, 151, 153–6, 158–60, 162, 171, 174–5, 177, 180, 186, 203, 205, 220, 236–7, 239–41, 244n14, 261
Green, Thomas F. 332, 336
Green, Thomas Hill 342
Grote, George 382, 397n4
Grotius, Hugo 202, 204–7, 215, 243n1, 246n24

Haackonssen, Knud 348n8
Hale, Matthew 373n22
Hampton, Jean 3, 182n9
Hart, H.L.A. 373n21, 398n14
Hastie, William 267–77, 270n1, 275n1
Hegel, G.W.F. 2, 4–5, 330–48
Heiman, G. 344
Herman, Barbara 332, 336, 348n13
Hill, Thomas 297
Hobbes, Thomas 1–4, 9–69, 84–107, 163, 178, 202, 238, 304, 319, 322, 336, 338, 361–4, 366, 369, 373n12–373n13, 381–2, 398n10
Homer (Poet) 237
Hooker, Richard 112, 148n2–148n3
Houlgate, Stephen 339
Hoy, Jocelyn B. 345
Hruschka, Joachim 285

Humboldt, Willhelm 335, 348n5
Hume, David 2, 4, 294, 303–28, 339

James II, king of England 215
Jephthah (biblical) 115, 237, 246n21
Jeroboam (biblical) 72
Jesus Christ (Saviour) 65, 70, 73–6, 78–9, 85, 99, 103–4, 150–2, 176–7, 179, 238
Job (biblical) 65
Julius Cæsar 245n16, 246n26
Jupiter 22, 24, 143, 237

Kant, Immanuel 1, 3–4, 163, 264–70, 267–97, 333, 335, 337–41, 344, 347n3, 348n7–348n9
Keynes, John Neville 343, 345
Kitcher, Philip 398n15
Korsgaard, Christine 289

Langton, Rae 289
Larmore, C. 375
Levinson, Sanford 330
Lieberman, David 373n28
Lincoln, Abraham 330
Lloyd, S. A. 2, 4, 83n1, 84–107
Locke, John 1, 2–4, 87, 107n51, 108–62, 148n4, 163–83
Lot (biblical) 121
Louis IX, king of France 205
Louis XIII, king of France 215
Lycurgus 216, 223, 244n11

MacGilvray, Eric 398n18
Machiavelli, N. 244n8, 244n14–244n15, 245n16
Mahomet 238
Marini, Frank 263n12
Marmor, Andrei 373n14
Matthiessen, Peter 347n2
McDonald, Forrest 331
Micaiah (biblical) 72
Mill, Harriet Taylor 379–80
Mill, John Stuart 2, 4–5, 105n15, 375–99
Milner, Rev. John 179, 183n23
Molesworth, William 373n17
Moloch 236
Montesquieu 200, 223, 235, 244n12, 343
Moses (biblical) 13, 73–4, 99, 237
Murphy, Liam 346

402

INDEX

Naaman (biblical) 75
Nagel, Thomas 289, 346
Nepos, Cornelius 245n17
Neuhouser, Frederick 262n6
Noah (biblical) 115, 119, 203
Nozick, Robert 181n3, 182n5, 182n7
Numa 216
Nussbaum, Martha 331

O'Neill, Onora 286, 288, 295, 335
Ostwald, M. 333
Otho 233

Paul, St 75, 79
Pericles 331
Peter, St (Cephas) 75, 77, 79, 150
Philo 202
Plato 69–70, 188, 200, 222, 338
Plutarch 243n2
Pogge, Thomas 288
Popilius Laenas, Gaius 243n3
Popper, Karl 399n21
Postema, Gerald 5, 324n5, 327n39, 354–74
Pufendorf, Samuel 195, 288

Quinn, M. 372n2
Quong, Jonathan 287

Rabelais, F. 204
Railton, Peter 397n2
Rawls, John 1, 173–8, 180, 182n9, 182n12, 248, 249, 253, 262, 263n16, 282, 283, 304, 324n5, 375, 395
Ripstein, Arthur 285
Robson, J.M. 398n9
Rogers, James E. 181n1
Rousseau, Jean-Jacques 1, 3–4, 163, 184–200, 248–63, 304, 333, 336, 338, 344
Russell, Paul 326n19

Saturn 24, 203, 236
Saviour *see* Jesus Christ (Saviour)
Sayre-McCord, Geoffrey 4, 303–28
Schofield, Philip 356, 372n7
Schultz, Walter 343
Sensen, Oliver 3, 4, 270n1, 282–97
Servius 216

Shapiro, Ian 324n5
Sidgwick, Henry 343
Silverthorne, Michael 373n12
Simmons, A. John 182n6
Singer, Marcus G. 348n13
Snellman, Johan Vilhelm 343, 348n11
Socrates 338
Solon 216
Sophocles 331, 333, 337
Stewart, Jon 347n3
Sulla 245n16

Tacitus 233, 244n15
Taylor, Michael 258, 263n13
Tetens, Johann N. 340, 348n7
Themistocles 331
Thucydides 331
Tiberius (Emperor) 245n16
Tronchin, Jean-Robert 260
Tuck, Richard 83n1, 373n12–373n13
Turner, Piers Norris 1–5, 375–99

Uriah (biblical) 42

Van Schoelandt, Chad 286, 287–8
Velema, Wyger 348n11

Waldron, Jeremy 175, 182n9, 182n14, 183n17, 183n23
Wall, Steve 183n24
Wallace, James 348n13
Warburton, W. 225, 239
Waszek, Norbert 345
Westphal, Kenneth 4, 330–48
Whewell, W. 384–5
Will, Frederick L. 332, 348n13–348n14
William III (of Orange), king of England 215
Williams, Robert A. 347n2
William the Conqueror 81
Wills, Gary 330
Wolff, Robert Paul 248, 262n3
Woodruff, Paul 331, 335
Wright, Crispin 335

Xenophon 245n17

Zeno 176
Zeus 237
Zhai, X. 372n2